PRAISE FOR *CL*  WHA??

"Christine Lavin is the unsung heroine of the latter-day folk movement. Her tireless support of talented songwriters has brought out the best in many, given chances to more than a few, and put her head and shoulders above most people claiming to be 'star-makers.' Her autobiography, like her life, is a work of art."

—Janis Ian, singer/songwriter

"When I see Christine Lavin in concert, I laugh and shed a few tears. Reading *Cold Pizza for Breakfast*, I laughed and shed a few tears. Just like her concerts, I didn't want it to end."

—Michael Stock, host, WLRN Radio

"Christine Lavin is not only a brilliant performing songwriter but she *can write*. . . . Joe Namath, Dave Van Ronk, and Bob Dylan may be some of the magic here, but really Christine's ability to find and tell a great story is what keeps the pages *turning*. Highly recommended."

—Robert Aubry Davis and Mary Sue Twohy,
"The Village," the folk channel on Sirius/XM satellite radio

"Christine Lavin is an artist who covers the gamut of performance in many genres; intimate of stars in the worlds of jazz, folk, and Broadway. . . . You join her in a most personal journey through her life and become her companion on a trip you want to go on unendingly."

—Bill Hahn, producer/host, *Traditions* and *Sunday Simcha*, WFDU-FM

"*Cold Pizza* is a creative and cozy journey through the warm and witty life of one of the finest singer/songwriters performing today. . . . [Christine Lavin's] point of view on her own world is as specific, witty, compassionate, and honest as her music. Through this book she has created a narrative that lets us in on the creative process of a writer who celebrates the joys of yesterday's pizza with the same gusto that she anticipates the joys of tomorrow's fresh surprises."

—Stuart Ross, writer/director, *Forever Plaid*

OTHER BOOKS BY CHRISTINE LAVIN

Amoeba Hop, illustrations by Betsy Franco Feeney, Puddle Jump Press (winner of a Best Book award from the American Association for the Advancement of Science)

The Christine Lavin Songbook, Cherry Lane Music

To Lisa & everyone at Posh!

Christine Lavin 7.8.10

COLD PIZZA FOR BREAKFAST
A Mem-*wha??*

CHRISTINE LAVIN

tell me
New Haven, Connecticut

Grateful acknowledgment is made for permission to reprint the following:
"It Was a Very Good Year," words and music by Ervin Drake. Copyright © 1961 Lindabet Music (ASCAP), Songwriters Guild of America, new lyrics © 2009. All rights reserved.
"Easy Street," words and music by Cliff Eberhardt. Copyright © 2009 Hank SR Music (BMI). Used by permission.
"My Autobiography," written by Janis Ian. Copyright © 2005 Rude Girl Publishing (BMI). All rights reserved. Used by permission.
Native American verse to "This Land Is Your Land," written by Peter Israel and Elizabeth Jones Israel. Used with permission.
"Arrow," written by Cheryl Wheeler. Copyright © 1985 Penrod and Higgins Music/Amachrist Music (ASCAP), ACF Music Group. "If It Were Up to Me," words and music by Cheryl Wheeler. Copyright © 1999 Penrod and Higgins Music/Amachrist Music (ASCAP), ACF Music Group. All rights reserved.
"Anita's Chili Parlor," "Ballad of the Hudson River," "For Every Old Stocking You'll Find an Old Shoe," "Gas Station Man," "John John & Princess Diana's Wedding Song," "Pirate," and "Why Do They Hate Us?" words and music by Christine Lavin.
"Another New York Afternoon," words and music by Christine Lavin. Copyright © 1999 Christine Lavin Music (ASCAP), administered by Bug Music. "Firehouse," words and music by Christine Lavin. Copyright © 2002 Christine Lavin Music (ASCAP), administered by Bug Music. "Ha Ha Ha Ha Tsk Tsk Shhh!" words and music by Christine Lavin. Copyright © 2009 Christine Lavin Music (ASCAP), administered by Bug Music. "Winter in Manhattan," words and music by Christine Lavin. Copyright © 2006 Christine Lavin Music (ASCAP), administered by Bug Music. All rights reserved.
"Damaged Goods," words and music by Christine Lavin. Copyright © 1984 CL2 (ASCAP), FSMGI (IMRO), and Rounder Music (ASCAP). "Good Thing He Can't Read My Mind," words and music by Christine Lavin. Copyright © 1988 CL2 (ASCAP), FSMGI (IMRO), and Rounder Music (ASCAP). "The Kind of Love You Never Recover From," words and music by Christine Lavin. Copyright © 1990 CL2 (ASCAP) and FSMGI (IMRO). "Ramblin' Waltz," words and music by Christine Lavin. Copyright © 1984 CL2 (ASCAP), FSMGI (IMRO), and Rounder Music (ASCAP). "Replaced," words and music by Christine Lavin. Copyright © 1991 CL2 (ASCAP) and FSMGI (IMRO). Worldwide rights for CL2 administered by Cherry Lane Music Publishing Company, Inc. (ASCAP). All rights for FSMGI (IMRO) administered by State One Songs America (ASCAP). Used by permission of Alfred Music Publishing Co., Inc. All rights reserved.
"Prince Charles" and "Three Months to Live," words and music by Christine Lavin. Copyright © 1981 PKM Music (ASCAP). "Gettin' Used to Leavin'," words and music by Christine Lavin. Copyright © 1986 PKM Music (ASCAP). All rights reserved.
Cover of *Amoeba Hop!* (p. 148) courtesy Puddle Jump Press.
Cover of *Fast Folk Musical Magazine* vol. 2, no. 9 (November 1985). Image p. 141 courtesy of the Ralph Rinzler Folklife Archives and Collections, Smithsonian Institution. Cover illustration by Libby Reid.
Cover of *Folk Guitar with Laura Weber* (p. 148) courtesy KQED/Northern California Public Broadcasting, Inc.
Cover of *Sing Out!* vol. 34, no. 3 (summer 1989). Image p. 148 courtesy Sing Out! (www.singout.org)
Photograph of Dave Van Ronk street sign (p. 141) © Otto Bost
Photograph of Speakeasy (p. 141) © Angela Page

Library of Congress Control Number 2010920290
ISBN: 978-0-9816453-6-0

Front cover photo © Bob Yahn
Back cover photo © Irene Young

Printed in the United States of America
First Edition
10 9 8 7 6 5 4 3 2 1

tell me

Published by **Tell Me Press**, LLC
98 Mansfield St.
New Haven, CT 06511
www.tellmepress.com

Editorial director: Lisa Clyde Nielsen
Art direction, text and cover design: Linda Loiewski
Editing: Justine Rathbun
Proofreading: Anita Oliva
Production and marketing: Jeff Breuler, Jeff Eyrich, Ian A. Nielsen
Publicity: Gail Parenteau

CONTENTS

FOREWORD

MID-1980S. ANN ARBOR, MICHIGAN. THE ARK. After an introduction befitting a member of the royal family, down through the audience tromped this woman lugging an acoustic guitar as big as she was. She climbed onto the stage and swung the guitar around like John Wayne reining in his horse. Fast behind that guitar came a smile as wide as the stage. And then that laugh—like a drunken sparrow she cackled, sharing this wonderful moment in life with a roomful of strangers who, before anyone knew it, had become her friends.

I don't know why Christine Lavin does what she does, but I'm glad she does it. Whether she's recording an album solely of her favorite recipes (with an accompanying cookbook), hosting knitting circles before her shows, or, in this case, writing a "mem-wha," she is what every artist yearns to be: an original. Whether she's singing songs or merrily spilling her life onto these pages, to be in her audience is to be grabbed by the lapels, expertly led around, and—when it's all said and done—laughed out, genuinely moved, and thinking differently. Days after one of her live performances, you'll find yourself remembering one of her lyrics or hooks or what-was-I-thinking observations, and you'll say, "You know why that's so funny? Because it's true." This book is no different.

Christine Lavin writes about things we didn't know we knew, makes us feel what we didn't know we felt, and, in the end, helps us understand life in a way we never thought we could. That's what a true artist does. And we're the better for it. So do yourself a favor. Read this book. For those of you who've never met her, it will be like sitting down with an old friend. For the rest of us . . . well, all good things should be shared.

If only the world were more like her.

Jeff Daniels

PREFACE

I've been a touring musician since 1985, though my adventures really started two decades earlier, in 1964, when I first picked up a guitar. That was also the year the Beatles made their American television debut on *The Ed Sullivan Show*—February 9, to be exact. Let's declare February 9 a national holiday! We have enough sad dates emblazoned on our souls—November 22, 1963; September 11, 2001—why not a happy one?

Instead of a business plan, I've followed hunches, my intuition, and my heart and have had the good fortune of meeting astounding people along the way who helped point me in the right direction. Okay, a few pointed me wildly in the wrong direction, but I always managed to recover somehow.

I've changed a few names to spare hurt feelings, but all these stories are true. Hey, I have eight brothers and sisters—you think they'd let me make things up?

I dedicate this book to four people: the late Laura Weber, who started me out on guitar; the late Dave Van Ronk, who taught me how to play it; Barry Humphries, a.k.a. Dame Edna, the most brilliant comedic performer in the English-speaking world; and Ervin Drake, one of the greatest songwriters in the English-speaking world.

There is an index (and song list) at the back of this book, and I encourage you to Google every single name listed there. You might make some life-changing musical discoveries. And you know I would *never* steer you wrong.

Christine Lavin

I'M TRYING
TO BLIND YOU ALL EQUALLY

P ack your bags!" he panted. "This is the one we've been waiting for. You're opening for Joan Rivers in West Palm Beach!"

West Palm Beach, Florida? *Joan Rivers?* This was the mid-1990s, and I thought, I'm just a folksinger! Joan Rivers? She's a huge star! This is too wonderful for words. I love my agent! I'm on my way!

I flew down from New York and pulled up in front of a brand-new, state-of-the-art, cushy 1,200-seat venue in West Palm Beach where a giant marquee flashed AN EVENING WITH JOAN RIVERS. The concert promoter met me out front. I asked him if they were going to add my name up there. No, he said, but they would insert an addendum sheet to the program, so I had nothing to worry about.

Joan and her people were so kind to me during sound check; they liked what they saw and heard. Her manager told me, "Joan does a voice-over from behind the curtain to begin the show. When you hear your name, *that's* your cue to walk onstage, where you'll do thirty minutes—not a minute more. Or less."

I went out to the lobby prior to the doors being opened to get a feel for the audience. This crowd was decidedly older—*way* older—than I was used to. Many of the women reminded me of someone; their outfits, their hair. I couldn't put my finger on it.

Uh-oh. *Nancy Reagan.* Not really my audience. No matter. The men were well dressed, a giddy rainbow of pastel pants, plaid sport jackets, white shoes, and shiny black toupees. I have a song called "Bald Headed Men" that I decided then and there to put in my set. Look at all these bald guys hiding their shiny domes. They'll *love* this song!

The doors opened, the hall filled, and the lights went down. I peeked out at the crowd from the wings, waiting to hear my name. I saw programs in the laps of all the audience members and imagined they knew they were about to see an opening act.

Suddenly, spotlights shot this way and that over the heads of the audience, and we heard Joan Rivers's voice. "Welcome to my concert. They say you can't take pictures or audiotape the show, but I say oh go ahead, what do I care? And now, please welcome the best opening act I could find in my price range, Christine Lavin . . ."

With that, I confidently strode out to the middle of the stage, preparing to hit the first chord of my first song . . . but I couldn't.

Joan was still talking.

I didn't understand what she was saying; all I could hear was the reverberation of her voice bleating on, punctuated by the audience's laughter. I stood there, frozen. They told me to walk out onstage when I heard my name. I heard my name. Why is she still talking?

I stood there and waited for her to stop. The only words I recognized were the final two: my name. I guess they meant I should have walked out onstage the *second* time my name was mentioned. Oops.

I hit the guitar chord and started my first song, "Good Thing He Can't Read My Mind"—"I am at the opera / I don't like the opera / but he loves the opera / and I love him . . ."—accompanied by the fluttering sound of program pages flipping and the occasional murmurs of "Who?" "Who is this?" "Is that Joan?" "Joan Rivers plays the guitar?" coming from the audience.

Addendum to the program? Ha!

That first song, one that in most situations is almost bulletproof, received what fellow singer/songwriter Cliff Eberhardt has dubbed the dreaded "golf applause," followed by more program page-flipping. I tried a quick joke after it—"I hope no one is out there thinking, 'She is playing folk music / I do not like folk music / but he loves folk music / and I love him,' "—which resulted in quizzical stares, more page-flipping, and more vocal queries from the audience. "Who the hell *is* this?" "Where's Joan?" "Are we in the right place?"

I charged into my second song, "Bald Headed Men," only to realize instantly what a mistake it was. Men wear toupees to create the illusion that there is hair up there. Did I really expect them to rip them off and toss them in the air? But I was committed to the song, so I sang it with gusto only to hear even *less* golf applause when it ended, and a very clear elderly voice from the front row say in a stage whisper, "That was AWFUL! I hope this part of the show doesn't last too long. Do you think Joan knows about this?"

I glanced at my watch. Only seven minutes had gone by. As I sang the next song, I became aware that the bright stage lights were bouncing off my shiny guitar and then hitting the audience in the eyes. Some were shading their eyes with their hands, some with their programs. I tried to move in such a way that I wasn't constantly hitting the same people in the eyes over and over again. During my next song (truthfully, I don't remember what it was—the show was going south, and at that point I was just hanging on for dear life), I squirmed a bit here and there to avoid blinding anybody.

When that song was done, to barely *any* applause, I was thinking that I should explain why I was moving in such an awkward manner. This wasn't what I wanted to say, but it's what I said: "I know I'm moving sort of spaz-like onstage. It's because I can see the stage lights are hitting my guitar, then hitting some of you in the eye. I'm moving like this because I am trying to blind you all equally."

I was done for.

A man near the front yelled out, "We don't even know who you are! We came to see Joan, and now YOU'RE BLINDING US?"

A voice from way back and up to the left in the rafters started chanting, "SPARE US! SPARE US!"

Then a voice from the right side took up the chant. "SPARE US! SPARE US!!"

"Where's Joan? We want Joan! We want Joan!!" cascaded from the balcony, along with more "Spare us! Spare us!" (which, you have to admit, is a rather odd insult to hurl at a concert). Then, of course, it got worse: "We hate you! Why are you here? Who are you, and what have you done with Joan Rivers?!" Next there was the all-purpose classic, "Boooooo! Boooooo!," which came from those with so little imagination yet so much disgust.

Maybe another performer would have taken the hint, but I ignored the pleas begging me to stop and continued my odd blindness-preventing spaz dance during each song.

At last I got to the finale, one of my favorites to this day: it's a back-track with a pretend sing-along of two classic songs from the 1960s, "All I Have to Do Is Dream," by the Everly Brothers, and "A Summer Song," by Chad Stewart and Jeremy Clyde, which segues into marching band music where I twirl batons—first one, then two, and then the lights go out and I twirl two green neon "light-stick" batons. It's usually a real crowd-pleaser, but all bets were off that night.

The music starts simply, but then there are intricate harmonies (my voice, prerecorded), and the audience normally joins in—very often many in the crowd don't realize the vocals are pretaped and think they magically sound like a well-rehearsed choir. There was no chance that was going to happen that night since I knew *nobody* was going to sing along.

I was so relieved to have gotten to this part of the show that I sang it all smiley like I was having the best time of my life. When the marching band music faded up and I picked up the batons, there was zero reaction from the crowd. How could they not react? But they didn't. When I picked up the first light-stick baton and cracked it so that it glowed bright green, that was the cue for the lights to instantly go out. We had rehearsed it at sound check. But the lights didn't go out. So there I was, twirling a neon baton for all it was worth . . . in full stage light. I yelled out "Turn off the lights!" as I twirled faster, but the marching band music was loud, and the spotlight operator was soooo far away. So I yelled it again, louder, as I twirled even faster. Then I screamed again: "*Please!* Turn off the lights!!"

The lights stayed on.

Then I picked up the second baton and cracked it. Oh man, in that setting, on that beautiful stage, it would have looked stunning in the dark. But with the lights still on, it looked like nothing. At the very end of the music I said to myself, "what the hell," and threw one of the batons as high as I possibly could. This baton totally defied gravity and reached for the ceiling. When it was at the very top of its trajectory, the entire stage suddenly went black. This was five seconds away from the end of the routine. Then the baton started its descent, spinning precariously back toward me onstage.

Now you're probably figuring I'm going to drop it, right? The light sticks will rupture and spew green goo everywhere. Everything else went wrong that night; why not this? But I *didn't* drop it. Not only did I catch it, but the timing was so perfect that I caught it right on the beat, and I got a huge ROAR from the audience as the lights came up. Now, I don't kid myself. It was a mock roar. They were thrilled that I was finished, that's all—and maybe a bit surprised that I didn't drop the baton. But it was a roar, and I quickly bowed, holding the batons in one hand and grabbing my guitar with the other, and dashed offstage into my dressing room, where I burst into tears.

I'm not proud of that. I should be more adult about these things. But never in my life did I have so many people hate me for an entire set. I should have locked the door to my dressing room, but who knew the promoter was going to come busting in and praise me? He was surprised to see me crying and said, "Oh, Christine . . . don't let a few rude people ruin it for you. You were *wonderful!*"

Wha?? I was there. I was THERE! They hated me. Was he insane?

"Would you like to stop off at Joan's dressing room to say hello before she goes onstage?"

I thought, *Are you kidding me? I never want to show my face in front of her again. Ever.* I declined.

I snuck out of the theater during Joan's set, first stopping in the lobby to collect the CDs I had hoped would sell after the show (fat chance!). I brought everything back to my hotel room, closed the door, sat in the dark for a few minutes, and then dialed my friend Andrew Ratshin in Seattle.

Andrew is the clever songwriter behind many musical projects—the trio Uncle Bonsai, the group the Mel Cooleys, and the one-man acoustic Electric Bonsai Band. I love to share funny backstage stories with him, but this experience had reached a whole new level of backstage-story grotesqueness! By then I was over the crying part, and I gave Andrew a quick blow-by-blow account of how the show went. He was very sympathetic—but what could he say except for the occasional, "Oh, no!" and "Oh, that's not good!" and "You're *kidding!*" I had hoped that by telling him everything I would get over it quickly, but I didn't. I didn't sleep the entire night.

The next day my flight back to New York was scheduled for 7:00 p.m. I had planned to go sightseeing before leaving town, but I abandoned that idea and decided to fly standby just to get back home. I was confirmed on the 11:00 a.m. flight. I boarded the plane, feeling like hell. When I am well rested I am a naturally happy person, but when I am sleep deprived I am not far from what Sally Fingerett of the Four Bitchin' Babes calls "a raving lunatic bitch of death." I was in the darkest, blackest of moods. But I had a window seat in the back with an empty seat next to me, so things could have been worse.

The doors on the plane closed, but there was a commotion up front. One of the flight attendants announced: "Attention passengers. We have a situation. There is a traveler onboard who is a very nervous flyer. Is there anyone with an empty seat next to them who will let this woman sit next to them and hold her hand during takeoff and landing? We really don't feel we can take off with this woman in the state she is in. If we must take her off the plane, we will be delayed. Is there anyone who can help?"

I volunteered. I had been a Girl Scout, and the truth is, at that point I was happy to find someone in a worse mental state than I was.

A teary, elderly, jewelry-encrusted woman toddled down the aisle and settled herself into the seat next to me. Her suit looked familiar and reminded me of someone: *Nancy Reagan.*

Her bottom lip trembled, so I took her knobby hand in mine and told her that I fly all the time; taking off is no big deal. The secret to dealing with takeoff nerves is to just lift your feet off the floor and tell yourself you are "sky surfing."

The plane rumbled down the runway, and she giggled when we both lifted our feet as the plane gently lifted off the ground. Calmed, she settled back into her seat and started to ask me the kinds of questions strangers ask each other on planes: Where are you from? What do you do for a living?

I lied. If she was in the audience the night before, I couldn't bear to relive it, so I told her I was a statistical typist from New York. (I *had* been a statistical typist once for a week, so it wasn't a big lie.) She asked me what I was doing in West Palm Beach. I told her I flew down to work on a job. She asked me how long I had been there, and I told her one day. (Hey, I was sleep deprived. I was making it up as I went along.) She seemed incredulous. "You flew to West Palm Beach to type numbers for one day? Couldn't they find anybody down there to do it?"

I told her I was very, very fast. "But still," she said, "the expense of flying you in . . . *How odd.*" I could tell I was in for a barrage of questions, so I cut to the chase. I told her it was a company controlled by the mob. The numbers were confidential, and they couldn't risk having a local type them—if the amounts were made public, *people could die.* She looked at me closely, leaned in, and whispered, "Well, what's to stop *you* from telling people those numbers?"

Good question. I thought for a moment, then said, "That's why they fly me back with an empty seat next to me, as a precaution."

She rang for the flight attendant and was moved back to her original seat. I fell asleep on the plane, woke up on the tarmac in New York, and have never been back to West Bomb Beach since.

2

LAW & ORDER
GIVES A SHOUT-OUT TO PETE SEEGER

S ome of my friends told me I should never tell the Joan Rivers story to anyone, ever. But it's a very real part of the life of a performer—I'm sure even Joan Rivers has her own nightmare stories. I can't write about what I do without mentioning the professional humiliations that smack me upside the head from time to time.

The fact that I've made a living onstage since 1985 is a surprise in itself. I've had no professional training, and even though as a young girl I dreamed of playing and singing my songs onstage, I had no idea how to make that happen. I had a destination but no map (much less a GPS system), and yet somehow I've earned a living as a musician. I've been signed by record companies and dropped by record companies. I've been signed to music publishing deals, and I've walked away from music publishing deals. I've made records in million-dollar recording studios, and I've made records that I engineered myself in my home studio in the middle of the night. I've learned how to manufacture vinyl albums, cassettes, and then compact discs, but those antiquated mediums have been kicked to the curb as digital downloading has trumped everything. The future holds more mysteries that I can only imagine. Everything's changed.

The one constant throughout my life has been the many musicians and performers I have worked with, learned from, collaborated with, been inspired by, been envious of, and at times commiserated with as we've been knocked about by the music business. Songwriting is a solitary process, but it's all the things that came after the songwriting that have shaped my career. It is more than likely that a new performer entering today's music world will need to learn the lessons I've gathered over the last twenty-plus years—building an audience not through one massive contract, but from the electronic grassroots. And if there is a God, my sense that it will take collaboration, mutual support, and reliance on the inspiration of others and sharing your own openly and freely will be borne out in the coming years. That's how I've lasted. I have no idea how I will fit in the new paradigm, but it's been an interesting ride getting to this point.

I was one of nine kids, and my parents thought it was important that each of us develop some special skill or talent, so they encouraged my interest in music. When I was in second grade I started taking piano lessons. My teacher had a very strange style—she hovered over the shoulder of her students with a long, unsharpened pencil poised in the air. If you played the wrong note she quickly rapped the offending hand on the knuckles.

It hurt. What made me—and many other students—practice was the fear of getting hit on the knuckles.

That fear eventually turned into resentment. Walking home with red, swollen knuckles, I began to hate the teacher, who became frustrated with me because she could see that I did have some natural musical instincts.

I lasted two years with this teacher, and for the last year of lessons I would cry on my way there and beg my parents to let me quit after each lesson. And each week I'd come home nursing my latest knuckle raps.

The day when my parents finally relented and allowed me to quit is still vivid in my memory—the sense of relief was palpable. Whatever I learned during those two years quickly evaporated, and I developed an aversion to reading printed music. To this day I can't read it.

Four years later, when I was twelve, Channel 13 (the New York City Public Broadcasting System station) began airing guitar lessons twice a week. I watched one of the lessons, mesmerized. The TV teacher was a woman named Laura Weber, and I was intrigued with the idea of learning how to play an instrument from a person on a television screen who couldn't possibly smack your hand if you played the wrong note. Plus you didn't have to be able to read music—it was more or less a "show and tell" system. It took some fancy talking on my part, but I got my parents to agree to rent a guitar for me to learn on for five dollars a month, and I bought a mimeographed booklet from the TV station for a dollar.

This was 1964, when TiVo was just a twinkle in the eye of some inventor, and even the VCR was still a *Jetsons* fantasy. My family lived in a house on the grounds of Peekskill Military Academy, where my dad taught speech and Latin. We had two TVs, one downstairs in my parents' bedroom and one upstairs for the children to watch. We kids were, in order from oldest to youngest, Louise, Gregory, Thomas, me, Edward, Jimmy, Mary, Christopher, and Josephine. My mom is also a Josephine, and my dad was also a Tom. So we had two Toms, two Josephines, and two Chrisses in one household. When the phone rang, chances were good there'd be some confusion.

Sitting in front of the upstairs TV, I would watch each guitar show broadcast twice—the first time on a weekday afternoon, and the second time on Saturday afternoon. Imitating Laura Weber caused an immediate problem, however. I am left-handed and she was right-handed, so she played right-handed guitar. I didn't know you could switch the order of the strings on a guitar so that a lefty could play more naturally, so I just did what she did—though it was quite awkward at the start.

Years later, when I moved to New York City and took guitar lessons with legendary New York blues/ragtime guitarist Dave Van Ronk, it turned out that he, too, was left-handed and played right-handed guitar, and he, like me, couldn't read music. He said that any left-handed guitar player who plays righty will always have a left hand slightly smarter and more dexterous than the average guitarist—but this is offset by a right hand that is always slightly dumber than the average guitarist's. A big plus, however, is that anywhere you go you'll be able to find a guitar to borrow if you're in a situation where you want to play but don't have your own. Left-handed guitar players don't often have that luxury.

So there I was, dutifully following along with my TV teacher, Laura Weber. Because rabbit-ear antennae were never very reliable, at least not where we lived, the picture would often "jump," which was annoying and made following along even harder. Luckily, my little brother Eddie could be persuaded to do almost anything for money. For five cents—the price of a Devil Dog, Eddie's favorite treat—he held the rabbit ears out the window for thirty minutes as I dutifully followed along with Laura.

Twenty-six years later, in July 1990, I got to meet Laura Weber. I was in San Francisco at the Great American Music Hall for the first tour of the Four Bitchin' Babes: Sally Fingerett, Megon McDonough, Patty Larkin, and me. The day before the concert, the *San Francisco Chronicle* ran my photo with a story that mentioned I had learned how to play guitar by watching lessons on public television when I was twelve. Laura was teaching guitar at San Francisco State. She read the article, looked at my photo, estimated my age, thought, "Well, I guess it must have been me she was watching!" and decided to go to the concert.

Five minutes before we were to take the stage, a crew member found me in the dressing room and handed me a business card. On one side it said LAURA WEBER—FOLK GUITAR, and on the other side she had handwritten, "Did I teach you how to play?" I took the business card onstage with me, and just before intermission I held it up and told the crowd that my TV guitar teacher, whom I had never met, was in the audience. I asked for the lights to be brought up and asked, "Laura Weber—where are you?" A petite gray-haired lady popped up and started waving her arms wildly. The crowd went crazy!

During intermission I went out to her table to meet her. She was more excited than I was. "You make up for all my live students who never practiced!" she squealed. Then she said something that was absolutely untrue, but it showed just how proud she was: "The best part is—you're the best guitarist onstage!"

What a sweet thing to say, but come on. Patty Larkin is one of the finest folk guitarists around. Sally Fingerett can also play rings around me.

Plus both Sally and Megon McDonough also play piano—so in truth I was the *least* accomplished musician onstage. But that's how gosh darn proud Laura Weber was of me.

I have since learned that folk/country singer/songwriter Nanci Griffith also learned how to play guitar watching Laura, as did Neal Shulman of the folk/rock duo Aztec Two-Step, as did Congresswoman Louise Slaughter of New York. There've got to be more of us out there, too. Wouldn't it be great if PBS organized a concert by performers who got their start watching guitar lessons on PBS, wearing clothes by people who learned how to sew from PBS, on a set built by people who learned carpentry from PBS, painted by people who learned how to paint by watching that fuzzy-haired painter on PBS? Seems to me that would be living proof of how important public television is, and it could be a good solid argument the next time the powers that be try to cut its funding.

I never saw Laura Weber again, though we did correspond. She died of cancer a few years ago, and I read that she continued teaching guitar up until just a few weeks before her death, so dedicated was she to her craft. I can't imagine what I would be doing with my life now if her lessons hadn't been broadcast on TV when I was just a kid.

By the time I was thirteen, I thought I knew enough to start writing my own songs. (Ah, the arrogance of youth!) Pete Seeger lived not too far away from us, in Beacon, New York. I had never met Pete, but I knew all about him, and I remember trying to write a song about the Hudson River to send to him. The only lines I remember now are, "Oh, my brown oil slicked waters / you once flowed so clear and blue . . . ," written from the point of view of the river. Reading those lines now, I see how naive they are. The Hudson River is much cleaner than it was, but I don't think you'd ever call its waters "clear and blue." But I was just thirteen, so what did I know?

Years later I would get to meet Pete Seeger and even work with him. Bob Sherman, who has hosted a radio program called *Woody's Children* for decades, plays the music of songwriters he considers musical descendants of Woody Guthrie. First he was on WQXR-FM, the radio station of the *New York Times*, but now he is also on WFUV-FM, the radio station of Fordham University in the Bronx.

In 2004, to celebrate his thirty-fifth anniversary on the air, Bob hosted a special concert at Merkin Hall at Lincoln Center that was taped for later broadcast. The lineup for the concert was Pete Seeger, Tom Chapin with Jon Cobert and Michael Mark, the Work o' the Weavers, Oscar Brand, Odetta, Doug Mishkin, and me. You probably know these names, though perhaps Doug Mishkin and the Work o' the Weavers are new to you. Doug Mishkin wrote the song "We Are All Woody's Children," which is the theme song of *Woody's Children*. Work o' the Weavers—James Durst, David Bernz, Mark Murphy, and Martha Sandefer—has meticulously studied the recordings of the Weavers, which was the first folk "supergroup," formed in 1948 by Pete Seeger, Ronnie Gilbert, Lee Hayes, and Fred Hellerman. Pete Seeger *loves* this group, whose sound is so close to the original. I sat next to Pete onstage that night and watched him close his eyes and smile every time they sang.

Bob Sherman was the first person to play my music on the radio, so he has always held a special place in my heart. I can't begin to describe the feeling songwriters get the first time they hear a song of theirs broadcast. Ever since then I have made a point of sending him CDs by brand-new songwriters. Bob always tapes his shows in advance and lets the songwriters know when their songs will air—there are not many radio people who will take the time to do that. I was thrilled when he asked me to be part of his thirty-fifth anniversary broadcast with such a stellar lineup.

Just before showtime we learned that Odetta had the flu and couldn't perform, and Oscar Brand was also a no-show, as he had come down with a wicked cold. No one was worried, however, since it was a round-robin format, and we were all capable of doing more songs than planned.

The first half of the concert went without a hitch, and then we took a fifteen-minute intermission. I went out to the lobby to say hello to some friends and ran into a songwriter named Garry Novikoff. I had met Garry when both of us had space-themed songs on a compilation album issued by the Mars Society in conjunction with the National Space Society. The album was called *To Touch the Stars: A Musical Celebration of Space Exploration*. My song, "If We Had No Moon," was about what the world would be like if the moon never existed, and Garry's, "Dog on the Moon," was a very funny stream-of-consciousness story-song about the vagaries of modern life. I loved Garry's song and had sent it to Bob Sherman, and he had played it on *Woody's Children*. Garry had hosted a "listening party" for his friends because it was his first-ever song to be played on the radio.

As I said hello to Garry, I suddenly got an idea. I said to him, "Odetta and Oscar Brand are no-shows. I wonder what Bob Sherman would think about having you come up onstage and sing 'Dog on the Moon'? If he agrees, would you do it?"

I watched a fleeting moment of panic pass through Garry's eyes, but then he took a deep breath and said, "Yes!"

I ran backstage, found Bob (by now, ten minutes of the intermission had gone by, and he was preparing to resume the second half), and quickly told him my idea. He thought for a moment.

"I remember that song—it's very good. Yes! Let's do it!"

Five minutes later we were all onstage. Bob told the audience how I came running backstage with the idea of inviting Garry onstage. He finished the speech with, "Where are you, Garry Novikoff? Come on up here!"

The house lights came up. Garry, who was sitting in one of the last rows, quickly ran up the aisle, leapt up the stairs, and then sat down at the grand piano. I think I was more nervous than he was. How did he stay so cool under pressure? I can't remember what he said to introduce the song, but I do remember he played it flawlessly; the crowd loved it and gave him a huge ovation. He bowed and then went back to his seat.

We ended that concert with all of us singing "Goodnight, Irene," but before we started, Pete asked Garry to join us onstage for the finale. Garry made the mad dash from his seat to the stage a second time that night, and I was just busting with pride on his behalf.

After the show, I went to an Irish pub on Columbus Avenue with Garry and some friends. We were all charged up, sharing pitchers of beer, and then Garry asked a very pointed question: "What if I had bombed? Did it cross your mind that that might happen?"

"Look," I said, "to be frank, it did cross my mind. But I thought even if you did bomb, it would still be an entertaining part of the show—a young guy comes out of the audience because two folk music stars couldn't make it. I knew the audience would be rooting for you to do well, and I would *never* have asked you if I thought it wouldn't work. My hunch was you could do it, and my hunch was right."

Then Garry said something I will never forget, and it explained that brief flash of panic in his eyes.

"I wrote 'Dog on the Moon' on guitar," he said. "I had never played it on piano. But I'm left-handed and play left-handed guitar. When you asked me if I could do this, I quickly thought of all the guitars onstage—they were all right-handed guitars. I had to think if I could transpose the song to piano on the spot, and I figured I could. That's what I did."

I was dumbstruck. He had performed at Lincoln Center in front of not only a sold-out house but also radio microphones, transposing his song in his head, on the spot, as he sang.

If there is a night you are not working yourself, you should always go to someone else's show. What happened to Garry Novikoff could never have happened if he had stayed at home. I'm not saying this kind of thing happens every day, *but it definitely can't happen to you if you're not there.* Livingston Taylor once said to me, "Woe is me if I sit in my dressing room all my life and no one ever knocks on my door. But worse is if they knock on my door and I'm not ready to answer it." Opportunity knocked on Garry's door, and he was ready.

One more Pete Seeger story:

Every year in June is the weekend-long Great Hudson River Revival Festival at Croton Point Park. A couple of years ago I was part of it, and I did a workshop of humorous songs with the clever British songwriter Zoe Lewis and the hilarious trio Modern Man—David Buskin, Rob Carlson, and George Wurzbach.

Over to the right of our stage was the Hudson River, and just a few feet from the shore was Pete Seeger, sitting on the grass. The mikes for David Buskin and Rob Carlson weren't set up yet, so we couldn't begin the workshop, but George Wurzbach started to talk to the audience.

"When I look at this gorgeous setting," he said, "the blue sky, the beautiful Hudson River, and Pete Seeger himself sitting right over there"—he pointed in Pete's direction, and Pete smiled—"I'm reminded of one of my favorite episodes of the TV drama *Law & Order*. Do any of you watch *Law & Order*?" he asked.

Pretty much the entire audience responded with a nod.

George continued, "This particular episode began with what they call a 'floater' being fished out of the Hudson River near the West Seventy-ninth Street Boat Basin. Lennie Briscoe, played by the late, great Jerry Orbach, says to the young officers pulling the dead body out of the water, 'Hey, I had your job when I was a rookie cop. It was the worst, most disgusting job on the force, but now, thanks to Pete Seeger and his friends, who've cleaned this river up, your job's not so bad!' "

The crowd laughed long and hard.

With all the great things Pete Seeger has done over the years through his wonderful music and generous spirit, this kind of sideways compliment—the improved condition of homicide victims floating in the Hudson River, resulting in less of a gross-out for the police—was one he'd probably never heard before. Or since.

3

PIGLET MEETS
JOE NAMATH

Since my family lived on the grounds of a military school and we ate our meals in the dining hall with the cadets, my mom still loves to remind me and my siblings, "When I was a bride, I was deprived of having to cook—all our meals were served to us by good-looking uniformed young men." That's Mom joking—she loved not having to cook. Keeping track of all of us kids was difficult enough.

As private military high schools go, Peekskill Military Academy was a good one—founded in 1833, with strong traditions and loyal alumni. (Coincidentally, the Martin Guitar Company was also founded that same year. Good karma, I guess—the guitars balancing the guns.) PMA's biggest rival was New York Military Academy. There was no love lost between the two schools, and I recently learned that Donald Trump went to NYMA. With military schools' strict haircut rules, it makes you wonder how he wore his hair back then.

Occasionally the top cadets, maybe one or two a year, would be chosen to attend West Point—the U.S. Military Academy—after graduating from PMA. West Point was a few miles up the Hudson, on the west side of the river. Two of the best cadets who ever attended PMA, Bart Creed and Mike

Kilroy—both fine athletes and students—went to Vietnam. Their names are just two of the 58,195 carved into the Vietnam Veterans Memorial Wall in Washington, D.C. I mention this because their deaths had a profound effect on my brother Greg a few years later when his number came up in the draft.

Growing up at an all-boys military school was often a lot of fun. The school had an excellent sports program, so I regularly got to watch football, basketball, baseball, and even swimming and wrestling matches. Sometimes I would bring girlfriends with me, and they loved being around so many teenage boys in military uniforms. Two of PMA's best swimmers, Carl Robie and Steve Rerych, won gold medals in the 1968 Olympics.

One day, when I was in fourth grade, all of this inspired an idea that I thought was a surefire winner: a dedicated cheerleading squad.

All the Lavin kids attended Assumption School from kindergarten through eighth grade. It was a very traditional Catholic school, with uniforms, no gym, no frills—but great basics in reading, writing, and arithmetic. The eighth grade did have a basketball team that competed in the Westchester County CYO (Catholic Youth Organization) League, so eighth-grade girls—the lucky ones—got to be cheerleaders. That was *it* for girls at that school when it came to sports: one year of cheerleading for a select few.

This wasn't enough for me, so I organized a cheerleading squad for the fourth-grade girls. We had nobody to cheer for yet, and it would be another four years until we were allowed to cheer for the basketball team, but holy cow, we would be *ready*. Then one morning I woke up with a brainstorm: I have a cheerleading squad with nobody to cheer for, and I live at an all-boys military high school that has no cheerleaders! I wrote to the head of PMA's athletic department, Victor Gabriel, offering to let the school have the use of my cheerleading squad at all football and basketball games for the coming season. I added that if the schedule allowed, we could also cheer for swimming meets and wrestling matches. (I knew that swimming and wrestling didn't normally have cheerleaders, but I felt that cheerleaders would make these sports much more popular.)

I carefully handwrote my letter in my best Catholic-school script and listed reasons why I thought this would work: it would raise school spirit, which in turn would help the teams to win more games, make the school more well known, attract more students, and increase enrollment, which meant better teams—my list went on and on. I told him how I would ask the parents of the girls if it would be okay, and maybe the parents would offer to drive us to the away games, too! An additional sign that this was a great idea: the PMA colors were blue and white, and so were our Catholic uniforms. Coincidence? I think not. We wouldn't even have to buy cheerleading outfits—we could just pin a large *P* on the front of our school uniforms!

I mailed the letter rather than hand it to Mr. Gabriel at dinner or walk across the campus to his home. Mailing it would make it look absolutely official and show how serious I was.

A few days later I heard my father chuckling on the telephone, and by the questions he was asking, I knew my letter was being discussed. He let out a big guffaw after he said, "The away games, too?" He could barely catch his breath, he was laughing so hard.

I received a typed letter back from Mr. Gabriel thanking me for my offer, but explaining that as PMA was an all-boys school, there were legal reasons why they couldn't have girl cheerleaders at their games. His letter was kind and to the point. I wasn't surprised by the rejection letter because of the phone call I'd overheard, but part of me was still stunned, because I thought it was such an obviously brilliant idea.

Lack of cheerleaders notwithstanding, the absolute best part about living on the grounds of PMA was that from 1963 to 1967 it was the summer home of the New York Jets. Sonny Werblin, who owned the team at the time, had two sons, Hubbard and David, who attended PMA, and during his visits in the early 1960s Sonny got the idea that it would be a great location for the Jets. There were dormitories, a dining hall, a locker room, and a playing field all in close proximity. When PMA was chosen, all of us kids—not just the Lavins, but all the faculty kids—were thrilled.

My brothers Greg, Tom, and Ed got jobs in the dining hall and in the dorms, serving meals to the players and also cleaning their rooms and making their beds every morning. Special beds had to be trucked in at the beginning of training camp because even back then, the players were much bigger than the average high school kid. They had assigned rooms—quarterbacks roomed with quarterbacks and defensive linemen roomed with defensive linemen, two and sometimes three to a room. They had a curfew of 10:00 p.m. during the week.

I got into the act, too, babysitting for assistant coach Buddy Ryan's young son. (I recently found out that the current coach of the Jets, Rex Ryan, is Buddy's son, so then I wondered, hmm . . . could it be. . . . I Googled him to find he was born in 1962. Holy crap—I was Rex Ryan's babysitter! Let's go Jets!)

Every day in summer I would go to the field and watch the Jets practice—and I mean *every day*. Sometimes I wouldn't stay for more than an hour, but I would always be there at some point in the afternoon. One day I had a stomach bug and didn't go, but the next day I did, and one of the players came over and asked where I was the day before. I think I was eleven at the time, and my face turned scarlet red. I so idolized the players that it never occurred to me that they would notice that a skinny young girl was absent one day. But it also showed how few people came to watch that the Jets recognized the regulars.

What I remember most about the summers when the Jets trained in Peekskill was the year Joe Namath and John Huarte joined the team. Everything changed.

Joe Namath, a quarterback fresh out of the University of Alabama, was paid $400,000—the most a professional football player had ever received—and John Huarte, also a quarterback, but from Notre Dame, was paid $200,000, also an astronomical sum at the time. The Jets were an AFL team, not an NFL team—the American Football League was still considered a bunch of upstarts.

John Huarte was a couple of inches shorter than Namath, and there were a lot of people who thought that his sidearm style of throwing wouldn't work against professional football's tall defensive linemen. (The skeptics were later proved correct.) Some of the players, however, were rooting for Huarte to get the quarterback slot since he was paid half of Namath's salary, and there was that whole underdog thing going on. But when they took the field, it was clear from day one that Joe Namath was something special. In every way. Suddenly, daily practices had a couple of thousand spectators instead of a couple of hundred. Dozens of press people were coming up from New York City. Lots of pretty young women would sit in the stands and feast their eyes on the players, especially Namath. When he completed long, impressive passes, they would clap and cheer as if it were a real game.

We heard a story once that when the team finished practicing one day, there were naked girls waiting for Joe in the locker room. I was so young and naive, I figured that if the players walked into the locker room and saw naked girls, they would turn around and run right out, screaming.

All the players were very nice to us faculty kids. On the days that players got cut from the team, we would feel bad for those who didn't make it. That part of summer training camp was always hard. We'd watch them pack up their cars and sadly drive away. But we knew Joe Namath would never get cut.

Joe had an Irish setter dog named Pharaoh that needed walking and a dark green Lincoln Continental convertible that needed washing. So besides serving him meals and making his bed, sometimes my brothers would walk his dog and wash his car. They said he was always a good tipper.

Joe often parked his car near our house, and one day when he was walking toward his car a bunch of us faculty kids were throwing a football around. Someone—I don't remember who—dared me to ask Joe to teach me how to throw the football. Normally I would be way too shy to do such a thing, but by now everybody knew he was a nice guy, especially nice to kids, so I screwed up my courage and said, "Excuse me, Mr. Namath, but can you show me how to throw a good spiral?"

I think the fact that I knew the word *spiral* helped. He stopped and said, "Sure."

I told him I was a lefty, but he said, "That's okay, it's the same principle," as he showed me how he spread his fingers out over the laces to get a good grip, then moved his arm back and then forward while he turned his hand slightly as he let ball go. It floated out over our yard and landed softly on the grass.

I ran and got it, then imitated what he had just done. Too shy to throw it back to Joe, I threw a slightly wobbly spiral in the direction of my little sister Mary, who was walking her pet albino guinea pig, Piglet. When Joe saw her little pet, he asked, "What's *that?*"

I told him it was my sister's guinea pig, and he asked if he could pet it. Mary was quite young—probably eight years old or so, and not really a football fan—but *everybody* knew who Joe Namath was, including her. She nervously picked up Piglet and carried him over to Joe.

He very sweetly tickled Piglet under his chin and stroked his head. Then Piglet bit him on the index finger of his right hand. Joe pulled his hand back, said, "Ow!" and Mary, cradling Piglet in her arms, ran as fast as she could into the house, up the stairs, and hid under her bed. I was just a kid myself and wasn't sure what to do. Piglet bit Joe Namath! This was a potential national catastrophe!

I ran into the house, too, and found Mary under her bed, sobbing. She was so afraid that Piglet was going to be taken away from her for biting Joe Namath. What if his finger got infected? What if he couldn't play football? Would our brothers be fired? Would *Dad* be fired?

I don't think Dad was worried about getting fired, but he did pace around the house a bit that afternoon. This was just the kind of unexpected disaster he always worried about.

"Do you know how much Joe Namath's hands are worth?" he said to no one in particular. "At least a million dollars! *Each!* How on earth could this happen?"

Mary stayed under that bed the whole afternoon, expecting at any moment to have Piglet snatched away. But nothing happened. Nothing at all. Life went on. (Not all that long for Piglet—he was an albino, after all, with a shortened lifespan.)

Mary's a schoolteacher now, with a husband named Tom (yes, another Tom in the family); two sons, Ian and Noah; and a golden retriever named Calvin. But to this day, if you want to make her flinch, just say "Joe Namath" and "Piglet" in the same sentence.

The guinea pig bite must not have had any lasting effects, because, as any football fan knows, the New York Jets won the Super Bowl in January 1969, defeating the Baltimore Colts 16–7—the first AFL team to beat an NFL team. Everyone at PMA—from Jean MacMichael, who ran the dining hall; to the kitchen cooks; to Renee, the campus gardener; to my brothers—felt they had a hand in helping them win.

I remember once when Howard Cosell was visiting the team. I was already a big fan of his—I listened to his Sunday-night radio program, *Speaking of Everything*, all the time. My brother Eddie told me that he waited on Howard Cosell in the dining room and that Howard ate an entire meal with an unlit cigarette dangling out of the side of his mouth. I checked with Eddie to see if that really was true, and he wrote to me:

Hi Teeny,

Was me. It did happen. But you are wrong about the cigarette: it was lit.

It was called "press day" for the Jets. All the media came to PMA to meet and greet the Jets. They put me, Brian Masella, and the Imhoff boys [other faculty kids] in white waiters' jackets, and we waited tables in the PMA dining room. We were each assigned tables, and we knew Cosell was "in the building" and were all hoping he'd sit at one of our tables.

Lo and behold, Cosell sits at one of mine. He was with some folks, don't know who, but he was definitely acting as the head of the table. At some point he lit up a cigarette and proceeded to eat his meal with it hanging out of his mouth. Never puffed it or took it out, just hung there the whole time. I was watching the ash as it got longer and longer, wondering if it would land on his plate. Never said a word to me except when I asked if he was done, and he grunted affirmative. End of story. Ash disappeared to who knows where, the ether of human experience. I take this memory to my grave. Just telling it like it is.

Each of us got a $5 tip from ABC Sports a week later. We were ecstatic. Bought a Ring Ding and can of Yoo-hoo from Chet's corner store for 25 cents and put the rest into the bank. Life was good.

FYI, Barbara Feldon was there, too, from *Get Smart*. She was making a commercial with Joe Willie. Don't be jealous.

Ed

When I ran into Howard coming out of the dining room (it may have been that very same day), I couldn't help myself—I ran up to him and said, "Mr. Cosell, I listen to your program every Sunday night. You are very smart!"

I didn't know what kind of a reaction I would get. There were stories that he could be rough on people, but he seemed completely taken aback. He laughed, shook my hand, and said, "That is so kind of you to tell me. You must be very smart to listen!"

I'm not such a big football fan anymore. It's too violent, and often players end up with debilitating and/or chronic injuries that can shorten their lives. But back then it was exciting to have the Jets in our own backyard for entire summers at a time.

4

THE CATHOLIC CHURCH
INTRODUCES ME TO MY FIRST ILLEGAL BEER,
AND TV INTRODUCES ME TO THE SMOTHERS BROTHERS

When the New York Jets left Peekskill Military Academy at the end of summer training camp in August 1967, we all knew they wouldn't be back. The Jets had outgrown the modest accommodations, and their front office wanted them closer to New York City during the summer months. We were sad that the Jets were gone for good, but much bigger changes were in store.

I was always a serious student and got good grades, but I was also a bit of an oddball when I took up the guitar at age twelve. By then I had already been a cheerleader-in-training for a few years—and I'd also become a baton twirler.

A red-haired classmate of mine at Assumption School, Marilyn Pomart, had been the mascot of the Peekskill High School Marching Band since she was very young (she started in first grade!). I *begged* her to teach me how to twirl a baton. The baton I learned on was cheap and unbalanced, but Marilyn had a real, professional baton; it was weighted, so when she threw it in the air, it spun in a perfect shiny circle. By contrast, mine made cockeyed loop-de-loops. It was enough to learn on, but I did have a big problem: that left-handed thing.

All baton-twirling squads have to work in unison, but my natural inclination was to do everything in the opposite direction from how Marilyn did it. I dreamed of being in a twirling squad, so I knew I had to learn right-handed. And I did. But whenever I was twirling alone I would twirl left-handed, and I was a much better twirler that way.

From the age of thirteen, I felt like I was on some kind of magic trajectory. My brother Eddie discovered Bob Dylan and started listening to WNEW-FM radio in New York City. I started listening to it, too, hearing the voices of Scott Muni, Roscoe, Jonathan Schwartz, and other young radio mavericks. I heard songs by the Stone Poneys, Judy Collins, Tim Buckley, Joni Mitchell, Leonard Cohen, Peter Paul & Mary, Glen Campbell, and Dave Van Ronk that were like nothing I had ever heard before.

I was learning how to write songs. I started performing in tiny local venues, and I remember buying my first record—a forty-five rpm vinyl copy of "By the Time I Get to Phoenix" performed by Glen Campbell. Jimmy Webb, the songwriter, was unknown to me at the time, but even as a young girl I knew that I was listening to real poetry set to great music. I played that record over and over and over. Plus the B-side—"Gentle on My Mind," written by John Hartford, another great song that has become a classic. I worked with John a few times—once was in Kentucky doing a public television show. Alison Krauss was also on the show. She was so young that when we all went out afterward, she ordered a nonalcoholic Shirley Temple. Working with John Hartford was a trip—he saw me twirling batons backstage and asked if I could teach him how to twirl his bow.

I said, "What!? Singing, playing fiddle, *and* clog dancing at the same time isn't enough for you?"

Of course I taught him how to twirl. He was a natural multitasker and picked it up quickly. John told me that he liked my songwriting because I write at a conversational pace, like he does. I didn't realize that was one of the things I loved about "Gentle on My Mind." You can practically recite it at the same pace you'd sing it. It also demonstrates the importance of rhythm in songwriting—it's got exactly the right number of syllables, perfectly matching up with the music. Another great thing about that particular song is that whether you sing it fast or slow, it always works—something true of the very best songs. A classic example is "Falling in Love with Love" from the Rodgers and Hart musical *The Boys from Syracuse*. Frank Sinatra recorded it early in his career at its original slow romantic tempo, then recorded it again many years later as an up-tempo swinging tune, and both versions work. Conversely, Joni Mitchell's original 1969 recording of her song "Both Sides Now" is at a moderate pace, but in 2000 she released a more stately arrangement, about half the speed of the original, with the new version trading youthful naivety for sad ennui.

I love playing around with songs and trying them at different tempos. One song that I reworked (and recorded)—though purists might object— was the Beatles' "All My Lovin'," which I slowed down and turned into the make-out music I always thought it could be. The way I see it, the original version is how a guy would sing it to a woman, but my slowed-down version is how a woman would sing it to a man. I hardly ever perform it live, because for me the arrangement in the recording with the strings (Robin Batteau on violin and Anil Melwani on cello) and the harmonies at the end really make the song, and I'm not satisfied without that luscious backup sound. When I was just learning how to play guitar back in the 1960s, I never dreamed that years later I would record a song from the very first Beatles album.

But that was still to come. My first performance ever was at a Girl Scouts dance. I even got written up in the *Peekskill Evening Star*. I don't have the clipping anymore (maybe it's somewhere out there on the Internet), but it said something like, "Miss Lavin played songs by Peter Paul and Mary and Bob Dylan, as well as her own composition, 'The World Is Coming to an End.' "

I finally did become a cheerleader in the eighth grade. (Do I remember a single score from any of the basketball games? Of course not, but I remember every cheer.) And in the ninth grade I went to Drum Hill Junior High School, where I made the freshman cheerleading squad. In the tenth grade I wasn't eligible because only juniors and seniors could try out for JV and varsity cheerleading, so instead I was on the twirling squad of the Peekskill High School Marching Band (a dream come true, since that's the band my idol, the red-haired Marilyn Pomart, was the mascot for).

I am not kidding, though, about being a bit of an oddball. Cheerleaders were popular and considered to be intellectual lightweights. I studied hard and enthusiastically, and I wasn't particularly popular. At my school, twirlers and cheerleaders didn't like each other very much. Twirlers felt they were superior because they had an actual skill, but they had to live with the fact that cheerleaders were higher on the high school totem pole, with no discernible skills involved (in the twirlers' eyes, at least).

So here I was, with a foot in both worlds . . . and I was a folksinger, too?

Besides the occasional Girl Scouts event, I once sang at a hootenanny that was put on in the gymnasium at PMA. I remember singing the Herman's Hermits song "Listen People." I also started singing at folk masses—the Catholic Church was trying to get "with it" by including folk music in church—and it was this aspect of my performing that landed me in the biggest trouble I had ever been in (up until then).

I was a devout Catholic from a very young age up to the point where I wasn't a devout Catholic anymore.

When I look at that sentence, I realize I'm paraphrasing Cliff Eberhardt's sentiment in the song "Easy Street": "Everyone's faithful until they're unfaithful / I'm living here on Easy Street." I can't put my finger on when I stopped believing, but it was a long, slow, gradual decline.

My first paying job (outside of babysitting) was as a switchboard operator in a convent in Peekskill during the summer of 1968. It was part time, and I wasn't there long. It was an impossible job, because it was back in the day when many nuns still wore full almost burkalike costumes; this order wore white habits with black veils, with white fabric circling their head and under their chins. (There must be a name for that piece of the outfit. Just imagine you had a head wound, and someone wrapped a white bandage around your head, then topped it off with a heavy black veil.) Multiply that by a hundred, and picture me answering the phone and someone asking if "Sister Gertrude" is there.

The last day I was there I answered a call from a man with a heavy Italian accent asking for Mother Superior. I was directed to tell him that she was busy, but he responded, "You tell her I am calling from the Vatican," so I put him on hold, and then I accidentally disconnected him. He quickly called back, and, unbelievably, I did the same thing again: I disconnected an Italian calling from the Vatican. Twice! I don't know if it was the Pope who wanted to talk to Mother Superior, but who else could it have been?

It didn't matter. By that time I was already on my way out the Catholic Church's door because of something that had happened a few months earlier.

I had been asked to play guitar at a folk mass at a weekend retreat of young Catholics like me—fourteen- to sixteen-year-olds. It was at a school not far from Peekskill. I was assigned a roommate for the weekend—a girl whose father was one of the chaperones of the retreat.

That first night (Friday) there was a folk mass led by a young priest, with two young nuns who also played folk guitar and sang with me. These nuns were part of the new youth movement taking over the church. Their habits consisted of a blue shift-style knee-length dress and a very small veil—really just a small black bandanna worn on the head and tied at the back of the neck. After the mass there was some free time, and they asked me if I wanted to go with them to get something to eat.

Now, I was one of the *kids* at the retreat, and I was being invited out by three of the adults *running* the retreat—how cool! Because I played guitar, they treated me as if I was more mature than I was.

A lot of people make assumptions about musicians and songwriters— like we all drink, take drugs, smoke, sleep around, that kind of thing—but I was an oddball in that world, too. I never did any of that, though as an adult, thanks to *Sex and the City*, I have developed a fondness for cosmopolitans—but come on! They taste sweet and fruity and just make you giggle. It's barely a real drink.

But back then I was a naive square. I said yes to the invite, and we drove around looking for someplace that was open. None of us were familiar with the area, and it was clear there weren't a lot of choices. The only place that we found open was a bar.

We pulled into the parking lot. The two nuns looked at each other, laughed, and then quickly whipped off their little veils. The priest undid his collar. I couldn't believe it. A priest and two nuns walk into a bar . . . with them an underage girl who had never been in a bar in her life.

We sat down at a table—it had one of those red-and-white checkered plastic tablecloths on it. We were looking at the menus when a waitress asked if we wanted anything to drink. They all ordered beers, and when it was my turn to order, the priest said, "Bring her one, too."

A live band was playing, and the two nuns went out on the dance floor with the crowd and started dancing. Our beers arrived, and I found myself sitting with this handsome young priest. Here I was, drinking my first beer with a priest who had just said a mass. And two nuns were on the dance floor. My life suddenly became interesting.

We all ate our burgers, the nuns danced some more, we had another round of beers, and then it was time to head back to the retreat.

Of course I was drunk. I had had two beers. Two beers can *still* get me drunk, and I'm older, wiser, and weigh more than I did back then. I don't think I was acting like I was drunk (you'll just have to trust me on this one), but I was goofy from the experience and by now halfway in love with the priest. I figured I would have a chance with him in a few years, when the Lord would appear to him in a dream to tell him he wasn't cut out for the priesthood.

By the time we got back to the retreat, everyone was in bed. My roommate was upset and worried because I had disappeared after the mass and then got in so late. I was so excited about what I had just experienced that I asked a question that no sane person should ever ask when they've been drinking: "Can you keep a secret?"

I told my roommate everything, and she acted like it was the most wonderful news she had ever heard. All the girls thought the priest was adorably cute in an oblivious pious way. She was envious but seemed genuinely thrilled for me. It took me a long time to fall asleep—first because I was tipsy, then because I was so excited about seeing the priest again the next day.

That didn't happen. My roommate got up very early the next morning, immediately went to her father (a chaperone, remember), and even before breakfast the priest and the two nuns had been dismissed from the retreat and my parents had been called and told to come get me.

I had to walk past the dining room as I left—all the other kids looked up silently from their plates as I walked by. My cheeks burned with shame. I don't remember how much of what happened was told to my parents, but a few days later that gorgeous young hunk of holy priesthood came to our home and personally apologized to my parents for what he had done.

I was embarrassed to my core—not at what I had done, but that he had to apologize to my folks for treating me like an adult instead of a kid. I loved how it felt to be out and about, sitting next to him, drinking a beer, listening to live music. Yeah, the nuns dancing was a bit weird, but all in all, it was fantastic.

I remember how remorseful the priest was, and how my dad sat there stone-faced and kept saying, "Uh-huh . . . Hmmmm . . . Yes, Father . . ." My poor mother—she didn't say anything and looked like she'd rather have been anywhere else in the world than witnessing *this*. I was such a good girl, a straight-A student, and not only had I been dismissed from a religious retreat, but it was because I went drinking with a priest and two nuns. Mom was an active member of the Assumption School Mother's Club. This was a very bad thing.

Eventually the young priest stopped apologizing. My parents accepted his apology, and he left.

For a few moments we all sat in silence. I wanted to get out of the room, but I knew there'd be some kind of stern lecture or grounding or *something* coming.

My father burst out laughing. My mother looked at him, horrified.

My father said, "Christine, you have always been such a sensible girl. You've never given us a moment's worry, and for your first time to go out and do something reckless—you do it with a priest . . . *and two nuns?*"

He tried to continue talking, but he kept laughing instead. I waited for the lecture I thought was coming, but he waved me out of the room. *Whew.* I ran up to my bedroom, grabbed my guitar, and tried to write a song about what had just happened (maybe someday I will, but I couldn't then). I could hear my parents downstairs talking, but that was that. Neither one brought it up to me again, and I didn't tell anybody about it for years. I'm not even sure my brothers and sisters know (though I guess they do now!).

That was probably the moment I started questioning the Church. A few months later, when I had the phone job at the convent, I noticed a lot of priests coming to visit some of the young pretty nuns, and that made me start to wonder even more.

When I think back about that whole incident, my father's handling of it still comes as a surprise. Dad was strict. People in Peekskill sometimes referred to us Lavin kids as "Major Lavin's Army." He maintained a bit of his military bearing, and even though he didn't wear a military uniform, as some of the PMA faculty did, he was always addressed as "Major Lavin."

Because he was serious and strict, a lot of the cadets kept their distance—he was never that popular with them. Nonetheless, to this day some of his former pupils show up at my concerts to tell me how much they grew to appreciate him years after they had graduated.

You can probably imagine how hard it would have been for a military man to preside over a household of nine children. We were never organized enough, neat enough, or quiet enough. Thank God we eventually figured out how to satisfy his need for control: we got him a dog. Not just any dog, but a *great* dog. A black Labrador retriever named Spanky.

Spanky had the run of the campus. During the school year all the cadets got to know and love him, and in the summer months most of the Jets knew him by name, too. You know you own a popular dog when people you don't even know greet your dog by name when you are walking him.

Dad taught Spanky many commands, but his favorites were simply "Yes" and "No." Dad would put a dog biscuit *on* Spanky's nose, and then he would command Spanky to "Sit!" Then he would say in a loud booming voice, "No . . . No . . . No . . . Yessss-terday" (Spanky would flinch), then more "No . . . No . . . ," then, finally, "YES!"

In one swift motion, Spanky would knock the biscuit up in the air and swallow it so fast it was a blur.

In a large, chaotic household there is always some kind of tension, some spats, feuds, or disagreements in progress, but having a dog like Spanky ensures that there's at least one member of the family who is loved by all, all the time.

Around this time I was preparing for my junior year at Peekskill High. At the end of my sophomore year I had decided to give up the baton-twirling squad (my left-handedness made me the worst twirler in the bunch), and I made "alternate" for the varsity cheerleading squad. If anybody couldn't make a game, I got to take her place.

The other members of the twirling squad couldn't believe that I would leave them to be an *alternate* on the cheerleading squad, but I did. Then that summer I got a call from the faculty advisor for the cheerleading squad that one of the girls who made the squad was moving away, so I was moved up to the full varsity squad. I was ecstatic!

I had also been elected to be secretary of the student council, and I was going into my junior year as a straight-A student—I was *on my way*.

To where, I didn't know, because music was always distracting me from other things. I had become a devout fan of *The Smothers Brothers Comedy Hour* on TV. The head writer for the show was Mason Williams, who at the time had a huge hit with his guitar virtuoso piece, "Classical Gas." A couple years later I bought his album *Sharepickers*—one of the first albums I ever bought—after I heard a song of his called "Godsend" on the radio. "Godsend" moved me to the core. I listened to it over and over again, and then I wrote a letter to Mason, care of *The Smothers Brothers*

Comedy Hour, telling him how much I loved that song. He wrote back, sending me the sheet music and encouraging me in my guitar playing.

Of course I couldn't read the sheet music, even though it also contained a printed chord chart—the song was sophisticated musically, beyond my abilities. But I was thrilled that he wrote to me.

Since then I've gotten to open concerts for the Smothers Brothers twice, and I told them my Mason story. They loved hearing it.

Once, a week prior to a solo concert I was going to perform in Eugene, Oregon, I did a phone interview with community radio station KLCC. When we went live on the air, the DJ announced what he had just played, and one of the songs was by Mason Williams. When we started to chat, I described my small connection to Mason.

The DJ told me that Mason Williams lived in Eugene, and that's all I needed to hear. I said over the air, "Please, Mason, if you are listening, please come to my concert next week at WOW Hall—I would love to meet you in person—I've been a fan of yours practically my whole life!" I added that if anyone who was friends with Mason was listening, please get the word to him.

I carried a gift for Mason to the concert in Eugene—a small round brass magnifying-glass paperweight. About midway through the show, I had the house lights turned on and asked if he was there.

Silence.

So I asked if there was anyone there who had a direct connection to him. A woman who looked to be about sixty raised her hand, and I asked her what her connection was.

"He was my babysitter," she said.

"You mean he babysat your children?" I asked.

"No," she said slowly, "he babysat *me*."

"Are you still friends with him?" I asked.

"I haven't seen him in a long time," she said, "but my daughter is a driver for Federal Express and knows where he lives."

So I deputized this woman to give the paperweight to her daughter to give to Mason.

When I returned home a few weeks later, there was a large envelope from him. In it was a CD of Mason singing "The Water Is Wide," which I played on my occasional XM/Sirius radio program, *Slipped Discs*, on channel 15, "The Village." I only play CDs that have been slipped to me in person by the artists—99.99 percent of the time I won't play a CD that has been mailed to me, but for Mason Williams I bent that rule.

Gotta love those Smothers Brothers for helping put Mason Williams on the map back in the sixties. In their concerts they play a twenty-minute video highlight reel of their TV show that is pure joy, reminding everyone just how ahead of the curve those boys were.

When I see the Smothers Brothers perform live, they look almost exactly as I remember they did back when their TV show was brand new. Sometimes I watched that show while holding my guitar, trying to figure out the chords to the songs as Tommy played. I know it's not the usual way to learn an instrument—staring at a TV screen—but it's the way I learned.

Anyway, there I was, gearing up for my junior year of high school as a budding songwriter and future cheerleader, when suddenly everything fell apart. Unbeknownst to almost the entire PMA faculty, Peekskill Military Academy had been financially mismanaged for years. It was announced that the school was closing for good, and we were told we had to move. Now.

My older sister, Louise, was a nurse at St. Vincent's Hospital in New York City, my brother Greg was a junior at Colgate University, and my brother Tom was entering Hamilton College. That meant there were still six of us at home, and suddenly our dad was out of work.

I recall that last stretch of summer as scary and hot, with most afternoons interrupted by thunderstorms. Living at that school, on that enclosed campus, was all we kids had ever known. We had had a worry-free child-hood. It was the only life our parents had experienced as a married couple.

Dad quickly started looking for another teaching job at other area private schools, hoping to find one that would include housing for his wife and large family. I was praying it would be within the Peekskill school district. I don't know how many schools he tried—but amazingly, he found one. But it wasn't nearby; it was way upstate—way upstate to us, anyway. Peekskill is in Westchester County, and back then we thought we *were* living upstate. But this new school was in Lakemont, New York: five hours' drive north, on the west shore of Seneca Lake, midway between Geneva and Watkins Glen. It was a coed boarding high school called Lakemont Academy that, yes, would take our whole family, even our dog. It had a big house on the grounds that could accommodate us, and all the Lavin kids could attend tuition free.

I didn't want to go. I begged my parents to let me live with a classmate so that I could finish out high school at PHS. I loved the school, loved all the activities I was in. I made varsity cheerleading, for God's sake!

But it wasn't meant to be. In late August 1968 we packed up all our things, and I said good-bye to my simple, happy life.

5

AND THE AWARD
GOES TO . . . THIS YEAR THERE IS NO WINNER

Our move up to Lakemont was done in the middle of the night so that we wouldn't have to stay in a motel—there were eight of us, plus Spanky, in our green station wagon.

When we arrived in Lakemont in the early morning, we were all a bit bonkers. We got there before our furniture did, so we spread out on the grass around the house and fell asleep. I'm sure the neighbors must have wondered about us right from that strange start. I remember waking up, not knowing where I was, stumbling around and whimpering. Spanky was the only one who was instantly at home in this new setting. He ran around and around the house, rolled on his back, wiggled in the grass, and was as happy as any dog could ever be.

The house the school had arranged for us was an old Victorian called the Manse. We'd never lived anywhere but the small house on the grounds of PMA—first we lived on the first floor, then as our family grew we moved out of the first floor and lived on the second and third floors. Now we had an entire house, and a house with a *name*.

This house wasn't on the grounds of Lakemont Academy; it was on a corner lot in the actual village of Lakemont. The school was a quarter mile away, down a narrow paved road that crossed Route 14. At this location Route 14 was a two-lane highway with a sixty-five mile per hour speed limit. Looking south you could see for almost a mile, but looking north you could only see about a quarter of a mile. We kids got used to crossing it, very carefully. Many of the cars went way faster than the speed limit. As long as you were vigilant, however, there was no big danger.

The entire campus of the school was approximately four hundred acres, bordered on the west by Route 14 and on the east by Seneca Lake. North and south of the campus was farmland. It was a beautiful setting. Across the lake was a patchwork of farms—some cornfields, some vineyards. On days when the sunlight hit it just right, it looked like a painting.

We still had a couple of weeks before school started, and I was determined to get something going in these new surroundings. I noticed a sign by a farm not far from the Manse that said BERRY PICKERS WANTED, so I inquired. The blackberries were ripe and the pay was ten cents a pint, so I showed up the next day and was pointed in the direction of the blackberry bushes.

I found out the hard way that blackberry bushes are homes for daddy longlegs. I hate bugs. HATE them. Whenever I came upon a spider I screamed, then went to the next bush.

An entire family was picking blackberries nearby—a mother, father, and three small children. They were very fast pickers and very serious. I had never met a family like them before, and they had never met someone like me. I was picking berries because I wanted to make some money and have a "country" experience, but they were picking berries because they had no other way to make a living.

The farmer's wife was intrigued by me—my fear of spiders and my complete inexperience with farm life. She gave me a jar of milk from their cows to take home. I gave it to my mother, who was thrilled, but I was afraid to drink it because it didn't come from a carton.

I lasted just one week as a blackberry picker. At the end of that week I took my card—with a hole punched by the farmhand for each full pint I delivered—to get my pay. My employer totaled up my pay card and gave me six dollars. (Sixty pints in a week isn't so bad, considering all those daddy longlegs!) The harsh reality of that payday was the end of my blackberry-picking career, but school was starting soon and I would have quit anyway.

We quickly found out why Dad was able to get this job at the last minute: the school had trouble holding on to faculty. The headmaster was a larger-than-life, eccentric, ego-driven—dare I say it?—madman. One of the first stories we heard was how he led a group of students into the woods for a nature walk near the lake shore, took a baby bird out of its nest, and squeezed it to death to demonstrate what life will do to you if you don't toughen up. Who knows if the story is true or not, but when it's the first thing you're told about someone, it's not a good sign.

There were only one hundred students at this school from grades seven through twelve, seventy boys and thirty girls. It was very expensive. My father was hired as dean, and what that came to mean was that when any of the students did anything bad that needed attention, the headmaster would usually disappear for a few days and tell my dad to handle the problem.

This school, small as it was, had a high concentration of streetwise teenagers from the New York City area who were hip to the drug trade. I was completely inexperienced with all of this and not really interested. I was all about studying, at least when I wasn't obsessing about cheerleading, baton twirling, and folksinging.

With so few boys, Lakemont's sports teams had little talent to draw from. Since there were even fewer girls, to be a cheerleader all you had to do was show up—no tryouts. There were six of us, and we were awful. And I mean AWFUL. We tried to whip up school spirit by making posters and taping them up around the school—Go LAKEMONT! CRUSH DUNDEE!—but the "heads" in the school (that's what we called the drug-takers) would draw peace signs on our posters, scratch out *Crush*, and scrawl *Don't! Love one another!* in its place.

Our football team was also awful. The local teams we played were from schools many times our size. One time we played a school that was much bigger than us, and the score was so lopsided that, one by one, our players started faking injuries to be taken out of the game until we didn't have eleven players left to play and the game was called off. We cheerleaders were still trying to whip up hope, and we were quite angry when the game ended prematurely. I think the score was 56–3 at the time.

Our basketball team was a bit better. We had a black player named Tony, and whenever he was fouled and would go to the free throw line, we cheerleaders would yell in unison, "Beep beep bang bang ooogawa black power!"

That cheer always silenced the gym. Tony was one of the best kids at the school—smart, handsome, and good-natured. I had a big crush on him and was hoping he would ask me out, but he never did. I had heard Janis Ian's song "Society's Child" a year or so earlier when we still lived in Peekskill, and ever since then I had thought the idea of blacks and whites getting together wasn't as impossible as before.

While the sports department at Lakemont was below par, so was everything else. The so-called Drama Department put on one play that year, Moss Hart's three-act comedy *Light up the Sky*. Except they never got around to learning the lines for the third act and ended it after two acts, with no explanation to the audience why the play just stopped.

It became clear to my parents that this school was not a good place for any of us, but we soldiered on. The Manse, with its marble fireplaces and quaint porches, was a beautiful house. It had been the parsonage for the Protestant church across the street and was the nicest place we had ever lived. My bedroom—it was small, but it was mine alone—was on the second floor and had a tiny porch with a fire escape attached (which made Dad happy, since he always worried about house fires along with a million other imagined catastrophes). In good weather I would spend hours on the porch playing guitar and writing songs.

All during that academic year bad things happened: students were dismissed; faculty members quit. When the student body took one of those standardized tests that show where you rank among all the other high school students across the country, I was the only one of all the juniors and seniors who even ranked above the fiftieth percentile.

It wasn't that these students were dumb; they weren't. They hated school, tests, the teachers, their parents, and the world in general, and they deliberately answered the questions incorrectly to protest the whole system. (And that's not even counting the ones who were high when they took the test!)

The school was so oblivious to the situation that when the yearbook came out, besides "best looking," "most likely to succeed," and the other usual categories, the Lakemont yearbook had "best heads." The faculty thought the term was a euphemism for *intellectuals*. Ha!

In the spring my parents decided that I would graduate with the seniors, then take one English course over the summer to officially complete my studies and get me out of that school.

At graduation every year the special Tower Award was given to the graduating senior who displayed leadership in sports, academics, and over-all student life. There was one student, "Ted," who everyone assumed would receive the award that year, except that he had become implicated in a group rape situation that led to the dismissal of a number of students. He wasn't kicked out—up until then he had had a clean record—but I'll never forget how his misstep affected the graduation ceremony.

At the graduation, when it came time to announce the winner of the Tower Award, the head of the school's board of trustees rambled off the list of qualities of the person it would go to. He opened the envelope, leaned into the microphone, and said, "This year there is no winner." He dropped the envelope on the floor and sat down in disgust.

Then diplomas were awarded to all of us, and we returned to our seats onstage. I opened my diploma to see that it was blank, which didn't surprise me because I knew I had to take a course over the summer to graduate. I laughingly showed it to the students sitting on either side of me, so then everyone started opening their diplomas—and a few unfortunates discovered that theirs were blank, too—in their case because they hadn't passed all their exams.

Lakemont wasn't all bad—we loved the Manse, and living in the tiny village was a new experience for all of us. I even picked grapes one fall—I did better at grapes than with blackberries—and during one spring break I tied grapevines with both my parents to make extra money.

And Spanky loved living in Lakemont big time. Spanky probably did more for the students at Lakemont than any human did. He was beloved by everyone on the school campus and in the village. But he was a dog, after all, and had his weaknesses.

Alas, one day his traveling ways caught up with him, and he was hit by a car on Route 14 a quarter mile from our house. He died, and the whole community mourned. But I can't help but remember what a wonderful dog's life he led while he was with us and think that, given the choice, he would have preferred to keep his freewheeling independence and take his chances.

6

DAMAGED GOODS

t took me five tries to pass my driving test. One of my first times behind the wheel was with my brother Tom on an unpaved country road. I buried the front end of the car in a mound of cow manure and had to be dug out. I started out a bad driver, and I still am. While I did finally get my license, and I suppose I could drive in an emergency (for example, if I was on a volcano being chased by a pyroclastic river of lava and rocks), it's not something I excel at.

A few years ago an eye doctor told me—in all seriousness—that part of my driving problem is that I focus twelve feet beyond infinity. This was during an exam in which I was desperately trying to get contact lenses so I wouldn't have to wear glasses onstage. After looking at my eyes this way and that, the ophthalmologist sat me down and told me that I was a "very poor candidate" for contact lenses, but a poor candidate "highly motivated by vanity."

I guess not motivated enough. Oh well.

In August 1969 my family traveled from Lakemont to Breezy Point, New York. My mom's parents' place was a couple of miles from the Marine Parkway Bridge, which we kids called "the singing bridge" because of the droning musical sound it made when you drove over its metal-grid road-way. We rejoiced when we heard that sound, knowing that the ocean and the beach were just a few minutes away.

As we drove south on Route 17, about 150 miles north of New York City, we started to notice more and more cars parked along the side of the road. Dozens of people were struggling with camping gear and large back-packs, and there were even tents pitched along the highway. It was the weekend of the Woodstock Music & Art Fair, and there were already news reports that thousands of people were headed toward it.

At one point Dad rolled down his window and shouted, "Take a bath, hippies! Take a bath!" at the people walking alongside the road. We kids hid our faces, embarrassed. Despite that, what we were witnessing was strange and wonderful—all these people heading toward a musical mecca that would become one of the landmark events of our era.

That weekend I remember all of us crowding around the radio at the bungalow. (There was no TV, so the radio was how we got all our news.) Public officials were begging people *not* to travel to Woodstock—word was that close to half a million were already there, which, of course, made even more people want to be part of it.

When we drove back to Lakemont a few days later, we passed even more cars left on the side of Route 17. There were still people camping, and there were lots of scraggly hitchhikers looking a bit worse for wear.

So that's as close as I got to Woodstock—driving by the area before it started and after it was over. I have listened to the Woodstock album a thousand times and wished I could have been there—but at the time I was only seventeen, and with my fear of spiders, the camping thing has never been high on my to-do list. (The song "Camping" on my 1986 album *Beau Woes and Other Problems of Modern Life* spells out my bug philosophy very clearly. To this day I won't eat anything that has more than four legs.)

I wouldn't be attending college for another year, so I went looking for a job, but I found nothing. The area was so sparsely populated that there were few businesses besides farms, a couple small grocery stores, and some beauty salons. I had a junior driver's license that wouldn't allow me to drive at night, so finding a job any farther away from home wouldn't work. I turned to plan B.

Plan B meant going to a state college that spring for one semester and then switching to Keuka College, a nearby all-girls school, the following fall. State University of New York at Brockport accepted me, and I enrolled in January 1970 as a nursing major.

I was assigned a room in a high-rise girls' dorm, and I soon got to know one of the other girls, Vicky, the only other student in the dorm who was a first-semester freshman like me. We were the only two girls in the dorm who had a curfew. We immediately bonded over the injustice of being singled out this way. Vicky even wrote a letter to the college newspaper complaining about it, saying, "How can we become acclimated to college life when we are the *only* two who have a curfew in the entire dormitory?" I was impressed by her use of the word *acclimated* and determined to use it myself at the first opportunity.

Vicky was one of the most beautiful girls I had ever seen. She had long, wispy blonde hair, big blue green eyes, the most luminous rosy tan skin, a dancer's lithe body, and a quirky yet mysterious spirit. There were lots of boys who lusted after her, and I got the feeling she enjoyed herself with a number of them. I was still inexperienced in that department—oh, I had had a couple of hot make-out sessions, but not much more than that.

Vicky and I were unlikely pals because we were so different, but she loved the fact that I wrote songs. She dated a fellow student who was famous for just being *at* Woodstock, and she thought my being a folksinger was *très* cool. I would often sit in the dorm's stairwell playing guitar and working on songs. (The natural reverb in any stairwell always makes voices sound better, and this can give a beginner confidence.)

I so wished that I could have looked like Vicky. The quintessential folksinger, to me, had long hair and an enigmatic air about her. Vicky was someone you couldn't take your eyes off of. Everyone wanted to know her and be her friend.

She quickly fell in with a crowd that was known to drink, smoke a lot of pot, and try other things, too. I went to one of their parties—people were dropping acid and giving each other naked massages, as well as discussing politics and art. Part of me was drawn to this group, but the inexperienced, conservative side of me balked.

Vicky convinced me I should change my major to something more artistic. At first I resisted—Brockport had awarded me a nursing scholarship, and I'd lose it if I changed my major. But since I was just taking core courses and didn't plan to be at Brockport more than one semester, officially changing my major at this point was moot.

Midway through my first semester at Brockport, I started to rethink my plan to transfer to Keuka College and become a nurse. I was making friends at Brockport and had discovered a coffeehouse in the basement of a church in town—a place aptly named the Crypt—where I started to hang out on weekends and sing at their open-mike nights. I liked the town of Brockport and the large campus—there were more than ten thousand students at that time, from many places, not just New York State. I liked the variety. The thought of confining myself to an all-girls college on a relatively small campus felt like a giant step backward.

My parents tried to change my mind—Keuka had offered me a substantial scholarship to continue nursing studies—but I'd cooled on the idea of nursing as a career. I wanted to change my major to theater—an odd choice since I had never been in a play in my life. But Vicky had convinced me that studying anything other than the arts would be a waste of my time. Since I couldn't read music, becoming a music major was out of the question. In any case, I decided to return to Brockport in the fall and change my major to theater.

That first spring semester ended in a way no one could have predicted, with the May 4 shootings of students by overzealous national guardsmen at Kent State University in Ohio. Four students were killed, and nine others were wounded. Some of the students killed were protesting the Vietnam War, specifically the invasion of Cambodia, but some of them were just walking to class. Many colleges and universities across the country closed because of strikes protesting the shootings. Brockport was one of them, so we had no final exams. It was a crazy way to end my first semester. I played guitar and sang at some protest events, though at the time I was ignorant about how all of this was affecting two of my brothers. Greg and Tom had both been drafted; Greg decided to take on Congress and the legality of the war, while Tom eventually served in Vietnam. Years later—in 1984—my younger brother Christopher wrote a cover story for the *Rochester Times-Union Sunday Magazine* about it. (You can find it on my Web site.)

That summer, when I was back living in the sparse badlands of Lakemont, my first college report card arrived. My grade point average was 2.3, the lowest of my life, highlighted by a D in Astronomy—my one and only D ever. In two short years I had gone from a straight-A high school cheerleader on the student council to a C college student making a dubious switch in majors. I had no idea what I was doing and began to wonder if college even made sense for me.

Soon after I returned to Lakemont, it was announced that the school was closing, and our family had to move again. Dad had found a job at DeSales Catholic High School in Geneva, New York, so we started to make trips to Geneva to look for a house. Geneva, at the northern tip of Seneca Lake, was home to Hobart and William Smith colleges and was a much bigger place than Lakemont.

That summer I got a job working at a local canning factory. I was a string bean inspector, watching the beans go by on a conveyor belt for ten and a half hours a day, pulling out anything that wasn't a string bean as it went by. That meant mice guts, twigs, and dead grasshoppers (Bugs! Dead bugs!!). Needless to say, I hated the job.

The string beans that passed me on the conveyor belt had just been blanched for sixty seconds, so clouds of steam continuously rose up into my face. The entire room was dismally hot and humid; we had to wear rubber boots because we were constantly standing in two or three inches of water. We wore plastic shower caps on our heads and plastic gloves on our hands, as well as earplugs (at all times) because of the noisy machines. The monotonous sound was so loud that the preferred mode of communication was to throw a fistful of beans at someone to get her attention, and then move your arms around wildly as you screamed.

A girl named Sherry and I were assigned to work on opposite sides of the same conveyor belt for a few weeks. While the work was pure torture, this girl intrigued me to no end. She had the flattest, most expressionless voice I had ever heard, but the odd stories she told about her family were fascinating. Her parents hadn't spoken to each other in more than ten years, she said; her father thought her mother had had an affair thirty years before, and her mother swore that she hadn't, but he didn't believe her. So her dad had staked out the first floor of their house—with the TV—as his territory, while her mother stayed on the second floor, where she worked on puzzles.

Almost twenty years later, a version of that strange tableau emerged as the first verse of what has become my most-requested song, "The Kind of Love You Never Recover From":

> I know a couple
> She sits in a rocking chair
> Working puzzles
> He watches TV upstairs
> She's got a secret she has never let out
> A man she thinks he never knew about
>
> She hasn't seen him in thirty years
> The mention of his name
> Does not bring on tears
> If you ask her
> "Are there any regrets?"
> She'll tell you, "No"
> But she never forgets . . .

One Friday afternoon, Sherry said she was quitting. I was surprised, since she had said she liked the job, but she declared that she was getting married. That surprised me to no end because I found her so exceedingly dull, and when I got home from work that day I told my mother all about her—as dull as she was, she was getting married!

My mother replied, "Well, for every old stocking you'll find an old shoe." That struck me so much that I immediately wrote a song with that as the first line of the chorus:

> For every old stocking you'll find an old shoe
>
> My heart was going flip flop 'til I fell in step with you
>
> For every shoe you'll find an old lace
>
> I love you with my soul [Get it? Sole!]
>
> You can see it in my face

Fortunately I never recorded that corny song.

Every day at the factory there would be dented cans—they weren't thrown away but were put aside, stamped SALVAGE. Employees were allowed to take them home since the string beans inside were perfectly good, as long as you didn't wait too many years before eating them.

A few years later, when I was living in Manhattan, my brother Tom, who was then working at the same canning factory, drove down to visit me. I was sick with a horrible cold and couldn't come home for Christmas, so he surprised me and brought me a case of salvage string beans.

After he left I turned on the TV to watch *It's a Wonderful Life*. It was the lowest I had ever felt in my life—sick as a dog and surrounded by damaged cans of string beans. The next day I wrote the song "Damaged Goods." People still ask for it today, but it's too depressing for me to sing.

In the course of writing this, I listened to this song—the words of which I'd forgotten—for the first time in maybe twenty years. How could I have been so sad at such a young age? The last chorus goes:

> Now I think of myself as damaged goods
>
> So far no one's ever treated me as gently as I wished they would
>
> And I don't hold my head up quite that high
>
> And I'm longing for the simple days
>
> I wonder how things got this way
>
> I'm longing for the innocence of times gone by
>
> Oh those times gone by

Back in the late 1980s I opened for Odetta at a club called the Iron Horse in Northampton, Massachusetts. I sang "Damaged Goods" that night and introduced it by telling the story of working at the canning factory, pulling out anything that wasn't a string bean as it passed me by on the conveyor belt.

Between shows Odetta really let me have it. "Don't ever tell people there might have been mice guts mixed in with the string beans! Oh my God, child, you never ever *ever* tell people things like that from the stage!"

I was always in awe of Odetta and felt terrible that she yelled at me like that. I never knew why that story upset her so.

The experience of working at that horrible job no doubt helped to keep me in school. I thought that if I didn't get a college degree, I might end up stuck in a factory for the rest of my life. It's ironic that a job I hated so much inspired two of my better songs. Whenever I'm in the canned vegetable aisle of the supermarket and see the string beans, I flash back to that hot, humid, deafening canning plant. And since everybody's looking for a bargain these days, here's a tip: the cans of julienne-cut string beans are usually a little bit heavier than the regular cuts—chances are there's a few more beans in there.

7

I WONDER
WHOSE UNDERWEAR SHE'S WEARING NOW

My college career didn't turn out the way I hoped. Of course it didn't—I had six different majors over four years. I went from nursing to theater to political science to English to something called CLAM (contractual liberal arts major), then back to English. The only consistent thing I did over the four years was play guitar and write songs. But I never thought music could be a career; it was just something I couldn't stop doing.

Despite my lack of focus, I managed to have a good time in college. Brockport was the only state school at the time that offered a major in dance, so many of the prominent American dance companies made the university a stop on their concert tours. I had never been to a dance concert in my life, and suddenly I was discovering Alvin Ailey, Lar Lubovitch, Alwin Nicholai, Garth Fagin, Daniel Nagrin, and other legends of the dance world.

Daniel Nagrin was in residence at Brockport for a short time, and I took one of his classes. He was a bit of an eccentric. One of his performances was a solo piece called *The Peloponnesian Wars*. Dressed in a toga, he pointed an M-1 rifle (I recognized it because the cadets at PMA carried the same gun in parades) at the audience, aiming first at one person, then another. Some people squirmed in their seats, others yelled for him to stop, and some actually ran out of the auditorium. To this day I can't remember if he ever pulled the trigger.

Besides welcoming Nagrin and other standouts in the dance world, SUNY Brockport was host to John Houseman's Acting Company for one week. His theater troupe was made up of recent graduates of the Julliard School in New York, and the star of the company was a young unknown named Patti LuPone. There was great buzz about her already, and I got to see her in a different production every night. David Ogden Stiers was also in that company, and it was clear that he was on his way to a major career. I ushered for theater department events so that I could see plays over and over again—and I watched how productions changed over time and how the actors handled situations when something went wrong onstage.

During my one semester as a theater major, I took an acting class. *Tartuffe* was being performed each night, and the set was on the main stage. The acting teacher assigned each one of us a piece of furniture, and our task was to introduce ourselves to it.

I was assigned a fancy bench covered with a beautiful embroidered fabric and trimmed with an elaborate silk fringe. Others in the class were assigned to tables, chairs, mirrors, paintings, walls—I don't know how they introduced themselves to their furniture friends, but what I did was first stroke the bench, then run my fingers along the fringe. Then I lifted up the fringe to look under the bench, and that's when the teacher yelled, "Freeze!"

He had been watching all of us from the audience. He ran over to me and screamed, "What are you doing?!"

"I—I'm getting to know the bench," I said meekly.

"WHY are you looking UNDER the bench?" he demanded.

"I—I want to see what it looks like under there?"

"Well," he bellowed, "It's very important to know how well hung a man is, but is it polite to pull down his zipper when you are first being introduced?"

I had never heard the term "well hung" before, but I knew it had to be something sexual, and my face felt like it was on fire.

That's my one and only memory of acting class.

Oh, I did try out for every play and musical that went up that semester, but I never made it past the first round, where everyone would line up onstage in front of the director, not moving or saying anything, and he would decide which students would get to read for a part. I was eliminated on my looks alone. It wasn't pleasant, but I take comfort in knowing I wasn't rejected because of anything I actually *did*.

Because the theater department didn't want me, I found other creative activities to throw myself into. I teamed up with a fellow student, a tall, lanky guy named Eric Lowen who played guitar and wrote songs, and we performed together as Lowen & Lavin. He'd wear a white suit and I'd wear a prom dress, and we'd play at dorm functions and down at the Crypt. After college we lost touch, but years later we came across one another and were surprised to find that we were both still at it; I was with the Four Bitchin' Babes at the time, and he had partnered with Dan Navarro as Lowen & Navarro. What are the chances that two folkies playing dorm parties at a state university could both end up making a living in music?

A few years ago Eric was diagnosed with ALS, though he continued to perform for a long time. The last time I saw him was at the Falcon Ridge Folk Festival. Dan Navarro had a bunch of musicians (including me) join Eric onstage to sing his song "Learning to Fall" as the finale of their set. The weather had been cloudy and a bit chilly most of the day, but just before Lowen & Navarro took the stage, the clouds parted, and by the time we got up there it was warm, sunny, and beautiful.

It broke my heart to see Eric, once so tall and strong, now in a wheelchair, but he was having more fun than anybody else that day, so I felt foolish for my sad take on things. When we played together in college I never dreamed that a robust guy like him could be hit by such a devastating disease. When you're in college you don't feel invincible, you think you *are* invincible.

One night there was a five-hour jitterbug contest on campus. I was a pretty good jitterbug dancer, so I had my eye on the fifty-dollar first prize. Another student, Vinny from Staten Island, was one of the best male jitterbug dancers around, along with another student, Larry Gostin. (If I ever ran into Larry in the student union, he would run over to the jukebox, put in a quarter to play "Rockin' Robin," and we would wildly jitterbug to the song.) Larry wasn't around the night of the contest, but Vinny was, and I wanted to be his partner. The way the contest worked was that you'd dance for fifty-five minutes, then take a five-minute break, then start dancing again.

However, there was another girl, Irene Marshall, who wanted to enter the contest with Vinny, too. He couldn't decide whom he should dance with, so he practiced his moves with me for a few minutes, then did them with Irene, then went back to me, then back to Irene—he really was torn. There were just a few minutes left before the contest started. A dozen couples were already on the floor ready to go, numbers pinned to their backs, and Vinny was still undecided. He told us he was going to the men's room, and by the time he came back he'd have made up his mind.

Irene and I eyed each other suspiciously. I could see that she was an excellent dancer. I was a little smaller and lighter, so Vinny could throw me around more easily, but she had better moves. We decided to shake hands and wish each other well no matter what his decision was.

As we were shaking hands, the music started to play. We started moving to the beat, then dancing, and both instantly had the same idea—we knew we danced better with each other than with Vinny, so when he returned from the men's room we informed him he was too late—we were entering the contest together.

We won. We were the only girl-girl couple, which made us distinctive, and Irene's roommate, Judith Friedman, did her best to whip the crowd into cheering for us.

I'll never forget the next day—the elevator in my dorm was broken, and I lived on the thirteenth floor. I was too sore to walk downstairs to the dining hall. I soaked in a hot bathtub all afternoon, then spread Tiger Balm on every muscle I could reach. I was happy to win the prize money, but it was the first time in my young life that I realized that maybe I wasn't as strong and fit as I had thought.

Irene and I became fast friends and had a ridiculous series of adventures over the next few years. Judith and I also became friends, but Irene had a mischievous streak that I found irresistible. We became pals with two guys who worked in our dining hall—best friends who were both named Jim. One day one of the Jims started calling Irene and me "Boom Boom" and "Trixie," and those were the names we subsequently used whenever we found ourselves in unlikely situations.

One of these situations was a talent contest on the college radio station—students came from all over the campus to compete, and listeners called up to vote for who was best. Irene and I went in as Trixie and Boom Boom, go-go dancers. The DJ played a rock 'n' roll song, and we danced. All the radio audience could hear was the occasional clapping sounds we made. The other contestants sang, read poetry, played instruments—we were just goofing around. When the next performer went on, Irene and I went into another room at the radio station and called the number to vote.

We said, "We are at a party with thirty people, and we just LOVED those go-go dancers, so all thirty votes go to them." We assumed they knew it was us calling—but they didn't, and they announced over the air that the go-go dancers just got thirty votes.

We made a few more phone calls like that—they even put our call over the air, and we figured someone would realize it was us voting for ourselves, but they didn't. Then we actually got real votes—Jim and Jim were listening in the kitchen of the dining hall, and they called in the votes of all the cafeteria workers there. So we ended up winning that contest, too. (There wasn't any prize, just bragging rights.)

Jim and Jim had just moved to a house off campus and were planning a housewarming party, but they had no furniture. So we suggested they have a BYOF—bring your own furniture—party, and they loved the idea.

Irene and I bought matching wooden kitchen chairs at a secondhand store and, dressed in pajamas, walked from our dorm dragging these two chairs behind us. When we got tired, we sat on the chairs and hitchhiked until someone with a truck stopped. We put our chairs in the back and piled into the cab, and the truck dropped us off at Jim and Jim's. They had so many friends that they outfitted their entire house during that party.

My grades improved after my first rocky semester, and I was able to save a lot of money by working in the dining hall and as an RA in a dorm from my sophomore year on. Sometimes Eric Lowen and I would even get paid for performing, though it was never more than fifty dollars. But life was good.

I was now living in my all-time favorite dorm. It was on a high floor in Mortimer Hall, facing west. Winters were brutally cold in Brockport, but I loved sitting in the window seat at the end of the day with a cup of hot tea, studying while watching the sun set over the snowy fields and listening to Judy Collins's "Secret Gardens of the Heart." It's one of those powerfully sweeping tunes that encompass a lifetime's worth of emotion within a single song, and it's among the most exquisite, achingly beautiful pieces of music I've ever heard.

One night, a young guy visiting a girl in our dorm was selling guitars. At the time I was still playing the same guitar I had learned on when I took lessons from public TV—a really cheap steel-string guitar, very tinny sounding. This guy seemed a bit on the shady side, but he offered me a small, really pretty Spanish-style nylon-string guitar for thirty dollars. To me that was a lot of money. I didn't know how to tell a good guitar from a bad one, but it did have a lovely sound, so I was tempted.

Irene came from a wealthy family and couldn't believe I wouldn't jump at the chance to buy a new guitar for thirty bucks. I had the money, but I wasn't one to make quick decisions like that. The guy said he'd throw in a cardboard case, so Irene ordered me to buy it. And I did. Over the subsequent years I was told that the guitar was worth a lot more than thirty dollars— and had probably been stolen!—but that never occurred to me at the time.

My new little nylon-string guitar sounded particularly sweet when I played it in the stairwell, and it also sounded good next to Eric's much larger steel-string guitar. I was writing songs all the time, but I never recorded any of them and rarely wrote them down. I sang them over and over again, never had any trouble remembering the lyrics, and didn't imagine that all these years later I'd have no memory of the vast majority of them.

One that I do remember was inspired by one of the girls in my dorm the year I lived in Gordon Hall. She wasn't particularly pretty, but she was tall and thin, had reddish brown hair, wore eyeglasses, and was a total slut. (I don't know how else to describe her.)

Not only did she sleep around, she had a habit of stealing the underpants of the guys she slept with. She bragged about her collection, and when I knew her she had thirty-four pairs. Very often she would wear a pair under her skirt and loved to flash people to show off her latest acquisition.

A famous musician came through our school to do a concert, and sure enough, the next day she was wearing his underwear and flashing everybody in sight, whether they were interested or not.

So I wrote a song called "I Wonder Whose Underwear She's Wearing Now." I can't remember if this is one that Eric and I did together.

I took a lot of English courses at Brockport, and while still a sophomore I somehow got into a graduate poetry class that I had no business being in. I wrote one incomprehensible paper about a poem whose meaning completely eluded me. I was so desperate to make sense of it that I made up terms like "cyclopean vindictive" and "diminishing parallels" to describe it.

When the paper was returned to me with a giant red F at the top and a handwritten note that said, "This is the most solipsistic bit of writing I have ever read," I spent the whole class praying that "solipsistic" was a compliment. (Of course, that F should have been a clue.) Years later I used the word in my story/song "The Shopping Cart of Love." After I say it I pause and tell the audience, "Yeah, I didn't know what that word means, either." Now you know why.

A few weeks after I wrote my underwear song, the beat poets Allen Ginsberg and Lawrence Ferlinghetti stopped in Brockport on their poetry-reading tour. One of the English professors, Al Poulin Jr., had edited an excellent anthology of modern American poetry, and many of the poets included in this book made a point of visiting the campus when they went on reading tours.

Allen Ginsberg played an odd instrument onstage—it was shaped like a book, and he pumped it back and forth to make a very simple accordion sound. One of the poems he read was called "Don't Smoke," and it consisted of him saying over and over "Don't smoke don't smoke don't smoke don't smoke" as he pumped the accordion-book in his lap.

Lawrence Ferlinghetti read a humorous poem he had just written called "Underwear," and I naturally felt a funny connection with him.

At a party for the two poets after the reading, I saw Ferlinghetti standing all alone. I screwed up my courage, boldly walked over to him, and asked him about his underwear poem. Then I told him that I was a songwriter, and—what a coincidence!—had just written an underwear song.

He wanted to know all about my song, so I told him it was about the slutty, men's-underwear-collecting girl in my dorm. He must have gotten the wrong impression, because he asked me if I would like to spend the night with him in his hotel room.

I got all flustered, told him I couldn't possibly do that, and just slipped away. I circulated for a while and talked to some other people, and about a half hour later I saw that Ferlinghetti had put his coat on and was leaving. A bunch of students gathered by the door, and I joined them.

He said good-bye to all of us, and then he looked over at me and motioned for me to come closer. I walked over to him, and he leaned down and whispered, "I wonder whose underwear she's wearing now?" And with that, he was out the door, the rascal.

It's no tragedy that early songs like that one have disappeared into the ether. Dave Van Ronk told me that many singer/songwriters often started recording years before they should—then had to deal with their early cringe-inducing songs coming back to embarrass them. Oh, don't get me wrong—I have lots of songs that I wince at when I hear them now, but there could have been a whole lot more.

That's one of the reasons why I am such a big fan of Pete Nelson's album *The Restless Boys' Club*. He was already forty when he put that first album out—so his debut CD showcases a fully formed songwriter with a smart, original point of view.

Another favorite debut album is Ray Jessel's *The First 70 Years*. He was actually seventy-two when he released it, but "70" sounded better in the title. The optimistic working title of his next album was *The Next 70 Years*, though its final title is *Naughty or Nice*. On Ray's album you'll also hear the glorious voice of Maude Maggart. I'm crazy about her work. She has made some elegant recordings and performs in the most expensive cabarets in New York, London, San Francisco, and Los Angeles. She reminds me a little bit of my college friend Vicky, except that she's brunette, not blonde. But she's got that same magnetic, mesmerizing quality.

Speaking of Vicky, she left Brockport after one year and transferred to another college closer to New York City. At first we corresponded, but then gradually we lost touch, as often happens with college friendships.

In 1976, a few months after I had moved to New York City, I called the last number that I had for her. I wanted her to know that I was finally committing to music and to thank her for nudging me in that direction way back during my first semester in college.

Her mother answered the phone. I asked if Vicky was there, and then there was a long pause.

"Are you there?" I asked.

"Yes, I'm here," her mother answered. Then she said, "Vicky is dead."

"What happened?" I asked, shocked. "Did she have an accident?"

"No. She committed suicide."

I'm sure I must have said something like, "I had no idea—I'm so sorry—" What do you say when you get news like that?

Her mother said good-bye, then hung up the phone.

I didn't have a stereo, but I did have a small cassette player and a few cassettes. One of them was Jackson Browne's *Saturate Before Using*, which included "Song for Adam," one of my favorites. I turned the lights off, lit a candle, played that song over and over, and said prayers for Vicky.

To this day it breaks my heart to think that such a talented, sweet, artistic beauty could take her own life. When you grow up plain looking, feeling invisible, you often think how wonderful your life could have been if only you had been lucky enough to be born beautiful. It's a smack upside the head when you realize how naive that kind of thinking is. Nobody has it easy.

8

SO YOU
WANT TO BE A PIRATE

S o you want to be a pirate
You've golden-ringed your ear
Your ship is on Lake Ontario
Have they taught you how to steer?

You said your mother was a gypsy
Said your father was a priest
Now's the time to celebrate
Come on in and join the feast

It's not often that I write songs that I don't understand, but this is part of one of them. I wrote it in December 1972, just prior to my twenty-first birthday, when I was at my family's home in Geneva, New York, during the Christmas holidays. A few days later, at a local hangout called Cozzies, owned by a beloved Genevan named Cosmo Fospero, I met a man who fit the description of the character in the song.

He had a small gold hoop in his ear, and he lived in a boat in dry dock on a canal off Lake Ontario. Over our first beer he told me that his mother had gone out on her own at a very young age and traveled all over the country, and that his father was one of the elders of his church. Since I don't believe in coincidence, I invited him to dinner at my parents' house.

I fell fast and hard for Gary. I remember the first time he kissed me, in the hallway off the kitchen at my parents' house. It was dark, it was a quick kiss, and it buckled my knees. I'd never felt anything like it in my life. This guy had complete power over me, and I knew my days of innocence would soon be over.

It happened on his boat on my twenty-first birthday. There you go.

I didn't realize that no one thought it was a good idea that I date this guy. Nobody knew his history—he was vague about *everything*. I didn't care. I was in love. The fact that I wrote that song *before* I met him meant that it was destiny.

Gary split his time between that boatyard and Syracuse, where he renovated apartments as his second job. He was eleven years older than me. I never met his parents or his younger brother, but none of that bothered me.

When I returned to Brockport in January for my last year of school, I went on the birth control pill, a new kind called "sequential" that was supposed to be easier on the body. Immediately something went wrong, though at the time I didn't realize it was the pill that had caused it. It was the first week of classes, and I was looking forward to my last year, which should have been a breeze. I had a job in the dining hall and was an RA, so I had no money worries.

But suddenly I was nervous and anxious, and I felt like the world was closing in on me. I quit my job in the dining hall; I quit my job as RA. I then had to find a new place to live, because the dorm master had to replace me. I moved out of my favorite room—the one with the beautiful view of the sunset—and to an apartment in town shared with a theater major I knew only slightly, a girl named Julie Sheinman. I now had to deal with a roommate, something I hadn't had to do since freshman year. I was irritable and borderline crazy. I was going to class and doing my assignments, but I was completely out of sorts. All of this took place during the first four weeks of classes, my first four weeks on birth control pills. I didn't make the connection.

When I got my period, it was heavier and more painful than anything I had ever experienced. I was light-headed and woozy. I called the doctor at the on-campus clinic where I got the pills, and he said that it was just my body adjusting and I'd be fine in a few days. But the next day I collapsed and was taken to the hospital.

My friends Irene and Judith were waiting for me just outside my room. All my friends, including them, knew about my new boyfriend, Gary, and one of them called him at the boatyard. He said he'd be right there, but he didn't come. My friends were furious, but I forgave him. I knew he was working two jobs and that the little jeep he drove couldn't do more than forty-five miles per hour. I was going to be fine, and I was generally embarrassed by the whole ordeal. I wanted it to be forgotten—the sooner, the better.

Gary was working so hard because he needed to save money for his grand plan: to sail around the world, starting in Florida. I crocheted him a blanket I hoped he could take with him. He was five feet ten inches tall, so I made him a giant five-foot-ten-inch afghan. It took me a long time. I would sit on his boat (still in dry dock) for hours and play songs for him. I also made him pillows for his boat, which I embroidered with his initials intertwined with mine. I would have done anything for this guy. First I had to get through school, though. Once I was off the offending birth control pills, clarity returned—with the realization that I had quit both my jobs. If only I had known at the time what was going on with me! But it was too late—I had already been replaced.

I now had to acclimate myself to my new surroundings, living off campus with a roommate and apartment mates. My roommate, Julie, was an immensely talented actress, and she was cute but not pretty in a conventional way, so she struggled to get small parts in college productions, all the while knowing that she had loads more talent than most of the conventionally beautiful lead actresses.

I continued to play guitar and sing at the Crypt, see Gary whenever I could, and keep up with my studies. I wanted to meet Gary's family, but he was always too busy with work to make it happen. The summer between my last two semesters I got an office job in downtown Brockport and moved into a house on College Avenue. I was living with a new bunch of girls and it was a lively place, but I could tell something wasn't right with my body again. I started to feel progressively worse, and since this had happened before I made sure to go to the doctor before the bleeding was out of control.

I was admitted to the local hospital and was released a few days later. I resumed my work and studies until I suddenly started running a high fever. When I went back to the local hospital, they transferred me to a bigger one in Rochester. I had developed an infection the local hospital didn't feel it could treat. Luckily I hadn't waited too long, and within two days the infection started to clear and my temperature dropped.

All the girls from the College Avenue house came to visit me at the hospital, and like last time, one of them called Gary, who said he'd be right there. Again he didn't show, and again I forgave him. My friends were furious. I told them it was my responsibility for going on birth control pills. We couldn't assume the men in our lives would come swooping in to rescue us. It's my body, my decision, I said. I would have liked it if he had shown up, but I knew his work schedule kept him too busy.

I finished my last semester of school in December 1973. My friend Irene had accelerated her classes and also graduated that semester, and then she moved to Miami to get away from the cold. I didn't want to be far away from Gary, but Irene, clever girl that she is, convinced me I should come to Miami to learn to sail in preparation for Gary's around-the-world adventure. He *loved* the idea and encouraged me to do it immediately, so I packed up my stuff, just took what I could carry and would need in a warm climate, and headed for Miami.

Irene and Vinny—yes, Vinny the jitterbug dancer—picked me up at the airport. Vinny had recently reconnected with Irene and had also come to the realization that he was gay, and he was having the time of his life enjoying Miami's wild nightlife scene. I was going to stay with Vinny until Irene could find an apartment for the two of us plus her new friend Amy, a modern dancer.

I started temping right away, working tedious jobs as a typist, file clerk, receptionist—but I was in Miami and the weather was beautiful, so the boring jobs would have to do for now. Once in a while I sang and played guitar at a club in Coconut Grove called Monty's Conch.

Irene found a small house to rent on Almeria Avenue in Coral Gables. It was for sale, so we didn't know how long we'd get to live there, but it was a thin slice of heaven while it lasted. The house was built in 1948 and had solar panels on the roof that heated the water. (Back then all the houses were built with solar panels to take advantage of the free hot Florida sun.) In the backyard were a banana tree, an orange tree, a grapefruit tree, and two hibiscus bushes. We could pick the fruit and eat it right there, and I would gather the hibiscus blossoms, dry them in the oven, and make tea. After suffering through arctic upstate New York winters, this was magical.

There were two bedrooms and a screened-in porch off the back with jalousie windows that we turned into a third bedroom. That was my room. Tiny lizards ran up and down the screens, but I didn't mind once I was told that lizards eat bugs.

On Saturday Irene and I would pack up our laundry and drive over to the Miamarina to wash our clothes in the laundry room used by those who docked their yachts at the marina. We hoped to meet some boating people who could teach me how to sail, and the bar at the Miamarina sold coconut shrimp for eleven and a half cents apiece. We could eat a delicious meal for less than a dollar.

Sometimes we would take little sailing jaunts with people we met— complete strangers. I remember one idyllic Saturday in the late afternoon, out on someone or other's boat. The sun bounced off the water, the boat gently rocked, and the radio was tuned to Minnie Ripperton singing, "Loving You," with that impossibly high vocal riff at the end of the chorus. It was one of life's perfect moments.

This was way back in the last century, when the world wasn't as dangerous as it is now. Once Irene and I even hitchhiked to Key West and back. What trusting souls we were. I had my guitar with me and got a gig at some bar that was supposed to be Ernest Hemingway's favorite hangout (though in Key West every bar seemed to boast that). I was singing when I suddenly saw a giant cockroach on the table right in front of the stage. It was running this way and that; I stopped singing and screamed.

A waiter came over and very casually put a beer can on top of the bug— a light aluminum Budweiser can (yes, I even remember the brand)—and then the can started to move around the table! That was the moment I knew I couldn't live in Florida for long.

I was in touch with Gary during that time—letters and the occasional phone call. He was always broke, and this was way before cell phones, so we didn't speak nearly as often as I wished. But I was still madly in love with him.

In mid-June, during one of our laundry jaunts at the Miamarina, Irene spied a flyer on the bulletin board looking for a "female crew to sail to the Bahamas for the summer." What perfect luck! We answered the ad, which had been posted by the owner of a thirty-five-foot fin clipper. It would be the owner and his first mate, and he wanted two female crew members to cook and clean for the months of July and August. We admitted that we had no sailing experience, but we were great cooks (a lie), very tidy (another lie), and willing to learn (the truth). They agreed to take us for an overnight cruise to try us out.

The next Saturday we met them at the Miamarina. The owner, Henrich, from the Netherlands, looked to be in his mid-sixties. The first mate, Carl, in his mid-twenties, was from Miami. We passed initial inspection, and then we took off.

We did no background check, nothing. We didn't give anyone Henrich's phone number or name; we just took off on a boat headed out into the open ocean with two strangers. We sailed way out to the point where you couldn't see land, which Henrich told us was called the ragged keys. It was beautiful.

Our first "test" was to make dinner. We went down into the galley and opened the cupboards, and immediately everything fell out. We had no clue how you were supposed to do anything on a boat. But Henrich and Carl ate the dinner we made (canned spaghetti), and then we watched the sun go down and went swimming. This was the year before the movie *Jaws* came out. The water was so clear and beautiful—if you ran your hand through it, thousands of microscopic plankton lit up. It felt almost supernatural.

Irene and I served dessert (canned pudding), and then we all sat on the deck, had drinks, and gazed at the moon. I imagined what it would be like to do this all summer—until Henrich said to me, "Let me show you where you and I will sleep."

Wha??? There were two sleeping areas—one under the front of the boat and one toward the back—and he said that he and I would sleep at the front, and Carl and Irene would sleep in the back.

Duh. THIS is why they wanted female crew. How stupid could we be?

I told Henrich I couldn't possibly do that. I was in love with Gary and wanted to learn how to sail so that I could go around the world with him. Henrich was unfazed.

"Oh, don't worry, I promise I won't touch you. This is how we live out on the open sea."

Well, I didn't buy it, and neither did Irene. But we were nowhere near land and it was late at night, so what were we going to do?

Irene suggested I sing a song for Henrich, who had told us he was an agent for Universal Artists Exchange—an organization that sounded like United Artists, or Universal Studios, but was neither. He claimed to book performers all over the world, so Irene had convinced me to bring my guitar on the trip.

I brought out the guitar and sang as many songs as I could think of in the hope that it would make Henrich and Carl sleepy. Eventually I stopped, and Henrich again asked if I wanted to sleep in his compartment with him, but I refused, and Irene refused Carl. So Henrich told us we could sleep up top under the open sky.

There were two small benches with cushions on them that you might call beds in an emergency situation like this. And there was a marine clock that banged and clanged every fifteen minutes. We stretched out on those cushions and closed our eyes. Five minutes later I heard Irene whisper, "Trixie?" And I whispered back, "Boom Boom?" We sat up and laughed ourselves silly.

Thankfully, Henrich and Carl were all business the next day. They sailed us back to the Miamarina and told us they'd be choosing another crew for their trip. Henrich gave me his business card and told me to get in touch if I ever wanted to do a musical tour.

We were bleary-eyed from not sleeping, but we stopped at the bar to get a couple of dozen coconut shrimp to go. We drove back to Coral Gables, woke up Amy, and sat around the kitchen table, devouring shrimp and describing our stupid adventure in the ragged keys.

Today, whenever I see coconut shrimp on a menu I have to order it, and I instantly think about that Minnie Ripperton song.

9

ARE YOU
A REAL GIRL?

During the first two months I lived in Coral Gables I regularly worked as a temp, but I was always on the lookout for ways to make extra money. I got occasional singing gigs—*very* occasional—and I sold Cracker Jack at the Orange Bowl, home of the Miami Dolphins. (I even sold Cracker Jack during the Orange Bowl game itself on New Year's Day.)

I wasn't a very good Cracker Jack vendor—I liked football too much and spent a lot of time watching the games. I wore a green vest with the name of the vending company, Zum Zum, on the front and back in big letters. I made only a seven-cent profit on each box of Cracker Jack I sold, and eight dollars a game at most. One of my best pitches was, "Attention football fans! News flash! While touring the Cracker Jack factory yesterday, Elizabeth Taylor, in her haste to eat as much free Cracker Jack as she could, by accident dropped her famed engagement ring sporting the Hope Diamond." Then I'd shake a box of Cracker Jack and say, "Why, it might be the free prize in this very box that I hold. For fifty cents you might become a millionaire! Look at that lovely lady with you—haven't you always wanted to get her a giant diamond ring?"

One of my worst sales pitches came back to bite me at one game. I guaranteed that if someone who bought Cracker Jack from me didn't like the free prize in the box, I would cheerfully refund their money. I thought it was the perfect sales pitch because back then Cracker Jack came in cardboard boxes covered with foil, and it took a couple of minutes to get the box open. In the time it took to find the prize, unwrap it, and figure out what it was, I would be long gone.

During the first quarter of one game where I was giving my "personal guarantee" pitch, I sold a box to a little brother and sister who were at the game with their parents. The boy was maybe six, the girl all of four years old. Almost two hours later I was back in that section again, and I heard a tiny screeching voice squeal, "Hey! There's the girl who sold us the Cracker Jack with the crummy prize!" I tried to pretend I didn't hear that and moved quickly in the opposite direction, but the two little kids chased after me, so I had to stop. I asked them what their prize was, and they told me it was a tiny cardboard coloring book with an even tinier cardboard brush. You had to spit on the coloring book and then move the brush around in it to see colors.

Eww. Spitting on a cardboard coloring book? Not a good prize. But I wasn't serious about giving the money back. I walked the kids back to their seats, and their parents glared at me. I told them I didn't think it was a bad prize, and they *had* eaten all the Cracker Jack.

I now feel ashamed about this, even though it was so many years ago. I should have just given them their fifty cents back, but that was the profit for more than seven boxes! What was I thinking?

The little boy said, "Well, you said you'd give the money back if WE didn't like the prize, not if YOU thought it was okay! *And we don't like the prize!*"

I suddenly saw that this could be a very important lesson for these children, so I told them that when they grew up, people were going to tell them all kinds of lies to get them to buy all kinds of things they didn't really want or need, so this should teach them that they shouldn't believe everything they hear.

At that point their parents told me to go away or they were going to call security. People sitting near them had been eavesdropping, and they started to boo me. (Hey, wasn't it also in Florida, two decades later, that I'd be getting booed opening for Joan Rivers? Coincidence? Maybe not.)

I had learned about being a Cracker Jack vendor from a guy that Irene was dating—a tall, red-haired guy named Ben. He and Irene didn't last very long, so she decided to check out the personal ads in the *Miami Phoenix,* the weekly alternative arts newspaper. Irene was really pretty and never wanting for male companionship, but she had a bit of a wild streak, and finding dates through the personals appealed to her.

Because there was no fee to run them, there were loads of personal ads. We used to read them out loud to each other—some were funny, some were sad, and some were just strange. For example, one was run by a woman with a "unique body design" looking for her soul mate. Another ad, posted by a guy named Derwood, caught Irene's fancy. She answered it and planned to have dinner with him one Saturday night.

But first he would come to meet her at our house. This way Amy and I could meet him, too, to make sure he wasn't a murderer or a serial killer. (Our little sailing adventure had taught us to be a bit more cautious.) Derwood seemed nice enough, so Irene left with him, returning a few hours later with a big doggie bag for us.

Derwood came in with Irene, and we all sat around talking. I could tell Irene wasn't interested in him; that was clear. It was also clear that Derwood wasn't happy he had spent so much money on dinner when there was not going to be any payoff for him, so I guess it was out of frustration that he told us our house was haunted. He walked around the rooms and stopped in mine, saying it was haunted most of all because of the jalousie windows. "Ghosts like to see their reflections," he said, "that's why they like your room best."

He got us all very, very scared, then left. We all ended up sleeping on the floor of the living room because we were afraid to be in our bedrooms alone. Especially me. "Oh great," I thought, "my room is the favorite hangout for ghosts."

The next day we all came to our senses and laughed it off. Derwood called Irene a few times, but she turned down a second date.

A few weeks later, Amy got a call from a man who claimed to have gotten her name from a dating service that said she was the perfect match for him. Amy told him he must have dialed a wrong number. Then I got a call like that, too. I also said it must be a wrong number. Then someone called asking for Irene, saying a dating service matched them up.

We got more and more calls, until we knew we had to figure out who was behind it. When the next call came in, instead of saying it was a wrong number, I asked what the name of the dating service was. He said it was the Dream Girls Dating Service that advertised on the back page of the *Miami Phoenix*. I felt like Nancy Drew. Our only connection with that newspaper was Derwood, Irene's date.

We pored over the pages of personal ads and found one for Dream Girls Dating Service, which guaranteed to match men with the girls of their dreams for no fee. The address was a P.O. box. That address looked familiar. Why, it was the same P.O. box listed for the girl with the "unique body design." Then we remembered that Derwood had said he dated her—and she was a midget. Irene called Derwood, demanding to know how our names had been given to a dating service with the same address as the unique body design girl.

Turned out the midget had fallen in love with Derwood. She was aware that he had gotten the names and numbers of a lot of girls from his personal ad, so she demanded that he hand them over to her. She opened the fictitious Dream Girls Dating Service to make sure that those girls would be taken so she could have Derwood all to herself. Derwood obliged, even kicking in the names of his dates' roommates, like Amy and me.

We continued to get calls for weeks, and even after explaining to these guys that they were duped, they'd still say, "Well, you sound nice. Would you like to go out?" But we always said no. I was still in love with Gary, and though we didn't have any set plans, I just *knew* he'd eventually come to Florida.

But then I got a phone call that changed everything.

It was on a Sunday. Irene and I had spent the afternoon at Crandon Park on Key Biscayne. It had been a beautiful, sunny day, and the water was luxuriously warm. The last time we had been there I had been stung by the detached tentacle of a poisonous jellyfish (who knew they could still sting you when they were dismembered?), so I was a bit leery about going back. But the weather was so beautiful.

The water there quickly got deep, but after about a thirty-yard swim there was a wide sandbar where the water was only about knee-high. Irene and I swam out there, deciding to walk to the white painted sign stuck way out on the sandbar. So we walked and walked, talking about nothing in particular. The water got a little deeper, up over our knees, and then a little farther on it was up to our thighs. Our steps were slower now, but we kept going. The water got a little deeper still, and then it was very slow going.

"I wonder what that sign says," Irene panted.

"I bet it says, THIS IS THE END OF THE SANDBAR; NO SWIMMING PAST THIS POINT."

We walked more and more slowly, as the water was now almost up to our waists. As we got closer, we squinted at the sign till we could make out the tiny letters:

DANGER. BEWARE OF SHARKS!

With that we both screamed, wheeled around, and tried to run as fast as we could back toward shore. It was like that bad dream where you have to run and suddenly your legs are made of lead. We were so far out that we hadn't heard the lifeguards blowing their whistles and waving at us, but now we saw them.

By the time we got back to the edge of the sandbar, we were winded and didn't have the strength to swim the thirty yards back to the shallow water. Everyone on the beach was watching us, and the lifeguards called out, asking if we needed help getting back to shore. We yelled back, "No, we just need to catch our breath." We were so embarrassed and scared, but then we started laughing and couldn't stop. We were Boom Boom and Trixie, two pinheads at the beach.

It's probably why I like the movie *Romy and Michele's High School Reunion* so much. It really lets you get in touch with your inner pinhead. My Aunt Patsy had a small but pivotal role in that film. She's the waitress who asks, "What kinda business you girls in?" when they're masquerading as businesswomen but haven't yet come up with the "inventors of the Post-it Note" idea.

Aunt Patsy had another small but pivotal role in another minor classic, *Piranha Women of the Avocado Jungle of Death*, which starred Bill Maher (of all people). She played the supply clerk who issues the scientists the equipment they need to make their trek into the forbidden jungle to study the piranha women. If she hadn't given them their gear, the movie would have been over.

Aunt Patsy (her proper name is Pat Crawford Brown) is a master at turning these small parts into memorable bits because she's a fantastic actress with boatloads of skills and decades of theater experience. She was also in *Sister Act* and *Sister Act Two* (doing her own singing), and for a few years she played the recurring part of "Ida Greenberg," the bad girl senior citizen on *Desperate Housewives*, until her character was killed off by that stupid tornado.

One of my most interesting backstage experiences occurred a couple years ago when a hearing-impaired man came to my show after watching a DVD of the film *Daredevil*, starring Colin Farrell (with the closed captioning visible). Aunt Patsy played a busybody on a plane who talks nonstop to Colin Farrell's character, who is some kind of private eye or assassin or something, and he gets so exasperated that he flicks a peanut against the back of the tray table in front of him, it ricochets into her mouth, and she instantly dies of an allergic reaction.

During this scene the captions said: "This part is played by Pat Crawford Brown, aunt of folksinger Christine Lavin." Now I know that my association with Aunt Patsy has sold at least one ticket to one of my concerts, and I hope my writing about her gets her a gig, too.

Where was I? Oh, yes. Pinheads at the beach. Irene and I finally caught our breath and swam across to the shallow water. We blended in with all the other swimmers for a few minutes, then slunk out of the water, gathered our things, and drove back to Coral Gables.

A few minutes after we got home, the phone rang.

It was a woman who asked me if I was the Christine Lavin who was seeing Gary. I said yes. And then she said, "Did he tell you about me?"

We talked nonstop for the next two hours. Her name was Gail; she lived in Syracuse. She told me that Gary lived with her there and worked in the boatyard where I had met him. Gail claimed that Gary had been living with her for five years—way longer than I knew him.

She asked me if I knew that Gary had a son—a son who was being raised by Gary's parents because he was not financially responsible. She went on and on about how Gary was a pathological liar, that she wanted to protect me from him, that he was a cheat, a scoundrel, a no-good bum. She had seen the afghan that I had crocheted for him and the pillows I'd embroidered, and she'd found my letters from Florida. She told me he would never be coming to Florida; he would never go anywhere; he was a big liar who spun tall tales out of the air.

I told her about the times I was in the hospital and he never showed up, and how I forgave him despite my friends' misgivings. I also told her about the time I was with him when another woman came by, and he quickly dressed and scrambled out of the dry-docked boat to talk with her. The woman had been wearing some kind of uniform—I thought she might be a waitress, but he told me she was a nurse who had come by to tell him about a good friend of his who was dying in the hospital. I believed him. I was an idiot! I had been a nursing major! I could tell a nurse's uniform from a waitress' uniform, but I gave him a pass on that one. There must have been yet *another* woman, besides Gail and me.

"You're right!" Gail squealed over the phone. "He can't help himself. He's a sex maniac! And a pathological liar! You have no idea how lucky you are that I was able to track you down!"

I cried. I told her I wanted to meet her, and that I still cared about Gary. Maybe if we got together, we could help him change his ways.

Her tone changed completely. "Oh, *no*," she said, "We are *not* going to meet. I've dealt with you, I've dealt with others before you, and I'll deal with a dozen more after you. He's *mine*. You stay away from him. *He* loves *me*. He doesn't love *you*. Who do you think gave me your phone number? He doesn't want to see you again." And with that she hung up.

I cried for hours and hours, and I wrote him ridiculously long letters. He was my first love. I couldn't believe I had been so duped. I was completely, desolately heartbroken for the longest time. I was in Florida *because* of him. What a disaster.

Now when I think about it, all I want is to get that afghan back. If you ever find a giant, five-foot-ten-inch granny-square afghan, please buy it for me, and I'll reimburse you. It's got to be out there somewhere. He can keep those stupid pillows with those idiotic entwined initials, but I'll die a thousand deaths if that blanket shows up on *Antiques Roadshow*. I can just see it now:

"This is an example of late-twentieth-century handiwork, known among collectors as 'the tragically naive American female crocheted love afghan' . . . notice the odd size, exactly five feet ten inches. . . ."

Thank God I met a nice guy named Dutch who took my mind off things. He was a photographer who had been the lead singer of a rock band called the Swags, which had had modest success in the Miami area. For a few years he managed nightclubs, but at that time he was starting a new business as a photographer. He was recently separated from his wife and had a young son named Jeffrey. It wasn't a perfect situation for either of us, but he was sweet, kind, and very talented.

There was one quirky thing about him, though. (Keep in mind that at this point in my life I had only been in love with one man.) Dutch told me his first girlfriend's name was Linda Borman. This didn't mean anything to me, so he said, "Maybe you know her by her stage name: Linda Lovelace. I was the first guy she ever went to bed with. She lost her virginity to me."

What an honor to be linked in this way to the star of *Deep Throat*. She passed away a few years ago, but she's probably looking down (or up) from wherever she is, thinking, "I sure as hell never thought I'd be connected to a folksinger!"

Dutch was as poor as I was—actually, poorer, since he was paying child support, too. After a few months of dating, it was clear that temping and selling Cracker Jack didn't pay enough for me to live on comfortably, so I took a full-time job with a large security company.

The only good thing about that job was that it was close to home—which came in really handy during the two weeks I was attempting to save the life of a baby bird that fell out of its nest in our front yard. I called the local ASPCA, and they told me what kind of food to feed it and how often—every twenty minutes during daylight hours. (They told me that baby birds eat one and a half times their weight every day!) During the workday I would run home to feed the little critter twice during the morning, then come home for lunch, and then run home twice during the afternoon to feed the bird again. It was the best I could do, and I figured that in nature there were times when the mother bird wasn't there at exactly twenty-minute intervals.

The little thing actually got stronger and started to grow feathers—at first I thought it might be a sparrow, but when the feathers started to come in, it was clear it was a woodpecker. After ten days I decided to take the little bird for a "walk" in the backyard. I was crawling along in the grass, encouraging my little bird to walk, when suddenly we were circled by big, mean, fully grown birds. They swooped in as close as they could, making threatening sounds as they got dangerously close to my little friend. I scooped him up, ran back inside, and put him safely in his box. The phrases "free as a bird" and "eats like a bird" are baloney. Birds are tough, territorial little scrappers who eat like pigs.

Two weeks into my baby-bird rehabilitation, the poor thing up and died. And yes, I cried. Irene, Amy, and I had a funeral and buried him in the backyard. At least he wasn't pecked to death by those other bigger birds.

Many years later, Broadway star Sutton Foster asked me to write her a song. I asked what kind, and she said she was completely open to suggestions, so I told her that if there was a story in her life that she thought might make a good song, she should write it out, and I would turn it into lyrics. Of all the stories she sent, the one that jumped out at me described her obsession with saving the lives of goldfish—at one point leading to her having eight fish tanks in her apartment—and how attached she got to the fish. Because of my experience with that pitiful baby bird, I connected with her story and wrote "The Goldfish Whisperer."

At my job at the security company, most of the girls were nice enough, though there was one who was a real pill. Phyllis was the wife of a military man who was deployed overseas, and she was pregnant. Maybe her swinging hormones made her so unpleasant, but nobody liked her.

One day Scotty, one of the bosses, told me that he'd heard I did unusual things for money—sell Cracker Jack, and play guitar and sing at clubs. He said he had an idea for me to make some easy extra money.

I said, "Great! What is it?"

And he said, "I'll discuss it with you over lunch."

That sent up a red flag, but I knew the lunch places the bosses went to were well lit and close by, so I figured it would be okay.

I told Dutch about it, and he decided he would also have lunch at that restaurant that day to keep an eye on things, just in case. I didn't think that was necessary, but I appreciated his concern.

When I met Scotty, we had a pleasant enough time—he talked about his wife and kids and the renovations he was doing on his house. After we had finished our meals, he got down to business.

"I run a small side business with a partner," he said, "a photography magazine. I'd like to take pictures of you for it—eighteen different poses, just the neck down, no immorality implied."

"You mean, with my guitar?" I asked.

"No," he said, slowly. "You won't be holding your guitar. You'll be naked. Eighteen different poses, just the neck down, no immorality implied.

"I'll pay you fifty dollars a pose. Nobody will ever know it's you—just the neck down, no immorality implied."

He was big on that phrase.

Of course I wasn't going to do it, but I didn't want to act like a prude since I worked with the guy. I just told him no, that's not the kind of thing I would ever do.

"What about seventy-five a pose?"

No. I excused myself from the table and told him I was walking back to the office.

"This is just between us," he said. I nodded and thanked Scotty for lunch, trying to act like what happened was no big deal, but my heart was pounding.

When I started to walk in the direction of the office, I heard footsteps behind me. It was Dutch. I had forgotten he was at the restaurant.

I told him what happened, but I made light of it. He asked if I wanted him to get some nightclub bouncers to beat Scotty up. Of course, I said no.

I didn't tell anybody at work, though I did tell Irene and Amy. At first they were angry, and then they laughed. We all laughed, trying to figure out what the eighteen poses would be. How much can you do without your face being in the photos? The whole thing sounded ludicrous.

Two weeks later I got an invitation to perform at a college in upstate New York near Albany. An old college friend of mine, Dory Johnson, worked at the college and thought I'd provide good entertainment when the freshmen arrived in September. I wrote back that I would take the job, and then I gave my notice at the security company. I'd have to travel 1,500 miles from Miami for a $150 gig, but I'd had all the heat, humidity, and craziness that I could stand. I knew that Dutch and I were not meant to be, so I called to let him know I was heading back north.

The same day I went into the personnel office to give my two weeks' notice, I heard that Phyllis, the pregnant military wife, had been fired, just one week before she would have been eligible for maternity benefits. Nobody liked her, but still, it didn't seem fair.

When the head of personnel—a very kind, grandfatherly man—asked me why I was leaving, I told him I had a great job offer in upstate New York (I didn't tell him it was for $150). Then I blurted out that I didn't think it was a very nice company. I said, "How can they fire Phyllis one week before her maternity benefits would have kicked in, while they keep on a guy who runs a photo porn business on the side?"

His eyes widened. "*What?*" he said. "Someone here runs a *photo porn* business??"

Uh-oh. Here we go. "Well," I said, "Scotty asked me to pose for him—eighteen different poses, just the neck down, no immorality implied. I turned him down, of course, but I can't believe someone who works here would run that kind of shady business on the side."

The next week was the worst of my life. Scotty was called in for a closed-door meeting with the head of personnel and two other higher-ups. He denied everything and said that I was a kook, a promiscuous nutball who didn't wear a bra and came on to all the men in the company. He said that I had come on to him and he had turned me down, so this was my way of getting back at him. He also said something that was supposedly so shocking, no one present at that meeting felt they could even repeat it to me—so I couldn't defend myself.

Rumors were flying all over the company—and most of them were about me and what kind of person I was to try to derail the career of such a hardworking family man. I didn't have much experience with office politics and didn't realize how ugly things could get. And it was all set off by the firing of Phyllis, a person I didn't even like.

After three days of this, I was so upset that they told me to stay home for the rest of the week. I spent some of that time packing things up, using empty boxes that I got from the local liquor store. One of those afternoons when I was home, and the living room was wall-to-wall liquor boxes, the head of personnel came to talk to me.

As soon as I saw him I started to cry, and I remember I said, between sobs, ". . . and you probably think I drank every bottle of liquor that was once in these boxes! . . ." I was a mess. He felt awful.

He brought up the shocking thing that was said about me at the meeting with Scotty, and he said that if it were true, I was not someone who lived a virtuous life and could never be believed. But he still felt that he couldn't tell me what it was—he was so embarrassed.

I took a deep breath and said, "I can't possibly defend myself if you won't tell me. I'm leaving the area, anyway, so you won't have to deal with this much longer. What are they saying?"

He couldn't look directly at me, instead keeping his eyes down on his fidgeting hands as he finally told me.

"Rumor has it that when you were in high school, you used to regularly 'service' the entire football team, but you told everyone that the quarterback, who was your special boyfriend, was such a dud, nothing you could do to him could help him get it up."

"*That's* what they're saying?" I asked him. "That's *it?*" I was so relieved.

"It's not true," I told him. "I was a virgin all through high school and practically all through college."

"I didn't think it was true, and I'm so sorry I have to discuss this kind of thing with an employee."

"Look," I said to him, "You are a security company. I'm sure you have ways to do background checks on people. Scotty is doing extensive renovations on his house. You know he doesn't make a big paycheck. How is he paying for the renovations? I'm not the bad guy here. I'm just the one with the big mouth."

I was asked not to work my last week, and I heard that Scotty was put on a leave of absence. I never heard anything after that, and since the whole ordeal left me humiliated and traumatized, I didn't stay in touch with anyone from that company.

Even though I wasn't going in to that office anymore, I was still upset about what happened, but Dutch had an idea that he thought would take my mind off things: a friend was starting up a new business—taking guests out on a large sailboat for a three-hour tour of Miami Harbor. To introduce the concept, there'd be a "shake-down" cruise that night, with invited friends and press, drinks, and hors d'oeuvres. Dutch would be photographing the event, and he asked me to come along with my guitar to sing to the guests as we sailed around the harbor. It sounded like fun, so I said okay.

There were approximately fifty people on board, and for the first hour the sailboat was docked as they ate and drank. I set up shop in a corner of the deck and sang songs. The sun slowly went down, and around 9:00 p.m. the captain said, "Let's take her out and see what she can do!"

The first half hour was idyllic, but then, for reasons I will never understand, the captain, ignoring the gathering storm clouds, headed the sailboat into the open sea. The weather quickly turned nasty—the ocean waves were swelling and breaking on the side of the boat, the sea spray soaking all the guests. I quickly put my guitar away, stashing it below in a closet, and then, like everybody else, held on to the rail in horror.

Now it was raining and there were claps of thunder and flashes of lightning accompanied by the sound of dozens of people vomiting over the rail. Thank God I hadn't drunk anything, and I have a strong stomach. Dutch put his photography equipment away (I guess it's not good PR to show guests blowing chunks from the railing of the boat) as he joined in the barf fest. He could see that I wasn't sick, and he begged me to find the captain and ask him to turn the boat around.

Bracing myself with every step I took, I made my way up to the wheelhouse. I screamed at the captain to turn the boat around. "Every single guest is sick! Even your crew is sick! PLEASE!! Go back to shore!"

But he just laughed maniacally as the sailboat rocked, the waves crashed, the lightning flashed, the thunder roared, the guests moaned, and the vomit flew in all directions. Walking was dangerous because the decks were slick with seawater and vomit. I found a relatively safe place to hang on, and eventually the boat turned back to land and we limped into port around 2:00 a.m. So much for a "three-hour tour."

I went down below to retrieve my guitar, where I encountered a whole different kind of horror. The toilets had overflowed, covering the decks below with something way worse than vomit. I scrambled back up top clutching my guitar, eager to get off the boat. I was convinced we had to have lost a few people overboard during the night, but miraculously, no one drowned. Every single person was angry, though, and gee, Dutch's friend's sailboat tour business never got off the ground.

I was furious with Dutch for including me in such a fiasco and refused to speak to him for the next two days. But then he came by and told me to get my guitar, saying he was going to make it up to me and swearing we wouldn't be leaving dry land.

He drove me over to Coconut Grove to meet a songwriter named Al Jacobs. Al cowrote the song "This Is My Country," and Dutch was hoping that Al might be able to give me some advice about songwriting and the music business. Al was an affable, much older guy, and he lived in a small sky blue bungalow with his wife. I played a few songs for him, and he got right to the point.

"You're a folk song writer," he said. "Don't let anybody try to change your style or how you write. You have a long way to go to make a living at it, but you have the necessary skills. Work hard. Don't get discouraged. You have talent."

It felt good to hear that, especially since I was still reeling from the awful situation at my job.

Before Dutch and I left, I asked to use the Jacobses' bathroom. On the sink was a small pink soap in the shape of a woman's high-heeled shoe. At the toe was a tiny upside-down bottle of perfume in the shape of a bow. When I came out of the bathroom, I told Mrs. Jacobs I thought that the soap was cute, and I asked her where she got it. She went into the bathroom, brought it out, and handed it to me.

"A gift for you," she said.

"From one songwriter to another," said her husband.

I kept that funny little pink soap for a long time—so long that the perfume inside the little bow-shaped bottle evaporated. In my first New York City apartment, it sat on my bathroom sink for maybe ten years. Then one day, when I was out of regular soap, I used it. And then I used it again. Before long, it didn't look like a shoe anymore. Then it was gone. I wish I had kept it.

I hear that "This Is My Country" is played at Disney World every night after the fireworks show. It was very sweet of Dutch to bring me to meet Al Jacobs at a particularly low point in my life.

Now that I no longer had a full-time day job, I spent a few days with Vinny at the beach before I left Florida for good. He knew I was broke, so he told me he knew a way for me to make fifty dollars.

Uh-oh, I thought. Here we go again. But Vinny assured me it was nothing bad.

He told me about a gay bar in Hallandale that had a talent competition every Monday night at eight o'clock where fifty dollars went to the winner. He said I would have a good chance because most of the performers lip-synched to recordings, and if I brought my guitar and sang, I would stand out. He said he would drive me there and back and introduce me to everybody, so I said okay.

We got to the bar—called Billy's—around seven. Vinny switched off the engine to his car, and then turned to me and dramatically said, "There's something I didn't tell you about this contest."

Uh-oh. "What?"

"You'll be competing against female impersonators. I didn't tell you because I thought that might scare you off, but I really think you can win this thing."

Oy. Female impersonators. I was wearing a long black satin moiré dress I had found in a thrift shop and had a silk flower in my hair. Thank God I dressed up.

"Are there any other women in the contest?" I asked.

"None that I know of," he answered, "but I never saw any rules saying women can't enter."

I hesitated, but we were there.

We went in, and there were young, tanned, handsome gay men for as far as the eye could see. Lots of them said hello to Vinny, and everyone was cordial as he introduced me around, but I did notice a few sideways glances in my direction.

By the time it was eight o'clock, the place was packed. Fifteen minutes later there was an announcement for all contestants to line up in the kitchen.

I stood in line between "Cher" and "Marilyn Monroe." The contestants also included "Carmen Miranda," "Diana Ross," and a few more I couldn't quite place. I guess one was "Mary" of "Mary Had a Little Lamb" fame, since she wore a frilly dress and carried a curly staff and a small, white, fluffy stuffed animal. All the other contestants were way taller than me, especially the ones who wore spike heels.

As the judges lined us up, I stood there hugging my guitar, trying to blend in. Of the dozen of us, I was in the middle of the pack. The judges went off to the corner of the kitchen, put their heads together, and whispered. Then they looked over at us and whispered some more. I got the sinking feeling that they were talking about me. I tried to look as blasé as possible.

Then one of the judges waved for me to come over and asked a very blunt question, "Are you a *real* girl?"

Oh my God. How do I answer? If I say yes, I may be eliminated. If I say no, I am lying. That's not the folk music way. So I split the difference.

"I don't know," I said.

"Well, that's good enough for us," he said.

Whew. I was in. The judges told us to wait in the kitchen in the order we were standing, and someone would come get us when it was our turn.

I went off to the corner to tune my guitar and to warm up as best I could. When the show started, loud Latin music blared in the other room, and you could hear the audience screaming and laughing and clapping. That was for "Carmen Miranda." It sounded like she had done well.

"Marilyn Monroe" was going to go on right before me. She was very nervous, so I tried to calm her down. She was fascinated that I was from New York and asked me a lot of questions about the city. At that point in my life I told her there wasn't much I could say since all I really knew was the neighborhood where my grandparents lived, Marble Hill, and Breezy Point, where their summer bungalow was.

"Marilyn" was very pretty, wearing a skin-tight black sequined cocktail dress, black patent leather pumps, long red nails, and a blonde wig. She also wore more makeup than I had ever worn in my life—I mean *cumulatively* in my entire life.

She was going to lip-synch "I Wanna Be Loved by You," but she hadn't done it before and was worried that she would forget the words. I told her that if that happened, all she had to do was wiggle and giggle and all would be forgiven.

I guess she did okay—I could hear the crowd laughing and clapping—and then it was my turn.

I came out onstage, and the room suddenly got a lot quieter. I sang a song I did a lot in those days, "Gas Station Man." I wrote it during my last summer in Brockport, the first (and only) time in my life I had a junker of a car to drive around in. There was a cute guy who worked in the local gas station where I'd fill up every now and then—one of the girls in the house had a thing for him, so whenever I went to get gas, if she was home she'd come along. The chorus went:

> You are her gas station honey bunch dreamboat
>
> Pump it easy, mmmm, pump it slow [I sang that line like Mae West]
>
> Fill her up, baby, 'cause she's way down low
>
> And she's got nowhere in particular to go

Well, luckily, I guess gay men in Florida also have a thing for gas station pump jockeys—they really liked the song, especially the Mae West part. I got a good hand, then went back into the kitchen to wait with the other contestants.

When the performing part was over, it was time to pick the winner. They brought us all out onstage together, then, one by one, a judge put his hand over the heads of each contestant and the audience applauded.

Vinny was out there with his claque, trying to whip them into a frenzy. After the first pass, the contestants were narrowed down to three—"Cher," "Marilyn Monroe," and me.

Again the judge did the hand-over-the-head thing, and the audience made noise.

Holy crap, I won.

I was so happy, but Cher and Marilyn stomped off the stage. The judge handed me a fifty-dollar bill. I thanked him, bowed, and then went back through the kitchen into the ladies' room.

And who was in the ladies' room? Marilyn Monroe. Crying. When I came in, she looked up at me and said, "You're a girl, aren't you? Well, *aren't you?*"

I admitted that I was.

"Then don't you DARE come back here next week to defend your title. This kind of competition isn't meant for you. You're a ringer! You're a girl! I should have won—did you hear them? I almost did win. *I would have won if you weren't here.*"

She went into one of the stalls and slammed the door.

"Look, Marilyn," I said, "I am so sorry. My friend took me here because he knows I'm broke and thought I might win the money. He didn't tell me until we got here that I'd be competing against female impersonators. I wouldn't have done it if I had known. But I didn't."

Her whimpering slowed down a bit, and then she came out of her stall.

"Do you think I'm pretty?" she asked.

"My God, you're gorgeous!" I said. "Look at you! You're ten times more woman than I am."

"Do you think I could have a career in New York?"

Oh, boy. What to say.

"I don't see why not. Everybody loves Marilyn Monroe."

"You promise you're not coming back next week?" she asked.

"I promise you," I said, and I meant it.

She hugged me.

Vinny and I drove back to Coral Gables, me fifty dollars richer. I never thought one of the last things I would do in Florida was enter a talent contest for female impersonators, or that "Marilyn Monroe" would ask me for career advice.

I wouldn't have had any of these adventures if I hadn't written that damn song about the pirate. I guess Gary did turn out to be a pirate—a liar, a schemer, and a cheat. I don't know if he's alive or dead, but I won't give him the satisfaction of including his last name here.

10

FATE FINDS
A WAY

I saw Gary one more time. We rendezvoused in a shopping mall in upstate New York.

He told me he loved me, not Gail, but she was supporting him financially and kept him on a short leash. He still looked good, and I knew I was just one margarita away from making the same huge mistake I'd made before. But reason prevailed—as he flirted and lied and insulted his meal ticket, I finally realized that he was the worst kind of trouble. I wouldn't let myself be fooled again.

A few days later I did a concert at a small college near Albany, after which I returned to Geneva, trying to figure out my next step. I actually considered working at the string bean canning factory again! But then I received a phone call that set the wheels in motion for something new.

It was from Henrich. Yes, the sailboat owner who had been looking for female crew. I had sent him my résumé, and he called because one of his artists had walked off a contract. Would I take over the tour? It would be two shows a day, five days a week, for five weeks, in schools across Iowa, Illinois, Indiana, and Ohio, for $400 a week. Could I be in Clear Lake, Iowa, in three days?

Why did that town sound familiar?

I would have to drive, but I didn't have a car. My parents kindly let me borrow one of theirs, and I was off.

Before I left, I went to the library to look up Clear Lake, Iowa, and found that it was the place where Buddy Holly's plane crashed—the crash that killed him, Richie Valens, and the Big Bopper. I couldn't believe I was beginning my life as a touring musician in the town where Buddy Holly ended his. Was this a good sign? A bad sign?

Over the next five weeks I realized why Henrich's original singer had bailed out on this tour. Yes, I was singing at schools, but it was *elementary* schools, and the route of the tour made no sense. I spent hours and hours crisscrossing and doubling back over the same territory.

When I started out I stayed in chain hotels, but after a few days I began looking for more interesting places. In Fairfield, Iowa, it was the Bates Motel—yes, a place that shared the name of the motel in Alfred Hitchcock's movie *Psycho*. As I checked in I said to the desk clerk, "You want to know why I chose your motel?"

"Yeah yeah yeah," he said, "there's postcards at the end of the counter. Send 'em to all your psycho friends."

Then he asked me how many there were in my party. I told him it was just me, so he said, "Oh, a young girl on the road all by herself? I'll put you in the room right next to the office so you won't be scared."

That's just what Norman Bates did with Janet Leigh! So he could spy on her through the wall! Nothing like that happened to me—the walls were concrete—but I could hear the office TV on all night and slept badly.

The show I was doing had to retain the title given it by the musician I was replacing: "This Land Is Your Land." I sang some traditional folk songs as well as some of my own, and figured out how to make it a show for kids. Because I was a replacement, Heinrich had (unbeknownst to me) assured all the schools that if they didn't like me, they would get their money back. I did fifty shows in five weeks, and only one school asked for a refund.

That school was in Ohio, where the principal who introduced the show warned the students that they weren't allowed to applaud because the sound is very disruptive to performers. (*Wha?*) He also told them they weren't allowed to laugh. It was like performing in a children's prison, under the watchful eye of the mean old warden. The principal subsequently rated my performance unsatisfactory; no one enjoyed it, he said. (Yes, because you wouldn't allow them to laugh or clap, you mean bastard!)

Funny little things would happen every now and then. On one of my stops I drove into a town so small that it had only one traffic light—a blinking red light in the town square. It was 7:00 a.m. on a Friday, and I was looking for breakfast before my first show. I pulled into a diner parking lot, and as I was getting out of my car a man came running across the square from the post office waving a red envelope.

"You're Christine Lavin, aren't you?" he panted.

"Yes, I am," I said, "but how on earth did you know?"

"I'm the postmaster. This arrived on Tuesday, said you'd be picking it up at General Delivery. Yours is the first car to drive through this week with out-of-state license plates, so I put two and two together and figured it must be you!"

Those five weeks on the road were both exhilarating and frustrating—all the extra driving, all the time alone on the road, all those shows for little kids. I crocheted a small afghan for my parents that trip to thank them for letting me use their car. I chose autumn colors for that blanket—brown, orange, yellow—and it is still on the bed in the guest room at my mother's house.

I finished up the tour in mid-October 1975. Although I did okay, I knew I wasn't the right performer for school audiences. But Henrich was pleased with how it went and asked me to continue after a two-week break—*to spend November and December in Minnesota and Wisconsin!*

I said no.

My friend Dory Johnson suggested that we take a trip up to Caffé Lena in Saratoga Springs. Caffé Lena was already famous as the longest-running live music coffeehouse in the country. It was started by Bill and Lena Spencer, and lots of notable things have happened there.

One of them was Bob Dylan's first out-of-town show, arranged by Dave Van Ronk (on whose couch Dylan was then sleeping). The audience didn't quite take to Dylan, so Bill Spencer jumped on the stage and harangued the crowd, "This kid is gonna be something special! Shut up and listen!"

It was also at Caffé Lena where Kate McGarrigle met Loudon Wainwright III; they later married and produced the musical prodigy Rufus Wainwright. Neal Shulman of Aztec Two-Step met his wife, Karen, there, too. Don McLean wrote "American Pie" in Saratoga Springs—not at Caffé Lena, but at a bar around the corner called the Tin 'n' Lint—so the town became known as a magnet for songwriters.

Bill Spencer eventually ran off with a Skidmore College girl, leaving Lena to run the Caffé by herself. She initially had no interest in folk music— she longed to be an actress—but Bill's departure meant she either had to keep the business running or find a new job.

I envisioned an Earth Mother type, wearing flowing robes and eating organic vegetables, but she turned out to be a chain-smoking, soap-opera-addicted Scrabble enthusiast. She showed us around the Caffé, and since I had my guitar with me, she asked me to play her a few songs.

Afterward, she asked what my plans were. I told her I didn't have any— so she asked if I had any experience taking care of sick people.

"When I started college, I was a nursing major. . . ."

That's all she had to hear.

"I have an old friend staying with me at my apartment," Lena said, "His name is Tom. He is bedridden, and I need help feeding him and keeping him clean. Could you do that kind of thing?"

I was thinking I should tell her how I switched majors from nursing to political science to English when she said, "I can't pay you, but you can live at my apartment. You'll have your own room, I'll feed you, and you can waitress at the Caffé on weekends to make some extra money. And if it works out, you can sing at the Caffé between the performers."

By the time I had gathered up my things in Geneva and returned to Saratoga Springs, Tom had had a stroke and was in the hospital. Lena didn't think to inform me, since she'd decided she would need my help anyway.

I moved into the apartment at 488½ Broadway (yes, that was the real address) in the third week of October. Lena told me Tom was probably going to die; she was quite upset, but something else on the horizon was distracting her. She asked me if I had a driver's license, and I told her I did. When I asked why she wanted to know, she wouldn't say, but she said she would explain things when the time was right.

That first weekend at the Caffé I helped Lena bake the desserts. She was famous for three desserts in particular: a revanée cake that was made of ground-up almonds soaked in rum, a sour cream coffee cake, and chocolate chip cookies. She showed me how she would use a little less rum and a little less sour cream and chocolate chips than the recipes called for to save money. (She was not a good businesswoman.) She never knew that behind her back I always added more when I was baking with her.

That first weekend a fantastic guitarist named Pat Webb played at the Caffé. He mimicked the sound of galloping horses by hitting his right hand on the body of the guitar while his fingers deftly strummed the strings at the same time. I had never heard of him before and couldn't believe such a master of the guitar wasn't world-famous. (During my time at the Caffé, I also got to see other first-rate musicians, like Kate Wolf, Jean Ritchie, the Central Park Sheiks, and Jay and Lynn Ungar.)

That first weekend I also met one of Lena's oldest friends and my all-time favorite Saratogian, Dorothea Brownell. The first thing Dorothea did when we met was to rummage through her purse, hand me a chestnut, and say, "Always carry a chestnut in your purse. It prevents rheumatism."

I loved walking around Saratoga Springs with Dorothea. Everyone knew her and loved her. By that time she was retired and in her eighties, but in her younger years she had been a social worker who placed babies with adoptive parents. As she walked around town some of those families would recognize her, and they hugged and kissed her, thanking her for all she had done for them. She was always embarrassed when people gushed over her like that.

Dorothea was a terrific crocheter. On the couch in her living room was a large crocheted panel that spelled out her favorite phrase: FATE FINDS A WAY. She had designed and made it herself. Every Christmastime she crocheted snowflakes out of very thin white cotton thread and sold them at craft fairs. At one fair she was awarded first prize, and she didn't even know there was a competition. When they handed her the trophy, she laughed and shrugged, and threw the trophy into the trunk of her little blue car.

She lived with her sister, Harriet, in a house their father had built on the outskirts of the downtown area. They were two old-fashioned spinsters who raised flowers, kept cats, and fretted about the Kentucky Fried Chicken that had been built too close to their home. I loved visiting them. They put out quite a spread for their tea parties.

Harriet never came to Caffé Lena, but Dorothea was always there for the Sunday night show, playing Scrabble with Lena at a back table during the concert. At first I thought it was disrespectful, but soon I learned Dorothea and Lena had seen all these performers numerous times, so they didn't need to keep their eyes glued to the stage. At least they weren't playing Sorry! or slapjack.

The Caffé's prices were very modest; still, many people chose not to order anything. The first weekend I made a grand total of fifteen dollars in tips, but I heard terrific music and loved the atmosphere.

I thought I could probably live in Saratoga Springs for the rest of my life. I would learn how to run the Caffé, and maybe that would be my contribution to the music world. I took it as a good sign that my initials were the same as Caffé Lena's.

The next day, a Monday, Lena asked that Chloe, another musician who was staying with her, and I meet with her to discuss something in secret. (As it turned out, this was why she had asked about my drivers' license.) She had gotten word that Bob Dylan was putting together a special "bicentennial tour"—the Rolling Thunder Revue—which would feature Joan Baez, Mick Ronson, Howie Wyeth, and possibly other top folk artists. Rumor had it they were not going to play large venues, just small ones. Lena, bless her heart, wanted them to play the Caffé.

Chloe and I glanced at each other, both thinking that this was futile. The Caffé seated just over a hundred. When Bob Dylan said he'd be playing "small" venues, he probably meant those that seated 2,500. But Lena was determined.

Word was that the musicians were holed up rehearsing in a secret location, but no one knew where it was. Lena, with all her grit and determination, got the number for a Massachusetts motel that *might* be the place where the musicians were. She asked if we'd be willing to go on a road trip with her, and we said yes. She needed both of us—Chloe had a car, and I had a license, whereas Lena had neither.

Lena picked up the phone, dialed the Sea Crest Motel, and asked for Howie Wyeth. She was smart enough not to ask for Bob Dylan, figuring he wouldn't be using his real name. But Howie was a drummer, not a household name. The operator put her on hold, then came back a few moments later and said that Howie wasn't in his room. That's all Lena needed to know.

We were going to go to Massachusetts to personally ask Bob Dylan to bring the Rolling Thunder Revue to play Caffé Lena. On the evening of October 31, 1975, Lena, Chloe, and I took off in Chloe's rust orange hatchback.

We were cruising along the Mass Turnpike—Chloe was at the wheel—when the car engine suddenly cut out. Chloe told us not to worry; this happened all the time. (Lena wasn't worried—she was in the back, sleeping.)

Chloe told me she needed my help to get the car started again. She opened the hood of the car, dug in her pocket for a book of matches, and handed them to me.

"There's two wires that I need to touch together to get the engine going again," she said, "but it's hard to see them in the dark. You strike a match and hold it down as close as you can to where I point."

I was hoping she was kidding. Strike a match, then hold it inside a car engine?

"Don't worry!" she exclaimed. "I do this all the time. Really."

So with grave misgivings I lit the match and held it as close to where she was pointing as I could. I closed my eyes, trying to distance my body from my arm, sure that at any moment there'd be a *boom*. But there wasn't. Instead, Chloe touched the wires together, the engine started, and we continued our journey.

This happened two more times before we got to the motel. Each time I was sure we were going to be engulfed in a fireball, but we weren't.

By the time we got to the motel, the sun was coming up. We checked in, but before going to bed I took a walk on the beach. Here I was, at a motel where some of America's finest musicians were rehearsing, on the edge of the Atlantic Ocean. I couldn't believe it. (I also couldn't believe that I had held a lit match inside a car engine three times the previous night.)

For the next three days we got to be part of the Dylan entourage and were able to watch a few of the performances. One of the musicians particularly fascinated me. He was no longer very popular, and it had been a long time since he'd played to such a big crowd. I wondered how it felt to go from people screaming for you one moment, to sparse crowds the next.

Lena finally found the right person to ask about the Rolling Thunder Revue playing the Caffé, though by now she knew that the Caffé couldn't even hold the crew. But Bob Dylan liked having her around, so she was welcome to stay.

We had to be back for the Caffé's weekend shows, however, so the Wednesday night concert would be our last. On Thursday we would have to leave the tour and go back to Saratoga Springs.

The tour was loosely organized—there were three big buses, a dozen or so cars, and a couple of trucks. We never got official paperwork; we were just told to follow the buses. After stopping at one rest stop, the buses got back on the highway going in the wrong direction, with all of us following. When they realized what they'd done, the buses all made a huge, wide U-turn in the grass to cross over the highway and go the other way.

I was driving at the time and had to think fast. If I didn't also make that big U-turn in the grass, we'd be lost, so I did the same. I still can't believe we didn't get pulled over, but none of us did.

On Thursday afternoon, Bob Dylan and some of his friends made a side trip to visit the grave of Jack Kerouac, author of *On the Road*. We all pulled into a rest stop along the interstate and went into the restaurant. When Chloe, Lena, and I sat down at a table to map out our route back to Saratoga Springs, Bob Dylan joined us.

He was kind of jumpy, always moving. I had been too shy to say anything to him at the shows, but there he was sitting at our table, so I told him how much I loved the concerts.

He said, "Thanks." He looked at the map and asked what we were doing, and Chloe told him we had to get back to the Caffé for the weekend shows. Dylan said, "Oh." His fingers drummed the table, and then he ran them through his hair.

I tried to think of something to say before he got up, so I blurted out, "I love how you end the show with 'This Land Is Your Land'—it's a nice touch how everybody takes a different verse."

"Thanks," he said, fidgeting.

I tried to think of something else, and then I knew what to say.

I asked him if he had heard the Native American verse that Pete Seeger had been singing.

"No," Bob responded. "How does it go?"

> This land was your land, it was not my land
>
> Until you sold us Manhattan Island
>
> We pushed your Nations to the reservations
>
> This land was swiped from you by me

"Wow, I like it," he said. Then he got up from the table and said, "Have a nice trip back home! Come back and join us anytime."

So that was my one and only conversation with Bob Dylan. I was hoping he would say something wise that I would remember forever, but instead *I* told *him* how a song went.

Lena joined the tour two more times over the next few weeks; by then Arlo Guthrie was part of it, as was Joni Mitchell. By that point I was more involved in my work at the Caffé and felt I'd had my chance to see the tour.

Lena eventually returned and settled in to her normal life—though not too much was really normal with her. One of her quirks was that she couldn't sleep in a bed—she slept sitting up in a chair. She also had very bad eyesight; at night she was practically blind and had to have someone hold her hand when she moved from place to place. She pretended she could see, but those of us close to her knew that she couldn't, so we helped her get around as best we could.

Chloe was a wonderful singer and songwriter, and a third musician, Bruce Forster, also moved into Lena's. He was tall, blonde, and skinny and wrote goofy songs about absolutely anything that crossed his mind.

On a lark we started a group called Brute Force & the Pushovers, and we called our tour the Rolling Blunder Revue. We took turns being the front person for the band. Chloe showed great promise, but every opportunity she could she'd duck outside and smoke weed. It really affected her performances, and not in a good way. I once took her aside and lectured her about it, which made her angry. We needed her car to get to gigs, but I didn't want her driving when she was high. Our shows were few and far between, however, so it wasn't a big issue at that point.

Besides running Caffé Lena, Lena was also hosting shows produced by an area concert promoter at the Saratoga Music Hall, a former church that seated eight hundred people. She made extra money by baking cookies for the concession stand, which I helped with, in addition to ushering. It wasn't a paying job, but I got to see the shows for free.

One of these performances was by comedian Robert Klein. The show was sold out, and two hours before the concert, the heating system in the hall conked out. This was in December. The promoter made frantic calls to get it fixed in time, and when the audience started to arrive, they were told to take their seats but keep their coats on.

Thirty minutes before the show it was only fifty degrees in the packed hall. I was in the large green room—where the heat was still working—and Robert Klein was there, too. He usually brought a tape recorder to shows like this so he could tape his performance, but he had forgotten it. He asked if one of us would be willing to sit on the side of the stage. If he improvised a line that got a laugh, he would point at the person, indicating that she should write down what he had just said.

I raised my hand and got the job. He gave me a pen and a pad of paper, and he told me to sit in the wings as close to him as possible, but not in the light.

I asked Lena if Robert had been told about the heating problem in the hall.

"Oh no," she said. "He's a big star. If he knows the heat is off, he probably won't perform. He doesn't know. He *mustn't* know."

I was just a volunteer usher, but I had enough sense to know that a co-median wouldn't refuse to perform to a full house just because the heat was off. I went over to him, pretending I was going to ask a question about the pad and pen he had given me. My back was to Lena and the promoter, and I quietly said, "The heating system in the hall is broken. It is only fifty degrees, and everyone in the audience is wearing winter coats. No one wants to tell you because they think you won't perform. Please don't let them know that I told you, but I thought you should know."

Robert Klein smiled, nodded, and whispered, "Cold is *great* for comedy. Heat is *death*."

He went off to the corner and started to scribble notes.

Just before he went onstage, he donned his coat. I followed him out and sat in the wings, well out of the light. The first section of his mono-logue was all about the cold. He jumped up and down and hugged himself, shivering—the crowd loved it.

Every once in a while he'd point over at me after a new line got a big laugh from the crowd. Later in the show he'd point at me and actually say, "Write that down," which also got a laugh. I carefully went through the notes with him after the show—he was pleased with my accuracy and thanked me for tipping him off about the cold.

He said he could pay me for the work that I had done (which would have been nice since I was living on practically nothing), but instead of money, he was going to give me advice worth lots more.

He asked me if I was a performer. I told him that I was, but not a pro-fessional yet. He said, "I'm going to tell you something I want you to re-member. Never use the 'F' word onstage. Ever. It gets you an automatic reaction, but ultimately that kind of language—what we call 'working blue'—cuts your potential audience by fifty percent.

"If you are serious about having a career, you don't want to do some-thing that is going to *guarantee* you'll miss out on half the number of peo-ple who might like your work, do you?"

Another good bit of advice I once heard is actually advice I *over*heard. Back in 1981 I recorded my debut album live at CBS Studio B in New York City. The cabaret trio Hilly, Lili & Lulu sang harmony on two of the songs. "Hilly" is Hillary Rollins, and her father, Jack Rollins, managed the careers of people like Woody Allen and produced *The Late Show with David Letterman.*

One night Hillary invited me to go with her and her father to see an up-and-coming comic named Steven Wright at a small comedy club in Manhattan. Everything he said was brilliant. It was a performance of one spectacular non sequitur after another.

After the set Jack Rollins went backstage to say hello to Steven, and Hillary and I tagged along. Jack told Steven he was one of the smartest comics he had ever seen, but he said the sign of a great performer is that the audience feels they get to know him by the end of the night.

"We don't know who you are, Steven," Jack said. "We know you are a genius, but we don't know *you.* The way to get the audience to know you is to have connecting threads that you weave throughout your set, here and there, to give it a context. Say something here, and then fifteen minutes later, refer back to it; thirty minutes later, refer back to it again—that kind of thing."

Steven stood there looking up at Jack, nodding, taking it all in. He showed not a bit of arrogance but was more like a student, understanding he was getting advice from one of the giants in the business.

I have never been to another Steven Wright show, so I don't know if he took Jack's advice, but this taught me to start putting connected moments into my concerts right away. If you are a performer, think about doing that same thing with your work. It will take a lifetime to perfect, but perfection always takes a lifetime.

A few months later I spent the weekend at the Rollinses' summer house in upstate New York. I remember it well because we went to see a fantastic summer stock production of *Fiorello!* Hillary had invited a few girlfriends for the weekend, but she warned us ahead of time to watch our language. "My dad can't stand vulgarity or cursing, so *never* use that kind of language around him."

I was surprised since he had been in show business for so many years. If you've ever seen the film *The Aristocrats*, you know just how filthy comics can get. Who knew that one of the biggest managers had such a dislike for coarse language? (That just goes to show you: you should *never* assume *anything* about *anyone* in show business.)

After the Robert Klein concert, the heating system was fixed in the Saratoga Music Hall, and Lena hosted four more big concerts there: Tom Paxton, Arlo Guthrie, Asleep at the Wheel, and then a special double billing of Rosalie Sorrels and Utah Phillips.

I had never seen Arlo Guthrie do an entire solo concert and was amazed at how funny he was and how spot-on his timing was. When Tom Paxton performed, he stepped away from the mikes during "Last Thing on My Mind," and when the entire audience sang the song back to him, the look on his face was pure joy. Asleep at the Wheel turned the Saratoga Music Hall into a homey honky-tonk. I couldn't believe how lucky I was: by ushering, I was able to watch the afternoon sound checks and *then* the entire concerts for free.

Because I was making so little cash, I looked around for other part-time jobs. There was a political newspaper that said they'd look at stories I wrote and pay me twenty-five dollars for every one they ran.

In January 1976 Rosalie Sorrels and Utah Phillips came to do their concert at the Saratoga Music Hall. They were the perfect duo: he was a political rabble-rouser with a million stories, and she was a cool, thoughtful singer with a silvery voice.

Utah had just announced he was running for president. It was all a big joke, of course. He was on the Sloth and Indolence ticket of the Do Nothing Party. His platform had provisions like ordering double-cheese pizzas for the warring factions in Angola in order to encourage a truce. He called it "Pizza with honor with Angola."

A PR man in Saratoga named Tim was helping to publicize the concert, and he had lots of connections. He sent out a press release about Utah

Phillips's presidential campaign, called the New York state capitol in Albany, and secured a room there where Utah could give a speech at noontime on the same day as the concert.

What Tim didn't know was that when the room was booked, the event was put in the official political pipeline, and press releases went out to the media, inviting them to a press conference to meet the new presidential candidate. The little newspaper I was a stringer for told me I should go and cover it. I got a ride with Tim.

The day of the event was snowy. Rosalie and Utah had performed in Boston the night before, where Utah had also done a radio interview in which he explained all of his political beliefs. Tim had a transcript of that interview, and I read it aloud as we slowly drove down to Albany. The roads were very icy and slick, so Tim drove carefully and laughed when I read things like, "Utah said, 'Our last president was so crooked, he had to screw his socks on in the morning!' "

When we got to the capitol, there were already three TV crews there, plus more than two dozen journalists. Tim started to panic. This event was really a joke, just to promote the concert. He didn't expect such a big turnout *at all.*

The press conference was supposed to start an hour after we got there, but Utah Phillips was stuck in a snowbank somewhere on the Massachusetts Turnpike. I joined the reporters milling around while Tim was in contact with the Massachusetts State Police, inquiring about getting a motorcade together to help Utah cut through the traffic.

The minutes ticked by, and the start time for the press conference passed. Tim was dashing about; big beads of sweat on his forehead became rivers rolling down his face and neck.

Fifteen minutes later Tim approached the podium, telephone in hand. All the TV cameras were switched on, and he was bathed in hot light, which made the sweat glisten on his face. He welcomed everyone to Utah Phillips's presidential press conference, then announced that he had Utah on the line, but Utah was stuck in a snowbank in Massachusetts and wouldn't be making it to Albany anytime soon. Utah *would* make it to Saratoga Springs in time for his concert later that night, but *not* in time for the press conference.

The reporters groaned.

Tim said, "Last night Utah was a guest on a radio program in Boston where he laid out his platform, and I have a transcript of that interview right here." He held up the typed pages for all to see, and the cameras zoomed in on them.

"I'm sorry our candidate isn't here, but at least we have this," Tim said, "which will be read aloud by . . . Christine Lavin."

Not a word of warning. I was standing there with the reporters scribbling notes.

I am sure there was a look of complete panic in my eyes, but it was superseded by the look of panic in *his* eyes. He looked at me and mouthed the word, "Please?" So I stuck my pad and pen in my skirt pockets, strode up to the podium, took the transcript of Utah's interview, and started to read, slowly and clearly.

Three of the TV reporters turned their backs to me, faced their cameras, and reported on what was going on at this press conference, with me in the background reading aloud. When I finished, Tim thanked them all for coming. The press conference was over.

But the reporters wanted to know what my connection was with Utah Phillips's presidential campaign. Before I could answer Tim took me aside and told me to come up with something official sounding. I turned back to the reporters and told them that I was Utah's East Coast campaign organizer.

That night the story ran on all the local channels, and there on the TV screen under my name it read: "Utah Phillips's East Coast Campaign Organizer."

When I met Utah later on, he laughed heartily and gave me a big bear hug. "My East Coast campaign organizer!" he bellowed.

After Rosalie and Utah's show in Saratoga Springs, there was a party at a nearby restaurant, and then everybody tramped up the street to Lena's apartment to get some sleep. But it wasn't meant to be. An old church just down the street on Broadway caught fire. It was a windy, frigid night, and everyone on the block—including us—had to be evacuated.

It was around 4:00 a.m. and bitterly cold. People were bundled up in winter coats over their pajamas. All the musicians were carrying their instrument cases—even after being awakened from the deepest sleep, their first instinct was to save their precious instruments.

The fire raged on and on, and we couldn't go back into the building, so some of us went to an all-night diner. Utah was laughing and joking—he never stopped entertaining. They finally let us back into Lena's apartment at 7:00 a.m., where we all went back to sleep.

The next day, on the front page of the *Saratogian* there was a picture of Utah sitting on the steps of city hall with a rubber chicken in his hand. The caption under the photo said, "Presidential candidate Utah Phillips saves his pet chicken from the flames."

The church burned down to the ground, though no one was injured. Dorothea and Harriet Brownell took it hard—their father was one of the men who built that church many decades earlier.

After all the excitement of Utah's press conference and the fire, I expected life would calm down a bit. That's when I learned, however, that when you traveled with Lena Spencer, you met interesting people—but when she stayed home, sometimes those fascinating people came to her.

One cold, snowy afternoon it was Kate and Anna McGarrigle, driving from New York City to their home in Montreal with the test pressing of their self-titled debut vinyl album. They stopped in at Lena's because they hadn't heard the album yet. A record label executive handed them the LP as they were leaving New York. They were so excited they couldn't bear the anticipation, and they stopped at Lena's to play it.

I asked the McGarrigles if I could listen, too, and they said yes. The four of us sat in silence in Lena's living room, listening to side one and then side two. I was amazed at the sound they had created: it felt like an acoustic version of Phil Spector's "Wall of Sound." The most fun was watching the McGarrigles listen to their first album in its entirety for the first time. I think they couldn't believe their ears. Nobody knew it yet, but it was a groundbreaking album. Lena was so excited for them—she realized this was much more than a folk record. This album contains "Heart Like a Wheel," which is now a folk standard (Linda Ronstadt recorded it, as have many others), and "The Swimming Song" that Kate's future husband,

Loudon Wainwright III, made popular. As soon as Kate and Anna finished listening, they hugged and kissed Lena and left, taking that precious test pressing with them to Montreal.

On another afternoon an itinerant folksinger from Minnesota stopped by Lena's apartment. Scott Alarik, a burly guy with a booming voice, was looking for a gig at the Caffé. Lena listened to him and hired him on the spot. For many years Scott traveled around the country singing traditional folksongs, but he has since become one of the Boston area's most distinguished music journalists, writing for publications like the *Boston Globe*.

One evening, just before dinnertime, folksinger Logan English came by Lena's to invite her to a surprise party he was throwing for a couple who had eloped. Logan was sweet and invited me, too, even though I didn't know the couple. Logan English was not only a wonderful singer, he was also a fancy cook. The party was an elegant buffet. I put something on my plate that I thought was creamed onion, but when I started to eat it, it was rubbery and funny tasting. . . . I heard somebody talk about oysters, and I realized it was an oyster in my mouth. I didn't know what to do. It was like a squishy rubber ball. I kept chewing and chewing and chewing. It took all my self-control to swallow it and not gag. To this day I can't look at an oyster without thinking about Logan English.

During the weekends I continued to help Lena make desserts and wait on tables, more convinced than ever that I should think about running a business like hers and give up any ideas of having a music career—even though I played the guitar every chance I got and constantly wrote songs. Every Sunday night Dorothea was there to play Scrabble with Lena, and it felt great to be part of a place that attracted the most interesting local characters. One of them was the young, dapper Tommy Flagg. He was the grandson of James Montgomery Flagg, painter of the famous Uncle Sam *I Want YOU* poster. Tommy was wealthy, dressed in a 1920s style, was absolutely mad for dance and dance companies, threw lavish parties around town, and generally loved to surround himself with artistic types.

One weekend the Balfa Brothers from New Orleans were playing at the Caffé. They stayed at Lena's, and one morning at breakfast they asked me to play them some songs. Their enthusiasm surprised me. Their music was Cajun, nothing like mine, so I couldn't believe they liked what I performed.

They told me I shouldn't give up my dream of becoming a professional musician, and they asked Lena to let me do a couple of songs during their intermission.

I did play that night, then went back to waitressing during the second half of their show. Afterward a number of people from the audience told me how much they liked my music. Lena subsequently put me onstage between other performers, and that seemed to go well, too.

Then Lena really surprised me—she said she was going to give me a co-billing weekend in February. Herb Gart, who had managed Don McLean and worked with Janis Ian, was crazy about this young piano player he'd worked with named Michael Devon. We would split the bill.

I started practicing like crazy for that weekend. Bruce and Chloe asked if I wanted them to sing on any of my songs, but I said no, I wanted to do this solo. Lena clearly didn't take our little "group" seriously. Bruce was fine with what I said, but I could see that Chloe wasn't.

Chloe was worrying me in a lot of ways. She appeared to be high much of the time, her hair was dirty and stringy, and her hands and clothes were grimy. One night she burst into my room in a panic and shook me awake, saying that Lena was planning to kill us. Chloe was trembling and crying, and I didn't know what to make of this. I thought maybe she had had a bad dream, but she assured me she was fully awake. She begged me to sneak out of the apartment with her and escape.

We jumped in Chloe's car and drove to the all-night Spa City Diner, where I tried to calm her down. Yes, Lena was a bit odd, but I didn't think she was dangerous or crazy. The more I talked this over with Chloe, the more I felt she might have deeper emotional problems. But I was too excited about playing my first official show at Caffé Lena to focus on this too much, so we went back to Lena's a couple of hours later and never discussed that episode again.

Herb Gart was traveling up from New York with Michael and would be there for all five shows. I was very nervous. I had been playing guitar and performing since I was thirteen, but most of that time I'd never thought that it was something I could make a living at. Although my set was planned out well in advance and I had timed it, I still raced through it during my first performance, conscious that Michael followed and worried that I'd go over my time. It's a common rookie mistake. I calmed down a bit as the weekend progressed.

On Sunday night Herb Gart gave me his business card. "You could have a real career," he said to me, "but you have to learn how to play guitar better. Here's my card. When you're a better guitar player, get in touch with me."

Lena and I went to the Executive Bar, just downstairs from the Caffé, to have a beer and talk about how the weekend went.

Who walks into the bar? Dave Van Ronk. I had never met him, but I knew all about him. I heard his music on WNEW-FM back when we lived in Peekskill. He was already a legendary character, known for mentoring Bob Dylan and for his own distinctive voice and intricate guitar style. He and his girlfriend, Joanne, were driving back to New York from shows in Montreal.

Van Ronk was a Caffé favorite and a dear friend of Lena's. She was overjoyed to see them both, and they joined us in our booth. Lena introduced us and told Dave that I had just finished my first weekend performing at the Caffé.

He didn't miss a beat and said, "Play me a song."

"Right here? Right now?" I asked.

"Yes," he said.

I took my nylon string guitar out of its cardboard case and quickly tuned it. It was awkward playing while sitting in a booth, with boisterous people nearby and a jukebox playing in the back room, but I managed to sing him this:

> Alone on the stage you're a cowboy in lights
>
> Charming the audience night after night
>
> They clap their hands for you, they all wish you well
>
> They go home to families you go home to hotels

> Well there's cranky bartenders and old chambermaids
>
> Young waitresses who might like to get laid
>
> Some treat you with contempt some with respect
>
> Their faces stay with you, their names you forget . . .

I sang the whole song for him. Halfway through I watched Van Ronk close his eyes as he was listening. Was he tuning me out?

When I finished, he opened his eyes, looked directly into mine, and said, "You should come to New York."

"Oh, I will someday. When I learn how to play guitar better."

"I'm a teacher," he said. "I'll teach you."

At that moment, my life changed yet again. The same night that Herb Gart told me to come to New York after I learned how to play guitar better, Dave Van Ronk told me that he'd teach me.

Fate found a way.

11

$250 FOR
A SET OF GUITAR STRINGS

It was March 1976. I had only two hundred dollars in savings and no job prospects, but I absolutely had to be in New York City if I wanted to pursue my goal of becoming a working musician. Julie Sheinman, my former college roommate, offered me an affordable room in her two-bedroom apartment.

The apartment was a walk-up on the third floor of 179 East Third Street, between Avenues A and B—definitely not a good neighborhood at that time, though the Hell's Angels lived one block away and kept the peace on the local streets. My bedroom was tiny. The bed was a door propped up horizontally by two small wooden horses. On top of the door was a torn, lumpy piece of foam rubber—my mattress.

Julie worked as a schoolteacher and drama coach. She was gone from early morning to late in the evening. I signed up with a temp agency and started working immediately in midtown offices—ad agencies, TV networks, book publishers, and pharmaceutical companies. I could spell well and type fast, so I got work.

One night a week I took guitar lessons with Dave Van Ronk. The first thing he told me was that I needed to buy myself a proper guitar. I didn't have the money at that point—but it was on my list. Dave was a larger-than-life character, the "Mayor of MacDougal Street" (a focal point in Greenwich Village), a Brooklyn boy who grew up to be one of the best blues and ragtime guitarists and singer/songwriters of his generation. He recorded more than thirty albums, and his influence on generations of musicians is incalculable. The list of musicians who studied under him, opened shows for him, traveled throughout Europe and Australia with him, and admired him goes on and on. David Hajdu quotes him throughout his book *Positively 4th Street*, and Bob Dylan raves about Dave in his book *Chronicles*. Suze Rotolo also writes extensively about him in her book *A Freewheelin' Time*.

Dave was a big man, well over six feet tall, and had enormous hands with long, slender, almost delicate fingers. He had dropped out of high school but was a voracious and intelligent reader, a self-educated man. He loved fine food and taught himself how to cook complicated dishes—some of which took two or three days of preparation. His taste in music was eclectic—he loved folk, opera, Balkan music, and jazz.

He couldn't read music, so he learned everything by ear. And because he supplemented his performance and record-sales income by teaching guitar, he came up with his own unique system of writing his arrangements down, based on the alphabet.

Capital E meant the low E string. A small e with a line next to it (e-) meant the E note on the second fret of the D string. An underlined e (e̲) meant the high E string. So his sheet music was small orderly stacks and gracefully curving lines of letters with additional curved lines here and there that indicated sliding up to or down to a particular note. Eventually Dave hired me to type up his sheet music, but it was painstaking work that took many hours to get right. Imagine every note of "The Maple Leaf Rag" printed out in Dave's way with a typewriter, not a computer, and on a plain sheet of paper, not a staff.

Many years later, after Dave had died and Allan Pepper was organizing a tribute concert at the Bottom Line, I was wracking my brains in a hotel on the road trying to remember how to play his song "Somebody Else, Not Me." I had learned it note-for-note years earlier, but I couldn't reconstruct it properly. I called his widow, Andrea, to see if she still had the sheet music to it, and she did.

I called the front desk to let the clerk know I was expecting music to be faxed and asking them to call me as soon as it came in. I waited and waited, but the front desk didn't contact me, so I finally called them and asked if they'd received the music.

"Well, we got *something* for you," the desk clerk said, "but I don't think it's music. It looks more like a math problem."

At first I was just another one of Dave's students. I practiced very hard, and I paid attention. Slowly we became friends. He would schedule my lesson to be the last of the night, and after the lesson he would play me tapes of music he wanted me to hear. He loved Louis Armstrong, Fats Waller, Billie Holiday, the songwriting of Dorothy Fields, Harold Arlen, Yip Harburg, Johnny Mercer. He adored Joni Mitchell.

He also thought the world of Janis Ian. He had a cassette of her song "Stars" that she had sent him right after she had written it. One night he played it over and over again, closing his eyes and smiling. He held court sitting on his couch, and I'd be in the rocking chair across from him. He'd instruct his then-girlfriend, Joanne, to "play this" or "play that," and she dutifully followed his instructions, shuffling through stacks of vinyl albums and piles of cassettes. He'd be puffing on a cigarette or cigar in one hand, sometimes holding an asthma inhaler in the other, often with a glass of wine or whiskey in front of him.

He'd offer me a drink, and sometimes I'd have a glass of wine, but I get hung over too easily and didn't relish the idea of stumbling home to my dicey neighborhood late at night, so I never kept up with him on that score. He'd grow increasingly giddy over the music—he loved some of it so much he'd play the songs over again, laughing with glee.

Around this time my college friend Judith Friedman invited me to dinner. Another guest was a woman named Anita Corey, who had just opened a Mexican restaurant on Columbus Avenue in Manhattan called Anita's Chili Parlor. It was the first eatery to offer outdoor seating on the sidewalk in that neighborhood.

I played some songs after dinner, and Anita asked me if I would consider performing at her restaurant on weekends. She invited me to come by the following week to look the place over.

It was a bright, airy two-story space between Seventy-third and Seventy-fourth streets on the east side of Columbus. I looked for the stage but couldn't find it— because there was none. Anita wanted me to wander among the tables with my guitar from 6:00 p.m. to midnight on Friday and Saturday nights—sometimes upstairs, sometimes downstairs, sometimes out on the sidewalk. And she wanted me to start in June.

Hmmm. I don't speak Spanish or sing in Spanish. Wandering around for six hours? Oy. But it would be steady work as a musician. I told her I would think about it.

At my next guitar lesson I told Dave what Anita had offered. He could see that I wasn't wild about the idea, but he understood steady work. Then he imparted these words of wisdom: *When someone offers you work you really don't want to take, demand more money than you think they could ever possibly pay.*

I called Anita, took a deep breath and told her I didn't think she'd want me for the job, because I would need fifty dollars a night. She agreed!

So every Friday and Saturday night I wandered around that restaurant and played songs for people—whether they wanted me to or not. I learned quickly that Carlos, the cook, would fix whatever I wanted at the end of the night if I sang Malcolm McKinney's song "Sometimes" (made popular by Jonathan Edwards a few years earlier) at least once. I also learned that some patrons would tip enough to allow me to take a taxi home after the restaurant closed (though more than once I encountered cabdrivers who refused even to *drive* to my neighborhood at that hour).

With the money I was making temping Monday through Friday and working as a wandering minstrel on weekends, I thought I should look for a new place to live. I had been in touch with Su Mead, an artist I met when we were both camp counselors at Greylock Camp in the Adirondacks in the summer of 1971. That was my one and only camp experience—I was the counselor for the seven- and eight-year-olds and taught guitar to all different age campers using the same "show-and-tell" system I had learned from Laura Weber.

Greylock was a Jewish camp; I was hired (at the last minute) because they thought my last name was "Levin." It was on Racquette Lake in the Adirondacks, a lovely spot. The thing I remember most was a terrible thing

I did as a joke. One day, while I was taking the little girls swimming, I guess my Catholic upbringing kicked in for a moment. These kids were so cute and sweet I was suddenly seized with concern about what would happen when they died, since they weren't baptized and couldn't get into heaven (I assumed there was a heaven). So on the spot I baptized them with lake water.

Word got around, and the camp owner was furious with me. I apologized profusely and told her I just thought it's better to be safe than sorry. I didn't get fired, though I know that was discussed. The other counselors, especially Su Mead, thought it was pretty funny, and we became friends after that.

Now, five years later, she was sharing a loft with four other artists on the sixth floor of a building on the corner of Sixth Avenue and Twenty-sixth Street. One of the artists would be gone for the months of July and August, and I was welcome to take over that space for $150 a month.

Julie Sheinman was making enough to afford the apartment on East Third by herself, so she was fine with my moving out. I moved into the loft at the beginning of July. I had a huge corner room, at least thirty by thirty feet, with large windows and a view of the Empire State Building. I was the only musician; the other residents were painters and sculptors. One also considered herself a poet.

When I would return from my wandering minstrel job with a large container filled with Mexican food, I would eat what I could, then put the rest in the refrigerator. Next day, more often than not I'd find most of it had been eaten during the night. No one fessed up to it, but the next day "poetry" would be taped to the fridge . . . something like this gem:

> I arrived hungry
>
> No morsel passed my lips
>
> No money in my pocket
>
> Don't hate the artiste in me

I worked a lot that summer and soon could afford to buy a good guitar. In the middle of July I went to Matt Umanoff Guitars in the Village and paid $750 for a brand-new Martin D-28 with a case.

Learning how to play this guitar was a whole 'nother story. It was a whole lot bigger than my nylon-string classical guitar, and its steel strings were much harder on my fingertips. With this instrument, rather than becoming a better guitarist or staying at the same level, I was actually getting *worse*. I continued playing the small nylon string guitar at Anita's on weekends, then I'd struggle with the steel-string guitar for the rest of the week.

In a spontaneous moment of extreme frustration I took the guitar back to Umanoff's, telling Matt that I didn't like how it sounded. I wanted to ask for my money back, but I wasn't sure he'd give it to me, so I told him I was on my way to Dave Van Ronk's for a guitar lesson and I'd come by afterward to figure out what I would do.

I went to Dave's and spent the entire lesson crying. Dave looked very uncomfortable. (Guys always look uncomfortable when women go on a crying jag.) I was whimpering, *"I can't do it. . . . It's too hard. . . . My hands are too small. . . . Why do I have to play steel string guitar? . . . What's wrong with me?"*

Dave sat there in silence and let me ramble and sniffle. Then he asked me a simple question:

"Have you thought of switching to light-gauge strings?"

Huh? Strings come in different gauges? I had no idea the guitar I was playing had heavy-gauge strings. Dave assured me that if I started using light gauge I'd have a much easier time of it.

I got up to leave, took twenty dollars out of my pocket (about the cost of a lesson at the time), and held the money out and said, "You probably don't want to take this since all I did was cry and you didn't get to teach me anything. . . ."

"Au contraire," Dave said as he plucked the bills out of my hand. "I should have charged you *triple*."

I was too embarrassed to go back to Umanoff's to tell him I wanted my guitar back with lighter strings on it. I told him I wanted a guitar with a bassier sound, so Matt let me try a few different guitars—other new Martins. When I found the one I wanted, it turned out to be $250 more than the guitar I had brought back. I told him I would have to come in two weeks with the money, so he put the guitar aside.

Two weeks later I came back with the money, and before Matt put the guitar in its case, I casually asked him if he could include a set of light-gauge strings, too.

I now use a gauge called "slightly lights," which are between "light" and "ultra-light" gauge. "Slightly lights" go from 0.011 for the high E to 0.050 for the low E. They are also sometimes called "custom lights," and a number of different manufacturers make them (including John Pearse Strings). I heard that "slightly lights" were specifically formulated for James Taylor, but I don't know if that's true. I do know that Janis Ian sometimes uses ultra-light strings—and she's a fantastic guitarist—so don't for a second think you are being a wuss if you don't use heavy- or medium-gauge strings. Especially when you are first starting out.

I now started playing this new guitar at Anita's, which helped to toughen up my finger pads. And it was louder, which was also good since there was no sound system at the restaurant and I had to compete with kitchen and dining sounds inside and street noise when I played outside.

I wrote a song about Anita's with the following chorus:

>Drink your margaritas up
>
>The temperature's going down
>
>Taxis are honking at the red lights
>
>They're heading into town
>
>Between the grumblin' of the traffic
>
>And the rumblin' of the trains
>
>I'm singing on the sidewalk
>
>And I hope it don't rain

The truth is, most nights I was hoping it *would* rain, because then the outdoor section would be closed and often I would be told to go home. It was pretty torturous to just wander around for six hours, interrupting people's meals with my songs. I got every kind of reaction—from elation, to disdain, to surprise, to complete noninterest—but if I sang "Sometimes" I would at least get that great takeout.

Since I would only be able to live in the loft through August, it was time to find a new apartment. The experience with that poet food thief had really bugged me, so I wanted to get a place by myself. I was intrigued with the Gramercy Park area in the East Twenties, where tenants who lived around the park also got a key to the park, which was closed to the public. The most I could afford was two hundred dollars a month, so, armed with the *New York Times* apartment listings I set out on a sweltering day to find a new place to live. As I stepped out onto West Twenty-sixth Street, the strap on my left sandal snapped. The elevator was out of order, and it was easier to walk to a shoe store across the street than to climb back up six flights of stairs to get my sneakers. I unwisely bought another pair of sandals. It was a hot day, and I wasn't wearing socks. In no time flat I had blisters everywhere.

I went into a drugstore and bought a box of Band-Aids. I wasn't even near Gramercy Park yet and had to put six Band-Aids on my feet.

This apartment search wasn't going well.

All the places that I could afford were horrible—and none had keys to Gramercy Park. I began to understand that the word *cozy* was code for "dark and cramped" and that *charming* meant "shabby." I was hobbling from block to block, applying new Band-Aids every few minutes. There was a newly renovated building that didn't face the park but had a sign that said a key to the park came with every apartment. Rents, however, started way beyond what I could afford. I could see an office on the first floor through the open door. A man was sitting at a desk and there was an empty chair next to the desk. I went in and sat down in that chair.

The man behind the desk bellowed, *"So, you want to live on Gramercy Park!"*

"No, I can't afford to!" I blurted out, "I'm a folksinger, I'm not rich, but my shoes broke and I have these new sandals and they hurt, my feet are bleeding, and I have to sit down, and I have to find a new place to live, and I don't know what I'm going to do!"

I figured the guy would throw me out, but he didn't. He leaned in close and told me he was an actor, and asked what I could afford to pay per month.

I told him two hundred a month, tops.

"Don't tell anybody I'm doing this," he whispered, "but my wife is a rental agent on the Upper West Side. You know that part of town?"

Yes, I did. It's where Anita's Chili Parlor was located. It hadn't even occurred to me to look there.

"I'm going to call her," he said as he dialed the phone. He told me that five minutes earlier his wife had gotten a studio apartment listing for $195 a month on West Seventy-fifth Street. He then asked me if I could afford her fee of 12½ percent.

"Yes," I said. My feet hurt so badly I figured it would be worth paying that money to end this search here and now.

I met the rental agent in front of a six-story brownstone between Riverside Drive and West End Avenue. The super, an old Irish lady named Mrs. Shugrue, was there, too, with the apartment key. We walked up a grand old-fashioned marble and mahogany staircase to the second floor, where it took Mrs. Shugrue several minutes of mumbling and key wiggling to get the door open. I knew I wanted to live there—if it took *her* this long to unlock the door, a burglar could never break in.

We entered a small studio apartment whose far wall was a giant floor-to-ceiling window that overlooked the street. There was a tiny windowless kitchen off the main room, and the bathroom had an angled floor-to-ceiling window that overlooked the street. Both windows had antique accordion wooden shutters that folded up into the walls on either side. When they were folded up, out of the way, the rooms were filled with light—not direct sunlight, but light just the same. When they were folded out over the windows, both rooms were dark.

The rental agent and I walked over to her office on Broadway (stopping to buy more Band-Aids on the way), where she sat down and worked out the math for what I would have to pay—first month's rent, last month's rent, and her 12½ percent fee.

When she slid the paper over to me with the numbers, I tried not to look shocked. I had thought the percentage applied to one month's rent, but it applied to a *year's* rent. Big difference. I knew what I had in the bank and knew that if I wrote these checks out I would have only thirty dollars left. But I knew I should take the apartment. Although I was temping all over midtown, my weekend gig at Anita's was now just a few blocks away—I could walk each way, saving money. I signed the lease, laughing to myself, knowing the broken strap of my sandal was a godsend.

On September 1 I moved into the first New York apartment that was mine and mine alone. This was never in my plans or dreams, yet here I was, and I loved it.

Lena Spencer (the owner of Caffé Lena) stopped by soon after I moved in. She had been invited to David Amram's wedding and asked if I wanted to go along. She stayed in a nearby hotel, spent her days playing Scrabble on the Upper West Side, going to clubs at night. David's wedding was in an East Side temple, and his reception was held in a huge space nearby. Steve Goodman was one of his ushers, and every hip musician in New York showed up to play in the pickup band. I don't remember David dancing, but I do remember him playing music for hours. He and his wife had met at Caffé Lena, and Lena was beaming with pride.

The next day Lena and I had lunch. She had bad news. Our old roommate Chloe had left Saratoga around the same time that I did and moved to Pennsylvania to live with relatives. When Lena called her to say hello, she was told Chloe had hanged herself.

I had never told Lena about that crazy night when Chloe woke me up saying we were in danger. Now, I didn't know what to say. I knew Chloe was troubled; I obviously never knew the depths of her angst.

Although I traveled back to Caffé Lena a few times over the following years to perform, Lena and I never became close. I was appreciative of the time I spent at the Caffé and had thought I would be there forever, but it wasn't meant to be. A few years later Lena fell down the stairs at the Caffé— she was navigating them alone, blindly, in the dark—on her way to see her good friend Spalding Gray do a one-man show in Albany. She banged her head and died several weeks later.

Lena was a mass of contradictions. On one of my trips back to Caffé Lena I saw her in a production of Sean O'Casey's *Juno and the Paycock*. I was amazed at how she totally disappeared into the part of Juno. She was a *really good actress.* As I watched her, I thought of her sitting at the back table of the Caffé at every performance, collecting the money, playing Scrabble with Dorothea on Sunday nights. In reality, she was probably as talented as—if not more talented than—most of the performers she presented. But she belonged to an earlier generation of women who had fewer choices than we do now.

I continued working temp during the day, taking my guitar lessons with Dave, and strolling around the chili parlor on Friday and Saturday nights, starting to build up my bank account. I also got some ideas that I thought might make good stories for *Mad* magazine, so I wrote them up and mailed them off.

I loved my tiny new apartment, became friends with my downstairs neighbor Martha, and for the first time in my life I had both my own telephone number in a phone book *and* steady music work.

Of course it couldn't last. In mid-October Anita let me know I wasn't needed anymore. Just like that. She explained that as the weather was cooling off, the outside section of the restaurant was going to be closed up. She couldn't afford to keep me.

I had gotten used to making that extra hundred dollars every weekend, not to mention the tips and the takeout at the end of the night. Though the job didn't thrill me, I was completely shocked to lose it. But since I was temping I knew I could stay afloat financially.

But then I got a letter from a writer at *Mad* saying that he liked my writing and wanted to meet me. I called him up. He asked if I could type, and when I said yes, he said that he wanted to interview me to see if I'd be suitable for working in their New York office. He suggested that we meet at a restaurant for dinner the next evening. I wondered why he didn't ask me to go to their office, but I didn't dwell on it.

The next evening at the restaurant, the hostess took me over to the table where the writer sat. He was very sloppily dressed, his hair was a mess, and he was generally unkempt. He looked up at me when I introduced myself, then he slowly looked me down and up again and said, "Gee, I'm sorry. I can't have dinner with you, but you can buy yourself a drink." He opened his wallet, took out a five-dollar bill, and tossed it on the table.

Unsteadily he rose from the table, and then slowly walked out of the restaurant. Through the window I watched him weave down the street. Later I found out that *Mad* didn't even have a New York office; all their writers were independent contractors. This guy had intercepted my letter and called me on his own.

I picked up the five-dollar bill, feeling embarrassed. But there was a restaurant on my way home that sold my favorite chicken soup, so I figured I would use the five dollars for dinner.

I walked down Columbus, right past Anita's, and there in the window was a black-and-white photo of a young guy holding a guitar. Underneath the photo it said, "Here every Friday and Saturday night." So it wasn't the weather that got me fired—I had been replaced.

The one-two punch of the *Mad* magazine writer and this news sent me reeling. I went straight home instead of buying that soup and threw myself down on my bed. I wanted so badly to cry; I felt I was entitled.

But I couldn't cry. I was just very disappointed. It was a Thursday night. I went to bed without eating, and the next morning when I woke up my throat felt sore.

I went to my temp job, but after a few hours my throat was now really painful and I had started running a temperature. I couldn't work anymore and left early.

As I approached my apartment building, coughing and sweating, I saw Mrs. Shugrue sitting on the stoop. She stood up and started wringing her hands. Whenever she was upset her lower lip trembled, and as I got closer to her I could see she was in full lower-lip-tremble mode.

"Oh, Miss Lavin, I did a terrible terrible thing," she said.

I just waved her off—I was feeling too awful to get into a conversation.

"I kept telling them you live here, but they didn't believe me."

What is she talking about?

I walked past her, unlocked the front door, and started up the stairs to my apartment.

"Miss Lavin, I did a terrible thing! Con Ed came here today and asked to get into your apartment. So I let them in. They said nobody lived there so they turned the electricity off.

"I said to them—look, there's a bed, and there's a guitar—a young girl lives here. *Don't turn the electricity off!* But they did."

I didn't know I was supposed to call Con Ed when I moved in. There was electricity when I moved in and I thought it was part of the rent. I immediately called Con Ed, but they told me I would have to go to their offices on Monday in person to have it turned on.

Mrs. Shugrue gave me two candles and a book of matches as she apologized over and over again. As the sun went down my apartment grew dark. I lay in bed coughing, sneezing, and sweating. Then my phone rang.

It was a regular from Anita's who was there now looking for me. His name was Craig, and he and a friend wanted to hear me sing. Anita told them she had let me go, so they asked her for my number. They wanted to know if I would meet them for dinner.

I told Craig I was sick, so he asked me where I lived; they would have dinner, and then bring food over to me. I gave him my address, and then I got up, straightened my apartment as best I could in the dark, and went back to bed.

Two hours later my doorbell rang. I lit a candle, let them in, and then got back under the covers. Craig introduced his friend Harry, who worked at the same law firm as he did.

I explained why my lights were out. My throat was so sore I could barely talk, but I told them that on Monday I had to go to Con Ed's office in person to straighten things out. I must have looked pitiful.

Craig and Harry sat there awkwardly for a few minutes, and then said good-bye.

Over the weekend Mrs. Shugrue and Martha stopped in a few times to see how I was doing. I was running a fever but didn't have health insurance, and the thought of going to the ER was out of the question—I felt too awful to move.

But on Monday morning I had to go down to Con Ed. I dragged myself out of bed, showered and dressed, then headed for the subway. As sick as

I was, I felt guilty spreading my germs in a subway car. But I couldn't afford a taxi.

When I got to Con Ed's offices, I found a cavernous room with more than a hundred people standing in various lines. I went to the information window. My throat was still terribly sore, and I could barely speak above a whisper. I asked the woman what I needed to do to have my electricity restored. She asked for my name and address, and when I told her she said, "Oh, you. I know about you. Go see that man"—she pointed to a man at a desk on the other side of the room. "Give him this," she said, handing me a card, and then added, "Don't stand in line. Go right over to him now."

I got dirty looks from the people who were lined up in front of this man's desk as I handed him the card.

"Well, Miss Lavin," he said, "you've got friends in high places. We apologize for shutting off your electricity. We need a deposit from you, and these forms filled out"—he handed me some papers and motioned for me to sit down—"and by the time you get home it will be back on."

I filled out the papers, showed my ID, gave him a check, and thanked him for helping me cut through the red tape.

"Don't thank me," he said. "Thank your lawyer friend Harry."

When I got home, my electricity was indeed restored, so I called Harry and thanked him for speeding me through the Con Edison system. I was in bed for the rest of the week getting over the flu, but at least I had working lights and a refrigerator. And since then I have never paid my Con Ed bill late, ever.

12

NOBODY'S FAT
IN ASPEN

Dave Van Ronk was always in and out of town performing concerts, and he asked if I would like to open for him at a club called the Salt in Newport, Rhode Island. I would travel with Joanne and Dave to Newport, a local musician named Paul Geremia would put us up, and I would drive back to New York with them the next day.

I can't remember what songs I played, but I guess it went okay because afterward the owner of the club asked me to sit with him and Joanne during Dave's set. I ordered a vodka and tonic and sat down at his table. I don't remember his name now, but I do remember that he had quite a scar on his forehead from brain surgery. (I'm sure someone reading this will know whom I'm talking about.) The surgery was successful—he was perfectly healed. And he was perfectly handsome and funny and charming.

Dave's set was spectacular. He played old chestnuts like "Green Green Rocky Road" (a song he played every concert of his life), "Moon of Alabama," and what I still consider the definitive version of "Mack the Knife." His performance of that song that night was particularly powerful, and when he ended it I leapt out of my seat to applaud, knocking my drink into the club owner's lap.

So much for making a good impression. He was a good sport about it—and I was glad it wasn't a Bloody Mary. I apologized and he laughed it off as he dried himself off with paper towels.

After the show was over and the audience gone, Dave sat down to have a drink with us. The club owner was going to be coming to New York in a few weeks and said he'd give Dave a call. I piped up, "Here's my number—call me, too!"

This was the age before answering machines—well, at least before I owned one. The weekend that the club owner said he'd be in New York, I made sure to stay near my phone. I ran out of things to do while waiting, so since it was now early December I decided to write Christmas cards.

I remembered how nice it was of those lawyers Craig and Harry to bring me food when I was sick and my lights were out, and how Harry helped me speed through Con Ed, so I wrote out two small UNICEF Christmas cards and then put them in a larger envelope together to save postage.

Just as I was writing out Harry's name on the small envelope, my phone rang. I jumped to answer it, praying it was the Newport club owner.

It wasn't. It was Harry. This was seven weeks after my Con Ed problem; I hadn't seen or spoken to Harry since, and he called me just as I was writing his name.

He asked me if I could meet him that evening for a drink. I declined, telling him I had plans. *(Yeah—what great plans—sitting around waiting for a phone call.)* I was also busy on Monday during the day, but agreed to meet him for drinks after work. He asked me to come by his office then.

The phone call I was hoping for never came. What a waste of a perfectly good weekend. Another lesson learned!

When I went to Harry's office, I was told he was delayed for a short time. Could I wait?

I settled into one of the couches with a book. Fifteen minutes later the receptionist asked me if I could continue waiting and I said yes. After another fifteen minutes she asked again. This went on for an hour and a half. Finally Harry stuck his head out of the hallway door. "I am so sorry," he said, "it's too late to have drinks now—"

I got up and started putting my coat on.

"We'll have to have dinner," he said.

It was a chilly, foggy night. We went to a lovely Chinese restaurant called Shun Lee Palace. It was the fanciest food I had ever eaten. After dinner we went to Michael's Pub, which had a live jazz band, with Woody Allen as one of the clarinet players.

After that we took a cab down to the Village, to a bar called the Lion's Head, near Dave Van Ronk's apartment. I called Dave and he joined us for a couple of drinks. Dave for the most part loathed lawyers, but he could tell this one was a good guy.

Harry entertained us with stories about Mafia dons and colorful scoundrels he had represented over the years. He also did a good amount of pro bono work and was active in the Legal Aid Society. We talked about writers and Harry and I discovered that we had the same favorite: Ring Lardner. We each owned vintage editions of *Ring Lardner's Collected Stories*.

We eventually said good night to Dave and then headed uptown in a yellow cab.

I have written a number of songs about Harry since that first night; the two most requested are "Good Thing He Can't Read My Mind," and "The Kind of Love You Never Recover From." He still works as an attorney and he's become my closest friend and confidant. He has also helped to guide the path my life has taken, like a guardian angel.

The following summer Irene, my jitterbugging college pal, invited me to Miami to visit. We spoke all the time on the phone and wrote constantly. I had a number of boring temp jobs where I often had very little to do, so I would write her long letters rather than sit there doing nothing. The letters turned into a short novel (never published) called *Letters to Boom Boom*, where my Ring Lardner obsession is painfully obvious.

When my flight landed in Miami, Irene picked me up at the airport and told me that the air conditioner in her guest bedroom had just broken.

This was *summer* in *Florida*. What was Irene thinking?! After the first sleepless night I knew that I had to either go straight back to New York or find another place to sleep at night. I called up Dutch, my Florida ex. Oh,

I wasn't interested in getting back together with him; my call was of a more pragmatic nature—did he have an air conditioner, and could I crash at his place for a few days?

He was now on a photo shoot in Orlando, so he said I could stay in his apartment, a studio over a garage in Coconut Grove. Irene dropped me off there on her way to work as a ballroom dance instructor.

Dutch had an extensive vinyl album collection, so I was alone all day in his apartment with three thousand albums lining the walls. The last day I stayed there, I picked up an album by a singer named Megan McDonough. It was called *In the Megan Manner*, and the cover photograph was gorgeous—Megan in a long, flowing dress, with shiny, lovely honey blonde hair.

I was transfixed. I played Megan's album over and over again.

That was the last time I visited Irene in Florida. She and I took different paths after that—she became a therapist, and I focused more on music—and we drifted apart. But I wrote two songs about her: "Sweet Irene the Disco Queen," a sort-of-true tale about how she and her first husband met (on the album *Future Fossils*), and a decade later a song about how they split up.

Happily, she eventually met someone else and is doing fine. We had so much fun when we were together that I'm sure our paths will cross again, probably when we're little old ladies and Boom Boom and Trixie start raising hell in the retirement home.

A few years after that Florida visit, in the fall of 1980, Harry made plans to take me to Switzerland on a ski trip. It was a ridiculous idea—I had never skied and it seemed extravagant to go all that way to put skis on for the first time. But I had never been to Europe, and it sounded like quite an adventure. We were going to leave around 10:00 a.m. from JFK on a Saturday in early December. The day before, I was standing in line at the bank to deposit money so I could write checks to cover my rent and utilities while away. Suddenly I got all dizzy and light-headed. I had to sit down and became nauseous—I had apparently gotten hit with some bug.

I slowly walked home. I put on my pajamas and crawled into bed, shivering. A few hours later I called Harry. I was hoping whatever I had was going away, but it wasn't, so I had no choice but had to cancel going to Switzerland with him. He was disappointed. I told him to go on without me, but he canceled the trip entirely.

The next morning my temperature dropped to normal and I felt fine. I simply wasn't sick anymore. I hadn't been nervous or worried about the trip—I couldn't believe that my temperature would return to normal at almost the exact time our flight would have taken off.

A few days later tragedy struck. John Lennon was shot and killed outside the Dakota apartment building on West Seventy-second Street, a few blocks from where I lived. Like many New Yorkers I tuned into the radio program of Vin Scelsa, who was on the air that night. He opened up the phone lines, and people called in venting their sorrow and frustration and rage. Around 2:00 a.m. I walked over to the Dakota and joined all the grieving people standing outside the building, some in silence, some weeping.

The following month, January 1981, Harry had to fly to Aspen to visit a client, and he asked if I wanted to go with him to make up for the European trip. We didn't know until we got there that there was no snow in Aspen—since he had to visit his client it didn't occur to him to check weather conditions. It was like a ghost town. The first day there we walked around and passed the Jerome Hotel. On the side of the building was a sign pointing down the stairs to the back that said, "Appearing Nightly at Richard's at the Jerome," with a picture of a beautiful blonde girl in a cowboy hat labeled "Megan McDonough" underneath.

I scrutinized the photograph—that Megan album I saw in Florida wasn't a country album. But I looked closely at the face and I knew it *had* to be her. I started jumping up and down and clapping.

"Harry! I know her! She's great! We have to go tonight!!"

Harry looked dubious. He is not a fan of country music, and in the hat she looked like a country act. But I told him *we were going.*

The show was scheduled for 8:00 p.m. We got there at 7:00. There were 250 seats on the main floor of the club, and up a few steps and off to the side was a bar area where patrons could watch the show without having to pay the cover charge. There were seven people at the bar. The rest of the room was empty—the lack of snow was affecting all businesses in the area.

I asked the maître d' to seat us as close to the stage as possible, right in the center. When the show started we were the only two paying customers. Megan had a four-piece band that played a couple of songs before she took the stage. When she walked out onstage Harry and I clapped like mad.

It *was* her. That voice was unmistakable. By now there were maybe ten people at the bar, and the two of us seated at the table right in front of the stage. Megan was singing a whole different kind of material from what I'd heard in Florida, but halfway through her set I started yelling out for songs from her album *In the Megan Manner*—I couldn't help myself. The look on her face was a combination of surprise and shock.

After her set I introduced myself and we exchanged addresses. Like me, she is one of nine Irish Catholic kids. We vowed to stay in touch.

Another interesting thing happened on that trip. One night at a restaurant, the wife of one of Harry's friends leaned over to me and whispered, "Isn't this the greatest town in the world? Nobody's fat in Aspen."

I know a good song title when I hear one. I never perform that song live anymore, but I'll never forget how checking into a hotel there a few years later the desk clerk, a woman of perhaps 350 pounds, leaned over the counter, looked me in the eye, and said, *"Miss Lavin, about your song . . ."* Then she burst out laughing.

Recently a countrywide obesity study concluded that the state of Colorado had the lowest percentage of overweight people in the country. I wasn't surprised, that desk clerk notwithstanding.

I also had one of my most memorably disastrous shows in Aspen, at the Paradise Theater. I was opening for Asleep at the Wheel, perennial favorites in that part of Colorado. At the time the girl singer was Mary Ann Price, and the leader, as always, was that tall good-looking cowboy Ray Benson. I had met Ray back in Saratoga Springs a few years earlier, but of course he didn't remember me.

Ray is a force of nature—way over six feet tall, huge booming voice, big cowboy hat—the kind of performer who, just by strutting out onstage, makes everyone start to have a good time.

Whoever thought it was a good idea to have me—a solo singer/songwriter—entertain the crowd before this hoppin' band was very wrong. I did the best I could but had to deal with crazy cowboy types leaving their seats to stand at the edge of the stage a few inches away from me, waving beer bottles in the air screaming *"WHERE'S ASLEEP AT THE WHEEL? Get the f*#k off the stage!"*

I just plowed ahead because I could see that there were a few people listening who seemed to enjoy what I was doing, so I focused on them. This was years before my Joan Rivers debacle, so you see there's no avoiding this kind of thing in this business. When my set was done I ran backstage, went into the bathroom, and locked the door behind me. I love that band and was so embarrassed.

But they knew exactly what happened—they were ten feet away the whole time, separated from the stage by only a flimsy curtain. Mary Ann knocked on the bathroom door and said, "Christine, you come out of there right now! Don't let those a##holes bother you. You are very talented!"

I thanked her, but I didn't come out of the bathroom. Then Ray himself knocked on the door. "Miss Lavin," he said, with that beautiful deep voice of his, "if there's one thing I like better than singin', it's an old fashioned rip-roarin' brawl. I want you to come outta there, point out to me which of those rude patrons out there gave you the hardest time, and then I will personally kick each one of their butts on your behalf."

Whenever I see Ray Benson on TV or hear his voice on the radio, I smile.

One last story about Aspen. A few years ago Harry was making the last ski run of the day. It's during the last runs of the day when most people run into trouble. They're physically tired, the light is waning because the sun is going down. Harry was skiing by himself on Aspen Mountain (what used to be called Ajax Mountain), on an expert black diamond trail, and he took a spill.

Falling down is no big deal, but he had no one to help him get up. His skis were wedged into the deep, soft snow. He hadn't been in Aspen for long and was not yet completely acclimated to the high altitude. As he struggled to right himself, he was practically out of breath.

Skier after skier after skier zipped by without offering help. Then fewer skiers went by, because the lifts had stopped. Harry didn't panic, but he became a bit concerned, wondering if the ski patrol was going to have to help him—or if they would even find him.

Then a woman stopped and asked if he needed help.

Harry let out a sigh of relief. "I'm embarrassed to say that I do," he said. "I just can't seem to get up."

The woman took her skis off and got down in the snow with him. She dug out the snow around his skis, then unbuckled his skis and pulled them off. She got behind him, put her arms under his and lifted him up to his feet, then knelt down to buckle his skis back on.

"Wait for me," she said. "I'm going to ski all the way down the mountain with you to make sure you are okay."

Harry was so grateful and waited while she put her skis back on. Before they took off he asked her what her name was.

"Carole King," she said.

"Carole King?" Harry said. "Are you a performer?"

"No, not really," she said. "I'm a songwriter."

"Well, Carole King, songwriter, I thank you for helping me in my hour of need."

Harry and Carole skied down to the bottom of Aspen Mountain. Carole even walked him to the shuttle bus to the hotel.

Could you possibly have loved her any more? She writes classic songs like "You've Got a Friend," and it's good to know that she walks the walk, not just talks the talk.

Last year Harry bought her latest album and said, "If you ever run into her, tell her she was mistaken that day on Aspen Mountain. She's a hell of a performer."

13

WHAT WAS
I THINKING?

Rewind back to 1977. I called Herb Gart, the manager who a year and a half earlier had told me to contact him when I was a better guitar player. His office was on West Fifty-third Street in Manhattan, and he had a reputation as a rather eccentric guru/photographer, but over the years he worked successfully with artists like Don McLean, Bill Cosby, the Youngbloods, Biff Rose, and Buzzy Linhart.

I went to Herb's office and played him some of my new songs. He wanted me to start meeting record producers, so he sent me to Steve Burgh, a musician who lived in Greenwich Village and had worked with David Bromberg, Phoebe Snow, and Steve Goodman, among many others. I was dubious about this, since I was a rookie in every way. But you have to start somewhere, so I followed Herb's advice.

I arrived at Steve Burgh's place in the late afternoon on a cold winter day, and as instructed I played him a few tunes. I guess he wasn't moved one way or the other, but he had another musician who was visiting—she was busy cooking in the kitchen—and he called to her and asked her to come and play us a couple of songs.

Her name was Sally Fingerett.

She sat down at his piano and dazzled us both with her dark, smoky voice and her liquid grace on the keys. Then she picked up her guitar and sang another song, and again I was impressed. Steve thanked her, and Sally went back to her cooking.

Steve thanked me for coming, and that was it. I put my guitar back in its case, put on my coat, and left. I stood outside the building and wondered what exactly just happened in there.

Was this his way of saying he wasn't interested in working with me? Or was he telling me, "Now *this* girl [Sally] is a real musician." Or what? I had never met a record producer before, so I had nothing to compare it to. But I walked away knowing I had just met an extraordinary musician with the unusual name of Sally Fingerett.

More than ten years later, in 1989, when I was on Rounder Records and performing on the road a lot, I had a series of dates in the Midwest. The night before I was to fly from New York to Milwaukee I could tell I was getting one of those annoying yeast infections that girls get (I can hear you guys wanting to turn the page—don't!). Now you can get over-the-counter medications that cure it, but back then you needed a doctor's prescription. I didn't have time to see my gynecologist, so I had him call the prescription in to my local drugstore.

When I landed in Milwaukee I went straight to the local public radio station for a live interview. I had dinner with people from the station and then checked into my hotel. The next day I'd be flying to Minneapolis, where I would do another radio interview that afternoon and a concert the following night.

So as soon as I got to my hotel room in Milwaukee I applied the yeast infection medicine—no big deal, I'd done this before—except *this* time, rather than solving the problem, it was like setting myself on fire *down there*. I filled the bathtub with cold water and jumped in—didn't help. I got ice from the ice machine, sat in a cold tub with ice—didn't help.

I got plastic bags from room service, filled them with ice, tried to sleep with ice packs around me—didn't help. Around 4:00 a.m. I called the front desk and vaguely explained my problem to the clerk, who said hotel policy was to tell guests go to the local hospital's emergency room. I dressed, took a taxi to the hospital a mile away, then sat there in agony for three hours until they could examine me.

The doctors said I had had an allergic reaction to the yeast infection medicine. They gave me a cortisone shot, then applied a topical medication, and finally I began to experience relief. But now I had to fly again, and I hadn't slept all night.

I called Rounder Records and asked if it would it be possible to have one of their reps—one of their *female reps*—meet me at the Minneapolis airport.

Walking through the Minneapolis airport I saw a woman at the other end of the terminal with a big sign with my name on it. I was *so* relieved.

She told me her name was Rikki Gale. We got my guitar and luggage and went out to her car as I explained what I was going through. She was very sympathetic. As we drove to a radio station, where I was to be interviewed before my concert, we talked shop about the music business. As she was explaining her duties, she mentioned that Rikki Gale was her rep name, but that her married name was Fingerett.

Now, mind you, I hadn't slept all night; I was basically a mess and doing my damnedest to keep awake so I could sound coherent for the radio interview—but did she say "Fingerett"?

I asked her if she was related to Sally Fingerett, and she said yes, Sally was her sister-in-law.

Wha??

I told her about that time years earlier that I was sent to Steve Burgh to "audition" for him, and all I remembered was this woman named Sally Fingerett who played two songs and left me feeling like a complete amateur. I peppered Rikki with questions about Sally. Rikki told me Sally was married, had one solo album and one baby, and had been in a group called *Buffalo Gals*. Sally was living in Columbus, Ohio, which was one of the cities I'd be playing on this tour! I was ecstatic.

I asked Rikki to tell Sally that I must meet her, that I would comp her for my show, and that I was dying to hear her album. I was babbling in my sleep-deprived state, but I couldn't believe I was going to cross paths with her again.

Before I got to Columbus I performed a concert in Cleveland, and the night after that concert I dreamed that I put together an album of winter songs by a dozen different artists. I remember vividly waking up in the hotel room in Cleveland with the idea—clear out of the blue. It was May or June—not anywhere near winter.

During my sound check in Columbus, Sally Fingerett arrived, with her solo debut album *Enclosed* for me. She shook my hand in a way that made it clear she didn't remember meeting me. But I was so happy to see her again that I went on and on about how I never forgot how brilliantly she sang and played that day at Steve Burgh's place and how thrilled I was to finally have her recording.

When I heard her song "Wild Berries" I knew it would be perfect for the winter compilation album I dreamed about in Cleveland. That collection came to fruition first in 1989 as a privately released cassette, then as a commercial release in 1990 as *On a Winter's Night*, first on North Star Records and then on Rounder. Sally became a part of that project, which led to the formation of the Four Bitchin' Babes. She still heads it up today, all these years later.

But it all started in 1976 in Saratoga Springs at Caffé Lena when Herb Gart gave me his business card, then a year or so later when Sally was visiting Steve Burgh's Greenwich Village apartment the same day I was sent to play for him, then my having an allergic reaction to medicine more than a decade later. There was no reason why Rikki Gale needed to tell me her married name—Fingerett—but she *did*.

How would life have been different if she hadn't? I don't even want to know. Sally is someone I know I will be friends with for my entire life.

When I met her that second time, in Columbus, she was married to the musician Dan Green, who now heads up his own recording company, Amerisound. Sally and Dan have divorced but have a lovely daughter together, and they remain close.

A few months after 9/11, while Dan was working alone with a band in his studio late on a Sunday night, the band pulled a gun on him and robbed him of every piece of recording equipment in the studio. They took his driver's license, tied him up, piled furniture on top of him, and said if he called the cops they would go to his house and kill his family.

Dan lay on the floor most of the night, unable to move, until early Monday morning, when his office manager found him and called the police.

The thieves were never caught, and Dan has since installed a state-of-the-art alarm system. He was traumatized by the event, but because it happened soon after 9/11, his overwhelming feeling was gratitude that nothing worse had happened. A few weeks later he wrote a song called "That September Morn," inspired, in part, by his traumatic experience.

Writing songs about 9/11 is a delicate issue. As Dave Van Ronk used to say, "It's very hard to write a good political song; it's very easy to write a bad one." Most of the better songs about 9/11 were written with some distance between the time of the event and the writing of the song, giving the songwriter some perspective. Similarly, Dave used to caution musicians about getting emotionally involved with each other, knowing it can become a very volatile relationship. Sally is now married to a great guy named Michael who has two sons—so for a couple of years there were three teenagers in Sally and Michael's household. Michael is not in the music business. Sally, besides heading up the Four Bitchin' Babes, continues to record solo and has recently branched out into theater *and* into the Jewish music scene. She has a smart, clever show called *Mentl Yentl* that she performs, and every year XM satellite radio plays a Hanukkah show that she created that includes a guest appearance by Dan Green.

One of Sally's most popular songs is "Home Is Where the Heart Is," which is not only on one of the early Babes CDs, but was also recorded by Peter Paul & Mary. Sally is also one hell of a cook. It makes sense, then, that way back in 1977 when I first met her, she was in Steve Burgh's kitchen. If you ask her very nicely, she might just give you her kugel recipe (fourbitchinbabes.com).

There's one story about Sally I love that she *hates* to hear, but too bad, I'm going to tell you. When I was in the Babes we were doing some Colorado dates. One night we were in Denver, and the next night we were due in Fort Collins, which is a few miles to the north. Sally was driving the rental van—she loves to drive. And truth be told, there is no one on earth who can pack a vehicle the way Sally can pack a car. (To touring musicians, this is a highly prized art. Word has it that drummers, with their exceptional mathematical sense, make the best packers.) She has a knack for fitting every oddly shaped suitcase and instrument case in such a way that when it's done it looks like a Chinese art deco interlocking puzzle.

Sally was working on an album at the time and popped a cassette of a rough mix in the van's cassette player. She was happily playing the song over and over and singing along until we passed a huge sign that said WELCOME TO WYOMING.

She had driven thirty-two miles past the exit we were supposed to take.

We all screamed, and Sally, laughing hysterically, did a giant U-turn and headed us back south.

If you want to make Sally laugh, just walk up after one of her performances and tell her, "Welcome to Wyoming!"

Cheryl Wheeler is another musician who hugely affected the trajectory of my life and career. I'll never forget the first time I saw her perform. It was during a horrible heat wave in New York in the summer of 1980. She was singing at a club then called "the Other End." (It had been called "the Bitter End" in the sixties and later went back to using that name.)

There were two sections in the club: the good side, with a cover charge, a stage with lights, and two shows a night. The bad section was a noisy restaurant with a makeshift stage, minimal sound, and no lights to speak of, where the performer did six sets a night and was paid only fifty dollars total.

That's the side Cheryl was on.

Despite the cooking clatter and eating roar, Cheryl's voice cut through and it was obvious to many of us that here was someone to be reckoned with. I was transfixed.

Cheryl was doing what I wanted to do, but she was doing it with a voice and an intensity I could never match. I walked out of there feeling very low indeed—and yet oddly inspired.

I walked down the block and stopped in at Kenny's Castaways. Bluesman Paul Geremia, Dave Van Ronk's friend from Newport, was playing there. I hadn't seen him since the night I stayed at his house after playing at the Salt. The heat wave had knocked out the air conditioning at Kenny's Castaways, yet there were candles on every table, making the room temperature hover somewhere around ninety-five degrees. I lasted all of twenty minutes and then left, my heart aching for Paul playing in that inferno, and still thinking about Cheryl's powerful performance in the bad section at the Other End.

When I got home I wrote "The Air Conditioner Song," a combined tribute to Paul Geremia's valiant performance and Cheryl's kick-ass style of singing. It's the first of my songs that Sutton Foster sang. She performed it at a "summer" concert at Joe's Pub in January 2006—it being a musical joke on her part to sing all hot-weather music during a cold snap. This was when she was between starring roles in two charming Broadway musicals, *Little Women* and *The Drowsy Chaperone*.

In 1982 I finally got to meet Cheryl Wheeler. I was still working as a temp during the day and doing music at night. This introduction came about because Cheryl's manager at the time wanted to meet me. We all gathered at an Upper West Side restaurant. I probably acted geeky since I was so in awe of Cheryl. She likely has no memory of that dinner, but I sure do. It changed my life as a temp.

During the meal Cheryl told the story of opening for Jonathan Edwards. He liked her music so much that he asked if she could play bass—and would she go on tour with him? As I recall, Cheryl immediately said yes, *EVEN THOUGH SHE HAD NEVER PLAYED BASS IN HER LIFE*. She simply went out, bought a bass, and started playing along with Jonathan's albums at home. When she joined him on the road it was obvious from the outset that she was not the bass player she had made herself out to be, but Jonathan kept her on tour anyway because he loved her music. He hired another bass player, she performed a bunch of shows with him, and everybody was happy. That's how I remember that story.

I was dumbstruck. I couldn't imagine pretending that I had a skill that I didn't, but Cheryl did exactly that and everything worked out fine. That night I vowed that the next time I was asked to do anything on a temp job, no matter what it was, even if I didn't know how, I would say that I could and let Fate find a way.

The very next day—*THE VERY NEXT DAY*—I got a call from my temp agency asking if I could take a one-day job that came with higher pay than usual because they needed someone with stenography skills. It was the annual board meeting for a church group in Greenwich Village. I don't have to tell you that I had no stenography skills whatsoever. You've already figured that out. But I thought about Cheryl Wheeler's bass playing and said, *"Yes! I can do it!"*

The next afternoon I showed up for the meeting at the church. At least twenty people were sitting around a big table. Some wore clerical collars.

I started to get nervous. I had purchased a professional steno pad, but I began to get a "What was I thinking?" feeling.

They seated me at the far end of the table. I took out my steno pad. I thought it best to hold the pad on my lap, not on the table, so they wouldn't see me scribbling like a madwoman when the meeting started.

Twenty people! A church! I had lied! I began to get panicky, nasty thoughts about Cheryl swirling in my head. But then the meeting started.

Now I don't mean to insult or make fun of anyone, but this is exactly what happened: the man who ran the meeting was a combination of slow talker, stutterer, stammerer, and one who liked to finish other people's sentences. He would repeat his own statements at least three times, at glacial speed. And after someone else would say something, he would repeat the end of his or her statement! I didn't have to scribble like a madwoman. In fact, I could have artfully calligraphied the words, xeroxed them, and filed them (as well as my fingernails) in the time it took him to finish every sentence.

Of course, this made the meeting take way longer than normal, but I was saved! Plus I was getting paid by the hour!

Next job: statistical typist. It was for the Museum of Modern Art's annual report. I vaguely remembered a mathematical formula for typing columns of numbers that I had learned in ninth grade, but I sure didn't know it now. But I said *"Yes! I can do it!"* If Cheryl can pretend to play bass, I can pretend to know how to type tables of numbers!

Again, Fortune smiled down on me. I was given a huge stack of papers—all numbers—and a desk with a typewriter in a room all by myself. I closed the door. I started typing out numbers in columns, simply eyeballing it to make the columns look even. Again and again. First time the columns were way off. Second time was a little better. Third time even better. Fourth time better yet.

When I took my lunch break I took all the papers out of the trash that contained my failed efforts, stuffed them into my purse, and threw them away in a street trash basket at least a block away from the museum. I did the same thing when I left at 5:00 p.m.

It took me almost an entire week to type the annual report for MOMA. I finished around 3:00 on a Friday afternoon and delivered it to my supervisor. She looked it over, was satisfied, and gave it to her boss. An hour later he called me in to his office, called his underlings in, thanked me for doing such an excellent job, and then *presented me with a booklet of free passes to the museum for the next entire year!* I thanked him profusely, and thanked Cheryl Wheeler in my heart every time I visited that museum.

The next job offer was to be a video game demonstrator and salesperson at the annual New York Toy Convention. So what if I had never played a video game in my life? *I can learn!* So what if I've never been a salesperson! *How hard could it be?*

I was assigned to a booth at the Toy Building in the Flatiron District downtown. I was given a calculator and was stationed between two video kiosks. One was a confusing video tennis game that was supposed to simulate some kind of 3-D effect but in reality made the player feel dizzy and slightly nauseous. (This was in the early days of video gamery.)

When I got tired of that I switched to demonstrating a game called Lost Luggage. A plane landed, then a luggage carousel slowly spun and went faster and faster as the game progressed. The goal was to control the little red cap guy, catching the bags as they flew off the carousel. If you missed a bag, it would open and underwear would float to the floor to the sound of trilling beeps. And if you missed the dreaded black bag that contained a bomb, it would blow up the airport, and the game was over. (Whoever thought this was a good idea for a video game? How naive we were back then.)

The weird thing was, no customers came in. There were at least fifty others like me, playing video games, order pads at the ready.

Ten o'clock . . . 11:00. Empty. A huge buffet lunch was rolled in at noon. We stuffed ourselves and chatted. Most of the other demonstrators were actors and actresses and models between gigs.

One o'clock . . . 2:00. No one came!

Turned out, this was where they booked the *overflow* game demonstrations. Ninety-five percent of all the game demos were happening a couple of miles uptown at Columbus Circle!

I did a concert with Cheryl recently and asked her about that first time we met all those years ago. It turns out that I had misremembered her story: she did *not* pretend to play the bass when she was initially asked, but she picked up the instrument and learned it just well enough in a few weeks—with help from Jonathan Edwards's bandmate Kenny White—to convince them to hire her as their bassist. As she told me:

> I could not believe I got the gig, but I did. I was blown away, and terrified. I knew I hadn't been hired for my bass playing, so that meant I'd been hired for my singing. Jonathan Edwards was absolutely my favorite singer and getting that gig was the first time I thought of myself as a singer. That tour was about three weeks and a total, riotous blast, just Jonathan, Kenny and me. My bass playing was barely adequate on my best nights and it was SO MUCH FUN singing the high part and playing the low part.

Obviously I misunderstood Cheryl all those years ago, but it doesn't really matter, because whatever it was she said, it inspired me to take chances in life.

So it was that many years and quite a few albums later I took a chance and hosted retreats for singer/songwriters on Martha's Vineyard in 1992 and 1993. I was so happy when Cheryl agreed to attend.

The first year I rented a bed-and-breakfast in Oak Bluffs for the month of September, invited some of my other favorite singer/songwriters to stay there, and arranged for a chef to make dinner every night. It cost a lot to do this, but I had just signed a publishing deal with Cherry Lane (including a songbook) that came with a hefty advance check. I have since learned that whenever you receive a large check, you should look at it as worth *half* the amount, and plan to use the other half to pay taxes. But I didn't know that then. I was so excited at getting such a huge check that I spent a big chunk of it on the Vineyard. A couple of years later I was stone cold broke again, but on the Vineyard that September I felt like Rockefeller.

Songs were written during the weekdays and a jazz guitar instructor named Howard Morgan gave workshops; on weekends we did concerts—which we taped—at the Wintertide, a small coffeehouse in Vineyard Haven. That first year resulted in a single CD, *Big Times in a Small Town,* on Rounder Records, engineered and produced by David Seitz.

The title song was written and performed by James Mee, a wonderful singer/songwriter who lives in Vermont. Before he went into music he was a prizefighter. Story was he got knocked out at a fight, woke up, and decided he wanted to become a folksinger. I love his work—it's thoughtful . . . yet *manly.* There's something very appealing about a masculine man singing gentle, beautiful songs.

The next year the songwriters' retreat would yield a double CD, *Follow That Road*, the title song written and performed by Anne Hills. Originally I was going to call it *Flying in the Face of Mr. Blue,* after a song beautifully sung by Vineyard resident Kate Taylor. But the title *Follow That Road* kept popping into my head. A few weeks before finalizing the packaging for the album, Dave Van Ronk left this message on my answering machine: "You know the Vineyard album you're working on? You should call it *Follow That Road.*" I knew he was right.

Jonathan Edwards joined us at the second retreat. I was thrilled because, like Cheryl, I was a big fan of his—and not just because I always got good takeout every time I sang his hit song in those long-ago days at Anita's restaurant.

But in the second year lots more musicians came to Martha's Vineyard than those who were officially invited. I just wanted the whole thing to happen on its own, but Dave warned me: "Unless you control it, it will turn into something you hate." I had no idea what he meant. But I found out.

The first year no one knew about the retreat except for the performers attending. The second year, though, the CD from the first retreat had been out in the world, and innumerable singer/songwriters showed up angling to get into the weekend shows. Whereas we were able to hang out, swim, and jam during the first year, during the second I found myself running away from musicians who were pestering me to put them in the shows. They wanted to get on the CD and get "discovered." By that time I had bought a tiny house on the Vineyard, in Oak Bluffs, and some musicians thought nothing of knocking at all hours to ask if they could sleep on my floor. Out of desperation I finally hung a Do Not Disturb sign on the front doorknob.

Besides Jonathan Edwards, Tom Paxton and Dave Van Ronk also came to the Vineyard that September. I loved having them there and did whatever I could to make their stay pleasant, but I also had to handle other duties that weren't so much fun, and I slept very little. By the time each weekend rolled around, I was a wreck. A young unknown performer named Dar Williams showed up, and I was told by others that she was really good and should be put in the weekend shows, but I was so overwrought I couldn't even think of listening to her songs. I will be always be sorry about that! By the end of that retreat I was borderline nuts.

I sold my tiny house the following month. Dave was right. The retreat had turned into something I hated because I simply didn't have the managerial temperament to run it properly—I wanted it to just "happen." But the CDs that resulted are wonderful.

One more story about the retreats. The first year Cheryl Wheeler had the room down the hall from mine at the Sea Spray Inn. I had a brand new Macintosh laptop that I was teaching myself how to use. Every time I made an error the laptop made a beeping sound, and I guess I said the same thing whenever this happened: *"What was I thinking?"* After overhearing this one too many times, Cheryl walked into my room and said, "Do you realize every time you make a mistake you say 'What was I thinking?' Why don't you program your computer to say it instead of that stupid beep sound? Better yet, why don't you write a song using that phrase, since it's practically your mantra?"

So I thank Cheryl for inspiring that song, too. A few years later Cheryl temporarily replaced Megon McDonough (who had previously spelled her first name Megan) in the Four Bitchin' Babes, so I got to travel with her and sit onstage with her every night, too.

And people who become fans of hers become enthusiastic fans for life. Last year I went with songwriter Ervin Drake and his wife, Edith, to hear Tony DeSare at the Oak Room at the Algonquin Hotel. It was a memorable night—revered jazz guitarist Bucky Pizzarelli was playing in Tony's band, showing that Tony had indeed "arrived." Near the end of the show Tony introduced some of the musicians in the crowd, including Ervin, who's written some of the best songs ever. I was surprised that Tony mentioned me, too. Being a folkie, I didn't think I was on his radar. But it's so much fun to be recognized when you're at someone else's show. The sound of applause *never* gets old.

After the show I was in front of the Algonquin saying goodnight to the Drakes when a woman grabbed my hand and squealed. "Oh my God! I couldn't believe it when Tony said you were in the audience! I'm your biggest fan! I've been to at least ten of your concerts in Boston. You are THE BEST!"

I tried my best to act humble and said, "Oh, thank you so much," but then she kept going.

"Your songs! Your songs are *amazing*—I have all your albums! I love that song about going through dead people's houses, the one 'Arrow,' where you sing, '*I wish I could fall in love / though it only leads to trouble / oh I know it does,*' the Mexican hat dance 'Potato' song you wrote with James, your dog, the Sylvia Hotel, the one about your cat's birthday. . . ."

I stood there smiling broadly, hoping against hope that she was actually going to mention one of *my* songs . . . but every one she mentioned was written by Cheryl Wheeler. *Every single one.* She was bubbly and ecstatic, and her friends were so happy that she was so happy, so you know what I did?

I hugged her and said, "Thank you! You've made my night."

Then I sent an e-mail to Cheryl from the cab on the way home, telling her I'm expanding my talents: "I did a *most* convincing Cheryl Wheeler impression tonight on the sidewalk in front of the Algonquin Hotel."

TOP LEFT: With my favorite violinist, Robin Batteau, in Central Park, 1986. Photo © Betsy A. Brody **TOP RIGHT:** When the first show at the Bottom Line ran late, I kept the folks who were waiting for the next show temporarily hypnotized by my baton twirling; mid-1990s. Photo: Christine Lavin Collection **ABOVE:** Singing a finale at the Bottom Line with Janice Kollar, Lillie Palmer, Gladys Bragg, Ginger Bennett, my brother Christopher, my sister Mary, Dave Van Ronk, Red Grammer, Chuck Romanoff, Tom Rowe, Steve Romanoff, Rod MacDonald, Nikki Matheson, O.J. Anderson, and Diane Chodkowski. This was the same night in 1986 that the Mets were playing the Red Sox in the World Series and Bill Buckner made an error that probably haunts him to this day. Photo © Betsy A. Brody **RIGHT:** See my hair? When this perm was new I looked like Art Garfunkel; late 1970s. Photo: Collection Christine Lavin **FACING PAGE:** This is the guitar with the $250 strings; 1984. Photo © Adina Sabghir

TOP LEFT: My aunts Carolyn and Patsy at Rockaway Point, New York; early 1930s. Patsy recorded the poem she wrote about Carolyn at the beginning of my song "Something Beautiful" on the album *I Was in Love with a Difficult Man*. **TOP RIGHT:** The brief moment (in 1952) when I was the baby of the Lavin family, soon to be replaced by a younger and cuter baby, brother Eddie. **LEFT:** The Lavin siblings in 1965 echoing the positions of the 1952 family portrait. **MIDDLE:** Grandpa and Grandma Crawford at Rockaway Point in the mid-1950s. On the album *Future Fossils*, the song "Rockaway" is about closing up their bungalow at the end of summer. **RIGHT:** The Lavin siblings on Mary's wedding day in 1990. From left to right: Tom, Jody (in Tom's lap), Christopher (standing), Mary (in Mom's wedding dress), Louise (standing), Gregory, Christine (in back), Edward (sitting on floor), and James (sitting). All photos: Christine Lavin Collection

144

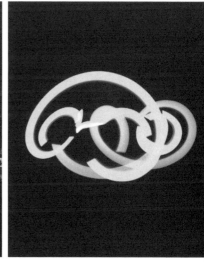

TOP LEFT: Backstage at the Philadelphia Folk Festival in the early 1990s. I talked these guys into being my "Lightning Bug Brigade" on the main stage. These are some brave songwriters: Hans Theessink, David Roth, Megon McDonough, Cliff Eberhardt, Fred Kollar, John Gorka, Kari Estrin, Sally Fingerett, Chris Smither, Eve Silber, Cathy Fink, and Marcy Marxer. Photo © Thom Wolke **TOP RIGHT:** At a party at Bellevue Hospital in 1984, I'm talking with Renee Katz and Senator Jacob K. Javits. Photo: Christine Lavin Collection **MIDDLE:** I tried (unsuccessfully) to blend in with the Star Attraction baton twirling squad in King of Prussia, Pennsylvania, in the early 2000s. Photo: Christine Lavin Collection **LEFT:** The thirty-fifth anniversary concert of *Woody's Children* in 2004: Bob Sherman, Garry Novikoff, Doug Mishkin, me (smiling at Garry), Mark Murphy, Pete Seeger, Tom Chapin, James Durst, David Bernz, Martha Sandefer, Jon Cobert, and Michael Mark. Photo © Steve J. Sherman **RIGHT:** What Joan Rivers's West Palm Beach audience never really got to see: late 1990s. Photo: Christine Lavin Collection

TOP LEFT: Another great night at this New York City club, 1989. Photo: Bitchin' Babes Archives **TOP RIGHT:** Backstage at the Bottom Line in 1992. I'm with former Yankee pitcher Jim Bouton, Julie Gold, and Paula Bouton. Photo © Teddy Lee **MIDDLE:** Me with John Gorka, Willie Nininger, and Jeff Hardy at a *Fast Folk* show at the Bottom Line in 1986. Photo © Teddy Lee **LEFT:** Phil Ochs Night at Folk City in 1985. That's me with Jim Glover, Dave Van Ronk, Thom Wolke, Sonny Ochs, and Tom Paxton. Photo © Teddy Lee **FACING PAGE:** At a *Fast Folk* concert in Central Park in the early 1990s. Photo © Jeff Nisbet

This group is spearhead... the opposition to nuclea... missiles based in New Yo... Harbor. Featured is CHA... KING, one of the finest... litical and cultural si... songwriters today, vag... reminiscent of the 60'... "Acres of Clams" & num... other songs covered by... tists as diverse as P... ger and Bright Mornin...

A Song
Christine La

Illustrations
Betsy Franco Fee

MOEBA HOP

Fax it! Charge it! Don't ask me what's for dinner!
THE FOUR BITCHIN' BABES

ALLY ROGERS
...bounded ene...
...t vocal preci...
England artis...
eat mixture of...
gs & work by ot...
ists' like Claudi...
Bob Franke. Her...
...m just out.

KEN KOSEK &
Glaser has...
corded with...
ark Sheiks"...
th Kenny...
ee School...
owned fo...
Hasty L...
Jazz vi...

24 HAP...
Ha...
have...
sin...
the...
pl...
r...

Christine Lavin & Don White
Friday, February 12th, 2010
knitting with christine: 7pm
doors: 7pm   show: 8pm
Steve's
BACKSTAGE PASS
Tix: $20

CHRISTINE
LAVIN

A Modest Proposal

A Birthday, they tell us,
Is only a number;
A number we run up,
Asleep or A-slumber.
And, since we all know The
Grim Reaper keeps reaping,
What sense does it make wasting
Precious time sleeping?
And so, Sweet Christine, I am
Begging in closing, you
Share my Motel Room
With neither One dozing.

Your Semi-Secret Lover, Ervin

Today as thousands of tourists stood at the edge f... ...lls an unidentified person conquered Niagara

ALSO LO JAI · 1989 FESTIVALS (part 2)
Songs · Columns · Reviews · & more!!!

FOLK GUITAR WITH LAURA W

...SERI... OF BEGINNING LESSONS IN FOLK
...ED BY KQED SAN FR...

NOVEMBER
1984

...ESDAY THROUGH
...DAY SHOWS AT 8:30+1

$6.00

The Sixth Floor
John F. Kennedy and
the Memory of a Nation
Dallas, Texas

THE FIRST EVER YELLOW TAIL RECORDS SONG CIRCLE

Electric Bonsai Band
Scott Katz
Christine Lavin
Patrice O'Neill
Katie Peterson
Matt Price
Uncle Bonsai

ONE NIGHT AT MILLER'S

Miller's Community & Arts Center
...7 Tolt Avenue in Carnation, Washington
...hursday, September 13th, 7:00 PM
Tickets $20 in advance

One Meat Ball
The Album   The Cookbooklet

OPEN
MIKE
$5.00 $9
EM CEES:
PALMER
ROGERS

14

STUPIDLY CRAPPY
MIND-NUMBING MUSIC BUSINESS DISAPPOINTMENTS

A journalist from Nashville once told me, "There's always a certain level of bullshit in the music business. When it gets bothersome, just rise above it, because it never goes away completely."

Hearing that has saved me many times, and it might save you. Yes, this is the chapter of music-business nightmares. Welcome to the dark side.

Ninety-nine percent of all the singer/songwriters I know never focus on the bottom line, and that includes me. It's not that I'm foolish or stupid; it's that I have always believed that if you do good work, the money will follow. I work as hard at a free benefit as I do at a fancy concert hall. My road managers will tell you that when I get paid at the end of the night, it's always a surprise, because I never know what it's going to be. (Hey, maybe I shouldn't be writing this. Oh, what the hell.) Luckily, almost all the promoters and presenters in folk music are upstanding, ethical people. I've been given maybe five rubber checks over twenty-five years as a professional, and all of the people who wrote those checks paid me in the end. (No, wait, not all of them; there *was* one who never made good. But one bad check over twenty-five years is a pretty good record.)

Having said that, it's almost a rite of passage in this business to have at least one horror story. I have a few.

In the late 1970s, before I had any recordings, I caught the eye of a two-man management agency. The older guy was very respected and had worked with a lot of wonderful musicians. He was past his prime, however, so he teamed up with a young up-and-comer—a fast-talking, snappy-dressing, walking cliché. The older guy gave them gravitas; the young guy gave them street cred.

The two of them were friends with a guy named Karl who owned a popular nightclub on Bleecker Street in New York. He started hiring me as an opening act whenever he had a headliner he thought I would be a good match for. It was two shows a night, usually Friday and Saturday, and I got paid fifty bucks a night. I got to open for Kenny Rankin, Henny Youngman, Dave Van Ronk, Tim Hardin, Arlo Guthrie, Jim Dawson, Aztec Two-Step, Livingston Taylor, and comedian Fred Willard. I loved working with all of them.

You're wondering where the horror story is? It's coming. I thought I did a pretty good job as an opening act. The way it worked, the box office stayed open until fifteen minutes into the headliner's set, so it was my job to keep the crowd entertained for thirty minutes or so as more audience members sat down. I had no delusions of grandeur—I was a support act.

One weekend I was opening four shows for Henny Youngman, the elder statesman of comedy, who would saw away on his violin in between saying things like, "Take my wife . . . *please!*" and "My psychiatrist tells me I'm crazy, and I tell him I want a second opinion, so he says, 'You're ugly, too!'" All four shows he did the exact same jokes in the exact same order, and all four times I laughed, even when I knew what was coming. He was a total pro who had a ball onstage. The first night he handed me his business card and said solemnly, "Darling, I want you to have a picture of my pride and joy." On the back was a photo of a can of Pride furniture polish and a bottle of Joy dishwashing liquid.

It was a hard weekend for me because I was getting over a cold, but I did the best I could. On Saturday night I walked into the dressing room five minutes before I was to go on. Henny was on the telephone.

He covered the mouthpiece and said to me, "Hey kid, I just got another gig tonight—I'm going to entertain at my stockbroker's wife's birthday party between shows. So I'm going on first for the first show. That okay with you? I'm going to open for you!"

I laughed and said, "Oh sure, Henny, that's fine with me!" thinking that he was joking.

He uncovered the mouthpiece of the phone and said into it, "Yes, she said it's okay. See you later."

He hung up the phone, put his arm around me, and said, "Here's a diamond pin."

He pressed something into my hand and closed my fingers around it. I looked down, and it was a safety pin with a dime glued to it.

"It's a dime and pin, kid," he said. "Now you're one of us."

And with that he walked out of the dressing room and, with no introduction, walked onstage. The crowd went wild. Karl burst into the dressing room and screamed, "What is he *doing???*"

I explained the situation to him, but Karl was enraged. Veins popping out from his head, he waved his arms around like a crazy man, screaming and spitting, "I have to close the box office! I have to close the box office *now!*" He pounded the dressing room wall with his fists, then stormed out.

Henny did his usual show and didn't even come back to the dressing room—he went straight out the front door to a waiting limo and disappeared. There was a very brief intermission, and then I took the stage. The waitresses were instructed that they weren't allowed to deliver checks to the tables until I was fifteen minutes into my set. I kept them in their seats. *Whew.*

I opened the second show—again it was packed, and Karl was again a wreck because Henny hadn't returned yet. (How did we ever live without cell phones?!) But he did show up in time, and even though Karl screamed at him, Henny just waved him off.

At all four shows Henny announced that that very night was his fiftieth wedding anniversary, and the crowd cheered. Six months later, I saw him on a TV show where he announced that that very night was his fiftieth wedding anniversary, and that crowd loved it, too. Next time you are out in a restaurant, tell them it's your wedding anniversary or your birthday—

who's going to question it? They'll all sing to you, and maybe even send over a bottle of champagne. Drink a toast to Henny Youngman.

Opening for all those pros was terrific experience, but it did have its down side. The two men who were "managing" me had very different ideas of what I should do onstage. The older one would take me aside and tell me which songs to sing, and then the young guy would take me aside and tell me what *he* thought. Often I would ignore them both and do what I thought best, and then they'd both be mad at me.

It was clear that they were not getting along, and their partnership lasted barely a year. Near the end, the older man confided to me that one of the problems with this business venture was that the younger guy couldn't read or write. He couldn't check the trades or do basic research or even write letters. He was young, handsome, and hip looking, but he was a functional illiterate who had been able to bluff his way into the music business. The older guy told me that he was retiring and that under no circumstances should I continue working with his partner. He was embarrassed to have been hoodwinked by this poseur at this stage of his career.

Before they officially split, Karl asked me to come to his office, upstairs from the club, for a meeting. I assumed those guys would be there, but they weren't. I walked in to see that he was alone. He stood up, pulled my jacket open, and said, "Show me your tits."

I flinched and jumped back, and he assured me he was joking. He asked me to sit down so that we could talk. Wary, I slowly sat down on the couch.

"You've opened a lot of shows at my club now and proved you can do it, so I think it's time to take this to the next level."

I thought—oh my God! He's going to book me as a *headliner?* I didn't see this coming.

"It's time for us to do the paperwork to make me your manager. Let's get it on paper, right now. I'm taking you to the top."

I stood up and said, "I don't think this is a good idea, but thank you, I'm very flattered."

"*What?!*" he screamed. "You're saying no to ME? *ME?* After all I have done for you? All the shows you have opened? All the opportunities I have given you!?"

"Karl," I said, trying to stay calm, "I think I did a good job for you. I never dreamed you wanted to be my manager. I thought you liked my music, that's all. I don't think you have the right temperament to be a manager."

He paced around his office, muttering, "Who the f*#k are you to tell me anything?? You stupid, ungrateful bitch. Where's my gun—where's my gun?" He stopped, put his finger to his temple, and pretended to pull the trigger.

"I'm going to kill myself if you say no," he said, pulling the imaginary trigger again.

"Karl," I said softly, "I don't need a manager. I'm not looking for a manager. What's to manage? I work as a temp during the day. If you had asked me, I would have told you that from the start. I had no idea you had this kind of plan."

He continued to pace and mutter, pulling the imaginary trigger. I got up and moved quickly toward the door.

"Yeah, run—get out of here, you stupid, selfish bitch!" he screamed. "Don't you ever set foot in my club again. If you ever come near me or my club, I will personally beat you to a pulp. Get the *f*#k* out of my *face!*"

I ran out the door, down the stairs, and down the street. I hailed the first taxi I saw, jumped inside, and then hid on the floor until I was sure I was clear.

To this day I have never set foot in that club again. I don't know if Karl would have beaten me up, but why chance it? I know now how lucky I was this happened. If I had kept working at that club, I probably wouldn't have had the nerve to approach the Bottom Line for work.

More than twenty years later, I ran into the fast-talking poseur from my "management team." He was on the sidewalk outside Zabar's on the Upper West Side, still a sharp dresser and a very handsome guy. He asked me what I was doing, so I told him I was writing, recording, and performing. While we were talking, a beautiful young girl stopped to say hello to him. He introduced me to her as "one of my acts," and when I gave him a look, he asked me if I was still signed to his company.

"No," I said. "As of twenty years ago I was no longer signed to your company. I guess you have so many artists that you didn't notice I was gone. But it was nice to see you."

As I walked away, I heard him say to the girl, "What a bitch!"

Whatever.

Not all the bad guys are so obvious. I had another agent who was smart, funny, sweet, and thoughtful—she seemed wonderful. But even nice, smart people can cave in to temptation. This agent managed the CD sales at my concerts, but she ran up a debt of $12,000 with the record company because she failed to pay them for the CDs, instead pocketing all the money. After numerous angry phone calls, promises of "the check is in the mail," and other such nonsense, I got stuck for the entire amount. *This* was some of that music business bullshit I had been warned about.

In 1991 I had a different kind of nightmare. That year my album *Good Thing He Can't Read My Mind* was nominated for a New York Music Award in the Folk Album of the Year category. The New York Music Awards were a project of Robby Wolliver, the man who took over Gerde's Folk City from original owner Mike Porco. Not only was my album nominated, but I was asked to be in the show, which was held at the Beacon Theater, just two blocks from where I lived. I invited the album's producer, Bill Kollar, and his wife, Janice, who also sang on it, to be my guests.

A local rock radio station had distributed the balcony tickets to teenagers, many of whom were fans of a glam metal band called White Lion that was also nominated for an award. Even before the show started, the fans chanted, "White Lion White Lion White Lion," stomping and clapping. The emcee for the night was an up-and-coming comic named Rosie O'Donnell. Whenever she came out onstage, she was able to quiet the White Lion fans, but she was the *only* one who had any power over them whatsoever.

Hilly Crystal, owner of the downtown punk club CBGB, was getting a lifetime achievement award that night, and even when *he* came out to give his acceptance speech, he had to stop and ask the kids in the balcony to shut up. (I played CBGB only once, and Hilly had no memory of me, but I sure remembered that gig. I asked the stage manager if it was safe to leave my purse in the dressing room during my set, and he said, "Are you kidding me? The only safe place is onstage right next to you, where you can see it. And it might be good to keep your foot on the strap, too." So that's what I did.)

As I watched Hilly Crystal dealing with the screaming teens, I started to get nervous. When the rock bands played, they were loud enough to overpower the balcony, but I would be performing solo on an acoustic guitar.

After Rosie O'Donnell introduced me—the kids quieted down for her—I was on my own. I walked out, and by the time I had plugged in my guitar—about five seconds later—the roar from the balcony all but drowned me out.

What could I do? I started to sing "Good Thing He Can't Read My Mind" as best I could as they booed from above. But then they started clapping along in mock fashion and started yelling "You You You You" in rhythm, some clapping, some pointing at me in rhythm. I thought that the best thing to do was to speed up the song and throw them off the beat, but then they caught up with me, so I slowed it down to throw them off, but then they slowed down. By then it was a disaster, and I feared that those sitting in the orchestra section would think I had no sense of rhythm, so I just finished as quickly as I could.

I took a quick bow as the "You You You You" grew even louder, then hastily ducked through the curtain. That was *it* for Rosie.

"How can you be so rude?" she demanded as she retook the stage. "That girl is a very talented songwriter. There is no excuse for your rudeness! Stop it. You should be ashamed of yourselves!"

The balcony fell silent. I was backstage and couldn't see, but I could hear. Over the years people have said all kinds of things about Rosie O'Donnell, but what she did that night was kind. I wrote to her afterward to thank her, and she wrote back, a handwritten note on yellow legal paper: "You are talented! Don't let the idiots get you down."

So there I was backstage after three minutes of stupidity, but since the White Lion fanatics were rude to just about everyone, I didn't take it personally. It was over and done with.

Or so I thought.

The plan was to announce the winner of the Folk Album of the Year category after my performance, and it turned out that my album had won. I didn't know this ahead of time. Because of what had happened when I performed, Robby decided on the spot to not announce that category. While I was still standing backstage looking rather bewildered, he walked over to me, handed me the award (a pretty Plexiglas tchotchke), said "Congratulations," and then pointed me in the direction of the stairs down to the China Club, where the press corps was waiting to photograph and interview the winners.

So I walked down the stairs with my guitar and with my award. There were already at least a half dozen bands being interviewed—there were press from all over the world at this event. They glanced at me, but no one interviewed me or snapped my picture. I went back up to the theater.

I handed the award to Bill and Janice Kollar, figuring that displaying it in their recording studio would do more for them than my putting it on a shelf in my tiny apartment. They were puzzled when I handed them the award—they expected it would be part of the event and didn't know why I had it when it wasn't announced from the stage. I didn't have a good answer for them.

When the evening was over, I tried to go out the stage door unnoticed. It was the only way out for the performers, and as I got closer, I could hear the noise and hubbub coming from just outside. It was the White Lion fans hoping to catch a glimpse of the band on the way out. I prayed that they wouldn't recognize me, and they didn't—for about five seconds.

Then someone screamed, "Hey, it's the folksinger!" and in unison they all started chanting "You You You You" and crowding around me. I was scared that my guitar was going to get crushed. There were security guards by the stage door who jumped in and made a space for me, but I was out-numbered, and I was scared. Oh, I didn't think those kids wanted to hurt me, but there were so many of them. . . . So you know what I did? I started chanting along with them, "You You You You," and laughing and jumping up and down, waving my arms around like it was all some kind of fun joke. (Well, it was better than crying, and it took some of the wind out of their sails.)

I ducked around one of the security guards and started to run down the street. I was just two blocks from my apartment. A couple of the kids started to chase after me but gave up when someone yelled, "Here comes White Lion!"

I got to my building, ran up the stairs, and slammed the door behind me. I took the guitar out of its case to see if it was damaged—it wasn't. That was a relief. I sat down on my bed and tried to process what I had just been through.

I was safe. I should have called it a day, but I didn't. My album had won an award, and I had a pass for the afterparty at the China Club. I had *won!* I shouldn't hide because of those rude kids! They wouldn't be at the

China Club anyway. So I caught my breath and went back up the street to the party.

I got a drink and started to circulate. Whenever I ran into someone I knew, they reacted like they were at a funeral.

"How *are* you? You *okay?*" I heard over and over again. I laughed it off.

I stayed at the party for about an hour, ignored again by the press corps, so I walked home and called my songwriter friend Andrew Ratshin in Seattle. I gave him the play-by-play, and he was as sympathetic as could be. Then I unplugged my phone and went to bed, figuring well, that's that.

The next afternoon when I plugged my phone in, there were a few messages on my machine—some from friends, some from relatives—asking if I was okay. Hmm, I thought. Why are they asking me that? Then my sister Louise called from Bakersfield, California, also wanting to know if I was okay. I asked her why she was asking, and she said she saw a report on MTV about the New York Music Awards that had a clip of me trying to perform while all the kids in the balcony were doing their "You You You You" chant.

An hour later, Robby Wolliver himself called to ask if I was okay, and I said, "Of course I am—they had nothing against me personally. I was just an easy target."

Robbie said, "Don't worry, this kind of thing will never happen again."

I said, "How can you be so sure? You can't control 100 percent of who gets the tickets for this kind of event."

"It will never happen again," he said, "because next year, and from now on, we won't have a folksinger in the show."

Oh, *great.*

I never saw the MTV report myself, but it seemed like everybody else did. I got calls for more than a week. A few days after the awards show the *New York Daily News* wrote a story about it—with the headline THE CROWD WENT WILD . . . UNFORTUNATELY and a big, smiley head shot of me. The article described how rude those kids were to everyone, but somehow I became the poster girl for the story.

I don't know what happened to the New York Music Awards; they seem to have disappeared into the ether. I assume that Bill and Janice Kollar still have my award on their studio shelf.

Here's another bad biz story, and this one is almost a standard rite of passage in the music business.

There was a man—let's call him Mr. X—who started showing up at all my concerts, chatting with me afterward and saying how much he wanted to work with me. This went on for almost a year. I had been making records with one company, but Mr. X told me that if I went with this other company, they would promote me like I have never been promoted, would quadruple my record sales, blah blah blah.

I had been working with Steve Rosenthal, the owner of the Magic Shop Recording Studio in SoHo. He'd produced some of my solo albums, a Four Bitchin' Babes CD, and the second Martha's Vineyard Songwriters' Retreat double album. Mr. X met with Steve and me at the Magic Shop.

We told him what we had in mind for my next album, and that we wanted to have creative control over the choice of the material and its production. He agreed to it all, saying, "Hey, you already have a good track record together. We're not going to mess up a winning combination."

He was going to give us a healthy budget, and we could record at our own pace. When we were ready to deliver it, they would map out a promotion schedule and budget—it all sounded promising. As Mr. X was pursuing me, I should have noticed that he wasn't the owner of this company, instead acting "on their behalf." But the record company I was with had never shown this kind of enthusiasm or prepared a detailed promotion plan.

After hiring a music business attorney recommended by a musician friend, I signed the contract—which also included clauses about future albums—and was given a $7,500 advance. Afterward, the first thing I did was go to the Magic Shop and record eighteen new songs—simple demos, live vocal and guitar.

Out of these eighteen, we would choose twelve to go on the next album. I gave a copy of the songs to Mr. X so he could weigh in. (Although we had creative control, I felt it was good politics to keep him involved from the start.) And weigh in he did: six songs could go on the album, but twelve he didn't like *at all*. He thought I should make an album made up of half original music and half songs by "newcomers" whom I would be credited with "discovering." He said that with my reputation for helping other song-writers, by recording their songs I could directly help them get on the map—and secure a piece of their publishing for myself and for him.

This came as news to me. I told him yeah, maybe I have this nice repu-tation, but it's because I send songs to singers—I send them songs recorded *by* the songwriter. Covering others' songs is not my forte. He was insistent and mentioned my connection to Julie Gold's song "From a Distance." (I was the one who sent it to Nanci Griffith, who recorded it first, and I also sent it to Stephen Holden at the *New York Times*, who suggested it to Bette Midler's producer when he was looking for something to follow up her hit "The Wind Beneath My Wings.")

Mr. X already had a cassette of a dozen songs he wanted me to listen to, but I refused, telling him this wasn't our deal; he had agreed that we had creative control. He came back with, "Do you have it in writing?"

I went back and read the contract—something I should have done before signing it. (Not reading contracts was another weakness of mine, along with my "not focusing on money" philosophy—I'm learning things just *writing* this book.) It turned out that although he told us in person we would have complete creative control, that's not how the contract was worded.

I was flabbergasted. The songs he rejected were songs I had been per-forming for a year. He was at many of those concerts—wasn't he listening?

All of this happened so quickly—within a week of signing—that I hadn't even cashed the $7,500 check. After talking things over with Steve Rosen-thal, who was also disgusted by this turn of events, I called Mr. X and told him I was going to rip the check up and that I wanted to call the whole thing off.

If only.

I got a call from the man who ran this record company, and he told me they would let me out of the contract if I returned the advance, paid them $20,000 in cash, and gave them a percentage of my next two solo albums—*and* the next Four Bitchin' Babes album. The Four Bitchin' Babes weren't even mentioned in my contract at all—how dare they make such a demand!

The next five weeks were torturous. I was on the road, so I had to deal with this on the phone between shows. I didn't have $20,000 in cash, and I didn't want to give them a percentage of future albums—something they had no right to expect. I was baffled as to why they'd rejected two-thirds of my songs—the whole thing was an embarrassing mess. I did my best to forget about it when I was onstage, but it occupied my thoughts every other minute of the day and made sleep more difficult than ever.

I wasn't practicing guitar, I wasn't writing songs—I was fighting with a record company. What a waste of time and energy. Nobody becomes a songwriter for this. It was maddening. I kept taking that check out of my purse, staring at it, and cursing myself for being swayed by these people.

But then one day while doing this, sitting in a diner somewhere in the Midwest, I noticed that the signature on the check was not that of Mr. X or the man who ran the record company—it was that of someone else altogether, the man who *owned* the record company. I was suddenly seized with an idea: I bet this man doesn't even know this is going on. So I called him up, told him what I was going through, and found out I was right. He had *no* idea any of this was going on, and he was angry—on my behalf. He said, "Oh, this isn't right at all. We'll rip up that contract and start over."

I called my guardian angel, Harry. I hadn't asked him to get involved since he was not a music business attorney, but I needed his help. He and I met with the record company owner at a restaurant on Lexington Avenue, and we sat at a back table for three hours and hammered out a contract. It contained a clause that said it would cover my next six albums, but it also said that if we hadn't sold 60,000 copies of my albums within nine months of the release of the second album, the contract was nullified. The owner of the company said that based on what I had already sold, reaching that goal would be a snap, since they would promote my albums in an organized way. Steve and I got creative control back, and I deposited the $7,500 check. I could get back to focusing on music.

When I finished that first album, I thought it was my best work; the sequencing of the songs (something I obsess over) was just right. I sent the company a tape of the album but heard nothing for two weeks. I finally called them up, asking, "What do you think?" and they told me they would have to have an outside consultant listen to it to know if it was ready for release.

Huh? Am I hearing right? You have to hire a consultant to know if a record is good? You can't listen and make that judgment call on your own?

I guess not. The consultant had an idea that one song in particular was going to be the radio hit, but I had it sequenced too far back in the album. He said it had to be moved up to track three or DJs would never get to it. So some faceless consultant who spent maybe two hours listening to an album I had spent months on forced the order of songs to be changed. And no, that track never got the airplay the consultant said it would. I was contractually obligated to do another album with them, and friends were telling me to pull a fast one—deliberately make a really crappy record just so I could escape—but it's not the folk music way to do anything so diabolical, so I made as good of an album as I could, hoping for the best.

There's a long, unhappy tradition in the recording industry of singers fighting with their record companies, and even I, a lowly folksinger, was continuing that tradition. About six months after the release of the second album—when none of those promised "organized promotion" efforts had materialized—I began to wonder how close we were to reaching that 60,000 sales goal. I asked Harry about that clause and said that if my numbers weren't anywhere near there, I wanted *out*. Harry advised me not to alert the record company to this fact. He said, "Maybe they've forgotten about that clause, and if you want out, you don't want to give them an opportunity to hold you to the contract."

But that's not the folk music way, either. These people might not be very efficient, but I didn't think they were evil. I just didn't want to be in business with them anymore. So I placed a call to the man who *ran* the company (a different person from Mr. X and the owner who worked out my contract) and asked him how close my sales numbers were to the sales goal in my contract. This was his response:

"What sales goal?"

The man who ran the company was unaware of the clause. He said he'd look into it and get back to me. A couple of days later he called and said, "Oh, we're nowhere near those numbers, but don't worry, we're not going to drop you."

I wanted to scream with laughter. He obviously had no idea why I was asking. But I kept my composure, thanked him, and did a little happy dance after I hung up the phone.

The day before that magic date—nine months after the release of my second album—Harry helped me draft a letter telling them I was out the door. We included a copy of the contract with that clause highlighted. I brought the letter to FedEx myself so that it would arrive the next day, and I could put the whole mess behind me.

A week later I received a long, rambling, handwritten letter from the man who ran the company saying how disturbed and hurt he felt, and how disappointed he was that I had chosen to leave their "family of artists."

I was stunned. He considered me part of his "family of artists"? In the two and a half years I was with them, they had never seemed interested in my music, attended my concerts, or made me feel wanted or welcome—is this how he thinks a family behaves? And now he's disappointed that I'm leaving?

My success in extricating myself from that situation is one of the reasons why I consider Harry my guardian angel. I've been told how lucky I was to be able to get out of that contract when I did, at least three years earlier than an artist normally would.

Here's another story—not truly a horror story, but a story of stupidly crappy, mind-numbing music business disappointment.

When I signed a music publishing contract with Cherry Lane, that contract covered most of the songs I had written up to that point, plus the songs I'd write over the next three years. When that three-year period was coming to an end, in the fall of 1994, I had to decide whether or not to stay with them. In that three-year period, none of my songs had made it into films or TV shows; if any of them were recorded by another artist it was through my own efforts, not the publishing company's. So even though I don't like to focus on the financial end of things, I wasn't sure it made sense to continue signing over 50 percent of the publishing revenue on my future songs.

The one important reason, to me, for staying was that I really liked Peter Primont, Dan Rosenbaum, and Mike Connelly, the three people there I dealt with most often. But I had to wonder if I was making a business decision because of personal feelings.

The date to sign—or not—was a week away. I was torn. Cherry Lane had just become partners with Dreamworks, the film company, so maybe that would open some new doors. I was leaning toward staying. When they paid me the advance when I first signed with them, it made my songbook and the first Martha's Vineyard Songwriters' Retreat possible, and I cherished both.

I had all but made up my mind to stay—but hadn't yet signed the papers—when I got in late one night and got this message on my answering machine:

Man number 1: *Why did you do that? I can't stand her voice!*

Man number 2: *Me neither, or her songs.*

Man number 1: *Why is that red light still on?*

Man number 2: *Uh-oh.*

That was it. I didn't recognize either voice and had no idea what the conversation was about. I had a dozen other messages, so it barely registered at all.

The next day I got a call from someone at Cherry Lane—I'll call him Mr. Y—apologizing for the message left on my answering machine. Before I could ask him what he was talking about, he quickly explained that he was having a meeting in his office with one of the rock musicians who worked there, one who had been given the job of writing out lead sheets for some of my songs.

This was being done for Stuart Ross, a theater writer/director best known for his long-running off-Broadway jukebox musical *Forever Plaid*, who had had the idea of turning my songs into a theatrical musical. Since I can't read music, Cherry Lane had agreed to supply the lead sheets to the singers. It was all very last-minute (and to this day, the project hasn't come to fruition), so some of the rock musicians were temporarily pulled off other projects to write out my lead sheets.

The rock musician who was in Mr. Y's office hated my music, and as a little joke, Mr. Y called my phone number so that he could annoy the guy with my voice on my outgoing message. Unfortunately, he had forgotten that it was an answering machine, and it had recorded their comments.

When my conversation with Mr. Y was over, I played the message again. Now that I knew who had left the message, I realized that not only did the rock musician hate my voice, but Mr. Y hated my voice *and* my songs. What are the odds that I would find this out just as I was about to sign a new contract?

There was no way I was going to sign it now, but I didn't tell the bosses why. Mr. Y felt terrible about what he had done, but I couldn't rightly say that he was the only reason I was leaving—he was the just the final nudge out the door. Though my relationship with Cherry Lane changed, they will always be involved in songs from my early albums.

In 2002 I got a call from Cherry Lane to let me know that they had been contacted by ESPN. A new morning TV show was in development for ESPN2, and the name of the show was inspired by my song "Cold Pizza for Breakfast," so they wanted the song to be the musical theme for the program. It was going to be a daily show, aired opposite the *Today* show, sort of a *Today* show for sports nuts. A daily morning show, and my song would be the theme!

But there was one problem. ESPN didn't want to pay for the song; they wanted it for free. Cherry Lane didn't want to give it to them for free. I understood that. Cherry Lane asked me how I felt about them trying to negotiate the price with ESPN, and I said go ahead—whatever it takes.

For a few days I fantasized how this song might be played under highlight footage of the Jets winning the Super Bowl. I wondered if they'd ask me to their studios to sing it live—maybe I could meet Joe Namath again!

They called me back a few days later saying that ESPN didn't have it in the show's budget to pay for the song, so it looked like it was dead in the water. At this point the show was still in development—it hadn't aired—so I asked, what if we let ESPN have the song for free for the first three months of airing? At the end of each show, they could include the credit, " 'Cold Pizza for Breakfast' by Christine Lavin © Cherry Lane/Dreamworks." Wouldn't that be worth something? And if the show was a hit, they would have advertising income, so then we could see if they'd be willing to pay some kind of royalty. The song would be associated with the program by then, and there would be reason for them to want to keep it as part of the daily broadcast.

But Cherry Lane stated that, as policy, they don't give anything away. Period. I told them how much it would mean to me—it wouldn't cost them anything to let ESPN2 have the song for three months, and if it created interest in my catalog, they would make more money down the line. But that's not how they work.

Is it because I had left them? I will never know. The show *Cold Pizza* aired every weekday on ESPN2 for five years without the song that inspired the title. That's a real kick in the head.

The music industry is different now and will continue to evolve. Many artists, except for the superstars, who operate on a different plane, are much more hands-on than we were back in the last century. Technology is different (Facebook, Twitter, YouTube), and there's a whole new generation of kids who pride themselves on never having had to pay for albums and think of music as something that's free, floating on the Internet. But those of us who keep writing and performing know that live performances are where we make most of our living, and CD sales at these shows—not in stores—are the source of the bulk of our CD money. So we will deal with the occasional music-business nightmare—and persevere.

I'll close this chapter with a true story about a wonderful Broadway singer named D.C. Anderson, who has spent years touring with the national company of *Phantom of the Opera*. Although he is best known for his musical theater and cabaret work, he also has a soft spot in his heart for folk music, especially Cheryl Wheeler songs (of which he's recorded a bunch). D.C. recently asked me to contribute to a compilation album titled *In My Room* to raise money for the National Multiple Sclerosis Society, and I was happy to oblige, recording Bob Franke's song "For Real." I jump at any chance to get good folk music in front of the theater crowd.

A few years ago, when D.C. was out in Los Angeles with *Phantom*, he went to the big Tower Records store there asking if they would take his CDs on consignment—meaning there'd be no risk on Tower's part. But they said no. They didn't know him, didn't know his music, and didn't care that he was in *Phantom*.

D.C. was disappointed, but he came up with a novel idea. He went to the section of the store he thought his CDs should be in—where singers like Barbara Cook, Betty Buckley, and Michael Crawford (the original star of *Phantom*) had record displays—and he traced the cardboard card that separated the stacks of CDs. He went home and made his own "D.C. Anderson" display card, went back to Tower Records, and slipped the card in with a half dozen of his CDs when no one was looking. A couple of weeks later he checked back in the store and was delighted to see that there were only two of his CDs left in the stack; he slipped in a couple more.

He did this for a number of months whenever he was in or near Los Angeles. He didn't care that he wasn't getting paid for the CDs that Tower was selling; he was just happy that his music was getting out there.

I wish this story had a happy ending. It doesn't. One day when D.C. was replenishing his stack, he was spotted by a sales clerk, who called security. D.C. was arrested. The police eventually let him go, after much anguish and explanation. The cops were incredulous. "You mean, you were putting *your* CDs on *their* shelves; they were selling them, keeping *all* the money; *you* were secretly restocking their shelves, *giving* your CDs away at Tower, and *Tower tells us to arrest you?*" Tower took out his homemade display card and told him to never set foot in their store again.

Maybe there is a happy ending after all: Tower went bankrupt, but D.C. Anderson is still out there singing.

15

AN ANGEL
SENT BY GOD

like to help people—it's in my nature; I can't avoid it—but I have learned that sometimes help can backfire. Back in 1977, when I had only been in New York for a year, the city was being terrorized by a murderous madman who called himself the Son of Sam. He targeted young couples parked in cars, and all of the young women he shot and killed had long dark hair. Now, that may have just been a coincidence, but it was noticed by the media, and it set off a wave of hysteria and fear. Women with long hair were getting their hair cut short. When all this was happening, I came up with an idea that I thought would crack the case.

I called the police, the 20th Precinct on West Eighty-third Street, and introduced myself. I said that I lived in the neighborhood and thought I had solved the Son of Sam case.

"Okay, go on," said the officer who had taken my call.

"Another way of saying 'Son of Sam' is to say 'Sam's Son.' Remember that Bible story about Samson and Delilah? His strength was in his long hair, and when his hair was cut, he lost all his power?"

"Uh-huh," the cop said.

"Well," I continued, excitedly, "put two and two together. The killer could possibly be a hairdresser—a very religious hairdresser—who recently lost his job and is now scaring young women with long hair into getting their hair cut off."

"You don't say," the cop said.

"Yes! So all you have to do is check with every hair salon in New York to see if any of them recently fired a hairdresser who maybe read the Bible between haircuts."

"A hairdresser who reads the Bible between haircuts?"

"Yes! And then check to see if someone applied for a job, and on their résumé it showed that up until recently he was working at a salon in New York, but he quit or was fired, and maybe—just maybe—he had a Bible with him when he was interviewing for the new job."

"A hairdresser carrying a Bible?" the cop said.

"Yes!" I told him. "Think about it—Son of Sam, Sam's Son, long hair—it all fits together!"

"You don't say," the cop said.

I started to not like his tone of voice. "Are you writing this down?" I asked him.

"Oh, yes," he said, and hung up.

Boy, was I surprised when the Son of Sam turned out to be a postal worker named David Berkowitz and that Sam turned out to be his neighbor's dog. That didn't make any sense.

In post-9/11 New York, we are always reminded to be on the lookout for any suspicious activity—the phrase the city uses is, "If you see something, say something." One evening I was walking with my friend Martha on the Upper West Side. At the intersection of West End Avenue and Seventy-fifth Street was a rental Ryder truck blocking traffic from continuing down the street to Riverside Drive, and near Riverside Drive we could see men working belowground through a manhole.

There was another truck parked where they were working, and it had three initials on it—but it wasn't an acronym I recognized (like EPA or

DPW). It was getting dark, and they were working with no lights. As we walked by all of this, I asked Martha if she thought this was the kind of thing we are supposed to say something about, and she immediately said yes. When I got home, I called the 20th Precinct and started to explain about the rental truck, and the guys working without lights in a manhole, when the cop said, "Wait a minute—this sounds familiar."

He put the phone down but didn't put me on hold, so I could hear everything he said. He shouted out, "Anybody know anything about a rental truck blocking traffic on Seventy-fifth and West End?"

I heard a different voice shout back, "Yeah, it's the city water department—one of their trucks broke down on the BQE, so they had to get a rental to finish up the rest of the day. They stopped by here to show us the truck on their way down to Seventy-fifth Street because they were afraid some wacko in the neighborhood was going to think they were terrorists."

"Some wacko." That would be me. I saw something, I said something, and now I felt like an idiot. I was just trying to help.

Late one Friday night in Ann Arbor, Michigan, I was hurriedly packing up my gear after a show at the well-known club the Ark. A young woman quietly approached me as I curled up quarter-inch patch cords and stowed them in my guitar case.

"I can see you're in a hurry," she said, "but there's been something I've wanted to ask you for a long time, so I hope you don't mind. . . ." Her voice trailed off. "Are you an ex-nun?"

What? I couldn't believe my ears. An ex-nun? Yeah, I thought to myself, that's the look I've been going for. What on earth could I have done to give that impression?

"Are you joking?" I asked.

"No," she said, "and I don't mean to offend you or anything, but some of my friends thought maybe you were, and I promised I'd ask you."

I laughed. "No, though I did attend Catholic elementary school and was taught by nuns, I've never been one myself."

"Thanks," she said. "Bye!"

And with that, she was gone. But her question lingered, taunting me.

I thought about this all during the weekend, and when I returned to New York City the following Monday, I got my hair cut at an expensive new salon in my neighborhood. I had been paying forty dollars for a haircut at a modest place, but this haircut and highlighting set me back three hundred. It was the first step in ridding myself of the ex-nun aura.

That day I also noticed that there were an unusual number of hang-ups and messages from unfamiliar people on my voice mail. A man named Joe left two messages to call him, but he didn't give his last name, so I didn't call him back. The next day there were more hang-ups on my voice mail, and a few more messages from voices I didn't recognize. It was a bit of a bother, but I didn't dwell on it. I had bigger things to focus on. Even with a new, improved haircut, I couldn't shake that ex-nun comment.

But then I thought, maybe it's a compliment. An ex-nun is probably still a very spiritual person, concerned about the world and her fellow man. And wouldn't an ex-nun have a lot of passion stored up, just looking to be released? She may be a mature woman, but a mature woman with the fluttering heart of a nymphet aching to experience worldly pleasures.

Who am I kidding? I went shopping.

When I returned, there were another half dozen hang-ups on my voice mail. Who were they trying to reach? Then the phone rang. I picked it up, and sure enough, it was a wrong number.

"Please, do me a favor," I said to the caller. "Tell me what number you dialed."

He told me it was area code 718, then the next seven digits were exactly the same as mine. Mystery solved.

"My area code is 212," I told him.

"But I dialed 718," he replied.

"Look," I said, "Dial again, and if you get him, tell your friend at 718 that I've been getting a lot of calls for him. Maybe there's something wrong with the phone lines."

A minute later, the phone rang again.

"Hi, this is Mickey," the man said. "I understand you have been getting calls for me?"

I told him that I travel a lot and had noticed lately that there had been a few dozen hang-ups on my voice mail, plus messages left that I did not return because I knew they weren't for me.

"Oh no!" he cried, "This is awful! I'm trying to run a business here!" he said.

"What kind of a business?" I asked.

When I heard him say Angel Wings Car Service, I felt bad. I've had an account with a car service, and I know how important the phone is to that kind of business. I've become friends with some of the drivers, and I imagined all the fares these Angel Wings drivers were missing because people were calling me instead of them. How many of their customers were missing airline flights? Important meetings? Birthday parties?

"I've got an idea," I said. "How about this—I will leave an outgoing message on my voice mail telling callers that if they are looking for you to dial again and make sure they dial 718. Will that help?"

"That'd be great," he said, "but I'm going to call the phone company and see if there's something they can do."

An hour later, Mickey called back on a conference call with a representative from the phone company. She said she would do some checking to see if somehow the area code prefix wasn't working properly.

For the next three days, I continued to get calls for Angel Wings. When I was home, I answered and told them to redial carefully, and when I was out, I left an outgoing message with those instructions, too. When I answered, I was as professional as could be, and I even started to recognize one voice— a shy young man.

On Friday of that week I was busy packing up for the next three scheduled shows. As part of my anti-ex-nun campaign, I planned not to wear the loose black linen two-piece that had become my favorite, instead opting for a long, copper-colored, cut-on-the-bias silk dress. A half hour before I planned to leave, the phone rang.

"Hi, Christine. It's me, Mickey," he said. "Any calls today?"

I told him there had been three so far, but I would put the standard rerouting message on my voice mail before I left.

"Thanks so much," he said, "you've really been a good sport about this—but we've decided to change our number completely. This problem is not going to stop, and you can't keep getting our calls forever. Could you put this new number on your voice mail?" He gave me a number that was nothing at all like mine.

"Sure," I said.

"You still may get calls for another week or so," he said, "because there are still those who will have the old business card with the old number. But it will stop. And thanks again for helping our customers find us."

"I was glad to help," I said, explaining how I use a car service myself and how I know what a difficult business it can be when you have phone trouble.

Long pause.

"We're not a *car* service," he said, "we're an *escort* service."

Another long pause.

"A what?" I whispered.

"An escort service. I told you that the first time we spoke."

I quickly thought back to that first conversation. I thought I heard him say Angel Wings Car Service, but—what is that called, selective hearing?—I guess that's not what he said at all.

He laughed. "I was kind of wondering why you were so accommodating and understanding. Your outgoing message was so sweet, in fact, that a few of my customers asked who you were and if you were one of my, uh, employees."

Another long pause.

"Have you ever thought of supplementing your income with this kind of work?"

I was stunned. My mind raced. What had I been doing all week? Why, I had been a pimp. A volunteer pimp!

"No, Mickey, I'm not the type," I said. I wanted to tell him that I had recently been mistaken for an ex-nun, but I decided against it.

"Does this mean you won't put our new number on your voice mail?" he asked softly.

"Yes, Mickey, I will. But this is the last time."

For the next three days, anybody who called my number asking for Angel Wings Escort Service heard me cheerily direct them to the new number.

I thought the story ended there, but it didn't. A week later I was home when my phone rang, and it was that young man with the shy voice asking for Mickey.

Without even thinking about what I was doing, I said to him in a soft, whispery voice, "You are a very sweet and kind man. You will never find love with any of these women. You must stop spending your money this way. They will take all of it until you end up old, broke, and very alone. There is a woman out there for you, but she is not here. You must never dial this number again."

"Who is this?" he asked, his voice quivering.

"I am an angel sent by God to put you back on the path of righteousness. God has great plans for you, and they don't include calling places like this. Trust me, there is a girl out there waiting for you. Now hang up the phone. Go find her."

Would an ex-nun have done that?

Yeah, probably.

16

CRYSTAL
THE PSYCHIC FOLKSINGER

O n June 29, 1981, I recorded my debut album, *Absolutely Live*, for Lifesong Records. We recorded it live, in front of an audience of a hundred or so, in CBS Studio B in New York.

The producer was Terry Cashman, who later went on to write the classic baseball song "Willie, Mickey & the Duke," about Willie Mays, Mickey Mantle, and Duke Snyder. That song became so popular with baseball fans that he eventually wrote a special version for every major league baseball team in the country, tailoring the lyrics to include each team's own stars. I mention this because by the time I was meeting with Terry and other producers about possibly recording, I had stopped taking guitar lessons with Dave Van Ronk. Dave and I were still friends, of course, but he could see that although I could learn the pieces he taught me, they were not sticking with me.

Dave had a very recognizable sound. To this day, when one of his songs comes on the radio, you can tell within a few seconds that it's him playing the guitar. Nobody else sounds like that, and in spite of three years of lessons, I never sounded remotely like him, not even when I painstakingly learned to play, note for note, his arrangement of "The Maple Leaf Rag."

After one of my lessons, Dave simply said, "I think I have taken you as far as I can. Now it's up to you." So I worked on my guitar playing on my own, and when I first auditioned for Terry Cashman, he suggested I find another teacher and learn more.

I signed up for a guitar class at the New School in Manhattan, one taught by a buddy of Dave's named Barry Kornfeld. When I went back and auditioned for Terry again, he saw that my guitar playing had improved and asked who was teaching me. When I said Barry Kornfeld, Terry called up Barry and asked to take lessons with him as well. It was after these lessons that Terry wrote "Willie, Mickey & the Duke," using a chord progression he had learned from Barry. So even though I had nothing to do with the writing of Terry's song, I felt that I played a tiny part in the process of its creation.

It was a few months earlier in 1981 that I saw the trio Hilly, Lili & Lulu on Tom Snyder's *Tomorrow* show, and I flipped over their sound. They were very retro looking and wore vintage dresses from the forties, sang close three-part harmony, and were very funny. I was dying to work with them. After tracking them down and going to their cabaret shows regularly, I got the idea of having them sing backup on my recording of a song I had written soon after Prince Charles announced his engagement to Diana Spencer, called "Prince Charles." When *Absolutely Live*, which included the song, was reissued as a CD on the Winthrop label in the year 2000, I asked that that song be left off.

CBS Studio B, where this live album was recorded, had quite a history. One of the technicians told me that it was where Simon & Garfunkel had recorded "The Boxer." He said that the session went on for hours because they couldn't get the exact drum sound they wanted, so they kept moving the drums around the very large room, positioning the mikes in different ways—this went on through the night.

Eventually they placed the drums out in the hallway, near the elevators, and that's how they got the sound they wanted. There were no speakers in the hallway, just the drummer seated at his drum kit. By now it was 3:00 a.m., and they were working on the part of the song near the end where they sing, "Li la-li [drum crash] Li la-li-li-li la-li—Li la-li [drum crash] . . . ," and the crashing drums echoed down through the elevator shaft. This scared the bejesus out of the security guard at the front desk, who thought it was gunshots and called the police, who suddenly burst upon the scene with guns drawn, in turn scaring the bejesus out of the drummer.

I don't know if it's a true story, but I can't imagine a sound technician making it up.

Where was I? Oh yes, the story about the song "Prince Charles." Barry Kornfeld played second guitar and Scott Spray played bass for the live session. One of the people in the audience was a producer from the *Today* show named Ally Acker. She was a friend of Hilly's (Hillary Rollins's), and after she saw us perform "Prince Charles," she decided it would be a fun song to do on the *Today* show. Here's the last chorus:

Oh Charles My Charles

Any girl looks good when she's nineteen

But think about her thirty years from now

When she's an old and ugly queen

Oooh—take a look at your mother, boy

And you'll know what I mean

So on July 13, 1981, I would be on TV for the very first time, with Hilly, Lili & Lulu behind me, singing a song warning Prince Charles that his marriage to Princess Diana was not a good idea. I suppose I could bill myself "Crystal the Psychic Folksinger."

At the ridiculous hour of 4:00 a.m., a limousine picked me up. I have long been a night owl, and I was so nervous that night that I didn't sleep at all. But I figured I could make it through a single song and a ninety-second interview.

Hilly, Lili & Lulu wore prom dresses and fake tiaras, and I wore a vintage black chiffon dress with sequins. We did a quick run-through around 6:00, and just after I finished singing the song a voice came over the sound system: "Miss Lavin, could you sing that last line again?"

"Take a look at your mother, boy, and you'll know what I mean," I sang.

"Oh no," said the voice, "You can't sing that. Rewrite the ending."

Wha?? Rewrite the ending? At six o'clock in the morning? I thought for a moment, and then sang this:

"Take a look in any royal history book, and you'll know what I mean."

"Hmm . . . that's good. Sing that," said the voice.

So now I would insult every queen who ever reigned, not just Queen Elizabeth.

We sang the song, and all went well. Afterward, Jane Pauley walked over for the interview. She thanked me for singing, and I said, "And I thank Hilly, Lili & Lulu, three of New York's most gorgeous women, who are also upset about Charles marrying someone else." Jane Pauley laughed and called them my "ladies in waiting and waiting and waiting." Then Jane said something like, "Why do you think you should have had a chance to become part of the royal family?"

I said, "I can't expect you to understand—you're the queen of the *Today* show. You already *are* royalty."

Then she said, "I guess I settled. Well, let's go see how Marian Burros [a food writer for the *New York Times*] is doing with those cookies."

And I said, "Oh, good! I haven't had breakfast. I'm starved!"

And that was it. The screen switched to Marian Burros out on the plaza, where her oven malfunctioned and her cookies were half-baked. Five minutes later, the show was over. I asked Jane Pauley what had happened to the rest of the interview, and she explained that it was live television and the show had been running long. I said good-bye to Hilly, Lili & Lulu, and a limo took me home, where I unplugged my phone, went to bed, and slept until mid-afternoon.

When I woke up and plugged my phone back in, the record company called. Everyone watched the show and thought I did a good job, but they couldn't understand why I never mentioned that the album was coming out.

I explained that the interview section was cut by two-thirds, but I wasn't told in advance. Phil Kurnit, the owner of the company, said, "You're on national television. You *don't* tell the millions of people watching that your debut album is about to be released, and instead you tell them you haven't had breakfast?!"

There you go. Live and learn.

When the album came out, the song got a lot of airplay around this country, though I was told it was banned in England. Too bad. Maybe it would have saved us all years of heartache.

Many years later, when Diana was single again and John F. Kennedy Jr. was dubbed the Sexiest Man Alive by *People* magazine, I fantasized about the two of them getting together and wrote "John John & Princess Diana's Wedding Song" for them:

> Women have pursued him because of his name
>
> Men have pursued her hungry for her fame
>
> Tall, good looking, but lonely despite all her wealth
>
> Longing to be loved by a mirror image of herself
>
> America's crown prince has finally found his princess bride
>
> All his former girlfriends have been pushed aside
>
> And all her former in-laws can't believe what she has done
>
> Another kick in the teeth of Britain's royal son
>
> So let's a drink a toast to the couple of the hour
>
> Let's hope this marriage, unlike most, has some staying power
>
> He doesn't need her spotlight, she doesn't need his name
>
> But if this doesn't work out they can still have us to blame

Needless to say, I never sing that one anymore, and it never gets requested since I never recorded it. But at shows people still ask me to sing "Prince Charles," and of course I don't.

However, another song from that first album, "Amoeba Hop"—about the adventures of one-celled creatures in a puddle of water—is still in my repertoire. The song was initially inspired by my ninth-grade biology class at Drum Hill Junior High School. A classmate, Betty Ann Murphy, brought in a bucket of swamp water one day, and to me it looked to me like a teeny tiny swingin' dance party under the microscope.

In 1998 a children's book illustrator named Betsy Franco Feeney approached me after a show and asked if she could turn the song into a kids' science/music book. Of course I said yes. This was seventeen years after the song was recorded. Who knew good things could take this long to happen?

But it took even longer than that. Betsy met with many children's book publishers, but the project was turned down again and again. She got comments like, "We don't know what this book is, or on which shelf in the bookstores it would be displayed. We can't tell if it's a children's book, a music book, or a science book."

It was all those things, and eventually Betsy and her husband, Jim, started their own imprint, Puddle Jump Press. Just as she was about to start the final draft, I got an e-mail from an organization called the Society of Protozoologists. Yes, an organization dedicated to the study of one-celled creatures! They wanted permission to post the lyrics to the song "Amoeba Hop" on their Web site. I said they could post my lyrics if they would do me a favor—look over the drawings for the proposed *Amoeba Hop* book. Not only did they agree, they put their logo on the book (though the organization has changed its name to Society of Protistologists, now separated into two groups—one that studies one-celled animals, the other one-celled plants).

The book *Amoeba Hop* wasn't published until 2003—thirty-seven years after Betty Ann brought that swamp water to class. I dedicated it to her and to Mr. Kristoph, our biology teacher.

Guess who showed up at one of my concerts in 2006? Betty Ann Murphy. She had no idea that I had dedicated the book to her, and I had no idea she was going to be there that night—but it was so much fun to bring her onstage, present her with a copy of the book, and finally get to thank her for carrying that bucket of swamp water to class way back when.

Later that year, Betsy and I were asked to perform at the annual convention for the Society of Protozoologists, and then in October 2007 Betsy and I were invited to perform "Amoeba Hop" in New York City as part of a concert called Operation Respect, in honor of teachers. The event was organized by Peter Yarrow of Peter Paul & Mary. I sang the song, Betsy turned the pages of a giant six-foot version of the book, and the book was held by Peter Yarrow and Noel Paul Stookey. I was thrilled!

Betsy now gives presentations at New York metropolitan area schools with a bucket of swamp water, a microscope, a slide show, and copies of *Amoeba Hop*. The American Association for the Advancement of Science has given *Amoeba Hop* its Best Book Award, which would never have happened without Betsy's talent, hard work, and perseverance, for which I am so very grateful.

The very first song on that first album was a song I wrote called "Three Months to Live." At the time, it was my favorite song to start shows with when I was the opening act. I knew everyone in the audience was there to see the headliner, not me.

> Record companies love it
>
> When their recording artists die
>
> They get to re-release all the albums
>
> That never sold back in July
>
> Well I don't have any records
>
> But I know the soundman's making a tape
>
> And in three months he'll be bootlegging copies
>
> For $7.98

When Michael Jackson died in 2009, twenty-eight years after I recorded that song, his album sales zoomed back to number one.

Crystal the Psychic Folksinger strikes again.

17

SPEAKEASY/*FAST FOLK*

Years from now, if someone writes a book about the American contemporary folk music scene of the late twentieth century, they will no doubt write at length about singer/songwriter Jack Hardy.

Since the late 1970s Jack has hosted a songwriters' dinner almost every Monday night in Greenwich Village (except when he's traveling). You can attend if (1) you are a songwriter, (2) you put two dollars in the pot (to cover pasta and wine), *and* (3) you have a new song to sing.

You'd be amazed at how many songs have been created because of those simple rules. (I remember frantically working to finish my song "Ballad of a Ballgame" so that I could go to one of his dinners.)

In February 1982 Jack (together with some other musicians) was part of a cooperative nightclub called the Speakeasy on MacDougal Street in Greenwich Village and started a monthly music publication that came with an album of songs. He called it *The Fast Folk Musical Magazine*.

I was impressed when I saw the first issue, because it was completely created by songwriters. It was packaged in a plain white cardboard album cover, and inside was a homemade magazine that contained the song lyrics and songwriter bios. The whole thing cost two dollars. Jack wanted to keep the price as low as possible so that anyone could afford it, but he had to raise the price to four dollars after the first few months. No one thought a two-dollar vinyl album could have anything worthwhile on it. (Boy, were they wrong. That first issue contained, among others, Dave Van Ronk, Erik Frandsen, and the debut recording by singer/songwriter Suzanne Vega.) Van Ronk introduced to me to Jack, and soon I was involved in both *Fast Folk* and the Speakeasy.

The owner of the Speakeasy was Josef, a short, grouchy, balding man with a thick Slavic accent. To get to the club you'd walk through a restaurant that served hummus and lamb dishes. As Julie Gold joked, "We thought we'd get discovered in a nightclub that had spinning meat in the window." The club, down a few stairs below street level, was a small, cramped room with mirror-lined walls and jammed with a chairs and tables. Lining the back of the tiny stage was Josef's pride and joy—a set of tanks filled with colorful, exotic fish.

Once, Andy Breckman—who would later create the TV show *Monk*—stopped in the middle of a song and slammed down a five-dollar bill.

"Five bucks says one of those fish won't live ten minutes outside of the tank!" he proclaimed.

He encouraged the crowd to up the ante—it went as high as twenty-five dollars—until Josef came screaming down the stairs. I don't think Andy was really going to torture a fish, but it was fun to watch Josef lose his temper.

Andy was just one of the musicians who passed through the Speakeasy during the 1980s. Most of the musicians were guitarists, including John Gorka, who used to joke that thanks to the mirrored walls, a performer could flirt with five different people at the same time. Piano players weren't as lucky—they had their backs to the audience, and the small upright was never quite in tune. One night Julie Gold gently asked Josef if he could do something about the piano.

"What are you talking about?" he screamed at her. "I just had it painted!"

Despite that, it was a wonderfully percolating scene, and it was where I saw many great musicians for the first time: Shawn Colvin, Nanci Griffith, David Roth and Josh Joffen (who were a duo at the time), the late Tom Intondi, Cliff Eberhardt, Lucy Kaplansky, David Mallett, Bill Morrissey, Greg

Brown, Uncle Bonsai (Andrew Ratshin, Arni Adler, and Ashley O'Keeffe), Lillie Palmer, Aztec Two-Step (Rex Fowler and Neal Shulman), The Smith Sisters, Rod MacDonald, Nikki Matheson, Peter Spencer, David Massengill, Richard Meyer, and Mark Dann—to name just a few.

At the Speakeasy we did everything except wait on tables—we booked, promoted, and emceed the shows; sold tickets at the door; seated the audience; ran the sound; and sold albums. There were concerts every night, and Monday was open mike. Many of the people who volunteered at the Speakeasy also helped out with *Fast Folk*.

For a couple years it was my job to bring the master tapes to Tom Coyne at the Frankford Wayne Mastering Labs. Tom was (and is) one of the most respected album-mastering artists in the business. I'm sure *Fast Folk* was paying him a fraction of what his standard fee was even back then, but he is one of those fantastic mastering engineers (like Phil Klum) who loves good music. Tom, God bless him, liked what we were up to—a bunch of renegade folk musicians creating our own scene—and took as much care mastering us every month as he did his major-label clients.

As subscriptions to the magazine grew, Jack threw "album-mailing parties" at his tiny walk-up apartment, where he also hosted the weekly songwriters dinners. One of the people who came to the mailing parties was a strange woman who shaved half her head; the other half was in dreadlocks. She told us she lived for free in a building on the Lower East Side with other squatters. She was very low-key and sweet and was eager to help, but since she never came to the Speakeasy, we assumed she wasn't a musician. Her name? Michelle Shocked.

Even with the magazine priced at four dollars, as time went on it became clear that the price needed to go up again. Local graphic artists wanted to design covers for the albums, and printing costs went up, so the subscription charge was raised. Then raised again. I think at its height it was ten dollars an issue—still a bargain when you consider what you got. A hundred years from now, someone is going to do very well with the old issues on *Antiques Roadshow*.

After the first year in New York, *Fast Folk* went on the road. I traveled to Boston with Jay Rosen, who worked during the day at J&R Music (and still does) but tirelessly engineered many of the *Fast Folk* issues in his spare time. The Boston area has always been very supportive of folk music. They've always had great radio—WUMB at UMass plays folk music every day, and they started playing the *Fast Folk* records as soon as they received them. Because of this, Suzanne Vega and Shawn Colvin became stars in the Boston area even before they did in their hometown New York area.

When Jay was recording the Boston artists, it was my job to collect their song lyrics, bios, and any publishing information on the songs. One of the songwriters on that first session was Tracy Chapman, who had never recorded before, but something went wrong with her recording: there was a loud hiss on her track from start to finish. It was extremely annoying and couldn't be eliminated, even by Tom Coyne. Jack Hardy didn't care. All he cared about was documenting songs, preserving them as they were being written. For that purpose, her recording was fine, he said. But I felt differently. I told him that no radio station would be able to play it with that hiss on it, and he scoffed.

"We aren't making these records for radio airplay," he said. "It's not what we're about."

Jack was always a purist, but I am more pragmatic, so I fought him. We went back and forth, and finally he said that the only way he would take that song off would be if I personally took responsibility: I would have to write to Tracy myself and explain. So that's what I did. I tried to put a positive spin on it—I told her I thought she was too good to have a bad recording be her debut. I hope she realizes that I was trying to do the right thing by her.

That recording was never used. It ended up on the cutting room floor, lost to history, I suppose.

I clashed with Jack over other creative differences—there are no piano songs in the early *Fast Folk* recordings because Jack didn't consider it a folk instrument—but I was such a fan of Julie Gold, who only plays piano, and Raun MacKinnon, who is a remarkable pianist (though she also plays guitar), that I finally wore him down.

Many of the studio recordings for *Fast Folk* were done in Mark Dann's attic studio—he lived on the fourth floor of his parents' home in Brooklyn, a big rambling Victorian house. But his parents were *not* fans of what we were doing, and so Mark didn't want them to know; we weren't even allowed to ring the *doorbell*. When we got off the subway, we would call from a pay phone, and Mark would run down to the front door just as we were walking up. If his parents were home and happened to see us, we were not to look at them—just keep moving.

I produced a few issues of *Fast Folk*—one of them was all humorous songs, and one of them was all women songwriters. Julie Gold and Raun MacKinnon were on the latter one—but the piano at Mark's parents' house was on the third floor. We had to wait for Mark's parents to go out, and one night after he gave us the all-clear, we raced there as fast as we could. Mark lowered microphones from a fourth-floor window down to the third floor, where I positioned them. Julie and Raun each had just one take to get it right. Julie sang her whimsical song "The Bus," and Raun sang David Buskin's classic "All in All." As soon as we were done, Mark pulled the microphones up through the window again, and we scrammed before Mark's parents returned. It seems almost comical now that Grammy winner Julie Gold had to record her early songs in such a clandestine manner.

Shawn Colvin is also on that issue, doing her song "Knowing What I Know Now." She went to Mark's to record it on a cold, rainy Sunday afternoon. She called Mark when she got off the subway, but he wasn't home yet, so she called me, asking what to do. She'd already waited fifteen minutes, huddling in a phone booth to stay dry. I begged her to give Mark another half hour (and to keep calling) before giving up. Eventually Mark did get home—he'd been stuck in traffic—and had her come over and make the recording. It's hard to imagine such a wonderful artist having to go to such lengths to record her songs.

But that's how we did it, and we all gained invaluable experience along the way. We also learned how much more power we had when we joined forces and created our own "scene." As more of us made our own albums and got radio airplay, we started traveling way beyond Greenwich Village. It's ironic that the *Fast Folk Musical Magazine* first created the scene and then helped dismantle it as the successful songwriters became solo artists. Regardless, I will be eternally grateful to Jack Hardy for starting it.

Everyone in New York wanted to play the Bottom Line on West Fourth and Mercer. For thirty years it was *the* club in New York for live music of all types, not just folk, but rock and jazz and even comedy. It was owned by Allan Pepper and Stanley Snadowsky, and after about two years of success with the *Fast Folk* recordings and all the Speakeasy shows, we approached them about doing a big *Fast Folk* show at their club.

I had met with Allan a year or so earlier, proposing the idea of doing a four-artist show at his club. At the time, none of us could fill the 350-seat club on our own, but together we knew that we could. That first meeting didn't go the way I had hoped, however. Allan pointed to one of the names and asked what I thought of that particular performer's music. I told him it wasn't anything I really liked, but I knew that the artist had a following and could probably fill a hundred seats.

"I'm glad you are honest with me concerning your opinion," he said, "but learn a lesson from this: *never promote something you have to make excuses for*. I don't like this person's music, either, and the philosophy of this club is that we only promote shows we believe in.

"When I saw that name on your list, I questioned your ears," he said. "I'm saying no to this idea, but try me again when you have a better handle on what you're doing."

I have repeated his advice to countless musicians: Never promote something you have to make excuses for.

And that goes for recordings. Instead of saying "It's not really finished yet" or "The guitar is too loud on this" or "My vocal is a bit ragged" or the like, wait until your recording is truly finished so that you can proudly hand it to someone, knowing it's the best it can be.

Later, Allan agreed to meet with Jack Hardy and me to discuss a *Fast Folk* show. I felt more confident with this idea—there were so many artists who had appeared on *Fast Folk* by then that I knew there were more than enough to put on a good, solid show. The highlights of that first Bottom Line Fast Folk Show were preserved as the April 1984 issue—I'm on that disk, along with Jack, Suzanne Vega, Frank Christian, Rod MacDonald, Erik

Frandsen, and others, with the disk closing with all of us backing up David Massengill on his groundbreaking song, "The Great American Dream."

That song became a sort of a local anthem for its time, but when David made his very first solo album, that song—arguably the best thing he has ever written—was not included. He had a manager who thought the song was so good and so powerful that they should hold it back, putting it on his second album once he was fully established. That first album didn't do what they had hoped it would, though I am convinced it would have had that song been included.

That's another lesson learned. It's never a good idea to save your A-plus material for the *next* album or your *possible* encore. When many musicians initially start to record, they have a first-rate collection of songs (because let's face it—you have your whole life to build up to your first album). There's this fear that if you put all the best songs on the first disk, you won't have great stuff for the next album. But don't think like that. You will keep writing, and you'll have great new songs for albums down the line. Always go with your best work right out of the gate.

One of the many important things about being involved in the Speakeasy cooperative and the *Fast Folk Musical Magazine* was being surrounded by so many other songwriters who were serious about what they were doing. There was a sense of competitiveness—that's bound to happen—but consciously or not, we were helping each other write better songs. (One of Dave Van Ronk's mantras was, "When music of quality sells, it's good for all of us. Never root against your competitor if what they are doing is good work, because ultimately you will benefit from it.") And we were learning about the music business.

When it was my job to choose and produce the music for a particular issue, I wanted every song to be great. I wanted each album to be a collection that could be played as a whole from start to finish, so "theme" collections struck me as a good idea. And I wanted the songs to be written *only* by songwriters who were pursuing careers, not dabbling. Jack Hardy didn't care who wrote the songs as long as they were good; he had a more magnanimous view of songwriting than I did. Stylistically, I was also drawn to lots of music that didn't fall strictly into the folk category.

It was just a matter of time before I would break away from the organization. It was Jack's project and vision, and it wasn't my job to be a thorn in his side.

All this time I had been working temp during the day, though in 1982, faced with a dwindling bank account, I took a deep breath and took a full-time job at Bellevue Hospital. I was hired as administrative secretary for the Bellevue Association, an organization of volunteers dedicated to helping the hospital chaired by New York Senator Jacob Javits. I had heard stories about Javits from my grandfather, Judge Thomas Crawford, so at our first meeting I introduced myself to Senator Javits as the judge's granddaughter. He smiled, shook my hand, and said, "Oh, I knew him long before he was a judge!"

Senator Javits had become involved with Bellevue Hospital after being diagnosed with amyotrophic lateral sclerosis (ALS), also known as Lou Gehrig's disease. Javits came there for physical therapy three times a week. He was a cantankerous man, and as the disease progressed, life got more difficult for him, though he did live at least a year longer than doctors predicted. He would dictate letters to me and I would dial the phone for him since his motor skills were deteriorating; at this stage he also had a full-time nurse with him since he was in a wheelchair equipped with an oxygen tank. His breathing was quite labored, and everyone at the hospital marveled at how determined he was to stay active.

As Javits's health declined, he came to the office less and less frequently. Sometimes I would bring work papers to him at his apartment on East Fifty-seventh Street, but often I had many hours in the office with nothing to do. I started bringing my guitar to work, and I'd close the door and practice for hours. The job was easy, I was well paid, and I had health insurance and a four-week paid vacation . . . but I was miserable. Two years after starting, I gave my supervisor two months' notice that I was leaving. I felt bad bailing out on Senator Javits, but I was really just a very replaceable secretary. I had never had a job with paid vacation or health benefits before, but I knew if I didn't make an honest effort to make a living as a musician now, it would never happen.

After quitting the Bellevue job in the summer of 1984, I produced my first solo studio album, *Future Fossils*, recording the whole thing in Mark

Dann's attic in Brooklyn. If you listen closely with headphones, you can hear the occasional car noise and bird chirp in the background, because the room wasn't soundproofed. I spent so much time preparing that when it came time to do the actual recording, I had the sequencing set so I could record the songs in the order they'd appear on the album. This way I wouldn't have to pay additional hourly time to edit it all together.

Mark worked fast and was very inexpensive. It wasn't until years later when I worked in other studios—some that were slow and expensive—that I realized what a bargain it was working with him. In folk music we are so used to squeezing as much as we can out of a dollar that we assume that when we can spend more money, we'll make much more expensive-sounding albums. But it doesn't always work that way. A lot of musicians return to their early producers after they've blown thousands with the bigger names in the business.

I had *Future Fossils* mastered by Tom Coyne, had the album cover designed by my cousin Maureen Bennett O'Connor, and had two thousand copies of the album pressed by the same company that *Fast Folk* used in Long Island City.

I held my record release party at the Speakeasy in November 1984, and a month later I visited my family in Geneva, in upstate New York.

Two days before Christmas, I started getting odd phone calls, which at first I thought were a joke. People who had bought the album before I left town (we're talking a vinyl album here) had put it on their turntable to play, but they couldn't get it off. It was stuck! They couldn't play the other side.

After the fifth call came in, I put one on my parents' turntable. Sure enough, I couldn't get it off. It was wedged down so tight that it snapped in two when I attempted to pry it off. I was frantic. I called the pressing plant, where another thousand were stored. On Christmas Eve they called me back and estimated that approximately eight hundred out of the initial two thousand had holes that were slightly too small. They were big enough to get wedged *on* to the turntable, but breaking the vinyl disk was the only way to get them *off*.

I was apoplectic. Even though the pressing plant promised to redo them, I had to deal with all the defective albums that were already sold—including about four hundred I had sold off the stage at concerts. When I told Tom Coyne about it, he laughed and told me about a major label that pressed 100,000 albums with holes that were way off center. That made me feel a little better. But it was Christmas, I wasn't in New York City, and there was nothing I could do. My father saw how perturbed I was, and he sat me down. At that point, the album had received good reviews, and he said, "What would you rather have, two thousand records with perfectly sized holes and bad music, or two thousand records with the wrong-size hole and good music?"

He was right. The problem could be fixed. I immediately calmed down. But I learned an important lesson about the nuts-and-bolts side of manufacturing.

All those early lessons learned with *Fast Folk* and my own early albums have come in very handy now that many musicians are again self-producing and self-manufacturing their own CDs. The music business is in a huge state of flux, and we now know the more business we take care of ourselves, the better off we will be.

Here's another interesting lesson I learned with *Future Fossils*.

Rounder Records was *the* folk music label of the 1980s, so I sent them a cassette copy of the album. No response. I sent them a vinyl test pressing. No response. I sent them a commercial copy. No response.

So I called them and asked if they had listened to it. No. If they would listen, I said, I would call back in a week to see if they would like to distribute it to stores. They said okay to that. A week later I called, and they said, no, not interested.

Meanwhile, I had gotten a list of all the radio stations in New England that played folk music, and I sent my album to them. The radio stations started to play it. Rounder Records had reps who would visit local record stores every week or so, and some of these record stores asked the reps if they knew anything about an album called *Future Fossils* some customers had heard on the radio. Of course, they didn't.

Rounder had weekly meetings with their reps, and at one of those meetings a rep mentioned my album. Another said he was asked about it, too, as did a third rep. The person who had told me, "No, not interested," was sitting there, and after the meeting he phoned me.

Rounder ended up selling a thousand of the first two thousand albums pressed. When I ran out of stock, it was an easy decision to put the album on their label, but it's good to know that at first I got "No—no—no—no" from them before I got a "Yes." I would not have asked them again after their last "No," but momentum was with me.

Jack Hardy kept at it with *Fast Folk* as singer/songwriter Richard Meyer took over a lot of the day-to-day work of the project. While many of the original songwriters who worked on it started to drift in other directions, Jack and Richard produced many more New York–based issues, as well as albums that showcased other cities. Besides Boston, there's an issue recorded at the Caffé Lena in Saratoga Springs, and others recorded in Toronto, Los Angeles, and Rhode Island. Plus, the yearly Bottom Line shows went on until 1994. In 2007 Smithsonian Folkways added every *Fast Folk* recording to its vast catalogue of material, so all those songs—including David Massengill's "Great American Dream"—now have a second chance to find an audience.

Jack continues to host his Monday night songwriters' dinners all these years later—and the rule that you must have a new song to sing to come to dinner still applies.

If you don't live in a big city like New York, you can start your own writing workshop wherever you live. The important thing is to pick a time and place and never vary from it, so that all local songwriters (or poets, or painters, or weavers, or knitters, or practitioners of whatever kind of art or craft you create) know that "every Monday" or "the second Tuesday of the month" there's a place to go to network/create with like-minded souls. Then, like at Jack's, many collaborations and friendships, and perhaps even occasional romances, will blossom.

I'm not going to go into any of those here. That's what songs are for.

18

OH . . . C—*EH?*

N—*EH?* D—*EH?*

Every summer there are fantastic music festivals all across Canada, and over the years I've been lucky enough to play a number of them—Mariposa, Summerfolk at Owen Sound, Winnipeg, Edmonton, Canmore, Vancouver—where I've met some of the wonderful people who keep the Canadian music scene so vibrant.

People like Richard Flohil, a transplanted Brit who lives in Toronto and works with folk, pop, and rock musicians from all over the world. And Michael Wrycraft, a graphic designer who creates inventive CD packages. The Canadian musicians I admire and have gotten to work with over the years include Nancy White (she's considered the "Tom Paxton of Canada"), Loreena McKennitt, James Keelaghan, David Francey, Eileen Laverty, Curly Boy Stubbs, Garnet Rogers, the late Joan MacIsaac, David Celia, Stephen Fearing, Eve Goldberg, Roy Forbes, Eileen McGann, Jann Arden, Bruce Cockburn, Murray McLauchlan, Lynn Miles, Ben Sures, and bands like the Arrogant Worms, Moxy Fruvous, the Barenaked Ladies, and so many others.

The first Canadian festival I played (which went belly up after only two years) was the Northwinds Folk Festival on Toronto Island. This was approximately eight months after I had released *Future Fossils*. Having an album played on radio stations in cities outside of New York suddenly opened up the world to me. I'm often asked how to get started in this business, and I can tell you for sure that you have to get your music played on the radio before you can travel. No matter how good you are, nobody will come and see you if they don't know who you are. Radio airplay changes everything. Of course, the Internet is changing everything even more—having a presence on Facebook, MySpace, and Twitter, and maintaining an up-to-date Web site are also important. But radio is still important.

About a month or so after the manufacturing problem with *Future Fossils* occurred and then was resolved, I received a letter from my father. He encouraged me to continue with my music, something he hadn't really done before. My parents had wanted me to have a safe career, like nursing, and my father had been especially worried that my musical aspirations were unrealistic. But now here he was—in writing—telling me to go for it. He also reminisced about when I was a little girl, recalling stories from my childhood that I had all but forgotten.

His letter perplexed me, because it seemed out of character. My father was strict and seemed—to me, at least—to be followed by a dark cloud, always worrying about one thing or another befalling him or his family. As he got older he developed a growing list of physical complaints that only added to his burden of worry. He liked order, did not like back-talk, and had probably not envisioned being the head of a chaotic household of nine children. But that was the hand he was dealt.

When we lived in Peekskill, Dad wanted us kids to do chores every Saturday. We'd wash the car, wax the floors, wash the dishes, do the laundry, and pick up trash around the house, all of which we hated—we were just kids who wanted to have fun. Every once in a while one of us would get spanked for misbehaving, but I was a good girl and have no memory of that happening to me. However, I remember one Saturday when I was full of spit and vinegar and refused to cooperate; my father followed me down the hall yelling at me, his hand raised like he might slap me—but I was sure he wouldn't hit me, his good little girl. I started up the stairs to the third floor, then stopped and turned around so that I was eye-level with him.

"Go ahead!" I yelled. "Hit me! You can't reason it out like a mature adult! You don't know how to have an intelligent discussion with your own offspring, so you have to use brute force!"

"Damn right!" he said as his right hand came down and smacked me right across the face. I burst into tears, ran up the stairs. So much for me thinking I was such an angel. I talked back and I got smacked.

I never got hit again . . . and come to think of it, I never talked back again. At least, not like that.

But Dad's reminiscences in the letter were not about that kind of thing. Instead, he reminded me of how he used to call me "Teeny Potter, lovely daughter." I have the letter here somewhere—I stuck it in a file folder so I wouldn't lose it. Of course, now I can't find that folder.

A few days after I received this letter, I spoke to my older sister Louise on the phone. I wanted to tell her about it, but I didn't want her to feel hurt that I had received such a personal letter from Dad. I brought it up near the end of our conversation.

"I got one, too!" she squealed over the phone. Hers was in the same tone as mine, but with personal details about her life. We quickly made a round of calls to our brothers and sisters and found out that we had *all* received these sentimental notes, and we all agreed it was out of character for Dad to do this and had no idea why he did.

We didn't know that he was dying.

He died on June 18, 1985, two days after Father's Day. He had been admitted to the hospital just a few days before he died, but by that time in his life he had been in and out of the hospital numerous times for various reasons, so we had simply taken it in stride. We did not know that he had been diagnosed with cancer the previous winter; he kept that a secret. All the Lavin kids flew in from across the country—California, Washington state, Florida, Illinois, Virginia, and New York City—for his funeral. Without discussing it beforehand, we all brought our letters from Dad, and we exchanged them and read what he wrote to everyone else. We decided that it would be a very nice part of his funeral service to have the letters edited together and read aloud.

The afternoon before the funeral, I remember sitting on the porch of our next-door neighbors, the Hurleys, with my brother Christopher, reading each letter out loud, deciding which sentences to include for the funeral. Of course, we cried as we did this, and we were practically dehydrated by the end of the afternoon. We knew that none of us would be able to keep it together enough to read the compilation of the letters aloud at the funeral, so we enlisted a family friend to read it for us.

When I think about those letters, I am so grateful that Dad took the time to write them. How many people die without having a proper will, or having their spouse and children looked after? Not only did our dad die with his house in order, he put his goodbyes to each of his nine children on paper, something we could hold and read for years to come. What a thoughtful, loving final gift he gave us all.

A lot of relatives came to Geneva for the funeral. It was held on a warm, sunny day at St. Stephen's, a large church near downtown with thick brick walls and stained-glass windows. We were all inside the church, the service going smoothly, when suddenly there was a tremendously loud crashing sound outside. It was so awful that I remember thinking that there must have been a car accident. I figured it would be just a matter of minutes before we'd hear sirens, but we never did. I forgot about it until the service was over and we started filing out of the church.

It was pouring rain, and it was cold. *Really* cold. The air temperature had dropped thirty degrees. The crashing sound we had heard was a bolt of lightning hitting a large tree across the street. We were all in a bit of a daze anyway—the way it is when families get together for funerals—but no one was prepared for this sudden, unforecasted change in the weather. Before we could go to the cemetery, we had to drive back to my parents' house and gather as many raincoats, umbrellas, sweaters—even blankets—as we could. This was the middle of June, and it was now hovering around forty-eight degrees and pouring rain. We muddled through, but it was odd.

The following weekend was the Northwinds Festival, and I debated canceling. My mother reminded me that Dad had written such positive words about my music and that he would want me to go. So I did. I was very sad, but I knew that working would be good therapy.

The festival grounds were on Toronto Island, so the only way on and off was via a short boat ride from downtown Toronto. I was very busy doing workshops and performances on the island, but while on the boat I thought about my father.

I guess when someone close to you complains about being sick more often than not, you begin to think that's just the way it is—rather than considering the possibility that he might die from his ailments. I'm sure I'm not the first person who has felt this way. As a parting shot to insensitive friends and relatives, more than one wag has said he would make "I told you I wasn't feeling well!" his epitaph.

I didn't tell any of the other performers that my father had just died. I didn't know any of them and didn't think it was appropriate to bring it up. But then I started running into the same guy every time I would take the boat to and from the island. He would smile; we'd both say hi. After repeatedly running into each other, we started talking. His name was Tom; he was a couple of years younger than me, worked for a concert-booking agency in Ann Arbor, Michigan, and had booked a number of the performers at the festival. There was something about him that I really liked, though I didn't feel the spark of a potential romance.

The last day of the festival, I ran into him backstage in the performers' tent behind the main stage. It was raining. I asked him where he grew up and what kind of a family he came from. He told me he grew up many places, including Brazil, because his dad's work included travel, and that he was one of eight children.

I told him I was one of nine. I asked him if his family got together often now that all of the kids were grown, and he hesitated for a moment, then said they had gotten together just a year earlier because their dad had suddenly died. I could see how upset it made him just saying those words.

So I told him that my dad had just died a few days ago. And then I told him about how the air temperature dropped thirty degrees during his funeral, how lightning had struck a tree, and how it was pouring rain when we left the church.

He looked at me in amazement. "At my father's funeral, the air temperature dropped twenty-five degrees—it went from being a beautiful sunny day to being cold and cloudy when we left the church."

We both sat there, staring at each other. What were the odds we would have such strange experiences in common?

Tom and I corresponded for about two years. When my girlfriends asked me if I was hoping this was going to turn into something, I told them that I didn't know why I kept writing to him. Someday the reason would either reveal itself, or I would just stop writing.

Well, the reason did reveal itself the day he met my sister Mary. Yes, Mary of Piglet and Joe Namath fame. He's the Tom she's been married to for years now—Tom Slothower. We used to joke about how Tom's dad met our dad out there in the Great Somewhere and said, "Hey, you know what I did at my funeral? Twenty-five-degree temperature drop *and* a whole lotta clouds!" And our dad said, "Oh, yeah? Well I'm going for a thirty-degree temperature drop and one clap of thunder, one bolt of lightning, *and* pouring rain!"

The last time I was in Canada, I heard that the couple who produced the Northwinds Festival mortgaged their house to do so, and then they lost their shirts. I am so sorry that happened, but I want them to know how their festival changed the life of my sister for the way better. I sure hope they recovered financially.

Two years after performing at Northwinds, I was invited to be part of the Summerfolk at Owen Sound Folk Festival, which is about a three-hour drive north of Toronto. It's a lovely small festival, with lots of craftspeople selling their wares. It was there that I met a wild group of guys called Friends of Fiddler's Green.

Fiddler's Green is a folk club in Toronto, and these seven guys own it and perform there. A high-spirited Scot named Tam Kearney is their biggest mischief maker, an irrepressible guy who lives for practical jokes and mirth making. I'll give you a few examples.

The festival took place in August, and the weather had turned awful one day—there were even hurricane and tornado warnings reported on the local news. (Ever since the first time I saw *The Wizard of Oz*, I have had nightmares about twisters. Very often the twisters are chasing me at Rockaway Point, where my grandparents had their bungalow.) On that wet, windy day, I made the mistake of telling Tam about my twister nightmares. Later on I had to use the port-o-john, and when I locked the door behind me and sat down to take care of business, Tam and another guy from Friends of Fiddler's Green started to rock it back and forth, screaming,

"Twister! Run for your life—it's a twister!" Thanks to Tam Kearney, that scene now sometimes pops up in my twister nightmares.

At that same festival, one of the performers I saw for the first time was Archie Fisher from Scotland. He's a tall, lanky man with a deep booming voice who plays the sweetest guitar and sings the most romantic songs. Tam organized a practical joke on CBS personality Bruce Steele as he introduced Archie, a prank that involved three thousand people.

At the Owen Sound festival, there are small stages around the grounds where concerts and workshops take place all afternoon, but at night everyone gathers at the large stone stage, where a few thousand people watch the show. Before Bruce got there, Tam got onstage and explained that at some point during Bruce's introduction Tam was going to secretly wave a white flag from behind the curtain on the left side, then wave the same flag from behind the curtain on the right side. These were the audience's cues to stand and scream and point—first left, then right—as if a streaker had dashed across the stage to disrupt Bruce's speech. Tam even had a run-through with the crowd to coach them on their screaming and pointing, after which he swore the entire audience to secrecy about the plan.

 A few hours later, when Bruce was mid-speech, the crowd started screaming and pointing—first left, then right—and then laughed hysterically as Bruce whipped around in bewilderment. The uproar lasted for a good three minutes, Bruce looking this way and that, but then Tam came out to save the day, asking everyone to calm down and take their seats. As everyone obediently sat down, Tam vowed to find the naked perpetrator and punish him for ruining Bruce's speech. Bruce thanked Tam for getting things under control, and then finished his introduction. For the rest of the festival, everyone in the audience kept up the ruse that a streaker had interrupted Bruce's speech, and Bruce was telling everyone about it, too, adding that, yes, he saw the streaker himself. To this day, I still don't think he knows it was a joke. That's how serious Tam is about these kinds of things. (So if you ever meet Bruce Steele, don't bring this up!)

At Canadian festivals all the volunteers, sound crew, and performers eat in the same big tent. Everybody stands in line and waits their turn for food, famous headliners next to volunteers, volunteers next to unknown songwriters making their first appearance. It's where we all get to know each other, and you might find out that the person who is ladling out the soup is a bus driver or a surgeon or an accountant by trade. At the Canmore Festival, north of Calgary in western Canada, literally half the town comes out to volunteer.

Once when I was at the Winnipeg Folk Festival, my fellow performers included the Washington Squares, a Greenwich Village trio of former rock musicians who donned black berets, black pants, and black-and-white-striped shirts to spoof the beatnik scene of the 1950s and early 1960s. Because they were experienced, sophisticated rock musicians, they had negotiated themselves some "extras"—including a private eating tent so they didn't have to stand in line with everyone else.

So there I was, standing in a long line waiting for lunch, when one of the Squares saw me. He said hi and invited me to have lunch with them so I wouldn't have to stand in line. I was tempted, but I had heard enough backstage grumbling about the unfair and un-festival-like special treatment the Squares were receiving. As I waved to them and declined their invitation, I was aware of at least a hundred eyes watching. While the Squares probably thought it was great to arrange special perks for themselves, it didn't do them any favors with their fellow performers or the staff.

I had mixed feelings about the group: I liked a few of their songs and thought the whole beatnik spoof thing was funny, but their cynical, opportunistic take on folk music ultimately left me cold. They were very good at creating photo opportunities for themselves—I remember a photo where one of the band members held a hammer out to Pete Seeger. (Get it? If I had a hammer?)

At the last concert Steve Goodman did in New York before he died, at the Bottom Line, the Squares got to open for him. Steve's music and recordings live on—he was a truly original genius—so what a break for the Squares to be on the same bill with him. Their set was professional and charged with energy, but what I remember most was that at the end of Steve's set, they came out onstage and joined him. Steve looked surprised, and I figured he was acting like it was a "spontaneous" moment when it really was planned, but I found out later that it *was* spontaneous—on the part of the Squares. They had a photographer in the house and wanted to be snapped playing with Steve Goodman. Give them points for chutzpah, but take away points for arrogance.

When the Squares broke up, let's just say they were not missed by the folk scene. They were good at marketing, but what draws people to folk music in the first place—truth and concern for the greater good—was not an integral part of their music. They did get a lot of work and a lot of exposure, probably at the expense of less savvy groups. But many of those less savvy groups are still working, while the Washington Squares are now a footnote in folk music history.

So, back at the Owen Sound festival, I sat with Tam at one dinner, having forgiven him for rocking my port-o-john. He was entertaining us with tales of his favorite pranks. One of his stories really impressed me.

He said that one of the other guys in Friends of Fiddler's Green, a very methodical, organized fellow, was shopping for a new car. He told the other guys about each detailed step he was taking in his quest to buy the best possible car.

"It started to really grate on our nerves," Tam said, "and finally we couldn't take it anymore. We said, 'Come on, man, just pick one, for God's sake!' And finally he did. He bought the best car he could find—according to him it had the best miles per gallon, the best resale value, the best of *everything*."

Tam's eyes lit up. "Then the fun really began," he said.

"Every night, for the next three weeks, we took turns sneaking into his garage."

Someone interrupted, "So what did you do—siphon gas out of his car?"

"No!" said Tam. "This was the beauty of this prank. We siphoned gas *into* his car. We started from the first day he owned the car. Every night we snuck into his garage and put just enough gas in his car to top off the tank.

"As he drove more and more and yet the gas needle was still at full, he began to worry that the gas needle was broken. He brought the car into the dealership to have it checked, but we had the guys at the dealership in on the prank, too. They reminded him that he had done more research than any other customer, ever, and congratulated him on making such a brilliant choice of a new car.

"When he figured out he had driven close to six hundred miles and still his gas tank was full, he decided it had to be some kind of miracle from

God. I kid you not! He calls me up and tells me he's calling his pastor and the local TV station—he's going to invite them over to examine his car.

"That's when I knew we had to stop," Tam said sadly. "It was one thing for us to have a good laugh, but we didn't want the whole bloody city of Toronto making fun. Not to mention the Catholic Church. So we told him the truth. You should have seen the look on his face. We had a jolly good laugh about it all."

The last day of the Owen Sound festival in August 1987 coincided with a worldwide event known as the Harmonic Convergence, a so-called global awakening to love and unity through some form of divine transformation. There were a lot of New Age–y folks at Owen Sound who were totally into this thing, but I wasn't one of them. But I was so inspired by Tam that I saw an opportunity to pull a prank of my own, using the Harmonic Convergence as the excuse. Instead of "Harmonic Convergence," we'd call it "Harmonica Virgins." Dressed in white sheets and playing harmonicas, we'd crash the set of one of the performers in the final Sunday-night concert, circling her a few times before disappearing into the dark offstage. We'd tip off the emcee to what we were doing, and he'd jump on the mike as we were leaving the stage and say to the audience, "Oh my God! How privileged are we to have just witnessed THE HARMONICA VIRGINS!"

I rounded up a dozen performers, the harmonicas, and the sheets. (With pranking being practically a Canadian tradition, the head of housekeeping at the hotel said it was okay to borrow a dozen white sheets.) Then I looked at the roster of performers for the final night's concerts, and that's where I ran into a problem. There was no one on the list whom I knew well. It's a point of honor to be chosen to play the main stage at Owen Sound—some performers wait years. There was nobody on that roster who I knew for sure wouldn't be thrown by being crashed by the Harmonica Virgins. Except one.

Me. I was performing on Sunday night. If they didn't crash my set, I didn't know how else we could do it. I have no memory of what I opened with or what I closed with—all I remember is wondering when the crashers were going to do it. Suddenly, people clad in sheets droning on harmonicas appeared from the wings and slowly circled me. I stopped playing and did my best to act confused. At first, no one in the audience knew what to make of it. The pranksters plodded along, breathing in and out on their harps—then I suddenly said, "Oh my God . . . I know what it is! It's the *Harmonica Virgins!*"

The audience roared.

The next day at the hotel, as I was preparing to leave for the airport, one of the festival organizers took me aside and said, "You know, it's actually quite an honor to have a prank pulled on you on the main stage. You should be very proud. Means you're accepted."

One year later I went to the Winnipeg Folk Festival, the largest of all the summer folk festivals held in Canada. Twenty-five thousand people from all over North America attend over a weekend in July. Twenty-five thousand folk music fans, many of whom I'd love to meet, and yet I seemed to continually run into the only two people I didn't want to see that weekend—or ever.

One of them was my ex-fiancé. He and I had been engaged to be married, but we had broken it off in February. Valentine's Day, to be exact. Since musicians are booked months in advance, however, we were both scheduled to perform at Winnipeg, thinking at the time how sweet it would be to attend as a married couple. When the wedding was called off, it was too late to undo our concert bookings.

The first night of the festival, we ran into each other at the hotel. I had such pangs of regret when I saw him, mixed with an undeniable longing. By coincidence, we ended up in the same bus going out to the concert site—a forty-five-minute ride. We talked, and it felt like old times. We held hands for a moment. I kept thinking, *maybe we made a mistake. Maybe being together again will show us we erred.* My heart pounded as my mind galloped. *He is a great guy. He is sweet and kind, and I am nuts about his music. Maybe we should give this another try.*

We also shared a ride coming back that night—a private car rather than a bus—and that's when he met . . . *her.* I was sitting in the back seat, and they were seated together in the front seat, next to the driver. As we all laughed and talked, it became clear that these two had a great deal in common. Way more in common than he and I ever did. In three minutes I knew this! They even looked alike!

Have you ever experienced love at first sight? Can you imagine how it felt to see it happening to two people sitting directly in front of you, one of whom you thought you might still be in love with? That's when the most torturous weekend of my life began. I was scheduled for a number of workshops at various stages around the festival grounds, as well as some solo concerts. My friend Andrew Ratshin was also at Winnipeg with his trio Uncle Bonsai; I complained to him that as I walked from one stage to another, I'd pass a few thousand faceless strangers, yet my ex-fiancé and this other woman seemed to be in my line of sight. Every time I saw them I got angrier. How dare he? The first night we had talked so sweetly to each other, and now I no longer even existed. Andrew tried his best to calm me down and kindly offered to hang out with me between performances.

All logic flew out the window. This guy and I were through. I knew that. We hadn't seen each other in five months, nor had we spoken during that time. He had been hurt way more than I was when we called it off, so why was I so upset to see him with someone else?

Because he wasn't mine anymore—a situation I wrote about in my song "Replaced":

> I have been replaced in your life
>
> The turning of the tides
>
> Has washed away your heartache
>
> Opened mine up wide
>
> Now I feel an old familiar hurt from years ago
>
> And I know I've gone through this before
>
> A different battle, a distant war
>
> When the odd man out evens the score
>
> It leaves you craving just a little bit more

The last night of that festival, I didn't sleep at all. I packed my bags, headed to the airport, and boarded a plane for the Vancouver Folk Festival in a near-psychotic haze. Thank God *he* wouldn't be there. When the plane lifted off, I remember that I was stepping on an imaginary gas pedal, trying to make the plane go faster, faster. *Get me the f*#k out of here!*

I was due to arrive in Vancouver one day before the university dorm would be open for performers. I had planned to stay in a hotel, but the festival organizers arranged for me to be billeted with a Canadian couple I was told were big fans of my music. I was also told that a volunteer from the festival would pick me up at the airport.

We landed in Vancouver uneventfully, and I found the volunteer, a rather forlorn young woman named Valerie. It was raining, and she looked waterlogged. After I got in her car and she switched on the ignition, she turned to me and said, "I don't make left turns."

"What do you mean?" I asked. "You don't make left turns—literally or figuratively?"

"Literally. I just got my license. If you're driving on a busy road and try to make a left turn, you're just inviting the oncoming traffic to slam right into you."

I couldn't believe it. The festival sent someone to pick me up who can only turn in one direction? I decided to think of this as a challenge.

"Look, Valerie," I said, "it took me a few tries to pass my driving test, and I had a lot of people help me. Now I can help you. You simply wait for a break in the oncoming traffic, then make your turn."

"Thanks," she said, "and I appreciate what you're trying to do. But if you want me to take you, you'll have to accept how I drive."

I decided it was best not to talk. I wasn't familiar with Vancouver's layout, so I could be of no navigational help. It soon became clear where the left-hand turns were supposed to be, based on all the right-hand turns and turnarounds Valerie made. I noticed that Valerie actually did make a left-hand turn every now and then, but never on a busy street.

We finally pulled up in front of a brown, three-story house in a quiet neighborhood. "Here we are," Valerie said.

I thanked her, and then the two of us unloaded the trunk and rang the doorbell. A young girl, perhaps ten or eleven years old, answered the door.

"Are your parents home?" I asked.

"No," she said.

"Well," I continued, "I'm the American performer who will be staying with you tonight."

"Oh, come on in," she said brightly.

Valerie and I walked into the living room. It was a nice house, a little on the messy side, but in a charming and lived-in way.

"When will your mom and dad be home?" I asked the girl.

She shrugged. "In a couple of hours. They're at work."

As we put my luggage down in the living room, my physical and mental exhaustion hit me all at once. I needed a nap *bad*.

"Can you show me where my bedroom is?" I asked.

"Oh sure," she said, leading us down a long hall. She switched on the light in a small pink bedroom, the floor littered with games, dolls, and comic books. The bed was unmade and covered with more kid stuff.

"Are you sure this is where I'm supposed to sleep?" I asked.

"It's the quietest," she said. "It's my room, and I can sleep on the sofa in the living room. I don't mind."

That was it for me. I turned to Valerie and said, "I can't do this. I had a rough night, I need sleep so badly, and I can see this is not going to work."

To the young girl I said, "Thank you so much for your kind hospitality, but please tell your parents I had a change of plans."

"No, don't leave!" she yelled. "You can stay in my room. It's okay with me!"

I thanked her again but declined.

With that, Valerie and I left. I had made a mental note of a Holiday Inn a couple miles back and asked Valerie to drive me there.

"I don't know why you are being so snippy about your accommodations," she said. "That was a perfectly nice house."

I apologized and explained that I was in a fragile state of mind, terribly sleep deprived, and would be much better off in a hotel.

"Suit yourself," she said.

After she dropped me off, I shook her hand and said, "Valerie, please let the festival know I am staying here instead, and whether you know it or not, you did make a few left turns. You can do it on busy roads. Just wait for a break in the traffic. They won't hit you."

She just shook her head, hopped in the car, and drove off, heading back to the festival organizer's office.

I checked into my room, unplugged the phone, and then promptly fell asleep. When I woke up hours later and plugged the phone in, the message light blinked.

It was the festival director. "Christine Lavin, why didn't you go to your host's house?" he asked. "They waited all afternoon, you never showed up, and now you've gone to a hotel instead! They had fresh flowers for you, and a quiet room in the back of their house with a private bathroom. They are so disappointed! Please call me. You have some explaining to do!"

No, *Valerie* did. As did the little girl who would let in anyone who knocked, even if her parents weren't home. Valerie, wherever you are, I hope that you have learned how to turn left by now. And put one of those GPS devices on your Christmas wish list.

I really can't complain, though. If I drove myself, I wouldn't have these odd little adventures.

The performers at that year's Vancouver Folk Festival included the Flying Karamazov Brothers, an expert group of juggling artists. Every three hours they put down their juggling toys, picked up musical instruments, and marched with a baton twirler around the perimeter of the festival grounds. I noticed that the twirler not only looked unhappy but had limited skills, so after one of their parades I took her aside and showed her a few moves.

"They make me twirl," she whispered, "but I'm the glockenspiel player. I don't like to twirl, but they insist we have a twirler. Could you become our twirler?"

I was taken aback. I was there as a songwriter, but I agreed to show up three hours later to twirl the baton for their next little parade.

The Flying Karamazov Brothers didn't know what to make of it when their twirler handed me her baton, but when I started to twirl, they smiled broadly. After my first parade, they took me over to their tent, and with great fanfare they brought me inside and pointed to all the costumes pinned to the tent wall. "Choose your costume!" they said.

For the next two days, every three hours from sunup to sundown, I donned green lamé shorts and a gold lamé vest as the official baton twirler for the Flying Karamazov Brothers' marching band. I had so much fun that I decided I had to figure out a way to incorporate twirling into my own shows.

Now I tell performers, if you have *any* other skills besides singing, writing songs, and playing an instrument, work them into your show. I recently did a group concert in New Jersey that included a yoga instructor/singer/songwriter named Daniel McBride (who also goes by the name of Dalian). He started out his set by leading the audience in a sixty-second yoga exercise. The audience loved it, and he really stood out from the rest of us, because who does yoga with an audience as part of their show?

Although I was in the darkest, most horrible mood when I arrived in Vancouver that rainy day, I was flying high by the time I left, thanks in part to the Flying Karamazov Brothers.

My all-time favorite Canadian musical discovery is a man named Grit Laskin. I first heard him sing and play guitar at Northwinds way back in 1985, and I had no idea at the time that he had actually built the guitar he played.

The more Canadian festivals I went to, the more fantastic Laskin guitars I saw being played by many of the best performers. At first I didn't know they were Laskin guitars—I just knew they were different from anything I had ever seen in the States, and I started asking a lot of questions.

The sound of his guitars is sweet and clean, and the inlay work is sophisticated, artistic, and very often playful. I even saw one Laskin guitar that had intricate inlay work on the *back*. I am now the proud owner of a Laskin guitar—it's my most cherished possession. I asked him to design me a guitar that was inspired by our solar system. That was all the instruction I gave him. He knew of my song "Planet X," about the trials and tribulations of Pluto's planetary status, and he also had a great interest in astronomy, so I couldn't wait to see what he would do.

I had to wait five years (yes, there's quite a waiting list for Grit's guitars). It arrived in 2002, and I just *love* it. It has the nine planets on its neck (yes, nine! Pluto counts! Don't get me started!) and the Pioneer Spacecraft on its headstock. Grit also included a certificate that stated if another planet is discovered in our solar system within my lifetime, he will put it on the neck for free. But he didn't say anything about taking Pluto off, and I appreciated the sensitivity he displayed there. In 2009, Neil deGrasse

Tyson, director of the Hayden Planetarium in New York, wrote a book called *The Pluto Files* about Pluto's demotion and the uproar it caused—and he included the lyrics to "Planet X." I sure hope that makes up for that D I got in Astronomy at Brockport!

Grit won't sell one of his prized guitars without a Calton guitar case. Calton cases are made in Calgary, and I swear by them. I used to have to buy a new guitar case every year, but not since I started using Caltons. If they get dinged up, you send them back, and the company will repair and restore them until they are as good as new.

The guys who build the Calton cases also work as volunteers at the Canmore Folk Festival every year. One of my older Calton cases has a unique striped-velvet interior, and the last time I was at Canmore, the new guys from Calton all came over to see my fancy case. Al Williams, who runs the company, smiled when he looked at those stripes. I didn't ask for stripes; they did it as a little surprise and were almost sorry they did.

"It took a ridiculous amount of time to do the striping," Al said, "and we never did it again. But it sure is nice to see, especially when it's cradling such a beautiful Laskin guitar."

Grit Laskin is one of the most sought-after luthiers in the world. There is a coffee-table book of his work called *A Guitarmaker's Canvas: The Inlay Art of Grit Laskin,* published by Back Beat Books, and I am so tickled that my guitar is in it. Four of Grit's guitars are on permanent display in the Canadian Museum of Civilization in Ottawa, the Canadian equivalent of our Smithsonian. His instruments have also been exhibited at the Boston Museum of Fine Arts, the American Craft Council in Manhattan, and the Museum of Making Music in Carlsbad, California. Grit is also a first-rate singer/songwriter, as well as the founder of Borealis Records, a company that showcases the music of many of his countrymen.

Before I received my precious Laskin guitar, I owned a lovely Larrivee, which I bought secondhand at Matt Umanoff Guitars in Greenwich Village back in the mid-1980s. Around that time, in addition to my twister nightmares, I started to have guitar nightmares, always worrying something was going to happen to my Martin, my only guitar. I had a recurring dream that the legendary guitarist David Bromberg invented a machine that was like a radio-tracking device for Martin guitars. In my dream, Bromberg would drive the streets of New York at night, when everyone was sleeping, with his machine—which looked like a woman's leather clutch from the 1950s—mounted on the roof of his car, slowly revolving. When it would hone in on a Martin guitar in the vicinity, a light would flash on the dashboard. He would then sneak into the apartment of the guitar's owner, open the guitar case, remove the expensive Martin guitar, and replace it with a Mickey Mouse guitar with a little hand crank on the side that played "Pop Goes the Weasel" when you turned it. He'd then close the case and sneak out. When the guitar's owner woke up the next day, he'd see the guitar case and think nothing was wrong—until later in the day when he opened it to find that his beautiful Martin guitar was missing and a cheap imposter in its place!

Nightmare! Nightmare! Nightmare!

When I told Dave Van Ronk about this dream, he suggested I get a second guitar so that if something *did* happen to my main guitar, I'd still be able to work.

So I went to Matt's and played a couple dozen different guitars—mostly Martins. But then I picked up this used Larrivee—I didn't even know the name Larrivee at the time—and I instantly fell in love with it. It's a very plain guitar, with no fancy inlay, but it has a warm, deep, rich sound. And eventually I stopped having my Bromberg nightmare.

For a short time I also owned a small-body Larrivee that had beautiful inlay work, with a gryphon on the headstock. Also for a short time, fellow folksinger John Gorka owned a larger-body Larrivee with the exact same inlay work on it. He left it in a car parked outside a diner in Pittsburgh, and while John and his friends were eating, the car was stolen. As my schedule would have it, I was doing a free outdoor concert two weeks later in downtown Pittsburgh at a large open square amid the Pittsburgh Glass buildings. I promised John that I would do what I could to try to find his guitar.

Midway through my concert, with about eight hundred people in the square, I told the crowd about what happened to John's guitar. Since my guitar had the exact same inlay work, I encouraged audience members to come backstage after the show to look closely at my guitar, take a picture of it if they had a camera, and use that to help John get his guitar back. As I took a breath mid-speech, a man near the front of the crowd yelled to me, "They found John's guitar!" so I repeated it into the microphone so everyone could hear. The crowd cheered.

So I asked, "Does John know they found his guitar?" and the man yelled back, "No, John doesn't know yet." (I repeated into the mike, "JOHN DOESN'T KNOW YET!") So then I asked, "Why doesn't John know?" and the man yelled, "Because the police are setting up a sting operation." (I dutifully repeated into the mike, "BECAUSE THE POLICE ARE SETTING UP A STING OPERATION.")

That explains right there why my dream of becoming a spy never came true. There was a happy ending, though: John did get his beautiful Larrivee back.

I don't have my small-body Larrivee anymore—I gave it to guitarist Frank Christian after he played it on one of my albums. Frank is such a fabulous guitarist that he got sounds out of that little baby that I knew I would never be able to get. I felt the guitar would be happier with Frank than with me, and I didn't need three guitars. My Laskin and my Larrivee were enough.

Grit Laskin learned how to build guitars by apprenticing with Jean-Claude Larrivee, starting when he was eighteen years old and staying for eight years. Larrivees are now made in western Canada, in Vancouver, while Grit works in the east. Larrivee has a whole team of builders and makes approximately a hundred guitars a year, while Grit builds just a dozen, by himself.

On my album *Cold Pizza for Breakfast*, I rerecorded "The Kind of Love You Never Recover From." If you listen on headphones, you can hear the Laskin guitar in your left ear and the Larrivee in your right. They were built twenty years apart, but I decided it was time to musically rejoin the master and his now-star pupil, a master in his own right.

In 2000, I visited Grit in his studio, and he showed me two guitars in different states of completion. There's a lot of "curing" time that needs to take place, so he works on one guitar while the other is "resting." The most complete one had partial inlay work depicting none other than Tam Kearney on the neck. The inlay depicts a hand turning the crank of a jack-in-the-box, and Tam has sprung out, playing his banjo. It's on a twelve-string guitar, made for a mutual friend of Tam's and Grit's. You won't see Tam Kearney on a guitar every day. Wait, that's not true. Grit's book *The Guitarmaker's Canvas* shows Tam's guitar in its completed form.

(Thinking about the "Tam in the Box" guitar brings back memories of my Bromberg nightmare. As Dame Edna might say, "Ooooh, spooooky, spooooooky!")

Last time I was in Toronto, I asked Grit about Tam, and he told me Tam was getting on in years and was in a wheelchair, but he was still performing and was as feisty as ever. We laughed about the legendary "Bruce Steele Streaker" prank at the Summerfolk at Owen Sound Folk Festival, and then I brought up my favorite Tam prank, the one he pulled on the guy who drove them all crazy researching his car purchase—but Grit interrupted me.

"That was *me*, Chris!" he said. "They did that to *ME!!*"

I knew there were seven guys who owned Fiddler's Green, but I had no idea that Grit Laskin was one of them.

Now every time I pick up my Laskin guitar, I smile, knowing that Tam's meticulously planned out and well-executed three-week Canadian prank was pulled on the incredible genius who built my guitar.

19

IN SEARCH
OF DAME EDNA

Many international concert promoters go to Canada to scout artists to book in their countries, so I was looking forward to traveling even more after going north of the border. As it turned out, my next international tour took me to Australia. I've now been back a second time, but the first trip couldn't have started any worse than it did.

No, it could have been worse. I could have died. I had a number of cities booked, mostly around Melbourne, Canberra, and Sydney, in the southeast part of the country. But my first performance was to be at the Port Fairy Folk Festival. To get there, I flew from Newark to LA to Honolulu to Sydney to Melbourne, and I didn't get *any* sleep on the way. I was met at the Melbourne airport by Andrew Pattison, a concert promoter who owns and runs a winery outside the city. I stayed with him and his family for a day (to get acclimated to the time change) before heading off to the festival, where I was one of only two Americans booked at the festival; the other was John McCutcheon, whom I had not yet met.

The next day we drove to Port Fairy, a tiny, sparkling jewel of a town on the rocky coast. I checked into my hotel and went to the opening-night concert, which featured some of Australia's top folk performers. I wish I could say who played that night, but my head started to pound and my throat was getting scratchy. I knew I had to get to bed, but I stopped at a pizza parlor and got a small pie to go (with a whole sunny-side-up egg, peas, and pineapple rings—really). I ate some of it and went to bed.

I woke up a couple hours later feeling very bad (no, it wasn't the pizza). My throat felt like I was swallowing glass, my head felt like it was a water balloon, my nose was clogged up, and my lungs were horribly congested. And I'm pretty sure I was running a fever. I say "pretty sure" because, although there was a doctor at the festival, he was volunteering as a sound man. He lived a few hours away and hadn't even brought a thermometer.

By the way, though I love Australia, and I love Australians, I have to say this was the worst hotel room I had ever stayed in my life. It was so small that I could reach out and touch both walls. (Though I didn't want to touch them, because they were peeling, water damaged, and covered with fluffy mold.) The bed was lumpy, but at least the sheets were clean.

So the next morning, the festival organizers, who'd heard that "the American girl" was sick, sent a young, strapping Aussie doctor to my hotel to check up on me. By then I was in agony. I could barely speak, I was on the verge of a migraine, and I was so sleep deprived that I felt like I was about to hallucinate, and in came this young doctor. He asked me to lift the back of my pajama top up so he could put his ear on my back, and then he asked me to breathe. (Can you imagine? My first Australia folk festival, and a doctor put his ear against my bare back. This could have been the opening scene for a twisted B movie.) He felt my head and thought I was feverish, but he didn't think I needed to be hospitalized. (I didn't either— I just felt *bad*.) He suggested I just try to get as much rest as I could. He would tell the festival organizers I would not be able to perform.

Then he left. For the next twenty-four hours I lay on that awful bed, moaning and groaning, staring at the peeling walls, and listening to the strains of far-off music and occasional applause and laughter that would drift in on the breeze as the Port Fairy Folk Festival went happily on without me.

For me, migraines usually end in barfing, and this time was no different. I ran down the hall to the dorm-style bathroom (that's right—no private bath) to throw up. Even though the barfing was horrible, especially with a sore throat, it signaled the migraine would be coming to an end, so I actually felt hopeful. I lay on the bathroom floor for a couple of hours until I barfed again, my only entertainment watching the barf swirl down the toilet in the opposite direction than it does in the Northern Hemisphere. To this day, I have never seen another pizza with a sunny-side-up egg on it, and if I even see a pineapple or a pea near a pizza, I get queasy. That day ranks as the worst day I ever had on the road.

Word had gotten around that I was sick, but since the other festival performers were fully booked with workshops and performances, they couldn't come visit me. That was fine, since I felt bad, looked bad, had a bad attitude, and—let's face it—didn't have my best game face on. Performers should avoid people with contagious illnesses at all cost, anyway. You'd be amazed at how many sick performers have gone to see other performers' shows; gone backstage to hug them, kiss them, and wish them well; and then said, "Oh, by the way, I am so sick. I can't believe I was able to get out of bed to come see you! But that's how much you mean to me!"

I knew someday I'd have to write a song about that kind of thing. Instead of hugging and kissing, I figured bowing would be a better way to greet people when you're not feeling well, and I even had a line written for the song: "if you're sick and touch me—ka pow! / Come on, sick people, BOW!"

Although I was lonely and blue that first horrible day, the next day couldn't have been more different—a steady stream of visitors brought food and flowers. Even a veterinarian came to visit—a veterinarian who did acupuncture on animals. The doctor might not have had his bag of tricks, but the vet had hers, so she did acupuncture on me using the same technique she uses on horses. Hay hay hay!

I met many people who tried their best to cheer me up, and I found that I was experiencing the festival in a whole different way, based on the critiques—and gossip—from the other performers. One sold more albums than all the other festival performers combined, and those performers, half of whom I met, talked about him with a mixture of wonder and envy.

There was one strange man who visited me a number of times. I was told that he was a bit of a stalker who was obsessed with one of the young

Australian folk stars (whom I also met). When I was clued in that some people were a bit worried about the strange man's obsessive behavior, I tried to do some sly detective work, asking him questions to see if I could figure out if he was a real threat to the folk star or not. I became sure that he was not—he just *loved* her music so much. Later on I came to understand how that feels, to be so passionate about someone's work that you want to see her show again and again—in fact, I can blame Australia for that happening to me a few years later.

But at that point in time, in Port Fairy, I was useless—coughing and wheezing, and moaning and complaining. But the doctor who came every day and put his ear on my bare back, my visitors, and my Miss Marple sleuth work were a welcome distraction. The performer who sold more albums than everyone else also came to visit me. It was John McCutcheon, the only other American at the festival. He plays many instruments—guitar, banjo, piano, autoharp, even the hammer dulcimer—and there's no one quite like him. He's also a first-rate songwriter.

When I got better, he and I did joint concerts in Melbourne and Geelong, so I got to watch firsthand what a brilliant entertainer he is. Twenty years later, he's even better. My brother-in-law Tom Slothower became his tour manager in the mid-1990s and is still on the road with him today. Who knew when I first met him in Port Fairy that we'd have such a connection all these years later?

After that festival he went west, and I went north to Sydney.

The rest of that tour is a blur except for the night I saw someone named Dame Edna on Australian TV. Dame Edna is the larger-than-life character created by Barry Humphries. Barry started his performing career in Australia as a classically trained actor, and he and Zoe Caldwell were in an acting troupe that introduced classic plays to theater audiences all across the country. In each city, town, and village where they performed, they were sponsored by the local arts club, which more often than not was headed up by a local woman who was well versed (or *thought* she was well versed) in the arts. Backstage, Barry took to mimicking some of the more memorable of these doyennes, much to the delight of his fellow actors, who encouraged him to develop this comic bit into something more.

His creation started as the humble "Edna Everage" from Moonee Ponds, a suburb of Melbourne, married to her beloved Norm (now deceased). Fifty years later, she is the magnificent international megastar—no, gigastar—Dame Edna Everage.

For my money, Barry Humphries possesses the most creative mind in the English-speaking world. I have now read his books, ogled his paintings, watched his films and television programs, and attended his Tony-winning Broadway shows over and over again, but back in 1988, all I knew is that he was the funniest performer I had ever seen, and I was eager to see more.

A year and a half later I was invited back to Australia to do another concert tour. The first one was a month long and ended up being a break-even venture, so I wasn't sure it made sense to do it again, but because my interest in Dame Edna was greater than ever, I went.

This second trip had its own quirky adventures. I started in Sydney, and the concert promoter there was a psychiatrist whose wife had just had a baby. (Literally—the baby was one week old.) The psychiatrist/promoter was a bit scattered, as you might imagine. He had arranged for me to be put up at the house of a friend of a friend, and he took me straight there from the airport. We pulled up to the house, a rambling white-brick structure that was being renovated.

We were invited in by a big beefy guy, dripping wet and wrapped in a towel. In the hallway, you could look up and see the sky. There was no roof! The guy shook hands all around and gave us a quick tour of the downstairs, which included the one working bathroom in the house.

He explained that the house didn't have automatic hot water. Instead, it had a heating system attached to the pipes. You had to turn this handle, then that handle, then this handle, then strike a match (he demonstrated), which lit the fire—it was an open flame—that heated the water. He then turned the handles off, and the flame went out. I asked him to demonstrate again—this handle, then that one, then this one over here, then the match. He then turned the handles off in the proper order.

If I turned the handles in the wrong order, could I blow up the house?

He thought for a moment and said, "Yes . . . but you won't do that! You look like a smart girl."

He brought me upstairs to my room. There were leaves scattered everywhere. There also seemed to be animal droppings in the corner. He explained that the window had just been installed that day in honor of my arrival.

After dropping off my bags, I went out to dinner with the shrink/promoter and his wife (and their baby—yes, the one-week-old baby went with us everywhere). We chatted about all things American—Australians are very concerned with what happens here. As they say, "When America sneezes, Australia catches a cold." However, the whole time I was trying to remember the order for turning the levers, wondering what would happen if I accidentally blew up the house.

In the middle of dinner, I blurted out, "I just can't stay at that house. I'm scared I'm going to blow it up!"

The shrink laughed and said, "I was thinking the exact same thing. But there's no money in the budget—"

I told him that I didn't care about the cost; I would cover it. After going back to get my bags, I booked a room at the hotel on Rushcutter's Bay where I had stayed the last time I was in Sydney.

The next day was a rest day, so I went for a walk in the park along the bay, and there was a bloke there who was teaching people how to throw boomerangs; he had a gunnysack full of them. I joined in, and soon there were about twenty of us throwing boomerangs this way and that—mostly out of control. As I'm a lefty, it was a bit tricky. I had a couple of very close calls before I gave up. I didn't want to tell people I got clocked in the head with a boomerang in Australia. It's too much of a cliché.

For a few days I did radio and TV programs to promote the weekend concerts. The first day I took a cab to an ABC radio station. ABC radio in Australia is like our NPR—except that everybody listens to it. This was November 1988, and George H. W. Bush had just defeated Michael Dukakis in the American presidential election. One of the first questions I was asked during the interview was if I was pleased that Bush had won. I wasn't, but I didn't think it was appropriate to vent on Australian radio, so I said, "I didn't vote for him, but I hope he does a good job."

The next question was a surprise—the host asked who I was hoping would run to oppose him in four years. I told him that I particularly liked the Democratic senator from Maine, George Mitchell, who seemed smart, fair minded, and able to work with people on both sides of the aisle and who was about to be elected Senate majority leader. The Bush-Dukakis race was rather contentious, and I said that the United States needed a leader who would rise above all the partisan politicking.

Next we talked about music. My latest album at the time had a version of the Petula Clark song "Downtown" that I recorded as a duet with Livingston Taylor. During the interview, the host played that song and told me that Tony Hatch, who originally wrote "Downtown," lived in Sydney. I decided on the spot that I was going to find him while I was there, and that afternoon, back at my hotel, I took the Sydney phone book and called every T. Hatch listed in there. (Keep in mind that there were four million people living in Sydney.) Each phone call cost me seventy-five cents.

No luck, so I started with the "A. Hatch" listings, and I found him! I told him that I was an American performer on tour and that I had recorded his song on my most recent album. Could I take him to lunch?

No. Not interested.

So I asked if I could ask him some questions, and he agreed. Our exchange went like this:

"I had no idea an Australian wrote 'Downtown.' What inspired it?" I asked.

"Well," he said, "for one thing, I'm not Australian. I'm British, but I have lived here for years. Back in the 1960s I was assigned to write songs for Petula Clark, who was making the transition from child star to legitimate actress and singer.

"I wrote the song about my first visit to America—I flew in to Idlewild Airport (now JFK Airport), then took the airport bus to Times Square. I arrived at night, got off the bus, and was delighted by the bright neon lights and the life and buzz and activity all around me, and the song just appeared. In my mind, I wrote it for the Drifters. It never occurred to me that a white woman could even sing it. I heard it as a sort of doo-wop R&B song.

"I sat down and played for Petula what I had at the time: just the melody—'da da da-da da da da da-de-da-da-da-de-da da-da-dah . . . downtown.' She liked it and said it sounded like something she could do. So I finished the song, and the rest is history."

I asked if the Drifters ever recorded it.

"Not to my knowledge," he said, "though I know of at least three hundred different recordings in dozens of languages."

Being a New Yorker, I was so happy to know that it was Times Square that sparked that song. And as a songwriter, I understand why it often takes fresh eyes to see the unique beauty and charm in a setting that local songwriters probably walked through, uninspired, many times.

Over the years, I have told everybody I've met who might have a connection to the Drifters to let them know "Downtown" was written with them in mind. I hope they finally find out.

I did a few more radio interviews over the next few days and was surprised that the one question they all asked was, "Who is this George Mitchell, and why do you like him?" This was before the Internet, so I was caught a bit flat-footed every time Mitchell's name was mentioned. I sent Mitchell a postcard from Sydney telling him that I was an American musician on tour who had mentioned his name in a radio interview—and now there were Australians wondering if he had plans to one day run for president. When I returned to New York a few weeks later, there was a letter from him saying he didn't have any such plans, but he was very flattered. I am still a great admirer of his.

The day after that radio program, I did a live early-morning network TV show—the Australian equivalent of the *Today* show. I had had a bad night in my hotel—there was some mix-up, and I was switched to the side that faced train tracks. Every twenty minutes trains rumbled by, so I ended up with zero sleep. The next morning I was standing on the street, looking rather bedraggled, in search of a cab to the TV station. I was in a rotten mood.

I made this trip in part because I had this crazy idea I might get to meet Dame Edna, only to find that Barry Humphries was in England. The whole trip I was reading *Dame Edna's Bedside Companion*, a wonderful book whose pages are specially treated to, as Dame Edna proclaims on the dust jacket, "resist bedroom stains." But she was on the other side of the world.

I was feeling so blue, so lonely. At least I wasn't sick on this trip, though I did have a nagging earache that seemed to come and go. I stood there on that street, clutching my guitar, waving my arm around trying to attract a taxi, and wishing I'd see a familiar face.

A cab finally stopped. When I told the driver the address of the TV station, he whipped around and said, "Oh, you're that little American girl singer. I picked you up yesterday and took you to the ABC. And I listened to your interview. Did you find Tony Hatch?"

Four million people in Sydney, Australia, and I get the same cab driver just at the moment I was hoping to see a familiar face.

I told him how I did find Tony Hatch, and I also told him everything I had learned about the song "Downtown." After our nice talk, I was in a much better mood, but I didn't look so good from lack of sleep. So at the TV station, even though they spackled me but good, when I did the interview I wore a pair of teal-colored sunglasses that had pink and white palm trees on the sides. I decided that the glasses made me look a tiny bit like Dame Edna, so during the interview I mentioned I had come to Australia to find her, because I was adopted and Dame Edna was my biological mother.

I thought it was funny, but I think they thought I was slightly nuts. I was talking like I was serious, and I think they wondered if I knew that Dame Edna was really Barry Humphries. But it ended up being a fun interview—I played a song live that went over well, so I knew it would help sell tickets for the weekend.

I had three concerts scheduled at a club called the Three Weeds in the suburbs of Sydney, and I had a mid-afternoon sound check on Friday for the eight o'clock show. The concert promoter told me to be careful there until he arrived, and not to speak to the owner, who tended bar, because he was out on bail for murder. Holy crap. And he told me that under no circumstances should I go to the second floor, because it was a whorehouse. There was a small space behind the stage, behind the curtain, where I should change my clothes. I was not to go upstairs, period.

After my sound check, I needed to get some dinner, and since the main dining room wasn't open, I went into the bar to order food. So I had to talk to the owner. He seemed like a nice enough guy, and as I ate my food, we chatted. He asked me where I was from, that kind of thing, and if I was going back to my hotel before the show. I told him no, I wasn't. So he told me I should go upstairs and use one of the rooms up there as my dressing room.

I said I was told not to go up there because . . .

"No, it's not right now," he said. "There's nobody up there—it's completely empty. You can go up there. It's clean. Nobody will bother you."

He could see I wasn't convinced.

"Look," he said, leaning over close to me, "I've got some, let's say, *legal* problems. I'm not doing anything that could cause me any *more* trouble right now. Trust me, you'll be safe up there."

I *was* curious to see what a whorehouse looked like, but it was just a long, dark corridor of cheaply furnished hotel rooms. At the far end of the hall was a small bathroom, and it was bright and clean, so I chose that as my place to dress. I had a couple of hours to kill before the show, so I took my time dressing and putting on my makeup. Around 6:30 I was finished, and I figured I would go down to the performance room early and say hello to the early arrivals. I gathered my things and grabbed the bathroom doorknob . . . which came off in my hand. I shoved it back into the door, but I heard the knob on the other side fall out onto the floor. I wiggled the handle in the opening and tried to catch it on whatever it is it catches on, to no avail.

I was stuck in the bathroom of a whorehouse owned by a man out on bail for murder.

I'm such a good girl. How did this happen? The psychiatrist told me *not* to talk to the owner. Did I listen?

I spent about ten minutes monkeying around with the doorknob, but it wouldn't catch. I tried throwing all my weight against the door. That did nothing but hurt. (And it was foolish since the door opened inward.) So I yelled out the window, "Help! I'm stuck in the bathroom. Help! I'm up here on the second floor stuck in the bathroom!"

I could see nothing but trees out the window, so I didn't know if anybody could hear me. But then I thought maybe I should use the Australian word for "bathroom," so I changed my plea to, "Help! I'm stuck in the loo! I'm stuck in the loo upstairs in the . . . upstairs! Can anybody hear me??! I'm stuck in the *looooooooooooo!*"

I did this for about twenty minutes, but I didn't want to blow out my voice, and it didn't seem that anybody was within earshot anyway.

By now it was 7:15. The psychiatrist/promoter would be there in fifteen minutes. When he couldn't find me, how would he know where to look?

The bar was on the other side of the building from where I would be performing. He wouldn't think of asking the owner. My mind raced. How long would I have to wait to be found? How would I explain what I was doing in a whorehouse bathroom? What if they couldn't find me and called the police? They would eventually look upstairs and find me. I'd be embarrassed, but I'd be found. But what if the TV news was listening to the police scanner? What if the owner got in more trouble?

I sat down on the edge of the tub to figure out if there was anything else I could do. That's when I saw a wire coat hanger sticking out from behind the wall heater. I wiggled it free, bent the curved part tightly together, and stuck it in the doorknob hole, jiggling it up and down, this way and that. Miraculously, it caught, and the door opened. It was 7:25. I dashed down the dark hall and then casually walked down the stairs. Two minutes later the psychiatrist/promoter walked in. No, I didn't tell him.

It was a fun weekend. After one of the shows, an older man asked me to sign a cassette for his daughter.

"Please sign it to 'Elle,'" he said. "She's a model in America—Elle McPherson."

Years later I was a member of the Equinox gym on Amsterdam Avenue and Seventy-sixth Street. One day I was on a treadmill, trudging along, when Elle McPherson came in and got on the treadmill directly in front of mine. I wanted to tell her I had met her dad at the Three Weeds the same day I got locked in the bathroom of a whorehouse owned by a man out on bail for murder. (The bad girl in me likes to type that sentence.) But I didn't say anything to her. Sorry to disappoint you! But I didn't.

Before I left the states for that trip, I had asked my *Fast Folk* friend Jay Rosen to make me a cassette tape of all my favorite songs from the magazine, so I could have something to play before my concerts. During that trip, especially at the show at the Three Weeds, many audience members asked if that music was for sale. That convinced me to start making compilations that I could sell as I traveled. I can talk myself blue in the face about the talents of Don White, or Red Grammer, or Lynn Miles, but it's so much easier to hand people a disk so they can hear for themselves. Over the years I have given away more than I have sold, but every one of those compilations wins fans for life.

During that tour in Australia, I did some shows with Judy Small, one of Australia's finest singer/songwriters, who is now an attorney in Melbourne. She still sings—wonderful songs like the antiwar ballad "Mothers, Daughters, Wives"—but now she also fights the good fight in the courtroom. On that trip I also did shows with a hilarious Brit named Martyn Wyndham-Read who was a font of useless misinformation. One night after a show, we were standing out in a field—there were no lights anywhere except for the sky above, which held more stars than I had ever seen in my life. With different constellations visible in the Southern Hemisphere, I was shocked to look up and see Orion, one of the few constellations I can easily identify.

I blurted out, "Wait a minute! How come I can see Orion?! That's a constellation in the Northern Hemisphere!"

Martyn looked at me and said solemnly, "Because there's two of them."

"No!" I said. "Two of them? Are you kidding me?"

And with that he burst out laughing. In case you don't know, Orion is one of those constellations that can be seen in both hemispheres, depending on the time of year.

Another night, sitting around in the dressing room, we were talking about Australia's unique flora and fauna. I had had a slight run-in with a kangaroo that day. At a petting zoo, I paid twenty-five cents for a wafer ice-cream cone filled with pellets to feed the kangaroos—but nobody told me that they're smart and mean. Eye to eye with one of the kangaroos, making baby talk ("Come here you cute little kangaroo, I just want to be your friend. . . .") and holding out a pellet, I was startled when he snatched the ice-cream cone right out of my hand, the little bastard. I yelped and tried to grab it back. To spite me, he crushed it in his handlike paws and sneered at me. This happened in front of a kindergarten class, and the kids screamed with laughter.

Martyn told me Australia has all kinds of wily animals, like the Australian hoop snake, which lies in the grass waiting for an unsuspecting tourist to come traipsing through. When the snake finds a victim, he rears up, throws himself forward until he forms a hoop, bites his own tail, lassoes his victim, and squeezes him to death. And this snake can go up to thirty miles per hour!

Don't waste time Googling. It turns out there *is* no Australian hoop snake. Martyn is a big liar.

I also visited Bondi Beach, where there are nets to keep the sharks away from the swimmers and where men wear the smallest bathing suits in the world. That's one of my most vivid memories of Australia. And back then all the stores closed at five and were closed all day Saturday and Sunday. I still managed to do a fair bit of shopping when I was there—buying Dame Edna books, cassettes, albums, and sunglasses. But it would be years until I would finally meet her.

20

THE BIRTH
OF THE FOUR BITCHIN' BABES

When I returned from my second tour of Australia, I started thinking about putting together a compilation of all my favorite contemporary songs. It was later that year, during the summer of 1989, when I dreamed about making it a winter compilation album. I would include one of my songs and as many other songs as I could fit.

My song was "The Kind of Love You Never Recover From," which has become an audience favorite. When I originally recorded it, I put the capo on the second fret of the guitar, then played a G chord to start it off—so the song was really in the key of A. Years later I reworked the guitar chart to put the song in the key of A without using the capo. It's more difficult to play this way, but the guitar voicing is much more interesting. It's something I learned from Dave Van Ronk but didn't put into practice until many years later. He thought I used the capo way too much and encouraged me to rework the guitar charts for many of my songs.

I have heard many stories from strangers about this particular song of mine, which I've put in the "hard for me to sing *and* play" category. (Why do I do this to myself?!) Sally Fingerett said to me, "You hooked a big one"—meaning my song was the equivalent of catching a big fish. It was a song that was bigger than the experiences that had inspired it. I am still looking for the best way to perform it.

One way I introduce it is to say, "If you came with someone special tonight, this is the time to put your arm around them, look them in the eye . . . and think of somebody else." There was a time when I would light a candle onstage before I sang this song, then blow the candle out afterward. Other times I'd sing the song in total darkness. I stopped doing that after I got a letter from a woman who was at one of my shows that said, "Please don't ever turn the lights off again when you sing that song. You have no idea how it felt to be sitting next to my husband in the dark, hearing him cry, and know he wasn't thinking about me!"

I remember vividly the first time I sang it onstage, during a sound check at a big concert hall in Connecticut. This was before I had recorded it. I was one of the guest artists on a bill headed up by Tom Rush, who holds the distinction of being the first singer/songwriter to record a Joni Mitchell song—"Urge for Going"—before the rest of the world knew who she was. I thought the only people there were the sound and light crew. I wasn't planning on doing the song that night, and I didn't—but I wanted to see how it felt to sing it into a microphone in a big performance space.

Halfway through the song I noticed an older man in a suit and tie standing in the doorway at the back of the hall. After I finished my sound check, I went out to the lobby to check on the albums being set out, and I saw him again.

"Excuse me," he said softly, "but that song you sang—about that love you never forget—which album is that song on?"

I told him I hadn't recorded it yet.

He took my hand and said, "You must record that song. It's the story of my life. I couldn't believe when I heard the words. It's the woman I've loved my whole life, since I was twenty, but my parents didn't like her. I've never stopped thinking about her after all these years, and now, hearing your song, *that's my life! That's my life you sang!*"

He was practically in tears. I hugged him and promised him that I would record it. When I finally did, it found its way to Andrea Marcovicci, the first star in the theater/cabaret world to sing and record it, thereby introducing it to a new audience. A couple years later I received this letter:

April 1993

Dear Ms. Lavin:

I've wanted to write this letter for two years now to tell you how one of your songs prompted me to contact someone I've always wanted to meet.

The song is "The Kind of Love You Never Recover From." For me it described my mother and someone she was engaged to. They never saw each other again after she returned the ring, but growing up I always had his name buried in my mind.

After hearing that song, I called him. When I told him I was Katherine's daughter, the recognition after nearly forty years was instantaneous. We met for lunch and, with neither one of asking the other to do so, brought pictures. My mother's, frayed and yellowed, showed the passage of time. But his were in perfect condition. He offered me one, but not the photo where he held my mother in a loving bear hug, the hem of her dress pulled up, revealing her lacy slip. They were so young, a very handsome couple. I didn't take any of the photos, although I really wanted to.

He tried to keep lunch going as long as he could, and I was really glad he made the effort. He kept rubbing his eyes in disbelief. I felt such warmth and affection on his part for my mother. I wanted to explain to him why she made the decision she did (my interpretation of events). I wanted to make everything all right. But it already was all right. He waved his hand for me to say no more.

My story ends with a reunion. When I told my mother what I had done, she wasn't upset. In fact, she reacted like a schoolgirl. She called him. They met again one time, but never again after that. Neither felt guilty about their respective spouses because neither had regrets.

If I hadn't heard that song, I know I would never have met him. And I'm so glad that I did. Time stood still when I talked with him. I felt like I had met him before, like I was there when they dated, rather than waiting to be born in another lifetime.

Sincerely,

Bernadette

The first recording of that song appeared on the compilation cassette titled *On a Winter's Night* that also had twenty other songs by twenty of my favorite singer/songwriters. The first time I had it available at one of my shows was in Sanders Theater in Cambridge, Massachusetts, in December 1989. I shared the bill with Buskin & Batteau, the acoustic folk/rock band led by David Buskin and Robin Batteau. I like to describe their music as "the thinking man's rock 'n' roll." Near the end of my set I sang "The Kind of Love You Never Recover From," and afterward I held up the *On a Winter's Night* cassette. I told the audience, "If you like that song, it's not on an album yet, but it is on this cassette with twenty other singer/songwriters I think you will love."

That night 250 cassettes were sold. I knew I was on to something. I had made two thousand cassettes and paid $200 to each of the other songwriters to cover royalties. I sold a lot of the cassettes—but also gave away a lot of them. I basically broke even, but it was wonderful to get the music out there to a lot of potential new fans. It was also an inexpensive way to "test the waters" with this project.

Immediately I started talking to different record companies about a commercial release and planning a four-artist *On a Winter's Night* concert tour for the following winter. But now it was spring, and I was eager to get some kind of "group" thing going sooner. I met with Allan Pepper, owner of the Bottom Line club in New York, and we tossed around some ideas.

Allan looked at the list of songwriters on *On a Winter's Night* and asked if there were three other artists whom I could envision working with. There were: Sally Fingerett, Megon McDonough, and Patty Larkin. They didn't know one another, but I knew all of them and felt that our musical styles and personalities would mesh.

Then Allan said, "What you need to do is give a snappy title to the show. Once you've got that, you'll get work. I will book you."

Sally Fingerett had written a song called "Do Me, Show Me, Buy Me, Love Me, Give Me," which was very popular, and that inspired the show title *Buy Me Bring Me Take Me Don't Mess My Hair*, but Allan thought it needed a subtitle. The son of a friend of Sally's was into surfing and used the term *bitchin'* to describe everything he liked, so Sally suggested "Life According to Four Bitchin' Babes," and it stuck.

Allan Pepper always liked fun titles and found them essential for selling tickets to his club. I recently e-mailed him, asking if he kept a file of some of his favorite show names, and he sent me a lengthy list that included these:

> July 1–2, 1983
>
> "Coming Distractions"
>
> 50 years of movie trailers . . .
>
> "Sometimes the coming attractions were better than the movies!"
>
> Including such trailers as: *Citizen Kane, Rock Around the Clock, Werewolves on Wheels*
>
> All seats $5.00

> October 28, 1984
>
> "Promise Them Anything"
>
> 50 years of political campaign commercials featuring rare and extraordinary footage from campaign spots for FDR, Eisenhower, Stevenson, JFK . . . plus celebrity endorsements from John Wayne, Burt Lancaster, Chuck Conners, and Janet Leigh . . . plus the first known political film ever made (the presidential election of 1908)
>
> Hosted by John Hall
>
> All seats $6.00

> December 17–19, 1991
>
> "Who's on First"
>
> A tribute to opening acts . . . sometimes the hardest acts to follow

Black 47, the Reputations, the Stingers
Hosted by Vin Scelsa

October 31, 1992
"Corn on Macabre" [say it out loud]
A Halloween comedy bash with Emo Philips and William Shaw
All seats $15.00

A couple of the shows became long-running series. Having a good title, an excellent host, and first-rate songwriters meant that a lot of people came back again and again. Allan Pepper ran the venue for thirty years, so advice from him holds a lot of weight.

A couple days later I sent Allan another e-mail asking him to explain his philosophy of not booking the same headliner with the same opener twice, and this was his response:

Chris,

I always took the selection of an opening act very seriously because it sets the tone for the evening. Unfortunately, a miscalculation can make a headliner fight harder to engage the audience that paid money to see them. To answer your question, there were many reasons that I tried not to book the same opening act twice for the same headliner. Part of it had to do with the creative challenge it offered me. Some of the fun of putting a show together is combining different elements that might not have seemed obvious at first.

Another reason I didn't like repeating myself was that I always wanted it to be fresh for the audience, so that someone who came to the club for every Janis Ian show or every Chris Smither show or every Suzanne Vega show got an extra bonus by seeing someone new as well.

I always felt that an audience appreciated that little extra effort that goes into putting together a show where 1 + 1 = 3. It's like being invited to a dinner party at someone's home where the entrée is something that you have had on many occasions, but the appetizer makes it a totally different dining experience. It is an experience that is enhanced if you ask your host for the recipe for the appetizer. . . . I always thought of myself not as a booker, but as a producer. Anyone can book a show, but not everyone can produce one.

Allan

Amen. After reading Allan's words, you can see why, back in 1990, armed with our new *Buy Me Bring Me Take Me Don't Mess My Hair . . . Life According to Four Bitchin' Babes* title that he helped create, we felt confident booking concerts across the country that summer. For that first tour we shared the stage, taking turns doing songs on various topics. During the intermission we asked the audience to put suggestions in a hat, which we drew from during the second half of the show. We finished with a couple of group numbers. We had a ball everywhere we went!

For the first leg of the tour we started in Chicago, then played Boulder, Salt Lake City, Seattle, and ended up in San Francisco. The last night, after the concert at the Great American Music Hall (the show where I met TV guitar teacher Laura Weber), we sat in a hotel room and did the final accounting for the entire trip. We were stunned to realize we had spent more money than we had made, and here we were, thousands of miles from home. How was this possible?? We had another set of concerts that summer that would start at the Birchmere in Alexandria, Virginia. So we were already in the red and had three thousand miles to travel to do our next show.

I felt awful. This whole thing had been my idea, and though we'd had a ton of fun, none of us could afford to lose money. We decided we would have to tape our show at the Birchmere and release it as a live album in the hopes that we would eventually break even. We had no plans for taking it beyond that brief summer tour—all of us would continue to work solo.

A few weeks later, at the Birchmere, Billy Wolf, the sound man, ran a tape directly off the board and gave it to us after the show. Dan Green,

Sally's husband at the time, edited it down at his recording studio in Columbus, Ohio. Rounder released it the following January, and then we started getting inquiries about doing more Four Bitchin' Babes shows, especially after the album was nominated for Folk Album of the Year by NAIRD, the National Association of Independent Record Distributors. Since both Patty and I were on the *On a Winter's Night* tour with David Wilcox and John Gorka, the idea of more Babes shows wasn't possible for the time being.

On a Winter's Night was released commercially by North Star Records, a small indie label out of Providence, Rhode Island, but the company insisted the compilation be shortened to fifteen songs. Since I was the producer, I had to make the cuts, and it was difficult to have to disappoint six songwriters. CD manufacturing was still very new and cost more than it does now, so twenty-one songs on the disk would have made it too expensive. Unfortunately, the cover artwork was less than thrilling. It was an oil painting of a snow-covered cottage in the woods, but the printing process made it look like the house was surrounded by yellow snow—not exactly appealing.

The four of us—Patty, John, David, and I—did a thirty-six-city tour, and I quickly learned that two women and two men traveling together was very different from four women traveling together. David and John are two of the most talented songwriters around, but there was a bit of good-natured competitiveness between them, so the shows didn't quite feel like the traveling pajama party the Babes shows felt like. Very often we traveled separately, meeting up at the concert venues, then going on separately to the next city—so we didn't develop the rapport the Babes did, though the shows themselves were very well received, and we all liked each other and got along well. All the venues we played asked that we do it again the following year.

At the end of the *On a Winter's Night* tour, I turned my attention to the idea of more Four Bitchin' Babes shows—and I knew I needed to decide which group effort I would be part of. I probably could have continued to do both, but one of the most important reasons for these shows was to create a musical event that would promote not just the four onstage, but the others on the CD on sale in the lobby—putting to work Dave Van Ronk's motto, "When music of quality sells, it's good for all of us." By stepping aside from one of these group shows, I could create an opportunity for another songwriter to participate. I chose to go with the Babes.

In subsequent *On a Winter's Night* tours, Cheryl Wheeler took part, then David Wilcox stepped aside and Cliff Eberhardt took his place, then Patty Larkin left and Lucy Kaplansky came onboard. My hunch is that one of these upcoming winters, that tour will hit the road again—though I don't know who will do it next time around.

When North Star Records went out of business, Rounder Records took over manufacture and distribution of *On a Winter's Night* and the cover was changed. To me the dark pen-and-ink drawing of a house on a midnight blue background looked Halloweenish—not what I was hoping for. But it was still an improvement over the "yellow snow" cover.

Fifteen years after *On a Winter's Night* was first released, Rounder sold out of stock and contacted me to say they were going to have it repressed. I asked if I could make some changes to it, and they agreed.

By now Cliff Eberhardt had done the *On a Winter's Night* tour a number of times, but he wasn't on the original version. But he definitely deserved to be on it now, and his song "Your Face" fit in perfectly.

As long as we were making that change, I thought, "why not make a few more?" so I added more of my favorite songs and subtitled the album as a special fifteenth-anniversary edition. I have always loved Judy Collins's song "Secret Gardens of the Heart," and she allowed us to use a solo version of it. By the time we added "Last Night" by Lynn Miles, "Remember When We Were Just Friends" by Annie Bauerlein and Chip Mergott, "Another Time and Place" by Dave Van Ronk, "In Our Hands" by Kenny White and Shawn Colvin, and "Lancelot's Tune (Guinevere)" by Buskin & Batteau, we had a twenty-song compilation. The economics of CD manufacturing had changed, so now it wasn't prohibitively expensive to have that many songs on a single disk. And I was able to change the packaging.

A new cover was designed for this version of *On a Winter's Night* based on a close-up photograph of snowflakes snapped by a photographer named Jim Zuckerman. Again I ended up dissatisfied. The cover copy was white against a blue background, and unfortunately the style and size of the font wasn't large enough to be legible. The background color ink bled into the spaces where the type should have been, making the text difficult to read.

Since the cover just wasn't right, I had an additional one thousand promotional CDs pressed without the CD booklet, instead packaged in a cardboard digipak. I sent twenty-five of these to each of the artists because I didn't want the first image for them to see to be a bad printing job. (*Especially* Judy Collins. To get someone of her stature on this project took a lot of work, and I just couldn't bear her seeing a poor-quality CD package.) I asked the record company to hold off on sending out the commercial version to the artists until I had mailed out the promotional copies with the better cover, and they agreed. But somehow, it happened anyway. Everyone saw the bad one first. The best-laid plans . . .

Here's a challenge to all you music collectors: if you gather all five of the different versions of *On a Winter's Night*—the original cassette, the North Star "yellow snow" cover, the Rounder "haunted house" cover, the Rounder fifteenth-anniversary "snowflake" cover, and the special "promotional" digipak version—and show them to me, I will do a free concert in your living room.

All told, there will eventually be six different versions of *On a Winter's Night,* though it started its journey as a twenty-one-song cassette at Sanders Theater in 1989 and was also the jumping-off point for the Four Bitchin' Babes.

After the series of concerts the Babes did in the summer of 1990, the release of the live album in early 1991, and the requests for more shows, I knew I was up for it, as were Sally and Megon, but Patty Larkin had just signed a multirecord solo deal with Wyndham Hill and was booked solid. We started looking around for who else could be part of the group.

I had this grand notion that there would be a pool of twenty or so female singer/songwriters who could all be part of a Four Bitchin' Babes project. My thought was that whenever a promoter or presenter wanted a Four Bitchin' Babes concert, we'd see which four were available for a particular date, and those four would do the show. The promoter would then make up posters using the photos of those four musicians. This way we could spread the wealth. We found out, however, that promoters and presenters only wanted one photo with four women in it. They wanted to know exactly who would be in each show and didn't like my idea *at all*. So we invited Julie Gold to be the official fourth Babe. Even though she had never been on the road before, audiences already knew who she was just from her song "From a Distance," and having a Grammy winner in the group was a nice boost for all of us. Julie was a lot of fun to travel with because everything on the road was new and exotic to her.

Sadly, Julie's dad died while she was with the Babes, and at every concert she carried a St. Christopher medal in her pocket that he had given her. It didn't matter that Julie was Jewish; it was a gift from her dad that she cherished. One of the concerts she did with us was at the Woodland Park Zoo in Seattle—we played for more than five thousand people one night, and later on at the hotel Julie discovered that her medal was missing. She was distraught, and the next day it was raining, but we all went back to the zoo and searched the stage and the grounds surrounding it. I thought there was no chance we'd find it, but Julie spotted it in the grass about fifty yards from the stage. We all felt it was a miracle.

Julie recalls:

> My stint as a Babe was fairly short-lived. I guess you could say I was "the reluctant Babe." I replaced Patty Larkin (though that is not really an accurate statement, as Patty Larkin is irreplaceable). I had already known Christine for many years, and over those years she had included me in many worthwhile musical productions. So when Christine invited me to be a Babe, I knew it was a good, original musical opportunity. I felt lucky to become part of such a talented, fun group.
>
> I am a very neurotic New Yorker, however, entrenched in my idiosyncrasies. I don't travel well, and I'm not a great "group player" . . . by that I mean I can't really "jam" musically. I am best suited to accompany myself when singing my songs. My singing is sincere, but I can't sing harmony at all, and I'm not comfortable "hamming it up." These were all issues that made me "the reluctant Babe."

But all that aside, it was an excellent, memorable learning experience. We played all over the United States. Indoors, outdoors, giant places, intimate places . . . It was scary at times.

For all the thrilling musical memories we shared, my favorite times were after the shows. We'd choose someone's hotel room and meet there after dropping off our stuff and getting comfortable. In those days we got paid in cash. I remember we'd buy a *ton* of candy, and there would be cash and candy on the bed, and we'd jump on the bed and eat our candy and count our cash. It was innocent and simple. We really had these fantastic "pajama parties" after every show. It was quite bonding.

I remember Seattle in particular. I had never been there, and when I saw Mount Rainier it absolutely took my breath away. I still think it is one of the most spectacular sights to behold. So as luck would have it, Meg's hotel room looked out at Mount Rainier. I, on the other hand, was on the second floor overlooking the parking lot. We did our "cash and candy" frolic in Sally's room, which was across the hall from Meg's. I asked Meg if I could please go into her room for a moment. She obliged.

I went in, hoping for a moment of serenity and a chance to gaze upon the magnificent Mount Rainier. Unbelievably, my naiveté and the fact that I'm a New Yorker to the core made me actually believe that Mount Rainier would be illuminated somehow, like the Empire State Building or the Chrysler building, which I see every night of my life.

Of course, I stared out the window into complete and utter darkness. I was *mortified* by my stupidity and sheepishly went back to the Babes. I never told them what I was doing in Meg's room. It took me *years* to finally share that story.

I've not been back to Seattle since my days with the Babes. We're all still friends; they're still going strong. It's a rich part of my history, and I'm very grateful to have been a part of it all.

One weekend out of each month the Four Bitchin' Babes did concerts, sometimes two or three cities in a single weekend. The other three weekends I did solo shows, so it was a nice change of pace. Both Sally and Meg were married with families, so being away one weekend a month fit nicely into their schedules. Although Julie had a great time on the road, she missed New York and let us know that she could do the shows for a year, at most, and that we should be on the lookout for a replacement.

I came down with the flu on one of the Babes show weekends, and at the last minute Sally asked Debi Smith, from Falls Church, Virginia, to fly in to replace me at a show in Columbus, Ohio. Debi had recorded five albums with her sister Megan as the Smith Sisters and had a stellar reputation on the folk scene. She was an immediate hit with the audience and with the other Babes, so when Julie was ready to move along, Debi took her place.

Looking back now on all the changes the Four Bitchin' Babes have gone through, it was Debi's joining the group that clearly revealed the secret to the group's longevity. Patty Larkin is a masterful guitarist with rock/jazz influences in her writing and performing. When Julie Gold took her place, her strengths as a songwriter and pianist with a definite pop sensibility expanded the group's sound. When Debi Smith replaced Julie, she brought her formidable vocal ability—she has a powerful soprano voice and is comfortable singing folk, pop, country, and even opera. Besides the guitar, she plays the Irish bodhran, a handheld drum, which was a brand-new sound for the group. When I saw how her unique skills jump-started us in a new direction, not only did I no longer worry about what would happen the next time one of us would leave the group, I realized that changes of Babes was essential to the group's continued success.

As Debi Smith recalled in 2009:

> I had been to see the Babes a number of times before I became part of the group. Sally and I were old friends from the NACA days (National Association of Collegiate Activities), which was an organization that helped book colleges. We would hang out at the conventions and do crazy things like jog through the Opryland hotel after eating too many M&Ms!

> I knew Chris through the Smith Sisters—we once played at the Speakeasy on MacDougal Street in the Village, and we met again at one of Dick Cerri's concerts. When I had my son Lee, my sister

became a lobbyist for renewable energy (the next logical career move after having been a folksinger!). I was thinking I was going to take a break from performing, but I missed it too much before long! I teamed up with Al Petteway to do a solo project, and we went to Martha's Vineyard for the singer/songwriters' retreat. Little did I know that the Babes were keeping an eye out since Julie was contemplating songwriting full time. I guess I must have done something right, because I was chosen to sub when Chris got sick in Columbus! That opened the door to being a member of the Babes eventually.

At the time I joined the Babes, I had just found out that my son had a form of autism called Asperger's. Having a child with autism is a blessing in many ways and is also very challenging. I was so grateful to be in a group where I toured on weekends a couple times a month but was home most of the time for my son. So I had the best girlfriends in the world to perform with and take a break from the stress that is part of being a parent of a child with a disability, while still being available to make sure my son was getting the care he needed. As Sally would say, it was like what they tell you on a plane—putting my oxygen mask on first so that I was able to help others! It made all the difference. Still does.

Lee was three then and is twenty-one now. I remember once he was on a baseball team and they called to chat with me. I had just joined the Babes. Lee answered the phone and said, "Here's my mom . . . she's a Bitchin' Babe!" That was an interesting conversation!

I stayed with the Babes from 1990 to 1997. The last year I was with the group, I felt a bit restless. At every show I would spend the intermission in the lobby collecting song suggestions from the audience, and more and more often people were asking me to do songs like "Shopping Cart of Love" and "The Kind of Love You Never Recover From." "Shopping Cart" was simply too long (almost ten minutes) to do in a group show, and "Kind of Love" was a long ballad that I felt would slow the show down. When it was obvious I was constantly turning down performing my most requested songs, I knew this group format probably wasn't the best option for me.

Some of my fondest onstage and backstage memories were with the Babes, however: every time we sang harmony on Julie Gold's anthem "From a Distance" and Sally Fingerett's "Home Is Where the Heart Is"; the time at Sanders Theater during sound check when Julie sang her brand-new "Good Night, New York," and one by one everyone—including the sound and light crew—stopped what they were doing to listen. Once, after our concert in Fort Lauderdale, a woman shyly came backstage to say hello. She told us her daughter was also a songwriter and maybe we knew of her— Carole King. We all squealed, embraced her in a big group hug, then, with her mom, silently sent good juju vibes to Carole.

We had many guest Babes as we traveled—in LA, Carolyn Hester joined us for a song; in Alexandria, Virginia, Mary Chapin Carpenter; in Seattle, Kristina Olsen; in New York, Mary Travers of Peter Paul & Mary.

PP&M recorded Sally's song "Home Is Where the Heart Is," which appeared on the very first Babes' album. Sally and Mary Travers had become friends—Sally was filmed as part of a PP&M program for PBS. Although I knew Mary, I get shy in certain situations, so I asked Sally to ask Mary to be a guest vocalist at the end of "What Was I Thinking?" for the next Babes' album, *Fax it! Charge It! Don't Ask Me What's for Dinner!*

A few weeks later Mary came backstage at our concert in Stamford, Connecticut. Sally had set up a portable recording station in the dressing room, and we had all worked on the script for Mary. She looked it over, tweaked it, then recorded it—before our show started.

Mary Travers is the voice that tells us what to buy on the Home Shopping Network, then later in the song she berates us for singing a song that had no ending ("Girls! Girls! What are thinking? / This is not a good career move! / I've been in this business a long time! / What are you doing??").

Mary refused payment, so we chipped in to get her a special thank-you gift. On my next trip to New England I stopped at the all-night LL Bean store. I picked the biggest, baddest Swiss Army Knife they carried and had it engraved Miss Mary T. She loved it.

A few months later we were performing at the Bottom Line and asked Mary to join us as a special guest. She brought her pianist, Russ Walden, and surprised us onstage by insisting Russ do a song in the show. Yes, it's been said many times about PP&M: they don't just talk the talk, they walk the walk. Up until that moment the Bitchin' Babes had been an all-girl affair, but Mary changed that—opening the door for future "Man-Babes" to follow (Jonathan Edwards, John Gorka, Dave Van Ronk).

Ten years later Mary Travers was diagnosed with leukemia and waiting for a bone marrow donor. I visited her at Memorial Sloan-Kettering Cancer Center, bringing along my all-purpose feel-good food: french toast bread pudding. Mary had lost a lot of hair and was wearing a funny Rocky and Bullwinkle–style hat. She was bored out of her skull. She loved bawdy jokes, so with her friend Paul Kehoe we set up a "getwellmary" project asking her fans to send messages and jokes. Eventually thousands of e-mails were received. Many fans told sweet stories and detailed remembrances of PP&M concerts. Paul printed out the e-mails, and Mary read every single one. They ended up in huge binders that she displayed on a table at her house in Connecticut.

That August I was invited to be part of an annual PP&M concert at a big outdoor venue in Ocean Grove, New Jersey. Peter Yarrow and Noel Paul Stookey were on the bill with the Chad Mitchell Trio. Mary was recuperating but not ready to return to the stage. Both Peter Yarrow and Noel Paul are perfectly capable of performing solo or as a duo, but it felt strange to not have Mary at the show. The concert was filmed for Mary. We all waved to her from the stage, and the audience waved and cheered from their seats. Even so, the night was slightly bizarre. The audience booed when Chad Mitchell talked about the number of Iraqis killed in the war. I got booed when I sang my sarcastic George Bush ending to "What Was I Thinking?" Who could imagine that political songs wouldn't be appreciated at a Peter Paul & Mary event?

About a year later I got tickets for Harry and me for the return of Peter Paul & Mary to Carnegie Hall. The audience erupted in whoops of joy when Mary walked onstage. She looked newly svelte in a flowing gown. Her trademark long blonde hair was now a short bob, but her voice was the same as ever—strong and passionate. She joked about learning that her bone marrow donor was a female Republican. It was the last time I saw Mary perform live with PP&M. She died in September 2009. I'm glad to remember her as vibrant and happy onstage.

Having Mary Travers as part of the Babes was a highlight that made up for the occasional train wrecks we had on the road.

We Babes still laugh about the disastrous performance sponsored by a radio station in Des Moines, Iowa. When we checked into the downtown hotel, the front desk clerk said to us, "We saved our most special room for you! The one with the ka-choosy tub!" When we got to that room, we saw that it also had mirrors on the ceiling. You had to wonder what shenanigans went on there. We all lay down on the bed together, looked at our reflection in the ceiling, and laughed ourselves silly.

Sally and I got a touch of food poisoning a few hours before the show but managed to play through it. The venue was a rock club that had no seats, decorated with mannequin body parts dangling from the ceiling. The audience had to sit on a cold concrete floor ringed with pool tables and pinball machines (yes, our music was accompanied by billiard balls clicking and mechanical pinging), and a thick fog of cigarette smoke hung in the air.

Halfway through the concert I asked if it would be possible for the smokers to put out their cigarettes, a request that elicited booing. At one point Julie put her head down on the piano; looked at Sally, Meg, and me; and mouthed, "This is DEATH!" Finally the show ended, and some people in the audience stood up and screamed, "Can we smoke NOW???" We ran backstage.

Not everybody hated us, however—there was actually brisk business at the merchandise table. We sold a lot of cassettes that night, but a few minutes later all the people who bought the cassettes came back demanding refunds because it wasn't *our* music on the cassettes—it was a fire-and-brimstone preacher giving a sermon! It obviously was a mix-up at the duplicating house. Our only way of making any money for that concert was through merchandise sales, so we watched our profit vaporize before our eyes.

That was a horrible night, but we got through it, and it made all of our successful nights all the sweeter since we knew how quickly bad things can happen in this business. Luckily, nightmare evenings like that were rare.

Over the years, as the Babes' reputation grew, in some ways it was becoming what I had always hoped it would—if there was a show where one of us couldn't make it, a substitute Babe would step in. The summer when Megon McDonough was pregnant with her son Denvir, Cheryl Wheeler took her place at a festival we played in Haines, Alaska, and then later on at the Philadelphia Folk Festival. A couple years later when Megon was starring in *Always . . . Patsy Cline*, Janis Ian stepped in.

I remember that show vividly because Janis Ian is one of my heroes, but also because it was the first time that Janis sold her own CDs directly off the stage. She had a been a music star for so many years on major labels that it simply wasn't something she did. So that night was an experiment for her, and she was stunned when the check for her merchandise sales had a comma in it.

Whenever the Babes traveled, Sally Fingerett oversaw all the details and any driving that needed to be done. She also advanced all the dates, went over the sound details before each concert, and took care of all the travel arrangements that a road manager or a travel agent would normally handle. Without Sally's behind-the-scenes work, the group could never have thrived. Because at any given time the four Babes could be in four different cities, it was no easy feat to have everyone arrive at the same destination at around the same time. But Sally made it work—and continues to make it work—beautifully.

In late 1996 I did a benefit concert in New Jersey, and it was there that I saw Camille West perform. I knew in my bones that she would be a good replacement for me. When I told the girls I thought it was my time to step away, they were all a bit concerned since I had started the project. More than concerned; I think they thought it was *the end*. But I knew they were worrying for naught, because Sally, "the business Babe," had become much more important to the group than I was. While I held up the comedic part of the show, I knew that Camille West could keep that aspect of the show going strong.

So in 1997, after having appeared on three Babes CDs, I stepped away, and Camille West stepped in. She was an instant hit with her song "Viagra on the Waters" and later with "Nobody Beats My B.O.B." (If you want to know what B.O.B. stands for, you will have to buy the Four Bitchin' Babes CD *Some Assembly Required*.) Camille's songs have become so identified with the Babes that a number of times people have asked me to sing "Viagra on the Waters," thinking it's my song, and I have to witness the looks of sad disappointment when I admit that I didn't write it.

As I expected, not only did the group *not* suffer when I moved on, the addition of Camille jump-started it yet again. I sat in a few times for "reunion" shows and watched Camille work her magic in front of adoring crowds.

In between Babes dates, Megon McDonough pursued theatrical work and writing projects, and soon she felt it was time to move on. Meg says:

> In 1989 I was playing with astrology and numerology, and heard from an astrologer the spelling of my name was a "hard vibration." So I put an *o* in place of the *a* just for fun, and Chris Lavin called me to join her on tour with some of her favorite artists! I'd say that *o* worked pretty darn well. The Babes were born.
>
> I toured with the Babes for twelve years. I loved every configuration of the group and had the best time you can imagine. And *got paid!* I mean . . . come on, how blessed is that?
>
> You never know where your life is going to take you, that's for sure. And I have learned to say, "Yes, and . . ." to life. I have learned to take it all one day at a time and not to take myself or life too seriously, but to love my life and the people in it deeply and gratefully.

Megon was replaced by none other than Suzzy Roche of the Roche Sisters, who were then on hiatus. Suzzy was an excellent addition to the group because, with her sisters Maggie and Terre, the Roches set a high bar when it came to vocal harmonies. With her in the group, the Babes' vocals were now tighter, and that was no coincidence.

But Suzzy had also been involved in acting projects, too (she is in one of my all-time favorite films, *Crossing Delancey,* written and directed by Joan Micklin Silver). For the next couple of years, Nancy Moran, a sassy and clever singer/songwriter from Nashville, subbed when Suzzy was in

Europe with the avant garde theatrical company the Wooster Group. Nancy brought a country influence that was new to the group, plus a very solid voice that's perfect for harmonizing. She proved to be road ready and the perfect team player, so when Suzzy was ready to move on, Nancy moved in.

It was at this time Camille needed to slow down. Sally, meanwhile, was a judge at a songwriting competition at the Kerrville Folk Festival in Texas, where one of the contestants was Deirdre Flint, a very funny songwriter from Philadelphia. Sally watched Deirdre's effect on the audience and made a mental note that she'd be a great Babe. She called her when Camille's seat was open.

It was clear that the Babes' format was a comfortable fit for Deirdre, plus she plays bass, an instrument the group hadn't used except in the recording studio. Besides bringing a new sound to the live shows, Deirdre brought her unique fashion sense, ratcheting up the Babes' bling factor.

Sally Fingerett remembers:

> I'll never forget that phone call. It was early evening, March 1990. I was chasing my four-year-old daughter, EJ, fresh out of the tub, as she ran around the house in nothing but a hooded towel, pretending to be "Princess Everything." I gave up trying to catch her so I could catch the ringing phone.

> It was my New York pal Christine Lavin. A few months before, Chris had included my song "Wild Berries" on her compilation CD *On a Winter's Night*. Now she was calling to ask if I'd like to do a couple of gigs "in the round" that coming summer. I went mental when she mentioned Patty Larkin and Megon McDonough, and I could not believe that Christine Lavin was calling *me*, offering to share her concert stages. There in the kitchen, I leaned my back against the cabinet, sliding down to a crumpled and astounded mess on the floor, as if I'd been poked in the eye by a winning lottery ticket.

> The thought of leaving my husband and young daughter to fend for themselves so that I might perform again seemed OUTRAGEOUS.

Fortunately for me, my (then) husband, Dan Green, a songwriter himself, couldn't have been more supportive.

As a family, we decided that I should give it a try. I would show up at gigs, shifting gears on a dime, one minute having just scrubbed crayon off a wall, and the next minute taking a bow for a standing ovation. I was so blessed to have these gigs that balanced my mommy thing. No Sylvia Plath hotline for me!

And yet I was so conflicted. I knew my EJ would miss me at night. I felt compelled to illustrate the importance of Mommy working and being away a few days a month.

Lightbulb!

Arriving home from a tour one Sunday night, I sat her down at the kitchen table. I laid out all the cash I had earned that weekend, stacking the bills into little piles.

"Okay, sweetie, here's the money Mommy earned while singing, and now we have to pay our bills. First, let's pay the people who let us live in this house," I said, scooping up a little pile of dough.

"Here's the money for the electric company; you know, lights, the cassette player, the toaster." Scooping stack number two.

"Got to pay the cable company so we can have our cartoons and CNN." Scooping stack number three.

". . . the phone company, so we can talk to Grandma." Scooping stack number four.

"Here's the money for the grocery store, for apples and cheese and cookies and milk." Scooping stack number five.

On and on I went until there was but a lone ten dollar bill on the table.

"Hey, EJ, look at this," I said, excited. "This is left over for us. Mommy's singing money covered everything and left us with a little extra for a McDonald's Happy Meal! Let's go!"

From that moment on, she understood that I never "left her" but rather "went to work" to support the family.

Now, almost twenty years later, I pinch myself every day. I'm grateful to have had this amazing opportunity, to have shared concert stages (and *stages of life!*) with all these amazingly brilliant and multitalented women who have comprised the Babes. But most importantly, I am grateful that my pal Christine Lavin included me in one of her wacky ideas that blossomed into a remarkable and enduring stage show. Thanks to the Babes, I've been able to make a living doing what I love while being able to take care of my very own Bitchin' Babe, EJ.

Thanks so much, girls, for sharing your thoughts. This can be a very lonely business—but not when we get together. Happily, two decades later, the Four Bitchin' Babes are still going strong—Sally Fingerett, Debi Smith, Nancy Moran, and Deirdre Flint. Their concert has evolved into a theatrical show—I was in the audience when they played B. B. King's in New York City last year, and I felt so proud knowing that I was part of the group's history. I hope someday we can do a reunion concert with all the Babes, past and present, onstage together, and swapping songs, stories, fashion tips, gossip, and recipes.

If you are a solo singer/songwriter trying to figure out how to make a living, think about teaming up with others who do what you do. It was my association with Jack Hardy, the *Fast Folk Musical Magazine*, and the Speakeasy cooperative that inspired me to produce my own compilation albums, like *On a Winter's Night*, that in turn spun off the *On a Winter's Night* tour and then the Four Bitchin' Babes. You can keep your solo identity while still being part of a larger group.

For the Babes concerts the four performers share the stage all night, but an alternate way to have a four-artist show is to have each performer do a miniset of fifteen to seventeen minutes in the first half of the concert, then after intermission sit side by side and swap songs. This way each of you has a chance to establish your music in a single set, and then it will be very interesting to see how you interact once the audience has a good idea of who you are as individuals.

I've only done that kind of format a few times, and I always found it quite satisfying. Crucial to the success of this format is that everybody stick to the strict time constraints of the first half. Tom Paxton taught me the best way to keep track of time onstage is to wear a watch on your left wrist, with the face of the watch on the inside of your wrist. Then you can keep track of time as you play your guitar without making it obvious. Normal time stops when you step out onstage, so you must wear a watch, especially when you are sharing the bill with other musicians.

A couple of years after *On a Winter's Night*, I put together an autumn-themed compilation on Rounder called *When October Goes*. Megon Mc-Donough sings that title song. She is one of the best singers I have ever heard, and she has a one-woman show called *HER WAY: An Interesting Bunch of Gals*, where she sings/tells the stories of some of the most influential female singers of the twentieth century. She is also planning more performances of *Always . . . Patsy Cline*, a show tailor-made for someone with Meg's vocal prowess.

Not long after meeting Meg in Aspen way back in 1981, I got her some gigs in New York. One of them was opening for Dave Van Ronk at the Bitter End. She brought me onstage during her set, and we sang "Air Conditioner" together. After the last show, we had dinner with Dave. He looked at us and said, "You know, if you two really want to make money in this business, you should work together."

This was way back in 1982 or 1983. I know I laughed really hard—as much as I adored Meg's work, I would never have dreamed we could work together. Dave saw something about us *years* before his prediction came true.

Meg stayed at my apartment that trip. She has always been very health-conscious—me, not so much. I remember she tactfully tried to give me tips on healthy eating that I pretty much ignored.

That last night, riding back uptown in a taxi, Meg and I were talking about how the shows went and who was there, when we were interrupted by the cab driver, who was looking at us in his rearview mirror.

"I know you! I know you!" he said, pointing at me.

Megon said to him, "Well, she's a well-known folksinger who does concerts around New York City. It's no wonder you know her."

"No," he said, "I used to work at the Pizza Joint. You came in there all the time!"

Megon had a big "I told you so" look on her face, and yes, I was embarrassed to be recognized for my fondness for pizza. But that's life in the big city. You think nobody knows your secrets, when everybody does.

I've tried to include Megon in every compilation project I have done because I know when she does have her huge breakthrough success, it will help sell all my projects (and you thought I was purely altruistic—nope!). In the back of this book you'll find a listing of all the artists on all the compilation projects I've worked on. I love them all. Buy their CDs! You'll thank me later.

I've been asked many times if I am going to do a spring and summer compilation as companion pieces to *On a Winter's Night* and *When October Goes*, but as of yet I haven't. There's something about cold weather that inspires songwriters more. But someday when I have time I'll find the perfect spring and summer songs to make it a complete seasonal set.

I know—I'll stick the compilation CD in a box with a packet of seeds, a tube of sunblock, a skein of wool, and a tin of cocoa.

Okay, maybe a martini glass, too.

21

YEAH, I'M
ALWAYS THE FIRST ONE YOU THINK OF IF SHE'S BUSY

Although I have made my living all these years onstage, you know I've never had formal training. I just play my guitar, tell my stories, and sing songs the best I can. My frugal Catholic elementary school never put on shows of any kind (unless you count mass), in high school I was too busy playing my guitar and writing songs to think about trying out for a play, and in college I ushered at plays but was never cast in one myself. So when I got a phone call in the summer of 1998 asking me to play the part of evil stepsister Minerva in a one-time-only benefit performance of *Cinderella*, I quickly said no.

It was my friend violinist Robin Batteau on the other end of the line, and he was calling from a small theater in Connecticut where his neighbor Paul was putting on a night of entertainment to raise money for a summer camp. The centerpiece of the entertainment was a spoof of *Cinderella*, and Robin was the musical director.

He told me he just got word that the actress who was cast to play Minerva had to drop out. He needed me in Connecticut in two days—which my routing had me traveling through anyway—so there really was no reason why I couldn't do it . . . I interrupted him, telling him I had zero theater experience. I was not the girl for the job.

"But Chris, it's a benefit for Paul Newman's Hole in the Wall Gang camp for kids with cancer."

Oh my God, how could I say no to that? Robin gave me the address of the three-hundred-seat theater, on the grounds of the camp, and told me to be there at two o'clock Saturday afternoon for rehearsal. My friend Lois Dino was road managing that weekend, so I called to let her know we had an extra stop.

Robin left out a few details that we learned when we arrived: The script was cowritten by Paul Newman (this was "neighbor Paul"!) and A. E. Hotchner, and the evil stepmother was being played by Carole King. (This was many years before she rescued Harry on the slopes in Aspen, but just a few years after her mom had come to a Babes show in Fort Lauderdale. I told Carole about our group hug with her mom, and she loved hearing about it.) One of the evil stepsisters was Carole's daughter, Louise Goffin. The narrator of the play was Joanne Woodward. The Fairy Godmother was Nathan Lane, and the Fairy Godfather was Paul Newman. There were two princes fighting over Cinderella—one was Broadway star James Naughton, and the other was beloved actor Tony Randall. And Cinderella was being played by Julia Roberts. Tickets cost $1,000, and it was sold out.

Now before you get all excited on my behalf, try to imagine how I might have felt walking into this situation. Some might think this was a dream come true, but it's more like an episode of *The Twilight Zone*. Did you ever see the one where the man finds a magic lantern and gets three wishes? At first he wishes for a million dollars. Poof! He's showered with bills, then an IRS agent comes and takes half of it away. So then he wishes he was the most powerful man in the United States of America. Poof! He's Abe Lincoln at Ford's Theater. So he's down to one wish, and he wishes he was the most powerful man Europe. Poof! He's Hitler. I would have been ecstatically happier being in the background in this production, but I had actual lines and had to sing. I was starstruck and terrified.

We arrived five minutes before the one and only rehearsal, so the stage manager thrust a script into my hands and told me to sit down on a bench next to Carole King and Louise Goffin.

Joanne Woodward stood at a podium on the right side of the stage. I mean the right side looking out at the audience, so is that stage left? Or stage right? (See? I have no idea about this kind of thing!) Joanne explained to the audience what they were about to see, and all I remember hearing was the end: "And here comes poor Cinderella. Her stepmother and stepsisters are so mean to her!"

That was Julia Roberts's cue to come crawling on her hands and knees across the stage. First she polished Louise's shoes, then mine, and then she moved on to Carole. I couldn't help myself. Even though I had no lines in this scene, I leaned down, pointed at my right shoe, and said, "You missed a spot!"

Without a word, she repolished my right shoe, and then went on with the scene. I was so proud! I ad-libbed a line to Julia Roberts! And she ad-libbed a response! I'm an actress!

Later on came my big moment. Joanne read, "Minerva is a singer and has dreams of going to Hollywood to become a big star!"

That was my cue to step forward with my guitar and sing the first verse of my song "What Was I Thinking?" Then I sat down again. Later on I had a scene with Tony Randall where he had all the women of the kingdom try on Cinderella's glass slipper (which was really a silver stiletto Manolo Blahnik). I was wearing lace-up floral tapestry boots, and there wasn't time to take them off, so he tried to put the shoe on over my boot. Of course it didn't fit, and I figured it would get a good laugh.

In this version of *Cinderella*, everything works out well for everyone in the end. Joanne read, "And the Fairy Godmother takes Minerva to Hollywood, where she becomes a big singing sensation!"

At that, Nathan Lane took me by the arm and swept me offstage. There were a few more loose ends tied up: Cinderella and the cute prince (Jim Naughton) lived happily ever after, and then we all sang a song—an old-fashioned standard to which A. E. Hotchner had written new lyrics to reflect this Cinderella story.

We all had to learn the song, so we gathered around the piano and were handed lyric sheets. I stood next to Nathan Lane, smiled at him, and told him I was a big fan. He said "Thank you," then we sang through the song a couple of times. Walking offstage, I said to him how nervous I was; how I had never been in a play before. He rolled his eyes and walked away.

Next we were all assigned one of two large dressing rooms—the guys in one, the girls in the other. Yes, I was in a dressing room with Carole King, Louise Goffin, and Julia Roberts. Julia wanted to put her hair up in pigtails as Cinderella, then shake the pigtails out as she was transformed for the ball, but she couldn't find any elastics. There were rubber bands, but she wanted two of those woven elastics that could slide easily out of her hair. I told her I would find them for her, then started searching high and low—I was even prepared to buy two elastics off someone if I saw someone wearing them. I was on a mission.

I looked in every corner of the green room, all the bathrooms, the small dressing rooms, the box office, and—voilà!—a woman in the box office found one. I ran it back to the dressing room, where Julia was in her underwear—thong underwear. Why does Julia Roberts wear thong underwear? Because she can. And she looks great.

I ran out in search of another elastic band and couldn't find one, but by the time I got back to the dressing room she had a second one that was found in a box of wigs. So Julia Roberts was all set to make her transformation onstage from grubby housemaid to glamour girl, and I helped! She graciously thanked me.

Since Minerva was supposed to be mean and nasty, I was given an ugly outfit to wear to make me look worse. I still couldn't believe I was going to be in this play. I felt like I had stepped through the looking glass, and I was just praying I would get through the experience and not do anything that would ruin the play or Robin Batteau's reputation. I wondered how many people he called before he dialed me. Why did I say yes?

The theater opened, and the seats quickly filled. I knew I really didn't need to be nervous; nobody paid a grand to see me. I chanted that thought in my head over and over to calm myself down. *They're not here to see you . . . they're not here to see you . . . don't be nervous . . . they're not here to see you . . .*

For the opening scene I took my place on the bench next to Louise Goffin and Carole King. Joanne Woodward made her speech, and Julia Roberts crawled across the floor and polished our shoes. I didn't ad-lib any lines this time; I was trying to be a professional. I admired Julia's hair up in those pigtails.

Later on I got up and sang a verse of "What Was I Thinking?" It got very little reaction from the crowd, but that was okay. They had no idea who I was. The first verse does little more than set up the song, and on its own it isn't very satisfying. I was just relieved that I remembered the lyrics and kept the plot moving forward.

Then came Julia's scene where she slid the elastics out of her hair, took off her housecoat to reveal a slinky gown, and became the ravishing beauty we all know and love. She was so right to insist on elastics instead of rubber bands. I felt proud for being part of the behind-the-scenes activity that made that scene work effortlessly.

Later Tony Randall tried the silver shoe on my foot—I stuck my booted foot out as he struggled with it. Not a laugh from the audience. But when he moved on to Louise Goffin's foot, I started to breathe easier—I only had one more thing to do. It was almost over! This wasn't so bad after all! I was an actress!

In the last scene, when everything works out, Joanne Woodward read, "And the Fairy Godmother brings Minerva to Hollywood, where she becomes a big singing sensation!" With that I stood up smiling, waiting for Nathan Lane to sweep me offstage.

I waited and waited. No Nathan. I waited some more. Joanne Woodward fumbled with her script and looked around. I looked around. Where was Nathan? *What was I supposed to do?*

Dead silence.

Joanne repeated the line, a little slower and a little louder, *"And the Fairy Godmother brings Minerva to Hollywood, where she becomes a big singing sensation!"*

I have no idea how much time ticked by. Maybe ten seconds, but it felt like an eternity. Since I was supposed to go off into the wings, spirited away by the Fairy Godmother, I went to plan B and started to spin myself there.

So I stuck my arms out and started to madly spin, aiming for the opening near the back of the stage to my left. (Is that stage left? Stage right? I still don't know!) As I got closer and closer, I got dizzier and dizzier. (I'm getting dizzy just typing this! I don't know how dancers "spot" as they spin—I was just spinning like an idiot.) Soon I was close enough to throw myself into the darkness, so that's what I did. I banged into a piece of furniture in the wings that fell with a big crash, and I heard the audience laughing. When I righted myself, who was standing in front me, holding a script and frowning? Paul Newman.

"What are you doing?" he whispered. "Making up your own lines? And who the hell *are* you?"

"Nathan—he, he was supposed to come get me," I whispered back, "but he didn't! He didn't come get me! I didn't know what to do! I've never been in a play before! I'm a folksinger! Robin asked me to do this! I've never been in a play before! I'm a folksinger—"

I stopped jabbering because the lights came up, and we all had to go onstage to sing the final song. I was so traumatized that I just moved my lips, closed my eyes, and pretended I was invisible. Nathan Lane was there for the finale, but why had he left me hanging? I wanted to ask him what happened.

There was a party following the play where audience and actors mingled. I saw Nathan dressed all in black, smiling and chatting with people. He looked happy and in a good mood, but I was too scared to talk to him.

Maybe I should not have told him I had never been in a play. Maybe he didn't want to share a scene with a rookie. Maybe he was teaching me a lesson. Maybe that part was changed and nobody told me. I will never know. But I do know that if in your first play you share a dressing room and a stage with Julia Roberts, there is only one direction you can go from there. My theatrical career began, peaked, and crashed and burned all on the same night—the night I got yelled at by Paul Newman.

More than a decade later I wrote a song inspired by the actress I was filling in for that night: Sarah Jessica Parker.

Yeah, I'm always the first one you think of if she's busy.

Ha Ha Ha Ha Tsk Tsk Shhh!

Even though I don't know anyone

Who knows anyone

Who can walk in Manolo Blahnik footwear

Even though I don't know anyone

Who knows anyone

Who can afford a Versace dress

I bought tickets for the very first day

Of the film *Sex and the City*

And I brought along a male friend

Was he straight? Take a wild guess . . .

22

THAT PART
IS TRUE. THE REST I MADE UP

When I first moved to New York, I spent five months on the Lower East Side, near the Hells Angels headquarters on Third Street between Avenues A and B; two months in an illegal loft with a bunch of artists on Twenty-sixth Street and Sixth Avenue (that building has since been torn down); then in the West Seventies between West End Avenue and Riverside Drive, in a small studio apartment in the building where Mrs. Shugrue, the elderly Irish lady, was the super. I lived there from September 1976—when it was a dicey neighborhood—until August 1994, but the truth is I had outgrown that apartment a good ten years earlier.

My theory is that at any given time, at least half the people who live in Manhattan are living in apartments they have outgrown but don't move out. Why? Inertia.

I always wanted to write a duet called "Inertia," a tribute to that mythical mistress who keeps us from fulfilling our destiny:

SHE: Why can't you commit to this relationship?

HE: Inertia.

SHE: Inertia? Who's *she?*

[CUE MUSIC]

HE: *Inertia. Always keeps me in place.*

SHE: *Inertia? I want to smack her in the face . . .*

My apartment was rent stabilized, so the rent could go up only so much every time I renewed my lease. I was getting more singing work, and for a few years I had money left over at the end of each month, which was a first. My apartment was quite small, just one room, a tiny kitchenette, and a small bathroom. But the downside was that it was on the second floor, overlooking the street, and hundreds of times I was woken up by a car alarm, a garbage truck, a police siren, a screaming neighbor, or someone ringing my bell my mistake.

Mrs. Shugrue's apartment was 1A, and the buzzer for my apartment, 2A, was right below hers. A few years after I moved in, Mrs. Shugrue retired, her apartment was rented out, and the building owner hired an off-site superintendent. Old habits die hard, so people who were used to ringing 1A looking for the super rang 2A when no one answered, often waking me up at odd hours. I pasted a sign up by the buzzers in the lobby saying, THE NEW SUPER IS MR. VELTRI, along with his address and phone number, but even that didn't help.

One night—around 4:00 a.m.—someone rang my buzzer and woke me up just after I had fallen asleep. It was a very quick buzz, not the normal length, and that was unusual, so instead of hitting the "talk" button, I hit the "listen" button. At first I wasn't sure what it was I was hearing, but I soon realized it was two gay boys in the outer lobby fooling around—one of them must have hit my buzzer by mistake in his groping frenzy. I was so mad at being woken up that I kept listening—hearing zippers unzipped, moaning, smooching sounds—and I waited until the moment when their love racket was coming to a crescendo to hit my buzzer long and hard.

They had been leaning against the downstairs door, which sprung open when I buzzed. I heard them fall to the floor of the inside lobby below my apartment, and they screamed. I kept buzzing, which must have really freaked them out. Then I stopped and ran to my window, just in time to see them tear out of my building, buttoning their shirts and zipping up their pants as they ran up the street.

I know that was *so mean* of me to do that, but that's the price you pay if you wake some New Yorkers up.

The loud nocturnal lovers were just one instance of the constant noise, and then one day in early 1994, as I went to answer the phone, I tripped over one of my two guitar cases, went flying into the wall, and broke my finger. That was it. I had to move. I could afford a bigger place. What I couldn't afford was to stay in a space so cramped and small that answering the phone became a bone-breaking ordeal. It was my friend Martha on the phone, asking, "Whatcha doing?" and I had to tell her, "I think I am staring at a finger I just broke answering this phone."

Martha is a fascinating person. When I first met her, she was working for a children's book publisher, but now she owns a charming store called Liberty House on 112th and Broadway. It's right across the street from Tom's Restaurant—the one that is famous for being the fictional Monk's diner where Seinfeld and company hung out, as well as being the Tom's Diner in Suzanne Vega's a cappella song about sitting in a diner waiting for a cup of coffee. Every day, tour buses still come by. The tourists get out, snap photos, and then get back on the bus. They never eat there.

Martha inspired my song "Shopping Cart of Love" the day we were walking down Broadway, between Seventy-fifth and Seventy-fourth Streets, and she told me she had recently been in D'Agostino's (which is now Fairway), in the express line, with thirteen items even though the sign clearly said TEN ITEMS OR LESS. When the checkout girl noticed that Martha was over the ten-item limit, she refused to check through the last three items and told Martha she had to put them back. Martha refused and asked the girl to make an exception—she wouldn't. The manager had to open up a separate cash register just for those three items. Martha said by the time she left, *all* the checkout girls were yelling at her, she was screaming at them, and she was afraid to shop there for months, thinking they might beat her up.

I knew instantly that this was the beginning of a song. So if you know that song, *that* part is true. The rest I made up.

Martha's bad day at the supermarket had helped me to write one of my most fun songs, and now her phone call set in motion a whole new series of life-changing events.

Because of my broken finger, I couldn't play guitar for a number of months, but I had a lot of concerts booked, so I hired Jon Gordon, a guitar player who had been in Suzanne Vega's band, to learn a whole bunch of my songs. It felt very weird standing there and singing without playing guitar. Every once in a while I would get lost in the lyrics, so I would run over to where Jon was, and he would hand the guitar to me. I would hold it for a second like I was going to play it, and the next line of the song would instantly pop into my head. It must have been some kind of "muscle memory" thing.

Eventually my finger healed and I went back to playing guitar for myself, but I knew I had to find a bigger apartment.

If you asked me at the time what my dream apartment would be, I'd say a sunny one-bedroom on a high floor, with a terrace facing west, in a building with a doorman and a health club, and plenty of restaurants nearby that delivered. I was paying about $500 a month for my studio, but figured I could pay $1,500 a month, which seemed to be reasonable for what I was looking for.

One Sunday afternoon I was reading the real estate section of the *New York Times*, circling all the potential apartments. It was clear to me that $1,500 wasn't enough for all the things I was looking for, but I started making calls.

Quickly I realized I was getting tripped up by the abbreviations in the ads, and asking questions just confused things until I got on the phone with a rental agent for a building near Lincoln Center. I told him what my budget was and what I was looking for, and he said, "If you can afford to pay that much per month, you'd probably be better off buying an apartment than renting one. Tax-wise you'll be better off, and the housing market is down right now, so you could probably pay less than the asking price. The housing market will eventually rebound, so when it comes time for you to sell, you'll actually make a profit instead of handing your money over to a landlord every month."

He even did some math for me, explaining that a mortgage and maintenance for a one-bedroom in a doorman building would probably be in the $1,500 range, if not lower. A total stranger said this to me. And no, he wasn't trying to sell me an apartment; he worked for a rental agency. Lucky me that I got him on the phone!

Buying was something I would never, *ever,* have considered. I'm a folksinger. Folksingers don't own property—especially not in New York City. But I thanked him, then flipped from the rental section of the *Times* to the co-op and condo sales section.

Right away, one apartment listing jumped out at me. It was on Riverside Drive, two and a half blocks from where I was living—a 675-square-foot, one-bedroom co-op in a prewar doorman building. I ran right over. The nineteen-story building was beautiful, with lovely pastel plaster filigrees on the front facing Riverside Park, with window boxes filled with flowers. Two sets of antique shiny brass doors led into an old-fashioned lobby with smooth marble floors and brass wall sconces. A uniformed man sat at the front desk. I asked him to buzz apartment 11B, but he smiled and told me the building didn't have any buzzers.

No buzzers? I already liked it. He called apartment 11B and told them I had arrived, and then we got into the manually operated elevator. The walls of the elevator were a lovely dark polished wood, with a gold domed ceiling. I got off the elevator. He waited until the door to 11B opened and then returned to the lobby.

This was the first apartment I was looking at in my quest to get more space and put distance between me and car alarms, garbage trucks, and late-night buzzers. I knew it was going to take a long time to find the perfect place, but I had to start somewhere.

The bedroom, hallway, and living room had beautiful oak floors trimmed with walnut and bird's-eye maple. I looked out the bedroom windows and only saw other brick walls. I couldn't see the street below, which meant no cars, no sirens, no trucks. *Heaven.* Same for the living room, the kitchen, and the bathroom.

I turned to the owners and said, "I bet I'm the first person who looked out your windows and liked what they saw." They laughed and said yes, I was.

I did go see many other apartments, but nothing compared to this place, so after two weeks of running all over the Upper West Side, I returned to make an offer. I ended up buying it for $23,000 less than the asking price. In that building there are three apartments per floor at a couple of different price points, mine at the less-expensive end, so it was like buying a small house on a really fancy block.

The one downside was the lack of direct sunlight. That apartment got no more than twenty minutes a day, usually around eleven o'clock in the morning. However, my studio apartment also didn't get any direct sunlight, so I was used to that. My dream of a sunny terrace and a health club in the same building would remain a dream.

There was another downside that I didn't fully understand when I made that move: a musician tripling monthly living expenses was a big deal. At the time I had no problem handling the extra expense, and I knew I'd be all right as long as I continued to work steadily and the economy was healthy. My finances were okay, but not great; I had never thought of buying, so I never focused on saving. All I cared about was music. As long as my bills were being covered, I didn't even know how much money I had in the bank.

Because this building was a co-op and not a condo, before the sale could be finalized I had to meet with the co-op's board of directors for an interview. Since it often took months before the actual closing, there was a stretch of time before I had to meet with the board and make the move, and during that interval something unexpected happened.

I discovered I had an intraductal papilloma, a benign tumor, in my right breast that would have to be removed. The surgery was relatively minor and would require just an overnight in the hospital; recovery time would be just a couple of weeks. I didn't tell anyone in my family about this until it was all over and done with. I didn't want to worry anybody.

I had the surgery, and the next day I was sent home, but then something went wrong. Over the course of the afternoon and evening I started to feel pressure building up in my breast. The pain increased, and soon I was sweating and nauseated. At first my breast felt swollen, but then it was hard as a rock.

As the night wore on, it got worse, and in the morning I knew I had to do something. I called Martha, who called Harry, and they both came up to my apartment. Harry called my doctor and then his car service, and, wrapped in a blanket, I was whisked over to the doctor's office, over in the East Sixties.

It was early morning, and the office had just opened. They walked me in, and I could barely stand up. I was in terrible pain and on the verge of vomiting. The doctor took one look at me and told me to immediately go to the emergency room at Lenox Hill Hospital.

The car had left, there was bumper-to-bumper rush hour traffic, and there were no taxis to be had. We were only a block and a half from the hospital, so we very slowly walked to the emergency room. It was really the best way to get there under the circumstances. Harry on one side, Martha on the other, I stumbled along as best I could.

At the ER they put me in a wheelchair, Harry barking orders.

I was put in a private room and told I would be prepped for surgery. Harry got in bed behind me and cradled me as I retched and heaved. I tried to stop myself from vomiting since the sheer act of it strained my stitches and put more pressure on my swollen breast. It was the worst I had ever felt in my life. (Even worse than in that hotel in Australia.) Then an IV was put in my arm, and I don't remember anything until waking up later that day.

I was in great discomfort, but the feeling of tremendous pressure was gone. I stayed in the hospital for a few more days. The doctor told me I had started to bleed internally after the first surgery, but she was vague about what she thought had happened. She said nothing like this had ever happened to any of her patients before. (I think she was worried I might sue.) I told her that one time earlier in my life I had very bad bleeding due to birth control pills, though I had no idea if that was relevant. This second surgery was more extensive than the first, and I had to wear a drainage bag for the next six weeks as I healed. I wasn't interested in suing anyone; I just wanted to recover.

I can barely remember the two weeks immediately following the surgery. It was one big fog of pain and drainage-bag drama. But as I slowly started to feel better and knew I was going to be all right, I called my mother. I didn't mention any of the complications, just telling her that I had surgery for a papilloma discovered in my right breast. My mother gasped and asked me what the date of my surgery was. When I told her, there was silence on the other end of the phone line.

My mother was startled because she said she had had a growing feeling over the years that when she was hospitalized for Paget's disease, there was something else going on that they didn't tell her. Her surgery was twenty-five years before mine was, but it was *the very same week* that I had my surgery for the papilloma that she had driven from Geneva to Penn Yan to look through her medical records at the Soldiers and Sailors Hospital.

She found that a papilloma was discovered in her right breast when she had surgery for Paget's disease, so it was also removed. But the Paget's disease was more serious, so they didn't tell her about the papilloma. My mother felt that her daughters should know, and she was about to call my sisters and me, only to learn that one of her girls was dealing with it in a New York City hospital.

It was now summertime, and wearing a drainage bag under my clothes was very uncomfortable. I wore very loose clothing so that it was less noticeable, but during that time I had to go in front of the board of directors of the co-op where I was hoping to live. I was told ahead of time that they were most concerned about my finances; they wanted to be assured that I could afford to live there. They knew I made enough to make a down payment and pay for the first few months, but they had concerns over the long haul, based on my tax statements.

I didn't want them to know that I was recovering from surgery—I didn't want them to have any reason to reject me, a self-employed person, if they thought my health wasn't good. So I prepared myself for their financial questions and wore a baggy floral jumper over a loose white blouse. In my left arm I carried three large books for the sole purpose of distracting them from noticing the drainage-bag bump on my right side.

I chose the three books carefully for the subliminal messages I hoped they would telegraph: *Vineyard Summer*, a coffee-table book of Martha's Vineyard photographs by Alison Shaw (one of Alison's most striking photographs is on the cover of *Follow that Road*, the second project done by the Martha's Vineyard Songwriters' Retreat); *Balanchine's Ballerinas: Conversations with the Muses* (the photographer for that book, Shonna Valeska, took the glam photo that is on the cover of my album *Good Thing He Can't Read My Mind*); and *Dame Edna's Bedside Companion* (for good luck; if any of the board members were Dame Edna fans, I'd be golden).

As I was warned, the board focused on my income and wondered how I could have such a healthy gross income and yet a meager net income.

I brought along my concert schedule for the coming year to show them that I was working steadily, and I explained that for years I had paid below-market rent, so I didn't focus on socking money away, though my business manager was forcing me to save in a retirement account that could be tapped in case of emergency (they liked hearing that). I promised them I was going to start to save now that I was tripling my monthly expenses, and then I read to them my list of reasons why I would be a good neighbor:

1. I have lived in the neighborhood since 1976 and already love it; however, I am desperate for quiet because I *am* quiet.

2. Since there are three people living in the apartment now and I am only one person, I'll be using the elevator a fraction of the time; hence, less wear and tear on the elevator and less energy used.

3. I'll be on the road a lot, so that means that not only will there be less frequent elevator use than before, but also that there will be less going to and from the front door: the front door will be opened and closed fewer times, and the floor in the lobby won't have to be cleaned as much.

They laughed at my list, then asked me to wait out in the hall as they took a vote. A few minutes later all the board members left, and then the president of the board asked me back in and welcomed me to the building.

When I moved in a month later, I ran into one of the board members in the elevator. He shook my hand, leaned in, and said, "I love Dame Edna, too."

My life in Manhattan improved quite a bit when I moved into that new apartment. Having an elevator was new, and having someone at the front desk keeping an eye on things was new, too. The building management kept apartment keys in the basement, so if anyone ever got locked out, there was no searching for a locksmith in the middle of the night. All visitors were escorted up to where they were visiting by the elevator operator, who spent the rest of his time at the front desk. The front door to the building was securely locked, and there were video cameras at the front door and service entrance. All during my time living there, there was never a robbery or mugging of any kind. I felt so safe there that I didn't bother locking my door.

And I had some intriguing neighbors. One was a newsman at CNN (who is now at another network), another was a Calvin Klein designer, and the most fascinating was the restaurant reviewer for the *New York Times*. She had to wear various disguises while doing her job, but I knew what she really looked like since she lived one floor below me. I got to know some restaurant owners over the years, and one of them asked me what she looked like. I told him I couldn't help him out on that score; it would not have been the neighborly thing to do.

Since I went from one room to two rooms, I had expanded my space, but not by all that much. I hired a furniture builder/artisan named David M. Sokol to make some changes. There were two closets in the bedroom, and I only needed one, so David turned the second closet into a home office. He also turned my living room into a living room/dining room/recording studio. This apartment was so quiet that I decided to make my next album at home.

With a home office *and* a recording studio in my apartment, I could simply roll out of bed at whatever time and work in my pajamas. Sometimes the whole day would go by, and I'd still be in my pajamas. Not that that was a problem. I have come to realize that my body clock likes going to bed around 4:00 a.m. and getting up at the crack of noon. Or 1:00 p.m. It only becomes inconvenient when I have to interact with the real world.

Steve Rosenthal, owner of the Magic Shop Recording Studio, designed a sixteen-track recording studio with two Tascam D-88 machines, Neve pre-amps, a Neumann vocal mike, various instrument mikes, a Mackie mixing board, and a few other pieces of equipment, that he and his assistant,

Scott Norton, taught me how to run. I engineered my vocal and guitar tracks for the album *Shining My Flashlight on the Moon*, then took those tapes down to Steve at the Magic Shop to record overdubs.

When you are engineering your own recording sessions, it can be humbling; there's quite a learning curve. During normal recording sessions the singer or instrumentalist is in a soundproof room separated by thick glass from the producer and engineer. The producer gives you a "go" sign and the engineer hits the switches, but invariably there are times when the engineer hits the wrong button, so the producer has to signal you to stop and start over.

Often these do-overs occur when you are singing the best any singer has ever sung in the history of music, and the idiot engineer has just ruined your potentially greatest musical moment *ever*. Chances are good that you give him a dirty look, roll your eyes, or sigh with despair and/or disgust.

You will never do that again if you engineer your own sessions, because you will make every mistake ever made by any engineer who has ever lived . . . and then you will go on to make new mistakes that no engineer has ever even dreamed of before. One of my bonehead moves was to take a strip of white labeling tape (where you handwrite the name of a project for ID purposes) and stick it on the DAT tape cassette over a part that moves when the tape is inserted into the machine. The tape jammed, and I had to call the studio and wait half a day for a real engineer to come uptown to extricate the tape. Steve Rosenthal told me later that they kept a running tally of the goofs I made while engineering my own sessions simply because they couldn't believe some of the ways I invented to ruin recording sessions.

One of the elevator operators in my building was a dapper older man named James L. Smith, who we all called Jimmy. He worked in the building for more than thirty years and was very popular with all the tenants. I really liked the sound of his voice and asked him to speak the part of "Professor Fish" on my song "Snackin.' " He had never recorded before, but I really wanted to take advantage of having a recording studio right in my living room, so I talked him into playing the part. It took many takes to get it right. A couple years later he retired, and we had a big party for him in the lobby. I am glad to have his voice on that recording.

Although I was very happy to learn how to record my own tracks, by the time that album was completed, the technology had already progressed to the point where my gear was on its way to obsolescence. Everything was getting smaller, faster, and cheaper. I ended up donating most of the equipment to a new downtown club that Steve Rosenthal opened, called the Living Room (which was where Norah Jones was eventually discovered). Those Tascam D-88 machines were installed in the basement, and there's no telling how many musicians used those machines to make live recordings. Now those machines are probably buried in some landfill or collecting dust in some back room, dreaming of being trotted out as curiosities on *Antiques Roadshow.*

I loved living in that apartment. They say once you become accustomed to a luxury, it's no longer a luxury—it's a necessity. I guess that's true. But for the first time I felt really safe living in New York. I had had my purse and keys robbed before, so I was very happy to live in a building where there was a real sense of security. Even with all the traveling I was doing, I didn't have to worry about my apartment when I was away. And outside my apartment in the hall was a mail chute that connected to an old-fashioned brass mailbox in the lobby. I loved to stay up at all hours writing letters and postcards, and it was great to be able to take just two steps out into the hall to mail them. I found out from my neighbors that many of them didn't trust the mail chute and never used it, but nothing of mine ever got swallowed up by it.

Very often when I would come back to Manhattan from the airport, I would leave my bags in the lobby, and when I'd return later they'd be waiting outside my apartment door. I always used a car service coming from the airport, and sometimes if there was a concert or a show I was rushing to get to, they would take my bags and bring them over to my building without me even being in the car. Now that's definitely one of those luxuries that quickly became a necessity.

I was getting spoiled.

My friend Harry's law firm had an account with a car service, and one day many years ago he told me that if I was ever in a bind, I could use it. I, of course, said I would never *dream* of doing that. One day I was standing in a long taxi line at LaGuardia Airport in a torrential rainstorm, however, and I broke down and called Harry's car service—and got a taste for how the better half lives in New York City. I wanted to reimburse Harry, but he refused, telling me I was free to use it whenever I wanted to. What a treat.

However, it seemed that many lawyers at Harry's firm were letting friends use the company account, so the policy was changed without warning: anyone using that account had to have a voucher *with* them and couldn't ask the driver to supply one (which is what was normally done).

That was long ago, when Ed Koch was mayor. And he liked folk music (go figure). I was asked to provide entertainment one night at Gracie Mansion—wait, I should go back a couple of years and tell you about the very first time I played for Mayor Koch.

It was at a big dinner party at Gracie Mansion, where I was hired to sing two songs for approximately a hundred guests. I was also hired to play the following week for a very small dinner party in honor of songwriter Paul Simon. I wasn't paid for these shows; it was an honor to be chosen to perform for the mayor and his friends.

This was a couple of years after my debut album *Absolutely Live* was released, which included the song where I warned Prince Charles about marrying Diana. I sang that as one of my songs at the big dinner, not knowing that the British ambassador and his wife were sitting with the mayor. The second song I sang was called "Don't Ever Call Your Sweetheart by His Name," which explains how using terms like *sweetie-pie, sugar lips,* and other endearments can keep you out of trouble if you are dating different people at the same time. I thought the songs went well, but the next day I got a call from the mayor's office telling me I was not needed for the Paul Simon event. My songs had been offensive to the British guests, and my second song had "raised the mayor's eyebrows" because it seemed to promote promiscuity.

At first I thought they were kidding, and I said, "It raised the mayor's eyebrows? Well, at least this way he has hair!" I shouldn't have said that.

I was embarrassed to be fired from the second gig, but I really felt bad for the mayor's aide, who was the one who suggested they hire me in the first place—*he* was on the hot seat. I apologized up and down and sideways to him, and for the next couple of years I went out of my way to recommend folksingers for the Gracie Mansion dinners who I knew would be well received. David Roth was one. Megon McDonough was another. The mayor loved them and wrote them glowing letters of thanks. I know there were at least a half dozen others, but I can't think of their names. (Hey, I'm over fifty!) I hoped that suggesting folksingers the mayor *did* like made up for my earlier faux pas.

So a couple years down the line that aide had moved on to another job, the mayor had a dinner party coming up that needed entertainment, and somehow I got called to do it. It was a new aide who didn't know what had happened the first time I performed for the mayor, and I didn't think I should keep that information from him, so I briefly explained that as far as the mayor was concerned, I was persona non grata at Gracie Mansion.

"That's all well and good," he said to me over the phone, "but we're desperate. Please take the gig. Just wear a different dress, don't sing those songs, and act like you've never been there before."

So that's how I found myself returning to the scene of my earlier crime. It was a small dinner party for eight, and I wasn't told who the guests were. I was instructed to eat in the kitchen with the mayor's chauffeur and bodyguard. That was fine with me. I peppered them with question after question about stalkers and scary situations they'd been in—it was a lively conversation.

When I was called in to sing for the mayor and his friends, I didn't say, "Nice to see you again, mayor!" I said, "Such an honor to meet you, Mayor Koch!" He gave no indication that he remembered me at all. *Whew!*

I was told that I would sing one song and, if the mayor liked it, to be prepared with a second one. So I sang "Amoeba Hop," guessing (correctly) that that song wouldn't upset him in any way. Right after that song, as he was clapping, he said, "Please, Miss Lavin, sing another!"

So I said, "Would you like a funny one or a serious one?" and he immediately leaned forward in his chair, his finger pointed at me, and blurted, "A serious one!" Maybe he *did* remember me after all.

So I sang "The Moment Slipped Away," I could see that he really liked that song, and my past sins were expunged.

I had made a reservation with Harry's car service to pick me up at Gracie Mansion following the dinner, which was a good thing because it was raining hard. Gracie Mansion is way over on York Avenue in the East Nineties, not an easy place to get a cab. The car was waiting out front, and the mayor walked out on the porch with me, shook my hand, and thanked me. I waved goodbye to his chauffeur and bodyguard (who were looking out the kitchen window), turned and waved to the mayor, and got into the car.

When I told the driver the account number, he asked me if I had a voucher, which of course I didn't.

"Get out my car!" the driver said.

"Why?" I asked. "What's wrong?"

The mayor was still standing on the porch, waiting for the car to leave.

"All da friends of all da lawyers use our car service, and now all you cheapskates in trouble. Da office say if you don't have a voucher, kick out my car! So I am telling you, *get out my car!*"

Oh, no. It was raining. The mayor was standing on the porch. I had finally made up for my bad behavior of a couple of years ago!

"Please," I begged him. "I will pay you cash. Please don't kick me out of your car. That's the mayor of New York. It's raining. Please don't kick me out."

"Show me your cash," the driver demanded.

I quickly looked through my purse and showed him I had twelve dollars. The mayor was still standing on the porch, a quizzical look on his face. I rolled down the window and yelled that everything was fine; the driver didn't speak much English, and I was trying to explain what my address was. The mayor waved and went inside.

"Why you tell the mayor I don't speak English??" the driver yelled. "I speak English! Why don't you tell him the truth that you like to cheat with your friend's car service? Why don't you tell him dat? No, you make fun of me. Get out my car!"

"Please," I begged him. "I am so sorry. I wasn't making fun of you. I couldn't think of what else to say. I will pay you twelve dollars to take me to a bus stop. Please just get me off the mayor's property."

So that's what he did. I was drenched when I finally got home, and the next day I called the car service and opened up my own account, which I still have to this day. I try to only use it when I have to (going to and from the airport with my guitar and suitcases), and they have saved me when I left my keys in the backseat one time, and my cell phone another. In a city like New York, where you are constantly among strangers so much of the day, it's nice to get to know the people you depend on to get around. Can you tell that's my justification for turning this luxury into a necessity?

One day, when I was coming back from Newark Airport, I was telling the driver the story of how I opened my account—in the pouring rain in front of Gracie Mansion after playing for Mayor Koch. The driver told me that Ed Koch is now a regular customer of theirs. Small world. Dr. Ruth also has an account with them—all the drivers love her and love talking about her, how she talks nonstop on the phone. One told me, "She ends all her phone calls the same way—she says, 'You da best! *You da best!*' "

I ran into Dr. Ruth one night at the theater, in the lobby waiting for the doors to open. I introduced myself to her as a customer of the same car service she uses and told her how much the drivers enjoy driving her around.

"Oh, I love my car service boys!" she exclaimed. "They come all the way uptown to get me every day. And they take me home every night. They da best! *They da best!*"

So even though I started life in New York way downtown, sleeping on a door, twenty years later I owned my own Upper West Side co-op and had a private account with a car service. In the back of my mind I knew to not get too comfortable with this arrangement. Writing songs and performing concerts is a wonderful career, but it's a luxury item on life's menu. My business manager had been forcing me to save money for my retirement (even though I've told him I will never retire), so even in those times I felt cash poor, I knew I was okay because I had a retirement fund for down the line—though now it *is* down the line, and it's worth a *whole* lot less than it was. Everybody's feeling the pinch.

Meanwhile, in the late '90s the value of my apartment started to rise as the New York real estate market rebounded (as predicted). Within a few short years it was worth double what I paid. But then the building needed a new roof, and then the bricks needed repointing, so the maintenance charges also started to climb. There was a debate about installing a modern elevator, but that was voted down by the co-op members. Having it manually operated also added to the security of the building, since the elevator operators knew the comings and goings of everyone.

For so long I had been blissfully casual about my finances—especially when I lived in that cheap walk-up studio apartment—but now I had to start paying attention to the bottom line. I continued to perform and make albums, but my business manager was regularly sending me e-mails, trying to get me to pay attention to the fact that I was doing better than breaking even, but not by much. He wrote that if I didn't get my finances under control, I would soon be in financial trouble if I continued to live in Manhattan.

I promised him that I would cut out all extraneous expenses, such as my weekly manicure at a lovely small day spa called Feline's on West Seventy-fifth Street. I didn't have my first manicure until I was thirty-five years old, and it was amazing how quickly I became accustomed to that luxury. But I had to let that go. I still miss that place! If you ever walk by, please tell Ingvor I say hello.

Around this time I became good friends with a man named Ray who lived in my neighborhood and owned a copy shop just down the block from the Dakota. Ray was an obsessed theater fanatic who took to devoting his shop windows to his current Broadway passion: first it was Linda Eder in *Jekyll & Hyde*, and then Deborah Yates in *Contact*. Not only did he see these shows over and over again—he played nothing but their music nonstop in his shop. I naively gave him a few of my albums, but he never played them. (I had to accept that his obsession was stronger than our friendship!) During the run of *Contact*, he took to sitting dead center in the orchestra section wearing head-to-toe yellow to catch Deborah's eye. Despite his obsessive nature, Ray was harmless. Now he lives with his partner, Warren, in Florida. Before they moved, Ray gave me the yellow bathrobe Deborah wore in *Contact* that he bought at a charity auction.

Ray's Copy Shop was beloved on the Upper West Side. He had a sign posted for waiting customers that said: SICK OF WAITING? OR JUST HATE RAY'S GUTS? HERE'S ALL THE COPY SHOPS WITHIN SIX BLOCKS. And there would be listed all their addresses and phone numbers.

Ray confided that Yoko Ono and John Lennon were regular customers, and he always made sure nobody bothered them when they were in his shop. He was heartbroken over John's murder and could barely bring himself to talk about since it happened so close by. Just before he and Warren moved south, Yoko stopped by and gave him a check for $10,000. I know that people like to criticize Yoko, but that one kind act speaks volumes.

I wrote a song about Ray's endearing theater obsession—I still haven't recorded it, but someday I will. The last couple of years he was in business, he made less and less money because it wasn't obvious it was a copy shop, with all the theater photos, posters, and programs—even that yellow bathrobe decorating the shop windows. He spent thousands of dollars on theater tickets, not to mention the hundreds of roses he'd bring to the stage door.

I could never *imagine* going to see a show over and over and over again the way Ray did.

Then Dame Edna came to town.

23

DAME EDNA
ARRIVES

Ten years after I first saw her on Australian TV, Dame Edna came to New York City and set up shop at the Booth Theater on West Forty-fifth Street in the center of the Broadway theater district. (Technically it might not have been the center of the Broadway district, but someone with Dame Edna's extraordinary talents naturally becomes the center of wherever she happens to alight.)

I couldn't believe my good fortune. It's one thing to read books, watch videos, and listen to her recordings, but now I was finally going to see Dame Edna *in person*. The day that I read in the *New York Times* theater listing that her show *Dame Edna: The Royal Tour* was in previews, I got two tickets for that very night. I called Harry and told him whatever he had planned, cancel it; I was *taking him out*.

Harry wasn't so sure about this. Like many people, he knew little about Dame Edna except that she is the creation of Australian Barry Humphries, and Harry had the common misconception that Dame Edna was some kind of "drag" character. She's not. She's a larger-than-life, self-proclaimed international mega—no, *giga*star. The fact that Barry Humphries is a man and Dame Edna is a woman is irrelevant. Like more recent creations—

Sasha Baron Cohen's Borat, and Robert Smigel's Triumph the Insult Comic Dog—Dame Edna is a being who can get away with way more than the rest of us because she's really not of this world.

It's difficult to explain a Dame Edna performance; it would be like trying to describe a favorite painting or film. Suffice to say, I never laughed so hard in my life, and judging by everyone else in the theater that first night, including Harry, they never laughed so hard, either. I knew I had to come back and see this show again.

Two nights later I did, this time bringing Martha. We had a great night—dinner at Sardi's, Dame Edna, taxi home. Martha was as enthralled as I was. The show was still in previews, no reviews yet, but I was raving about Dame Edna to anyone who would listen. I also got into the habit of mailing Barry Humphries a postcard after each performance I saw, raving about Dame Edna to *him*. As Barry later said, "My dear Christine, at first I thought you were a *stalker* . . . but then I realized you were an *acolyte*."

I went again and again, taking various friends with me, then I started going alone so I could totally focus on what was before me. (No, really it was because I ran out of friends willing to tag along.) Orchestra seats at the time were $65. This was an expensive hobby I was developing just when I was supposed to be saving money, so I made some adjustments. I took the subway to and from the theater instead of a cab, and instead of an expensive dinner at Sardi's, I found a soup stand not far away on Eighth Avenue. After 6:00 p.m., a big bowl of soup (with bread, a cookie, and an apple) was $4.31.

Then I stopped taking the subway and walked each way, but I always had dinner at the soup stand, where I met other theater fanatics who were, like me, cutting back on expenses so that we could see favorite shows over and over again. I saw *Dame Edna: The Royal Tour* five times during previews, and when it was finally reviewed, the critics (unanimously, rightfully) praised it to the skies.

I couldn't get enough of this show, and one day while standing in line to get a last-minute ticket, I checked to see if I had enough money to pay cash. I knew my business manager was going to question me about these new theater bills, so I thought if I paid cash, there wouldn't be a paper trail. (Uh-oh. I was in trouble now.)

The best way to explain my newfound addiction is to reprint this story that ran in the *St. Petersburg Times*:

Stop Me Before I Edna Again

by Christine Lavin

My name is Christine. I am a DameEdnaholic. Please help me.

I feel better already. Admitting your problem is the first step toward conquering it. It's just after 11:00 p.m. now, and I have seen this show nineteen times since it opened in mid-October. Yes, not only was I able to score a ticket tonight, it was fourth row center (one of the house seats they sell at the last minute if there is no friend of the cast clamoring for it). The first eighteen times I saw this show I laughed until my lungs ached, but tonight I actually laughed so hard I cried. Barry Humphries/Dame Edna, in my estimation, is the finest comedic performer in the English-speaking world. I simply can't get enough of him.

Do the math: nineteen times $65. Add in the handling fees for the times I've bought tickets over the phone. Add in the times I brought friends along (some more than once) and paid for their tickets. Add in cab fare. I have developed an expensive addiction, and I don't know how to stop it.

Oh, I have tried other shows—saw *Kiss Me, Kate,* loved it, but the whole time wondered how Dame Edna's show was doing just a few blocks away. *The Dead* mesmerized, and at the end I wept along with the entire audience while thinking I could have been laughing along with the audience if I was over at the Booth. I attended *Dirty Blond* and kept thinking how much Mae West would have adored Dame Edna and admired her fashion sense. I sat through *Putting It Together* happy for Carol Burnett knowing that the show was going to close—now her nights would be free and she could enjoy herself over at Dame Edna's superior show.

I don't go to other shows anymore. I simply can't concentrate on them when I know Dame Edna is in the vicinity.

I've seen the show from the mezzanine, from a box seat on the side, from the center of the orchestra, from the back of the orchestra, from the far left, far right, third row center, and tonight fourth row center. I've seen it with three different pianists at the keyboard, and a change of dancers.

The night I saw it for the eighth time, I took note of something that happened in the second act. After she sang a song about her beloved son Kenny, Dame Edna strolled over to the piano, picked up a single tissue that had been placed there, dabbed her eyes daintily, and said, "With that lovely song I even moved myself!"

I knew something had to be done. Broadway houses are unionized, and a prop man no doubt placed that tissue there. A prop man who might have, if you'll excuse the expression, *germs*. Dame Edna needed a sterile tissue anytime her emotions got the best of her, and she needed it in a tissue dispenser as glamorous as she is.

I would find one.

My shopping was in vain. Neither Gracious Home or Lechter's or Bed Bath & Beyond or Laytner's Linens had anything but ordinary tissue box holders. I was discouraged but undaunted.

I bought a plain white plastic tissue dispenser, and then headed to the fabric and trim district in Manhattan's West Thirties. I hit pay dirt—a trim store brimming over with sequins, rhinestones, sparkles, and beads. I bought yards and yards, along with the finest glue the store carried. How much did I spend? Let's just say more than the price of a ticket to her show.

I stayed up until 4:00 a.m. sketching, cutting, and gluing until that tissue box was itself a glittering jewel, the highlight of each side a giant, sparkling scripted *E*. I inscribed on the inside FOR DAME EDNA: THE ROYAL TOUR BOOTH THEATER, NYC, OPENED OCTOBER 17, 1999, TO UNANIMOUS RAVE REVIEWS. I included a brief note in the package, explaining my reason for the gift.

The next day my own work took me out of town, so on the way to the airport I dropped it off at Federal Express (ordinary postal service isn't good enough for someone as special as Dame Edna). I spent ten days on the west coast, intermittently wondering, Did she get the tissue box holder? Does she think I'm insane? Should I not have told her how many times I've seen her show? At 5:00 p.m. I'd look at my watch, thinking, It's 8:00 in New York—Dame Edna is descending the staircase. What kind of crowd does she have tonight? Which dress is she wearing? Why aren't I there? It was then that I should have realized I was developing an addiction, but all too often the person with the problem is the last to know.

A stack of mail greeted me on my return—magazines, catalogs, bills—but nothing from the Booth Theater. I sighed and shook my head. I was silly to do what I had done. I tried to put a positive spin on it: I'd already spent hundreds of dollars going to that show. Think of all the money I could now save . . . but then a plain white envelope, with no return address, caught my eye. Could it be?

Yes! A letter from Dame Edna herself! In a plain white envelope! Who knew? It read in part:

"I now cry onstage at least twice a night, and now, instead of dabbing my eyes with a germ-laden Kleenex placed upon my piano by a grubby props man, I have your tasteful monogrammed dispenser. It's lovely, Christine, and so thoughtful of you to make it for me. I only hope you didn't inhale as you were gluing on all those gems. I would hate such an act of kindness to lead you into substance abuse.

"My only fear is that this lovely bauble you have created might upstage me, so I hope I don't see any audience member's eyes swiveling to your creation. Thank you for writing the brief documentation inside. Only a few of us seem to think of posterity these days.

"My thoughts to you and your loved ones for the coming year, and my gratitude to you for solving so prettily the tissue issue.

"A joyous heart always, Edna"

I picked up the phone and ordered a ticket for the next night's performance. Could it be true? Could my tissue box now be part of a Broadway stage set?

As it was at every performance I've witnessed, that night the theater was packed. I had another good seat, sixth row, slightly to the right. When the curtain rose, as Dame Edna descended the stairs, I was afraid to look. Was it there? If I looked, would she see my eyes swivel? Should I just wait until she walks near the piano, then look? The tension was excruciating.

As the crowd roared her entrance, I couldn't bear it anymore—I glanced quickly toward the piano. Yes! It was there! But I immediately looked back at Dame Edna, praying she didn't notice the eye-swivel maneuver.

Her show was screamingly funny that night, and to my delight and joy, she dabbed her eyes not once, but twice—in both the first act and the second act. The tissues practically leapt out of that dazzling box into her hand, and I felt good knowing I was helping to keep her so daintily germ free. More important, I now had another reason to see the show again. And again. And again.

And tickets aren't all I've spent my money on: I've bought two Dame Edna pins at the memorabilia shop next door to the Booth (tiny rhinestone-encrusted eyeglasses—I had to buy two in case I lose one). At that shop I also purchased all twelve videotaped episodes of Dame Edna's hilarious British TV game show *Neighbourhood Watch*. I've spent hours at her Web site. I bought John Lahr's brilliant book *Backstage with Barry Humphries*—the expensive hardcover, not the paperback.

I want a Dame Edna refrigerator magnet, but no Broadway souvenir shops sell them! I know this because I have gone into every single one—at different times of day, more than once, always dressed differently—and asked. I am hoping that this will create a demand for Dame Edna magnets, and eventually some enterprising souvenir salesperson will get the hint.

I've met and chatted with the box office ticket sellers, ushers, lobby bartenders, stagehands, and tonight made friends with Paul, the coat checker. I'm thinking of quitting my job and asking them to hire me. No, I have never met Dame Edna personally, and at this point I'm afraid to because, well, look at what I've turned into! I have no history of mental disease, drug or alcohol abuse, so my behavior is as much a surprise to me as it is to my friends. I have always scoffed at Trekkies, Jekkies, and other what I considered bizarre types who became obsessed with a form of entertainment. What am I? An Ednaholic? An Edna-head? An Ednaddict? An Ednut?

Are there others out there like me? A support group I can join? I'm free to attend meetings anytime, though not between 8:00 and 10:30 p.m. Monday through Saturday. Oh, yes, Wednesday, Saturday, and Sunday afternoons are out, too. Though Sunday nights are okay.

Please. Help me. This show may run for years. And be forewarned: It may be coming to your town soon.

The *St. Petersburg Times* ran this story twice. First while the show was still running on Broadway in New York, and the second time a week prior to the show hitting the Tampa Arts Center after its Broadway run was over. I am thrilled to think that maybe my story helped fill seats for her.

All told, I saw this show twenty-eight times on Broadway—I know because I saved all my ticket stubs. I had never done that before; perhaps it was my Catholic upbringing reminding me it's important to hold on to holy relics when you find them. And I am not a crafty person; making that tissue box was a first. Having it become part of a Broadway set for Dame Edna brought me more pride and joy than I can put into words.

Although I started as a folksinger, after watching Barry Humphries's performances so many times, I felt moved and inspired to do more than just sing songs. At every performance of his I felt I was sitting at the feet of the master, learning something new every night. No two shows were ever the same. Every once in a while Dame Edna would stop whatever she was doing, look out at the adoring crowd, and say, "Ever get that feeling you are in the right place at the right time with the right group of people? I have that feeling tonight."

Amen.

When *Dame Edna: The Royal Tour* opened on Broadway, it was scheduled to be a limited run, but ticket sales took off, and the show was extended again and again (as Dame Edna herself declared, "I am the Spandex of Broadway shows"). The Broadway establishment itself was so taken with Barry Humphries's creation that they created a special Tony award just for Dame Edna, because there simply wasn't any existing category that encompassed all that Dame Edna is.

The year of these particular Tony awards was also the year that the film *Gladiator*, starring another Aussie, Russell Crowe, was huge at the box office. Dame Edna has always had a thing for the gladiola and has been known to toss hundreds out into the audience after each performance, so she arrived at Radio City standing up in the sunroof of a stretch limo, waving gladiolas, and declaring herself "The Gladdy-ator." During the awards ceremony, which was broadcast nationally on television, Dame Edna presented the Tony award for Best Costume Design to Martin Pakledinaz for *Kiss Me, Kate*. She planted two big kisses on him, leaving big red lip prints on both cheeks. He gave his entire acceptance speech with these colorful smooch marks on his face, not knowing why the audience was laughing. It was a typical Dame Edna move: creating comedy where there was none before.

Eventually they had to close the show—Barry had other commitments he couldn't postpone any longer—but I was one of the lucky ones who scored tickets for his very last Broadway performance that year. Dame Edna's show was one of those rare Broadway experiences: As the weeks went on, ticket sales went up, and when the closing date was announced, that show instantly sold out, the tickets bought by other Dame Ednuts like me.

It was a Sunday matinee, the show was funnier than ever, and I don't know if this is typical of Broadway performers or just Barry Humphries himself, but he sped from the theater straight to the airport and flew back to Australia that same night. Not before he got ovation after ovation, however, from an audience standing and cheering and stomping and, yes, crying.

The following Sunday morning I was scheduled to sit in for John Platt on Fordham University's WFUV *Sunday Breakfast* radio program from 8:00 to 11:00 a.m., and for the four weeks running up to that final performance, I tried to coax Barry into a recording studio to tape a "farewell New York" greeting that I could play for the radio audience. I had arranged with mastering engineer Phil Klum, who at the time was working at the Master Cutting Room mastering studio around the corner from the Booth Theater, to drop whatever he was doing should Barry show up. So even though Phil was mastering tracks for the album of the Coen Brothers' film *O Brother, Where Art Thou?* and the Broadway show *The Full Monty*, he promised that if Dame Edna darkened his doorway, he'd drop everything.

I called Barry's personal assistant, David Bruson, many times trying to make this happen. Barry had said he would definitely do it, but days, and then weeks, went by, and it still hadn't happened. I didn't want to become an annoyance, so I stopped pestering him.

But then I got the idea of having Dame Edna *call* Phil Klum's answering machine, pretending she was calling the radio station from her private plane flying back to Australia. It could all be done over the phone so Barry wouldn't have to go into the recording studio at all. David talked to Barry about it, and he said that would be fine, too. He asked that I fax to his hotel the phone number to call and a rough list of New York topics Dame Edna could riff about.

This I did four days before her final performance. Since I had been working on this idea for approximately three and a half weeks and it hadn't happened, I wasn't sure it would.

But guess what? *It did!*

Dame Edna bade farewell to us via Phil Klum's answering machine, rhapsodized about her time on Broadway, and even left some spaces in her monologue so that I could interject comments here and there, making it sound as if she *really* was calling the station live from her private jet.

Following the radio broadcast, I got e-mail from listeners who were amazed that Dame Edna not only called into the radio station, but did so from a plane. One person chastised me for taking the call, saying phone calls from planes jeopardize safety. I e-mailed them back, "Well, Dame Edna has friends in high places able to arrange such things."

After a break, Barry took *Dame Edna: The Royal Tour* all across Canada and the United States. It was a successful, satisfying experience for Barry to finally draw large crowds in North America after being wildly popular in Australia and the United Kingdom for decades.

To me, one of the most wondrous things about his work is how it stands the test of time and is almost spookily prescient. When the world calendar flipped from the year 1999 to 2000, a new American arts television network called Trio celebrated this new millennium by broadcasting tapes of Dame Edna's British talk show *The Dame Edna Experience* back-to-back for twenty-four hours on January 1, 2000. On one of the shows—originally aired on September 12, 1987—Dame Edna's special guest was "Kurt Waldheim," former secretary general of the United Nations, who began a grand entrance, but halfway down the staircase he abruptly fell through a trap door and disappeared. The band's fanfare suddenly stopped as Dame Edna explained she had decided at the last minute to "abort" Dr. Waldheim's appearance because it would have been "too political." On January 2, 2000, the real Kurt Waldheim fell down in the lobby of an Austrian hotel and broke his leg!

Besides his British talk show and his British game show (both total genius; watch them on DVD!), he has written many books, developed other indelible characters (Sandy Stone; Les Patterson; "Norm," Dame Edna's husband, who was never seen but often discussed; Madge Allsop, who was often seen but never spoke; her fictional gay son, Kenny; and her problem lesbian daughter, Valmai); and is a wonderful painter. If I were you, in this uncertain economy, I'd start amassing a Dame Edna collection right now.

A couple years after his Broadway triumph with *The Royal Tour*, Dame Edna returned with *Back with a Vengeance*, another show that was a hit with audiences and critics, and one that I saw many times in New York (I even flew to Boston to see it there, too, when it was touring).

Most intriguing to me is when Barry Humphries as Dame Edna takes on yet *another* role—he did this in Douglas McGrath's film version of *Nicholas Nickleby* when Dame Edna played Mrs. Crummles. On the fifth season of *Ally McBeal*, starring Calista Flockhart, Barry as Dame Edna played the guest role of Claire Otoms, a client of the law firm. For the life of me, I knew there had to be a story behind the name Claire Otoms—and there is. It's an anagram for "a sitcom role."

In 2004 Penguin Books published Barry Humphries's memoir, *My Life As Me*, and on page 336 of his book he writes about all the people who can't get enough of him and come to see him over and over again. I'm mentioned in the sentence that includes designer "Prince of Chintz" Mario Buatta, comedian Carol Burnett, director Mike Nichols, composer Stephen Sondheim, actor Helen Hunt, and Henry Kissinger.

That's the magic of Dame Edna. She has the power to bring together people from all walks of life and every conceivable political persuasion to worship at her feet, drink in her wisdom, and then leave the theater with a bounce in their step and love in their hearts.

On my Web site I wrote a rave review of Dame Edna's shows, and a year after Barry's second stint on Broadway, I was hired at the last minute to fill in at a one-person theater festival in St. Louis, Missouri, when one of the performers canceled. When my name came up as a possible replacement, the producer went to my Web site to see if I would be suitable. When he saw my Dame Edna review he hired me on the spot, in one night paying me way more than the money I spent on all those Dame Edna tickets combined, so my obsession paid off and my business manager stopped worrying. For the time being.

In 2006 I was putting the finishing touches on a cookbook project for Appleseed Recordings called *One Meat Ball*. It's a nineteen-song CD where all the songs are about food in one way or another, and each song has a corresponding recipe in the accompanying CD-size, ninety-six-page cookbook. It's one of the most fun recording projects I have ever worked on—it includes songs by some of my heroes, like Dave Van Ronk, Tom Paxton, Pete Seeger, and actor/singer-songwriter Jeff Daniels; my compatriots Cathy Fink & Marcy Marxer and Sally Fingerett; but also less-familiar names like Ray Jessel, Mary Liz McNamara, Marcy Heisler, and Zina Goldrich.

At the end of the CD there is a hidden track of faux phone messages supposedly left on my answering machine—Megon McDonough needs to borrow a stick of butter, Vance Gilbert says he's on his way up with a case of root beer, Jeff Daniels pretends to be my irritated landlord . . . and just before Phil Klum mastered the project, I e-mailed Barry Humphries and asked if Dame Edna could leave a phone message, too, to really polish the cookbook/CD off properly.

Well, she did. It's a classic, and Phil Klum is probably the only mastering engineer in the world who has captured and mastered the glorious voice of Dame Edna via telephone *twice*.

When *One Meat Ball* was completed—the CD mastered, the cookbook edited and ready to roll—there was one crucial detail I didn't have in place. I had the money to get us to that point—ready to manufacture—but not a single penny more.

On my way to a gig I sent an e-mail from my cell phone to Mark Hawley, a fan who had become a friend of mine and had recently retired from Wall Street. I told him I had a wonderful cookbook/CD project that needed an executive producer, and I included a list of artists on the project. Would he be interested?

I got this e-mail back twenty minutes later:

Dame Edna's on this? How much you need? I'm in.

I'm not saying *One Meat Ball* might not have seen the light of day without Dame Edna, but I think *One Meat Ball* might not have seen the light of day without Dame Edna. No, that's not a typo.

My fantasy is to produce an event that starts with a buffet of the entrees in the cookbook *One Meat Ball*, followed by a concert featuring many of the artists on the CD in *One Meat Ball*, at intermission have a buffet of the desserts in *One Meat Ball*, followed by a performance by Dame Edna.

A girl can dream, can't she?

24

FALLOUT

n times of crisis, I bake. Well, actually, I bake in good times, too. At 8:45 p.m. on Monday, September 10, 2001, I stood in line at Federal Express with eighteen little boxes, each containing a loaf of *petit pain au chocolat* I had promised to bake for anyone who contributed $100 to radio station WPKN during their call-in membership drive. This particular bread takes ten and a half hours to complete. I started it late in the evening of September 9 and finished the loaves in time for delivery the morning of September 11.

I heard the news about the World Trade Center from my answering machine. Harry had left a message at 9:39: "Turn on your TV. Something happened to the World Trade Center. Oh, my God."

Watching the television, I saw the devastating images of incoming planes and falling towers. I tried to call Harry and Martha, but my landline phone went dead, and my cell phone wouldn't work. So I headed out of my apartment.

I was one of thousands of people walking the streets of Manhattan that morning. A neighbor ran out to the street holding her cat, as if they were going to evacuate. The subways had stopped. Businesswomen were walking barefoot, carrying high heels. Some people were crying. There were parents with young children—the kids happy to be let out of school early. I passed long lines at grocery stores, where people were stockpiling bottled water. I kept walking, passing people eating lunch at outdoor cafes. *How can this be?* I passed a dry cleaner's—through the window I could see a man busily ironing shirts. *How can this be??*

I walked to Martha's apartment. We wanted to help, so we decided to donate blood. But when we could finally get a call through to the Red Cross, we learned that the blood bank was at capacity. I had to do something constructive, so I told Martha I was going home to bake bread.

Back home at 3:00 p.m., I worked on the bread, keeping an eye on the TV news stations—CNN, MSNBC, CBS, CNBC. Harry stopped by to watch the coverage with me. Many firemen were missing, and one of the companies mentioned was Ladder 25, two blocks from my apartment.

The next day, when Harry and I met for lunch, I had a chocolate bread for him in a shiny red shopping bag. I felt funny carrying this cheery little bag around—it didn't seem right. We went to the Mexican restaurant across the street from his office, and for dessert we ate the bread while watching Colin Powell stumble his way through a press conference playing on the TV above the bar.

The latest news report had said that seven guys were missing from Ladder 25 on West Seventy-seventh Street. So I decided to drop off a loaf of *petit pain au chocolat* at the firehouse. I did that again and again and again for the next two and a half months. We all did whatever we could to stay sane during this time. For me it was baking *petit pain au chocolat* for Ladder 25. One night, while shopping for the ingredients to make that bread, I was reciting in my head the list of ingredients, and the list started to sound like song lyrics. That's how I wrote the "Sunday Breakfast" song— just trying to remember all the ingredients in the bread for the firemen.

Writing songs about 9/11 seemed unthinkable at first, but I couldn't ignore the topic. The one overwhelming thought I had was "Why do they hate us?"

So I wrote a simple song using that refrain, and in between verses I would read newspaper articles that shed some light on what was happening.

> Why do they hate us
>
> Why do they hate us
>
> Why do they hate us so much
>
> Am I naive?
>
> It's so hard to believe
>
> Someone could hate us this much

I performed ten concerts in the month following 9/11—from Newport, Rhode Island, to Santa Cruz, California. The readings changed as the situation changed, and I'd include different op-ed pieces from the *New York Times* at different shows. My two favorites were written by USC professor Ronald Steel and Israeli writer Amos Oz, both run in the *Times* on September 14, 2001.

My song got mixed reactions. Some people were upset that a humorous songwriter brought this topic into her show. Some would tell me after the concert that they attended to forget about the state of the world for a couple of hours and didn't appreciate my reminding them.

New York was a somber place. The news reports heaped tragedy upon tragedy as the extent of the loss became clear. Jeff Hardy, brother of Jack Hardy, the musician who started *Fast Folk* and the Speakeasy Cooperative, was a chef at the brokerage house Cantor Fitzgerald on floors 101 to 105 of One World Trade Center. Jeff was also an excellent bass player, and during the 1980s and early 1990s he performed with just about every New York songwriter who was part of the Village scene. Every year when we did the group *Fast Folk* show at the Bottom Line, Jeff was the bass player for the house band. A few years earlier he had gotten married, stopped touring, and became a chef so that he could stay at home with his wife and two young sons. But he came out of retirement for those annual *Fast Folk* shows.

It was a treat when Jeff added bass to our songs. He was a solid harmony singer, adding subtle vocals. While Jack Hardy was a bit of a gruff character, Jeff was one of the most easygoing, popular musicians around. Hearing that he was killed just added to the heartbreak.

All the downtown businesses near Ground Zero were hit hard, and one of them was the Bottom Line. Going out to a show was the last thing on people's minds. Allan Pepper was hit financially, but he was most concerned about the effect on the whole city. He thought the best thing would be to hold a free concert to get people out of their homes and bring them back to life.

He called the show A Gift of Music: A Gathering of Friends. There would be no admission charge, and just about everyone Allan contacted said yes. So on Monday, October 1, I joined the list of performers that included Merry Amsterberg, Joy Askew, the Bacon Brothers, Richard Barone, Taylor Barton, the Beat Goes On, the Bongos, Jen Chapin, Tom Chapin, Martha Wainwright, Jackie DeShannon, Florence Dore, Margaret Dorn, Cliff Eberhardt, the Fab Faux, Julie Gold, Annie Golden, Meg Griffin and Train Wreck, Freedy Johnston, Lucy Kaplansky, Pete and Maura Kennedy, Lena Koutrakos, David Massengill, Felix McTeigue, Ann Marie Milazzo, Modern Man, Morley, Jenni Muldaur, Willie Nile, Rod Picott, Terre Roche, Phil Roy, John Sebastian, Pal Shazar, Jules Shear, Sheriff Bob and the Goodtimers, Slaid Cleaves, Antonique Smith, Phoebe Snow, Jill Sobule, Chip Taylor, Soozie Tyrell, and Dan Zanes and the Rocketship Review.

Radio station WFUV broadcast it live and supplied some of their popular program hosts to help MC the event: Delphine Blue, Darren DeVivo, Dennis Elsas, Meg Griffin, Rita Houston, Claudia Marshall, Corny O'Connell, John Platt, and Vin Scelsa. Other hosts included Bottom Line stage manager Neil Lifton, WFDU's Jerry Treacy, local activist the Reverend Bill Ayers, Doug Tuckman, and artist May Pang.

Backstage was a somewhat lively scene. We were happy to be working, though all still a bit shell shocked.

When the doors opened, the club filled quickly. The show started, but something wasn't right. Slowly we realized that everyone in the audience was shell shocked, too. They sat quietly, applauding but subdued. At one point one of the hosts asked people to order something—anything—the waitresses were standing around with nothing to do because hardly anyone was drinking. This had never been a problem at the Bottom Line.

Slowly people started ordering, and you could feel the room start to relax. I was anxious to do my part so that I could kick back and watch the rest of the show. I sang my "Dream Dream Dream/Summer Song" medley and twirled my batons. All went well. Then I stood by the bar handing out chocolate chip cookies that I had baked earlier that day. I watched a good portion of the show with Cliff Eberhardt and Julie Gold, drinking beer and eating cookies.

The performers were naturally sad, yet we rose to the occasion and did our best to cheer up the audience. As a performer, I never felt more needed than I did that night. Halfway through the show, however, during a changeover onstage, a fireman in the audience stood up and asked everyone to be quiet. The room fell to a hush. We strained to hear him, since he didn't have a microphone.

"There's a lot of funerals still going on for so many of the firemen who died," he said, his voice on the verge of breaking, "and there aren't enough firemen to go around to, you know . . . to attend each funeral. . . . If you can, if there's a funeral . . . in your neighborhood . . . please go. . . . It doesn't matter if you didn't know the guy. . . . Please just go." He sat down, and now the only sound you could hear were muffled sobs.

Allan Pepper later wrote to me about the impact of 9/11:

> I had five shows booked during the week of 9/11. All of them had to be canceled.
>
> The first show we did after 9/11 was on September 20 with Lucy Kaplansky and Catie Curtis.
>
> Many artists started to cancel upcoming shows. Some of them because they were having difficulty getting into the country, and others frankly because they were frightened to come to New York.
>
> We were approximately two miles from Ground Zero, and for weeks after 9/11 the odor of burning plastic was in the air. I found that during the day, if I stood outside in front of the club for any significant amount of time, my eyes would tear.
>
> One of the reasons I put together the free show on October 1 was because I felt that people had to reclaim their lives. Many musicians still had a hard time performing, and many of our customers

were either going to memorials or going to benefits to raise money for victims of 9/11.

I did not want this show to be a benefit or a memorial. I wanted it to be a celebration of life. I felt people needed to gather in a familiar setting and affirm collectively that life goes on, and it was time to affirm life by living it. Many of the performers who participated found this experience liberating. For many of them it was the first time since 9/11 that they had performed. I found it equally redemptive for those who gathered to see the show, because they were permitted to have a good time without feeling guilty. And they were able to laugh, perhaps for the first time in weeks. The simple fact is you have permission to move on if others move with you.

In mid-December 2001 the guys at Ladder 25 told me to stop baking for them. I had watched that firehouse turn into a shrine, with photographs, flowers, candles, drawings, and prayers taped to the door and windows. And offerings of food. Turns out I wasn't the only one feeding the firefighters. They had all gained at least twenty pounds. Nobody was cooking stews or meatloaf—just sweets. I was trying to help but was in reality just another well-intentioned stranger who wasn't helping at all.

In January 2002 I wrote a song called "Firehouse" that contained these lyrics:

> At first there was this slender thread
>
> Of optimistic hope
>
> The digging went on round the clock
>
> No one slept, but somehow coped
>
> The photos of the missing men
>
> Were posted on the glass
>
> Of the red door where
>
> We said a prayer
>
> Whenever we walked past

As we all know now, the crews working on what became known as "the pile" worked feverishly around the clock, many without the protective breathing equipment they should have been wearing, even though the ruins smoldered for months. Christine Todd Whitman, the head of the Environmental Protection Agency at the time, assured us that the air was safe to breathe.

Dave Van Ronk lived on Sheridan Square in Greenwich Village, about a mile from Ground Zero. In my mind, his story is firmly linked to 9/11, as I wrote in a February 5, 2005, article for the *Washington Post*:

. . . and the tin pan bended and the story ended . . .

by Christine Lavin

The 47th annual Grammy Awards will be handed out later today in Los Angeles. There is one nominee in an obscure category that won't be televised tonight—Traditional Folk—whose name is Dave Van Ronk. During his lifetime he performed concerts around the world, taught countless young guitarists how to play, recorded more than three dozen albums, received an ASCAP Lifetime Achievement Award . . . yet never a won a Grammy. He was nominated only once before, in 1996, but watched his friend Ramblin' Jack Elliott win it that year. This is his last chance. He died February 10, 2002.

The album . . . *and the tin pan bended and the story ended . . .* is Dave's final concert, performed October 25, 2001, at the Institute of Musical Traditions in Adelphi, Maryland. Three days before this concert he was diagnosed with colon cancer, his surgery scheduled for October 31—Halloween. "Not an auspicious sign," Van Ronk joked.

There's a lot riding on this for Dave—the Grammy is the official stamp of approval that could make more valuable the 60+ hours of archival tapes belonging to his widow, Andrea Vuocolo. In the first chapter of Bob Dylan's book *Chronicles, Volume One*, recently nominated for a National Book Award, Dylan acknowledges the great influence Van Ronk had on him. When Dave's own book The *Mayor of MacDougal Street* is published in May, a Grammy win would shine the spotlight brighter on that, too. And now there is Martin Scorsese's documentary film for PBS set to air later this year (working title "Bob Dylan's American Journey") where Van Ronk is prominently featured.

Looking back, Andrea now realizes that Dave knew it was going to be his last concert. She had been on the road with him for twenty years, taking care of him and the business side of his work, but that night he did something he had never done before: asked the sound engineer to run a tape off the soundboard, then afterwards gave the tape to her and told her to do whatever she thought was best when the time came. When they got home she put the tape on a shelf in the living room, then forgot about it as she went about the business of canceling his shows for the next two months, and then accompanying him to the hospital.

Van Ronk had asthma all of his adult life. He lived in Manhattan's Greenwich Village not far from Ground Zero, and immediately after September 11 his breathing became more labored. He rarely left his apartment, but when he did, could only walk for a block before he'd have to stop to catch his breath.

When he checked into the hospital the doctors discovered his lungs so badly congested they could not operate, so he was put on ever-increasing doses of medications, and the surgery was postponed three times. When they finally operated on Dave, the medications that enabled him to breathe left him open to infection. His long and torturous healing process began.

Word had quickly spread quickly throughout the folk music community that Dave was in trouble: no health insurance, no savings. The first check came from Arlo Guthrie. Then one from Janis Ian. At the North East Regional Folk Alliance (NERFA) conference in the Pocono Mountains in mid-November, Sonny Ochs, sister of the late songwriter Phil Ochs, passed the hat (well, actually a water pitcher) at each meal during the weekend, collecting over

$2,000 for Dave. Then Allan Pepper organized a benefit concert at his Greenwich Village club the Bottom Line on Sunday, November 25—Peter Paul and Mary, Arlo Guthrie, and Tom Paxton performed two sold-out shows, which included raffling off autographed acoustic guitars—an event that raised $34,000 in a single day for Dave, just five weeks after he had been diagnosed with cancer.

Dave was astonished. At the concert Andrea read a statement he wrote from his hospital bed: "I knew I could finally fill the Bottom Line; I just didn't know I'd have to go to such dramatic lengths to do it."

The New Year came and went. He got worse, but slowly he started to get better. At the end of January '02 his doctors discussed the possibility of letting him go home.

There was one more benefit planned: on Super Bowl Sunday, February 3. There's a rule that you NEVER schedule a concert on Super Bowl Sunday (for obvious reasons), but Pete Seeger, Oscar Brand, Danny Kalb of "the Blues Project," and lots of other musicians crowded into the Towne Crier in upstate Pawling, New York. The room was SRO. At the end of the show people were stuffing bills into the overflowing tip jar as they went out the door. Another $4,000 for Dave.

This was also the same day that Dave was released from the hospital. He was overjoyed, sitting in his usual spot on the couch in his living room, not ready for company yet, but dialing up old friends, scheduling writing sessions for his book. Everything was looking up.

Two days later everything changed. Dave ran a high temperature, was rushed back to the hospital. Two days after that he died. It wasn't the colon cancer; it was an infection. Doctors expected he would live at least another year. But he didn't. Andrea went into seclusion.

It wasn't until over a year later, Sunday, May 18, 2003, that a public event to honor Dave was held—at the site of the first fundraiser, the Bottom Line, and that day was also declared Dave Van Ronk Day by the City of New York. Lots of musicians participated—again Tom Paxton, this time with Suzanne Vega, Richie Havens, David Bromberg, Terre Roche, Odetta, Frank Christian, David Massengill, Eve Silber, Rosalie Sorrels, Patrick Sky, and a dozen others. That weekend more than eighty radio programs around the world also played Dave's music in tribute.

Prior to this show Allan Pepper met a number of times with Andrea to discuss what to do with the money it would raise. Andrea was crying, but she said, "I have the tape of his very last concert. Maybe that could be an album?"

That afternoon was a turning point in Andrea's grief. She decided that if the tape was good she would find the best label for it and try to get it nominated for a Grammy. Until she told Allan Pepper that day, nobody knew Dave harbored this wish.

The concert clocked in just over a hundred minutes, so it had to go on two disks. Andrea forced herself to listen. Friends of Dave's listened. The consensus was that his performance was brilliant: He sang knockout versions of all the songs, especially "One Meat Ball," "Green Green Rocky Road," "St. James Infirmary," ending the concert on a wistful note with Joni Mitchell's "Urge For Going." Between songs he discussed his early life hanging around with jazz and blues musicians in Harlem, his mother Grace Van Ronk, whom he called "the backbone of the Rosary Society," his tour of duty with the Merchant Marines, Bob Dylan.

Andrea took on the job of record producer. She hired Jigsaw Mastering sound engineer Phil Klum, widely known in the industry as a painstaking perfectionist, to see if there was a way to edit it down to fit on a single CD without cutting any songs or stories. Phil Klum brought it in at 78:59 without losing a single song or story. It took close to a thousand edits, but even listening on headphones it sounds seamless.

What to call the album was debated at length. Andrea's pragmatic friends, including me, thought of calling it *Dave Van Ronk's Final*

Concert. But Andrea didn't like that title. Instead she chose . . . *and the tin pan bended and the story ended* . . . a phrase Dave's Irish maternal grandmother used to end stories she told to him as a boy. Dave himself recorded that phrase, but only once, on the album *Going Back to Brooklyn*, following the song "Last Call."

Andrea wanted a label that would trust her choices. Smithsonian Folkways did, so she chose to go with them. Tom Paxton wrote the liner notes. Andrea worked with the Smithsonian designers, assembled photos for the CD booklet, and chose the most memorable Van Ronk bon mots to use throughout ("Take care of your vices and your virtues will take care of themselves"; "Never make the mistake of thinking someone you don't like likes you"; "I wanted to play jazz in the worst way—and I did").

Smithsonian Folkways released the album on June 30, 2004, which would have been Dave's sixty-eighth birthday, the same day New York City renamed the street in front of his apartment building Dave Van Ronk Street. Six months later the album was nominated for a Grammy.

One of the albums competing in the Traditional Folk category is *My Last Go Round* by Rosalie Sorrels and Friends. Rosalie dedicated her album to Dave, so if she loses to him, she'll be okay. The other three competing are Norman and Nancy Blake for their album *The Morning Glory Ramblers*; John Prine, Alison Krauss, Beth Nielsen Chapman, and others on *Beautiful Dreamer— The Songs of Stephen Foster*; and *Gitane Cajun* by the band Beausoleil. I imagine they'll be happy for Dave, too, if he wins.

As Tom Paxton wrote in the liner notes, "There isn't any counting the number of artists [Dave Van Ronk] affected positively; they'll be coming forth for decades to come to tell us about it. You are hearing Dave's final concert, and to say that is almost unbearably painful to me. Goodbye, Davey. You were the last Bohemian and the last 'Mayor of MacDougal Street.' You were a grace note in the lives of all those who were lucky enough to know you. We'll miss you for the rest of our lives."

If you watch the Grammys tonight on TV, try to resist your impulse to run to the fridge during breaks. In the "bumpers" in and out of the commercials will be the announcements of who won in the categories that don't involve any of the big stars in tonight's televised show. I know there are folk musicians all over the country, and one person in particular, living down on Dave Van Ronk Street in Greenwich Village, who are hoping that maybe, just maybe, this will be the night that Dave Van Ronk's secret wish is finally going to come true.

Dave's album didn't win. *Beautiful Dreamer—The Songs of Stephen Foster* did.

25

IF I DIDN'T
HAVE TO PLAY GUITAR RIGHT NOW, I'D BE KNITTING, TOO

Near the first anniversary of 9/11 I hosted a dinner in the wine cellar of Macelleria, my friend Sergio's restaurant. I invited all the musicians I had worked with that year, trying to distract everyone from sadness, having us focus on positive relationships. A week later I saw a news report about a knitting store in my neighborhood that was experiencing a boom in business. I called and signed up for a group class. I knew basic crochet stitches, but knitting was something I wanted to try. In the news story they noted that social psychologists thought this sudden interest in knitting was due in part to the unstable world we were all trying to cope with. We might not be able to control much, but we *can* control the yarn in our hands.

I was totally gung-ho. I thought of all the benefits of knitting, one being I would save money because I wouldn't have to buy sweaters anymore—*I would knit my own!* My very first project was a sweater I knitted out of an oatmeal-colored wool, and what a smack upside the head it was when I realized that just the materials—wool and knitting needles—cost more than a hundred dollars. Let's see . . . buy a sweater at the Gap for $39, or take a month to knit my own for more than a hundred bucks? For a girl who had grown up very modestly, I somehow had quickly developed a fondness for expensive yarn.

With heightened security at airports, knitting became a welcome distraction while waiting around. Nonknitters always seemed to be surprised that knitting needles weren't confiscated going through security—the joke was the airlines let us on with them as long as we promised not to knit an afghan. Flight attendants like having knitters on their flights, as we don't complain when there's a delay—more time to knit!

I got into the habit of knitting backstage before concerts. There is something soothing about the rhythm of the needles. I also do a lot of thinking about songs as I'm knitting. It's a very constructive pastime—no matter where I go now, I always carry along a knitting project.

One day I got the idea to let people coming to my shows know that I was knitting backstage beforehand, and if they were a knitter (or crocheter or quilter or bead worker), they should come an hour early and have a knitting circle with me in my dressing room. As word spread about this backstage event, I'd often have at least five or six knitters at any given show. Then, sometimes way more than that.

There's a wonderful group of women singers in the Seattle area called the Righteous Mothers who do an annual benefit concert at the Washington Performing Arts Center in Olympia for the Monarch Children's Justice and Advocacy Center. One year they invited me to be a guest in that show, and not only did they advertise the backstage knitting circle, they announced there would be a silent auction of hand-knit scarves in the lobby.

That was the biggest backstage knitting circle I have ever been part of—we had more than eighty knitters! And there were more than a hundred scarves in the silent auction. I remember that circle well—because it was so large, and because when I gave out prizes ("oldest project," "newest project," "largest project," "most unusual"), the oldest project was a blanket that a woman had started twenty years before and still hadn't finished.

"Most unusual" was a large, intricate shawl being knitted by a woman who had bought a big box of yarn at an estate sale of an elderly woman who had recently died. The daughter of that elderly woman walked by the knitting circle in the lobby, recognized her mom's yarn, and stopped to tell us she was so happy to see that it had found a good home.

When I started knitting and meeting other knitters, I felt like I was accepted into a supportive sorority I hadn't known existed. I have come to think of knitters as type A personalities who need to be doing something with their hands at all times. They also tend to be nurturing types who want to create something useful for those they love, as well as for those they don't even know. I've met knitters who make tiny caps for premature babies and prayer shawls for hospital patients. Though I have yet to meet a knitter making a shotgun cozy or a handgun warmer.

Uh-oh, I can hear you gun owners making *tsk-tsk* sounds after reading that. I'm constantly surprised to find there are often gun owners at my shows. How do I know they are there? Because of the e-mails I get afterward.

But first I need to backtrack. On New Year's Eve 2002 I was part of the First Night celebration in Raleigh-Durham, North Carolina. I love to work on New Year's Eve—for a musician I think it's good luck to be working as the new year starts, and over the years I have done many First Nights around the country. Most of them work the same way: you buy a button that gets you into every show, and then you go from show to show, usually in a city's downtown area. Most of the performances are forty-five minutes long, starting on the hour, so you have fifteen minutes to get from one venue to another. First Night celebrations are family oriented (there's no alcohol), and at midnight there is often a fireworks display.

So there I was flying down to Raleigh-Durham on December 30. The weather was bad, so I was stuck at LaGuardia for an extra three hours or so. I knitted for a while and then felt like reading, so I cruised around the terminal looking for discarded newspapers. I hit pay dirt when I found an intact copy of that day's *New York Times*. There was a lengthy article about this young senator named John Edwards, who was about to announce his run for the presidency. I was particularly interested in learning about him because he represented North Carolina, where I was headed.

For the First Night shows the next night I would be performing three forty-five-minute concerts. At the time I was working wireless, and near the end of each show I would put a miner's light on my head and go into the audience singing a song called "You Look Pretty Good for Your Age," searching for the best-looking man in the crowd, whom I would crown "Mr. Portland" or "Mr. Twin Cities"—whatever city I was in. Then I would bring the lucky guy onstage and either write a song with him on the spot or ask him questions to see if he was intellectually fit to wear the crown.

Since I was doing three short shows, I made three different crowns for that night—"Mr. Raleigh-Durham," "Mr. New Year's Eve," and "Mr. North Carolina." I had to make all three titles different in case they ran into one another later. Didn't want a fistfight to ensue. *(I'm Mr. New Year's Eve! No, I AM! Put up your dukes!!)*

The night prior to most shows I would carefully craft a crown out of newspaper, usually spending two or three hours on each one. I really did! After a while it all got to be too much, and I dropped that song because the crown making was really cutting into my practice and knitting time. But not that night. For that New Year's Eve in North Carolina, I'd be doing that song three times in a large room at the convention center, holding about a thousand people.

To test the intellectual ability of the chosen dudes, I made up four questions: one on sports, one on politics, one on current events, and one on the arts. The sports question caused a lot of debate. Who has a better basketball team: Duke or the University of North Carolina? Because I had read that article about John Edwards in the *Times*, the political question was, "Who is the forty-nine-year-old senator from North Carolina who is expected to enter the next presidential race?" At all three shows they got the answer right.

I had no idea that John Edwards and his wife, Elizabeth, were at one of those shows. I found out when the senator's office contacted my agent the following week requesting an autographed album for Elizabeth. They said that she had been a longtime fan of my music. And they also wanted to know if I would be interested in doing concerts for him should he run for president.

I signed a CD for Elizabeth, then wrote to the senator that I had to do more research on him and his policies, since I didn't know enough at that point to support him. I also wrote that my gut feeling was he should think about running for vice president. I didn't think he was old enough or experienced enough to run for president.

A couple weeks later I got a note from Elizabeth Edwards, thanking me for the CD. She mentioned that her favorite song of mine was "Fly on a Plane." "I never get on a plane these days without thinking of that song," she wrote.

Ever since then I have been sending Elizabeth my CDs when they are completed. I send everything to her through Sarah Lowder, director of the Wade Edwards Foundation (www.wade.org). It was founded in 1996 in memory of the Edwardses' son, Wade, who died in a car accident as a teenager. The mission of the foundation is to reward, encourage, and inspire young people in the pursuit of excellence. In her most recent book, *Resilience*, published in 2009, Elizabeth writes heartbreakingly about the death of Wade. It's difficult to read parts of that book, and it's amazing how Elizabeth Edwards has dealt with the difficulties she's encountered.

During the run-up to the presidential election of 2004, when John Edwards was on the ticket with John Kerry, I got the idea to knit a shawl for Elizabeth. A company called Prism makes one of my favorite yarns, and there is a color called Tea Rose that is soft pink, beige, and pale yellow—so beautiful. So my plan was to knit the shawl in this color backstage at my concerts, pass it around the knitting circle and let everybody add a few stitches, and then I would also add some silver and gold sequins here and there, too.

I felt certain the Kerry/Edwards ticket was going to win, and I knew that the last two months leading up to Election Day would be very exciting for Elizabeth. I thought that giving her a shawl knitted at that same time would be a beautiful reminder of such an important time in her life. Not surprisingly, most of the backstage knitters were Democrats who loved adding stitches to this gift for her. But Elizabeth Edwards is one of those political wives everyone loves, no matter what their party affiliation.

As you know, not only did the Kerry/Edwards ticket *not* win, the day after the election it was announced that Elizabeth Edwards had been diagnosed with breast cancer. That night I did a concert in Toronto with Tom Paxton, and the mood at the preshow knitting circle was somber indeed. The shawl for Elizabeth was about three-quarters finished, but now everyone adding stitches did so with an aching heart. Like Australians, Canadians probably follow U.S. elections more closely than half of the American population, and up north they were as shocked as I was that George W. Bush had been reelected.

The shawl for Elizabeth now represented something so different from what I had envisioned. For the next month I passed it around at all the knitting circles. I worked on it in airports, and when knitters would stop to admire it and I told them whom it was for, they would sit down to add a few stitches. One time a little girl, maybe four years old, was fascinated by what I was doing, so I put the needles in her hands and helped her make a couple of stitches. By the time the shawl was finally finished, hundreds of people had contributed to it.

I packed it up and sent it via FedEx to Sarah Lowder in Raleigh-Durham. Right around that time there was an anthrax scare involving the post office, so I figured sending it FedEx would be best. The next day I got a call from the Wade Foundation, telling me that due to the anthrax scare they weren't allowed to open any packages, even from FedEx, unless they knew exactly what was inside. I told them what it was, and they promised to send it on to Elizabeth.

A couple of weeks later I got a beautiful note from her. After she underwent treatment for her cancer, she wrote a book, *Saving Graces*, published in 2006, in which she wrote about the shawl and what it meant to her: "It is the gift of all those women whose names I'll never know. And it is, also at the same time, something in which I can literally wrap myself and something in which I can figuratively wrap myself, this huge community of people—spread out among the towns I toured—people who were pulling for me and who believed in the strength of that tiny knot they tied."

When I read that, I e-mailed Fine Points, the yarn shop in Cleveland where I had bought that Prism yarn, and Liz Tekus, the owner, made up a kit of knitting needles, Prism yarn, and silver laser disk sequins, calling it the Elizabeth Edwards Shawl Kit. (If you go to www.finepoints.com, you can buy one. Don't be shocked by the price of the yarn. I told you I've developed a weakness for the good stuff!)

Okay, now back to the guns. On April 26, 2007, Bob Herbert wrote a column in the *New York Times* called "Hooked on Violence" that, among other things, stated that since 1968, the year that Robert Kennedy and Martin Luther King were assassinated, more than a million Americans had been killed by guns. Not in wars overseas, but on our own soil—murders, suicides, accidental shootings. I'd become more sensitive to the gun issue after October 2002 when there were those bizarre shootings in the Washington, D.C./Virginia area, where my sister Jody lives. I learned Cheryl

Wheeler's song "If It Were Up to Me" and started doing it in my shows, but I didn't feel that was enough, so I ran a half-page ad in *The Performing Songwriter* magazine of Cheryl's lyrics:

If It Were Up to Me
by Cheryl Wheeler

> Maybe it's the movies, maybe it's the books
>
> Maybe it's the bullets, maybe it's the real crooks
>
> Maybe it's the drugs, maybe it's the parents
>
> Maybe it's the colors everybody's wearin'
>
> Maybe it's the President, maybe it's the last one
>
> Maybe it's the one before that, what he done
>
> Maybe it's the high schools, maybe it's the teachers
>
> Maybe it's the tattooed children in the bleachers
>
> Maybe it's the Bible, maybe it's the lack
>
> Maybe it's the music, maybe it's the crack
>
> Maybe it's the hairdos, maybe it's the TV
>
> Maybe it's the cigarettes, maybe it's the family
>
> Maybe it's the fast food, maybe it's the news
>
> Maybe it's divorce, maybe it's abuse
>
> Maybe it's the lawyers, maybe it's the prisons
>
> Maybe it's the Senators, maybe it's the system
>
> Maybe it's the fathers, maybe it's the sons
>
> Maybe it's the sisters, maybe it's the moms
>
> Maybe it's the radio, maybe it's road rage
>
> Maybe El Nino, or UV rays
>
> Maybe it's the army, maybe it's the liquor
>
> Maybe it's the papers, maybe the militia
>
> Maybe it's the athletes, maybe it's the ads
>
> Maybe it's the sports fans, maybe it's a fad

Maybe it's the magazines, maybe it's the internet

Maybe it's the lottery, maybe it's the immigrants

Maybe it's taxes, big business

Maybe it's the KKK and the skinheads

Maybe it's the communists, maybe it's the Catholics

Maybe it's the hippies, maybe it's the addicts

Maybe it's the art, maybe it's the sex

Maybe it's the homeless, maybe it's the banks

Maybe it's the clearcut, maybe it's the ozone

Maybe it's the chemicals, maybe it's the car phone

Maybe it's the fertilizer, maybe it's the nose rings

Maybe it's the end, but I know one thing.

If it were up to me, I'd take away the guns.

It cost me over a thousand dollars to run the ad, and the magazine got angry letters from gun-owning subscribers who canceled their subscriptions.

But reading in Bob Herbert's column that more than a million Americans had been killed by guns shocked me to the point where I couldn't do another thing until I wrote my own song about it. I'm all for *knowing* rather than *not* knowing the reality of any given situation, and I thought that if people heard this grim statistic once more, it might go a long way toward at least opening up the debate about gun control in this country.

I went into the recording studio with Brian Bauers, the lead singer of the acoustic rock band the WMDs, who produces other musicians on the side. I asked bass player Steve Doyle and violinist Robin Batteau to also play on this song.

Right around this time, John and Elizabeth Edwards held a press conference to announce that her cancer had returned. I put together a disk of some of my new songs in various states of completion, including this one about gun violence, and sent it to Elizabeth. She wrote back about that song in particular and encouraged me to put it out into the world, not just send it to her.

With all she had on her plate—a husband running for president, two young children at home, not to mention dealing with cancer—for her to write to me meant a great deal. Even though I had no plans to put out an album that year, I did so because of Elizabeth Edwards's letter.

That gun song is the only serious song on my Yellow Tail Records's disk *Happydance of the Xenophobe*. I put it near the middle so that whoever is listening to the album will be taken by surprise. I've never written a song quite like it. It just states facts and asks a few questions.

I have gotten more e-mail about this song than anything I have written in the last ten years, and 95 percent of the e-mail is angry. Yes, gun owners from all over the country have chastised me for writing this song. Some of their letters are bizarre, and more than a few have told me that I should "write a song about all the people who are killed in car accidents—cars kill people, so why do you blame guns and not cars?" One man wrote that of the million killed by guns, "900,000 of them are gang members, crack whores, and drug addicts, so guns are helping clean up our society." A firearms instructor was in the audience in Boston when I sang the song, and he wrote that I obviously have fear issues when it comes to guns, so he offered to teach me how to shoot for free.

Jeez Louise. Did he not get what this song is about?

If you insist on writing me an angry letter about it, I will write back and put the same ending I put on all the letters I write back to gun owners: "P.S. Don't shoot the messenger."

After another concert in Boston, a woman came backstage in tears to tell me that her sister was shot and killed by a boyfriend in 1989. She said she was so glad someone was acknowledging her sister's death and all the others who had died this way. Now when I get angry e-mails from gun owners, I tell them about this woman and write, "I hope you can understand why her reaction to the song means a million times more to me than yours."

I know it might be considered a bit foolish to anger gun owners, but I feel safe doing it. They know if they took a shot at me, my CD sales would go through the roof, and they don't want to see *that* happen.

So the recording of this song, and the whole album it is on, came about because of a string of incidences that occurred after I took up knitting after

9/11. When I'm in New York City, I stop in whenever I can to Knitty City on West Seventy-ninth Street between Broadway and Amsterdam to sit and knit with Pearl, the owner (yes, that's her real name) and her staff. If I have a day off in Cleveland, I drop into Fine Points. If I'm in Williamsburg, Virginia, it's Knitting Sisters. In Redding, California, it's Sew What? In Bath, Maine, it's Halcyon Yarn. In Denver it's Showers of Flowers. On Bainbridge Island it's Churchmouse Yarns and Teas. In Bloomington, Indiana, it's A Yarn Basket. In Tarrytown, New York, it's Flying Fingers; in Chatham, New York, it's The Warm Ewe. In Derry, New Hampshire, it's Yarn and Fiber Company, and in Flagstaff, Arizona, it's Purl in the Pines. Other great shops include the Yarn Shop in Geneva, New York; Bella Yarns in Warren, Rhode Island; and, in Massachusetts, Yarn It All (North Attleboro), Elissa's Creative Warehouse (Needham), Webs (Northampton), and Saftler's Fabric and Yarns (Whitman). I keep finding wonderful knitting stores and knitters everywhere I go.

At some concerts I have noticed knitters with light-up needles, knitting during the show. I love that! I look out at them and say, "Hey, if I didn't have to play guitar right now, I'd be knitting, too."

26

ERVIN DRAKE

've always loved sweeping songs that tell a life story—I mentioned Judy Collins's magnificent "Secret Gardens of the Heart," and there's also her song "The Blizzard." Amanda McBroom's "Errol Flynn" is another gem of a song, and speaking of gems, "Loose Gems" by Craig Werth, "Quarter Moon" by Cheryl Wheeler, "Stars" by Janis Ian, and "Are You as Excited About Me as I Am" by Jeff Daniels are beautiful, meaningful, meticulously crafted songs that I can listen to again and again and never tire of.

And at the very top of the heap is "It Was a Very Good Year."

Everything about that song is perfection—the simplicity of the lyrics, the melody between the verses, the unusual rhyme scheme. . . .

When I was seventeen

It was a very good year

It was a very good year for small town girls

And soft summer nights

We'd hide from the lights

> On the village green
>
> When I was seventeen

The song just thrills me—the lyrics go from the age seventeen to twenty-one to thirty-five to "the autumn of the year," spanning a lifetime in four and a half minutes.

I remember how personally so many people took Frank Sinatra's death. He was the skinny kid from Hoboken who grew up to be the defining singing voice of his generation, and a good actor, too. Lots of women adored him, and lots of men idolized him. One of them was a young guy named Stewart, who owned the Broadway Delights delicatessen on the east side of Broadway between Seventy-fifth and Seventy-sixth streets. For the entire week following Sinatra's death, Stewart played Frank's music non-stop in his store.

One of those afternoons I was in there. Stewart was making my sandwich, Frank's music was playing, and out of nowhere Stewart asked me if I knew any girls I could introduce him to. He wanted to settle down but hadn't met the right girl yet.

I was surprised by his question—I didn't know him well. We joked around a lot, but I never saw him outside of his shop, so I never expected he'd think of me as someone who could play matchmaker. I told him that offhand I couldn't think of anyone . . . but I could write a song about his predicament.

I left with my sandwich, and that night I started working on a song that I eventually titled "Another New York Afternoon," which ends like this:

> Now the man beside me is wearing headphones
>
> Is that music? . . Yes, Sinatra's voice
>
> The woman with him looks like she needs to talk
>
> But right now she is not first choice
>
> So I lean to listen in a little closer
>
> "It was a very good year" . . . my favorite tune

As we travel underground

The music curls around

Another New York afternoon

Stewart sings along

With Sinatra's song

It's another New York afternoon

To my knowledge, Stewart has never seen me perform, and now his deli has closed and he's not in the neighborhood anymore (neither am I). But I gave him a copy of the album that contains this song, and for a couple of years I sang it all over the country. Sometimes women would ask me for Stewart's number, and yes, I would give them the number for his deli. I said to Stewart in private, "If you meet your wife because of this song, and then if you break her heart, I will have to track you down and smack you."

I heard through the grapevine that he did find his heart's desire, though not through my song. I never even knew his last name. However, it was thanks to Stewart that I met one of our greatest American song-writers, the author of "It Was a Very Good Year," Ervin Drake.

One Monday night three years or so after I wrote the song about Stew-art, I was in the audience at a Manhattan cabaret called Don't Tell Mama for a show called *Monday Night Madness*, hosted by a stand-up comic named Angela LaGreca. At the time, during the day Angela was the warm-up comedian for the TV show *The View*, and often on weekends she would play comedy clubs around the country, sometimes as Joy Behar's opening act.

Angela's guests for *Monday Night Madness* would be other comics and sometimes singers (I was one of her guests a few months later). One of her favorite things to do in the show was to point out celebrities in the audience. The night when I was in the audience, she pointed out someone and mentioned that he was the author of the song "It Was a Very Good Year." Ervin Drake!

I almost jumped out of my skin. As soon as the show was over I weaved through the crowd to find him. I'd had a couple of cosmopolitans, so I was a little tipsy. When I finally found him, I started babbling. "I love *your* song so much that I have a song about how much I love your song!"

I don't know if he couldn't hear me well or just thought I was some nut, but he seemed to wave me off in a dismissive manner, and then I lost him in the crowd. Or maybe he was motioning for me to meet him outside? Whatever it was, I couldn't find him, and I couldn't believe how I had messed up meeting one of my heroes.

The next day I found an Ervin Drake listed in Great Neck in the Manhattan phone book. I wasn't bold enough to call; instead, I wrote to him. First I wrote out a postcard (my theory is that many people won't open mail from strangers—but who can resist reading a postcard?). In a separate envelope I sent him *Getting in Touch with My Inner Bitch*, with a note on the outside of the CD asking him to play track nine. I included my street address, my e-mail address, and my telephone number. I told him I would love to discuss songwriting with him, if he was interested.

Ervin and I have since become fast friends. He comes from a very creative family. His brother Milton wrote the songs "Mairzy Doats and Dozy Doats and Liddle Lamzy Divey" and "The Java Jive." His brother Arnold was a comic book writer best known for creating *Deadman* and *Doom Patrol*. Ervin knew and worked with many legendary singers and songwriters. He told me great stories about Frank Sinatra—how whenever he would come to New York he would call Ervin up and ask, "How are you doing? How's the family? Anything I can do for you?" How when any of his songwriters were in the audience when he was singing, Frank would always single them out, praise them to the skies, and make them feel like a million bucks.

Ervin Drake changed me as a songwriter. I can look at any one of my songs and know instantly if it was written before I knew Ervin, or after, based on the rhyming.

Ervin Drake is quite disciplined in his writing, is very much "old school." He was good friends with Johnny Mercer, who wrote songs we still know today: "Moon River," "One More for My Baby (and One More for the Road)," "I Remember You." Johnny used to say—and Ervin has repeated it many times—"If a song doesn't rhyme exactly, you aren't finished writing it," and now I agree. There are the rare songwriters who can rhyme odd words—Joni Mitchell comes to mind, as do Leonard Cohen and Lori Lieberman—but they are exceptions. Now I wince when I hear songs that rhyme *home* and *alone* or *time* and *mine*. Those are assonant, or "near rhymes," and it's not good songwriting.

Songwriting is a craft. Half rhymes, sloppy rhymes, and near rhymes are the songwriting equivalents of leaving loose threads dangling from your clothes or leaving rough surfaces on hand-built furniture. When I have been able to, I have gone back and fixed some of my songs where I used lazy rhymes, or improper tenses of songs to force a rhyme.

I know I keep coming back to "Good Thing He Can't Read My Mind," but I have been told it is my "signature" song, so it's a good one to demonstrate with. This is the bridge of the song I originally wrote in 1988:

> I am not complaining I'm just making observations
>
> Expanding your horizons is a sign of maturation

That rhyme bothered me *every* time I sang it, and I must have sung it hundreds of times (and winced hundreds of times). I knew *maturation* wasn't the right word, but *maturity* didn't rhyme, so rather than keep working on it, I forced a rhyme. After becoming friends with Ervin, I knew I had to rewrite that line. It's even more of a tongue twister now, but it *is* a better rhyme:

> I am not complaining I'm just making observations
>
> Expanding your horizons is a sign of sophistication
>
> Now I tolerate cigars 'cause he's a smoker
>
> I'm playing chess though I confess
>
> Sometimes I long for poker

At least the rhymes in the bridge are all good ones. I don't know if anyone has noticed that I changed *maturation* to *sophistication* in the song after singing it differently for more than fifteen years, but it's because of Ervin that I did. Of course there are other places in the song where I used assonant rhymes, but there's no way to gracefully fix them. For example, in the opera verse:

> I don't understand a word—even when it's English
>
> Everyone around me says, "This is divine!"
>
> I don't like the opera—look! I'm at the opera!
>
> It's a good thing he can't read my mind

Eeeew! I rhymed divine and mind—bad, bad songwriter. In the skiing verse I sing:

> There's no exhilaration—I am feeling terrified
>
> Everyone around me's having such a great time
>
> I do not like skiing—but look at me I'm skiing
>
> It's a good thing he can't read my mind

I rhymed *time* and *mind*—what a *shonda!* Uh-oh. Here's part of the sushi verse:

> Some say eating sushi is like chewing on your own cheek
>
> Or sucking down a bucketful of tentacled slime
>
> I am eating sushi—I do not like sushi
>
> It's a good thing he can't read my mind

Well, at least I'm consistent. I may have fixed the awkward rhyme in the bridge, but I haven't fixed the bad rhymes in all three verses, though I have learned to live with them. Recently, however, Rene Ruiz, from the a cappella group Toxic Audio, challenged me to write a "male" version of this song—which I did ("Good Thing SHE Can't Read My Mind: A Dude's Eye View" is on my latest album). When you hear it, you'll see that it's a much better crafted song than the original.

If you are a songwriter, I want you to go and look at some of your own songs. Look at them—as Ervin says—"with an unfriendly eye." If you are using assonant rhymes, now is your time to raise that bar—unless you are *absolutely* sure the exact meaning of the word is more important to you than the rhyme. (Or if you are Joni Mitchell, or Leonard Cohen, or Lori

Lieberman.) It's okay to go to www.rhymezone.com. There's no excuse for sloppy rhyming when a Web site like that is so convenient. Hey, I wonder if there's a lot of rhymes for the word *rhymezone.*

How about *pinecone?*

No, that's an assonant rhyme! Just wanted to make sure you were paying attention.

As I've said (and sung) before, I don't believe in coincidence. If you are a songwriter, think of this as a message coming from the Great Beyond from Johnny Mercer through Ervin Drake through me to you: the best songs that stand the test of time are the most carefully crafted ones.

And to give the flip side, it is also extremely difficult to write songs that *don't rhyme at all.* Annie Bauerlein is one of my favorite contemporary writers. She wrote a song called "Remember When We Were Just Friends," which doesn't have a single rhyme in it. I *love* that song and didn't realize it was completely unrhymed until I read her liner notes about the song, where she mentions that fact.

I think writing a completely nonrhyming song is a different kind of amazing feat. I'll have to ask Ervin if he's ever tried that.

Ervin wrote many other songs besides "It Was a Very Good Year," though before I tell you about those other songs, I should tell you *how* it is he came to write *that* song.

In 1961 the Kingston Trio was working on an album, and the music publisher they were working with, Arthur Modell, wanted a solo number for singer Bobby Shane. Ervin was at work at six o'clock one night, getting ready to go home, when Arthur stopped him in the hall and asked him if he had anything that Bobby could do as a solo. Bobby was coming in the very next morning. Ervin said no, he didn't have anything on hand, but he looked through his little notebook where he kept ideas for songs and came across this: "neo-folk tune, story of a guy's life told in wine vintage terms, possible title 'It Was a Very Good Year.' "

Ervin says, "I closed the book, sat down at the piano, and started writing the words and the music simultaneously."

He wrote the entire song in thirty minutes.

The Kingston Trio recorded it, and as luck would have it, a couple years later Frank Sinatra was driving through the desert from Los Angeles to Rancho Mirage, heard the song on the radio, and thought, "Hey, that would be great for *The September of My Years*," the album he was about to start working on. He pulled off the road and called the radio station to find out more about the song.

I once heard Jonathan Schwartz play a live recording of that song by Frank Sinatra, and Frank introduced it by saying, "Here's a folk song for you kids . . ." Because Frank first heard it sung by the Kingston Trio, he always thought of it as a folk tune.

My all-time favorite segue from song to song is listening to the Kingston Trio's version of "Very Good Year" side by side with Sinatra's because they are in the same key. The Trio is two guitars, one voice, and one guy whistling, and of course Frank's version is with a full orchestra with that powerful, lush arrangement written by Gordon Jenkins (and for which Gordon won a Grammy). Who knew that such an indelible recording started out as a simple folk arrangement?

But Ervin Drake wasn't a folk song writer. His first big hit was the Billie Holiday recording of "Good Morning Heartache," and the story behind *that* song has become legend.

Ervin was twenty-three years old, a struggling songwriter in New York. He had some very interesting jobs before he made his living as a songwriter—but he's writing a book, and I don't want to give any of it away. Let's just say they were not the kinds of jobs you'd put on your permanent résumé or tell your mom about.

He was dating a gorgeous Broadway showgirl who was twenty-one and a real knockout. Ervin was madly in love, and though he knew it was quite a risk, he proposed marriage to her. She not only turned him down; she broke up with him on the spot. She was having the time of her life in New York and was not about to be tied down, especially not to a penniless songwriter.

Ervin was devastated. He poured his sorrow into his work, writing the lyrics to "Good Morning Heartache." The next day he showed them to his friend Irene Higgenbotham, a pianist, who wrote music to accompany them.

Ervin Drake and Irene Higgenbotham sat on the floor of the recording studio when Billie Holiday recorded the song for the first time. They were too scared to tell her they were the authors—she was a big star, and they were nobodies. But they shouldn't have worried. She knew a great song when she heard one, and her recording of it not only was Ervin's first hit, it changed his life forever.

He went on to write the musical *What Makes Sammy Run* and *Her First Roman*. He wrote the Frankie Laine hit "I Believe" that thousands of schoolchildren have sung over the years. He wrote "Tico Tico," "Al Di La," "Widow's Weeds," and hundreds of others. He wrote music for the *Jane Froman TV Show*, eventually met a lovely woman, married, moved to Great Neck, and had a family.

One day in the mid-1970s he was drinking his morning coffee, reading the obits in *Newsday*, and saw that showgirl's name. Her husband had passed away, and she lived one town over. He had never seen her again after she refused his marriage proposal, but he had never forgotten her, especially because she inadvertently jump-started his career. He thought of calling her, but he didn't. He did smile wistfully, however, when he realized that she was living just one town away from him for all those years, and he had never bumped into her.

A year later that showgirl was drinking her morning coffee, reading the obits in *Newsday*, and saw Ervin's name listed in his wife's obituary. She didn't call him . . . for a respectable length of time. But she did call him eventually.

"May I speak to Mr. Drake?" she asked nervously into the phone.

"Hello, Edith!" Ervin exclaimed.

What happened next, in his own words: "Later I asked her if she was free that night, and she was, and I drove us to Elaine's in New York City, where we had dinner with my friends.

"Later I drove her home and stayed over. We discovered we had a lot in common—neither of us was a stamp collector."

Ervin and Edith married in 1982 and have been together ever since. All those years they were apart, Edith never knew that Ervin had written "Good Morning Heartache" for her.

Next time you hear "Good Morning Heartache," you are going to remember how Ervin finally got the girl thirty-four years after she broke his heart.

Ervin and Edith are fixtures on the New York cabaret and theater scene and quite the glamorous couple. (Edith—once a showgirl, always a showgirl. And Ervin cuts quite a figure himself.) They drive in to Manhattan at least twice a week to see live shows. Ervin continues to write, too. I recorded his song "I'm a Card-Carrying Bleeding Heart Liberal" on my 2005 album *folkZinger*—it's a live performance from the stage at Chicago's Old Town School of Music. I brought my cell phone onstage, and Ervin was on the line as I sang the song with the help of students from the school.

Ervin and I co-wrote the political song "The Peter Principle at Work" on that album, and both he and Edith's voices are on the fourth track of that disk, my version of "Winter in Manhattan." I made sure that song's rhymes were exact before I called him. The original first rhyme was, "When it's winter in Manhattan / you never know what to expect / some days it's a snowy Wonderland / other days it rains you get wet." I was able to fix the assonant rhyming by changing "what to expect" to "what you will get."

I also corralled Ervin into actually singing on a couple of my albums— the song "Sunday Breakfast with Christine (and Ervin)" on my 2002 album *I Was in Love with a Difficult Man*. In that song I sing the recipe for *petit pain au chocolat*, and Ervin sings the voice of the hungry, sleepy man. The following year he joined me on my holiday disk *The Runaway Christmas Tree*. As Ervin himself says, "You simply can't make a good Christmas album without a Jew." He sings the Hanukkah verse on the opening track, "A Christmas/Kwanzaa/Solstice/Chanukah/Ramadan/Boxing Day Song," and also "Scalloped Potatoes," track number eight.

Recently there was a workshop production of his musical, *What Makes Sammy Run*. Ervin wrote some new songs for it, and he hopes to bring a revival back to Broadway. Ervin is now in his nineties, and he's still tweaking a work that was a success on Broadway back in 1964. Writing for the theater is a fascinating process, and I saw the workshop version three times.

International cabaret chanteuse KT Sullivan threw a birthday party for Ervin in 2006 when he turned eighty-seven. I wrote a special poem for him and recited it at the party. You should have seen him squirm, then squirm and moan, then squirm, moan, and cry out in pain.

A Cavalcade of Near Rhymes for Ervin Drake on His 87th Birthday

Before I met Ervin I thought it was perfectly **fine**

When writing songs to use imperfect **rhymes**

If the line was "I'm doing the best that I **can"**

The next line could end with the word **"understand"**

But "can" and "understand" no, that's just plain **wrong**

You'll never see something like that in his **songs**

He says if the rhyme's not exact, the song is not **done**

So back to the drawing board, not for all but for **some**

Who take the craft of songwriting as serious **work**

And never give up, even if it **hurts**

To wrack their brains over the smallest of **nouns**

'Til the absolute perfectly tuned word is **found**

I know that Ervin wishes he could cover his **ears**

This imperfect rhyming just makes him feel **weird**

He's looking at Edith, thinking, please take me **home**

I can't take this bad writing, I must be **alone**

But it is your birthday, dear Mr. **Drake**

87 years gone, today starting **88**

You're fit as a fiddle, oh dear, that's a **cliché**

Like when you get lemons, make **lemonade**

You say if you avoid clichés like the **plague**

You'll go far in this world; your reputation will be **made**

> We hope on your birthday you have a fabulous **time**
>
> Yes, Ervin Drake, you are one of a **kind!**

That bad poetry took me about four hours to write—yes, eight times longer than it took Ervin to pen "It Was a Very Good Year." What does that tell you?

When Ervin was in Los Angeles a couple of years ago, he ran into the splendid cabaret singer Tierney Sutton.

"She walks up to me," Ervin said, "and asks, 'Are you the man who wrote "It Was a Very Good Year?"' Of course I proudly said, 'Yes, I am.' Then she says, 'You bastard!' I stood there wondering why on earth she would say that, and I'm thinking maybe she's going to make a joke, but she doesn't, so I ask her, 'Is there a problem?' "

"Yes," she said. "The last verse where you talk about an age is thirty-five, and then the next verse you say, 'But now the days are short / I'm in the autumn of the year.' I'm over thirty-five, and I can't believe I should be preparing for the autumn of my life at this point! There should be another verse!"

Tierney Sutton made such an impression on Ervin that he did write an additional verse:

> When I was fifty-two
>
> It was a very good year
>
> It was a very good year
>
> For trav'ling the world from
>
> Greenland to Greece
>
> I found inner peace
>
> As globally I flew
>
> When I was fifty-two

"I wrote this after Frank had died," Ervin said. "It's the only verse of the song he never heard."

Now Ervin's friends are hinting around that *another* verse to this song is needed. Life doesn't end at fifty-two, either.

In 2008, on the tenth anniversary of Frank Sinatra's death, I met Harry at Patsy's Restaurant on West Fifty-sixth Street for dinner. I chose it because the story was it was Frank Sinatra's favorite place to eat in New York, and I wanted to drink a toast to him there.

I arrived a few minutes early, walking from the west. There was a group of people who were getting out of a car, approaching from the east. We all arrived at the door at the same time, but since the door opened in my direction, I reached for the handle first and held it open for them.

The first two people walked through and thanked me, but the third person, a man, stopped, held the door for me, and said, "No, allow me."

I walked through the door, looked up, and said "thank you" to Frank Sinatra Jr.

He was there with quite an entourage, and the staff was ecstatic to see him. Word quickly spread. People started to look up from their food and whisper. Diners from the second floor casually walked down the stairs and strolled around the first floor just to get a peek at him before heading back upstairs. Frank Jr. looks a lot like his dad, though beefier, and obviously—since he wouldn't let me hold the door for him and insisted on holding it for me—he's an old-fashioned, well-bred gent.

His party was seated at a long table to the left, not far from the stairs, and Harry and I were seated right next to them. A few minutes after we were seated, the people at the table on the other side of us left, and the maître d' asked if we would move to that table—Mr. Sinatra's party was growing and needed ours.

Of course we moved.

I e-mailed Ervin on my cell phone that Frank Jr. was at Patsy's; would he like to send a message?

Ervin e-mailed back: "Yes. You might say that the day his dad determined to record my song, it was a very good year for this composer/lyrist. He was the best friend a songwriter ever had."

Then he followed it up with this: "You might add that any time he'd like me there for an appearance, I'd be ready. This old kid ain't a bad crooner himself."

Then a few minutes later, this arrived: "Today I bought 500 Frank Sinatra stamps!"

I wrote out Ervin's e-mails onto a postcard, then asked the maître d' if he would hand it to him. He refused. I tried explaining that it was a message from Ervin Drake, an old friend of Frank Sr., but he waved his hand, walked away, and wouldn't listen.

If I was bolder I would have walked it over to his table myself, but I didn't. I didn't want to intrude, though I think Frank Jr. would have loved to have received a message from one of his dad's favorite songwriters.

After we had paid our bill and were getting up to leave, I watched the waiter bring the bill to Frank Jr.'s table. I e-mailed Ervin: "Ervn—Frank Jr. jst grabd check b4 anyone else at his tabl had a chance. He turnd down all offrs 2 split it w/him."

Ervin replied, "Christine: Just like his old man."

27

JIM CARUSO'S
CAST PARTY AT BIRDLAND

O n July 19, 2004, the *New York Times* ran a story by a writer named Erik Piepenburg about an open-mike show, *Jim Caruso's Cast Party*, held every Monday at the jazz club Birdland on West Forty-fourth Street in Manhattan. It had been many years since I was part of the Monday-night Speakeasy cooperative in Greenwich Village, and based on what I read, it sounded like this show welcomed all kinds of performers and songwriters, not just Broadway/cabaret or jazz. I called and was told that performers who wanted to be in the *Cast Party* show should start arriving at 9:30 to sign up with host Jim Caruso.

Birdland is a lovely restaurant/club that seats 140 people at three tiers of candlelit tables and banquettes that surround the stage. The stage is small, and a good portion of it is taken up by a nine-foot concert grand piano. The bar area, to the left of the stage, can hold another fifty people or so, and the dark gray walls are lined with beautiful framed black-and-white photos of jazz greats, all snapped while performing there. The club is owned by Gianni Valenti, a twenty-first-century Renaissance man who's combined his love of restaurants with his love of music to create a club that has live music seven nights a week, with excellent acoustics, sound, lights, and food.

I arrived around 9:30 that first Monday night with my guitar, but I didn't plan on singing. I figured I should just watch the show once to see if someone like me might fit in. I introduced myself to Jim Caruso and was surprised that he knew who I was. He insisted I do a song in the show that night.

So much for inching my way in.

At that point *Cast Party* had been going for just over a year—in two different venues before it found a home at Birdland. It is unlike any other open-mike scene I had experienced before. For one thing, it starts late. At 10:00 p.m. Jim Caruso, an extremely funny, talented, versatile performer in his own right, is the host, ringleader, and cheerleader. He sings and dances, he has produced television shows, he has recorded albums, and when Liza Minnelli put together a stage show called *Kay Thompson & the Williams Brothers,* she cast Jim as one of the Williams Brothers. As one of the Williams Brothers, Jim Caruso has toured the world with Liza, but his *Cast Party* show is so well established now that it keeps rolling even when he is in South America or Europe with Liza.

At *Cast Party*, Jim, or whoever is hosting, decides *who* goes on *when*—makes up the running order on the fly. Your name could be called first at 10:00 p.m., or it could be called last at 1:00 a.m. You would never know, and it is *not* cool to bug the host. You'd have to sit there and sweat, prepared to hit the ground running.

There's a house band consisting of piano, bass, and occasionally drums. For the first couple years the house pianist was Billy Stritch, who is also Liza's primary accompanist, so as she traveled more frequently and he was less available, another pianist, Tedd Firth, took over. Tedd also records, performs, accompanies some of the best jazz and cabaret singers on the scene, and travels a lot, so other pianists have had to sub for him on occasion. One is Mark Berman, who has conducted the *Rent* orchestra on Broadway and played piano in the pit orchestra of *Avenue Q*. Another is David Budway, also a fantastic pianist who has toured the world and who also works with Liza Minnelli. On occasion Billy Stritch will still be called on for *Cast Party*. All these pianists are first-rate technicians at the keyboard and lively performers under the lights.

On Monday nights it's Steve Doyle who plays stand-up bass. He also fronts his own band, Men's Warehouse, singing and playing piano, but at

Cast Party he's just on bass. When he's not available, British musician Wayne Batchelor subs for him, as has Saadi Zain. Steve was absent when the arts minister of the Turks and Caicos Islands flew him down there because he wanted bass lessons. (I guess if you're the arts minister of a country, you can do things like that!)

It's quite a workout for the *Cast Party* onstage musicians. They have to be able to read whatever is put in front of them and usually have no more than a thirty-second powwow with each performer to set the tempo and go over any idiosyncrasies of the sheet music. If it's a well-known standard, Tedd and Steve know every one ever written in every key ever written, so sheet music isn't necessary. I'm sure many of the singers don't realize how lucky they are to have such experienced professionals backing them up. The singers who bring their own accompanists—feeling more comfortable, I suppose, with someone they've rehearsed with—don't realize what an opportunity they are missing by *not* using the house musicians. I mostly perform solo with my guitar—the house band gets a break—but if I have a song that would benefit from having them play along, I write up a chord chart, and I get to have a back-up band, too.

The quality of the singers ranges from starry-eyed newbies who've literally stepped off the bus at Port Authority earlier that day to legendary pros like Marilyn Maye, who holds the record for the most appearances on *The Tonight Show with Johnny Carson* (seventy-six). On any given night there will be thirty to thirty-five singers onstage, and the house band gives each one the best possible backing that they can. I've heard audience members marvel repeatedly at how much care the pianist and bassist display, even when it's a singer who possesses more chutzpah than talent. Credit Jim Caruso for creating a very supportive atmosphere, and Gianni Valenti for welcoming *Cast Party* to his legendary club. This is not *Star Search* or *American Idol*. There's no competition, which keeps the atmosphere fun. Over the years I have become friends with many of the regulars; most are singers, and some are songwriters. Very often we sit together, cheering each other when it goes well and commiserating when it doesn't.

Yes, I have a couple of "crash and burn" stories from *Cast Party*. One rule I set for myself—and I encourage other performers to heed—is that you simply cannot have a drink before you perform. You are working. Even though you're not getting paid to be in the show at *Cast Party*, if you are serious about what you are doing, you don't drink. After you perform is a different story, though even then you have to watch it.

So one night at *Cast Party* I got there right after it had started. There were no seats at my friends' tables, but there was an open table right down in front of the stage. I had my guitar with me, out of its case, so that when my name was called I could just jump onstage.

I was nursing a cranberry and seltzer as I waited for my name to be called. Time ticked by: eleven o'clock, then midnight, then twelve-thirty. There had been shows where not everybody got onstage if too many showed up, so I figured it was going to be my turn to end up on the cutting room floor. So I ordered a cosmo.

By that time it was 12:45 and most of the audience had gone home, but there were still thirty or forty people in the house. My cosmo arrived, I took one sip, and *then* Jim Caruso called my name. I was surprised, and in my haste while grabbing my guitar, I decided to take one giant step up to the stage rather than walking to the stairs on the side of the stage.

Instead of gracefully hopping up on the stage, I tripped and fell flat on my face, though my musician's instinct somehow had me cradling my guitar so that it wasn't damaged—though it did go completely out of tune. Jim helped me up, and even Billy Stritch, who was at the piano that night, leapt up to help. I was so embarrassed, and there at my table, right by the stage, stood that cosmo. I wondered if everyone thought I was drunk. I had violated my own rule. I had taught myself a lesson I thought I already knew.

Many months later I was in the audience when another singer took a tumble on her way to the stage. One of her high heels got caught on the hem of her coat, and she flew down four stairs and landed between the walkway. I ran over to her to see if she needed help, and Jim came running from the stage. She slowly sat up and moved this way and that to see if anything was broken. After she determined that she was okay, Jim escorted her to the stage. She did her song and then went back to her seat.

I went over to her table and said, "Congratulations, and welcome to the club: girl singers who fall down on their way to the stage at *Cast Party!*"

Her name is Barbara Brussell, and we became good friends right from the start. I immediately told her about my tumble, done in full view of the audience in full stage light, with my guitar getting a good whacking, too. I could see she was relieved to meet someone who shared such a professional humiliation. We both laughed. She asked me what my name was, and when I told her, she screamed.

"I sing 'The Kind of Love You Never Recover From'!" she exclaimed.

Since that first time we met at *Cast Party*, we have performed together a few times—the first time was at a Democratic fund-raiser in an Upper East Side Manhattan apartment. I did some funny songs, and Barbara sang dramatic theater songs, and then she sang "The Kind of Love You Never Recover From" with a pianist. Before she sang it, she let them know that I was the author, and it was one great moment, I can tell you that. It's a difficult song for me to sing, so I love it when really accomplished singers like Barbara take that song places my voice can't. She also came out of the audience at one of my concerts to sing it with me. That was a whole other kind of experience—I could concentrate on the new guitar chart I had written for the song without having to worry about singing it, too.

These experiences with Barbara Brussell are the kinds of things that have come directly out of *Cast Party* and demonstrate so clearly why having a regular public place for musicians to work on material helps to develop a lively music scene.

My all-time favorite performance Barbara gave of "Kind of Love" was at the monthly luncheon meeting of the Dutch Treat Club down at the National Arts Club on Gramercy Park. The speaker was Jane Fonda, who was promoting her autobiography at the time. Usually there is just one singer paired with a speaker, but KT Sullivan, who books the entertainment for the Dutch Treat Club, wanted "Kind of Love" to be part of the entertainment, and by then everybody knew that Barbara could sing it better than I could, so we both got the gig.

Jane Fonda was very funny—during the Q and A portion someone asked if she would like to marry again, and she responded, "Not a chance . . . but I *would* like to share my bed with more than my dog."

When Barbara sang "Kind of Love," she sang it so beautifully and powerfully that the packed room became hushed, then erupted with shouts, whistles, and applause when she was done. When she walked back to her seat, Jane Fonda gave her a big high-five and a hug. I was over the moon.

Afterward Barbara apologized to me because she didn't think enough people realized that I had written the song, even though she mentioned that just before she sang it—but I could not have cared less about that. When you write songs, you want them to be heard, that's all. And if someone can sing it better than you can, more power to them. I told her that from that point on, if she was *ever* in the audience when I was doing a show, she had to come onstage and sing it. She promised that she would. Right now she is living in Sacramento, so I have new reasons to travel and perform out west. We'll both be very careful walking on- and offstage so we never repeat our *Cast Party* pratfalls, however.

The audience that shows up every Monday night at Birdland is, for the most part, an intelligent, listening crowd. And they come from all over the world. The most memorable audience members I met were a wedding party from London—they came to *Cast Party* from the reception at the Plaza Hotel—and the bride, groom, bridesmaids, and groomsmen were all in their finery. They sat in the elevated section farthest from the door, drank champagne, and watched the show for more than two hours. When they had to leave, an impromptu receiving line sprung up by the door.

Every *Cast Party* show has its surprises. One night it was a fourteen-year-old girl from San Francisco named Lauren Haden who flew in that same day with her parents and younger brother. She sang Marcy Heisler and Zina Goldrich's "Taylor the Latte Boy." If there was a top ten list of the most-performed songs at *Cast Party*, this song would certainly be on it, so most everyone in the audience had heard it many times before. But this girl, with her youth and innocence, put a new vitality into it, and the crowd loved her.

Another night it was Earl Okin, who had just gotten off a flight from London to find that his guitar was smashed in transit. I lent him mine, and he stopped the show with his song "My Room." On YouTube there's a funny video of him doing that song. Earl is a very versatile, eclectic songwriter who lives in London, but once or twice a year he ventures into New York City and finds his way to Birdland.

About six months later he returned, this time with guitar intact. He showed me a photograph that he carries in his guitar case everywhere he goes—a picture of him with Paul McCartney's group Wings when Earl toured with them as their opening act. The photo was snapped on the ferry that crosses the Mersey River (yes, like that Gerry & the Pacemakers' song). By unbelievable coincidence, in the audience that night at *Cast Party* was Joe English, the drummer of Wings, so Earl and Joe had a nice reunion.

Another occasional Cast *Party*er is TV news journalist Budd Mishkin of NY1 (who plays a mean guitar, is a witty songwriter, and is brother of Doug Mishkin whom I mentioned back a few pages). And one night Tommy Flagg walked in—he was the flamboyant dance promoter I knew back in my Caffé Lena days—and I don't know which of us was more surprised to see the other.

So there are those performers who only occasionally make it to *Cast Party*, and others, like me, who try to make it every week. One is jazz violinist wunderkind Aaron Weinstein. Another is Lodi Carr, a phenomenal jazz singer in her midseventies. Jim Caruso has a strict "no ballad" rule at *Cast Party* (*"People,"* he reminds us, *"this is a party!"*), which he relaxes whenever Lodi shows up. One night after I performed, she asked me to write a song for her. I told her I would do my best, though really I was thinking it would never happen—she's a jazz singer, for God's sake. But then five minutes later she asked me if I knew of a twelve-step program for people who like whipped cream too much. I told her, "Lodi, I don't think so, but I think I have an idea for a song for you!"

Late that night I started writing "Whipped Cream," which took me a long time to complete since I was writing outside my comfort zone. When it was finally finished I had a chart written up, and I sent a tape of the song and the sheet music to her—but Lodi never learned it. I can't say I wasn't disappointed, but I decided to use the song myself. I rewrote the song to be *about* Lodi Carr, and I recorded it on my album *Happydance of the Xenophobe*, having Lodi sing lines here and there.

I also wrote another song about Lodi called "A Nonagenarian," but I never recorded it. She told me a big problem for her was that she would only date older men, and as she got older, there were fewer and fewer. I worked a long time on the song, but then I had a Christmas brunch where Lodi met Ervin Drake's brother Arnold. They immediately hit it off and became a couple, so the song wasn't relevant anymore. Arnold died a couple years later, but Lodi made him a happy man while he was still with us.

Another *Cast Party* favorite is Jeff Blumenkrantz, whose witty songs are sung by the likes of Broadway divas Rebecca Luker, Judy Kuhn, Megan Mullally, and Sutton Foster. Whenever he stops in to sing and play, everyone takes notice.

I've also become a great fan and friend of Ray Jessel, whom I saw for the first time at *Cast Party*. Ray lives out in LA but spends a good bit of time in New York, and whenever he's here, he makes a habit of coming to *Cast Party* on Monday nights, and usually he performs his own show on Wednesday nights at a nearby cabaret called Don't Tell Mama. He's a dead ringer for Einstein, and his music is just as smart.

When I was working on my *One Meat Ball* cookbook/CD, I really wanted Ray Jessel to be part of it, so I asked him if he had written any songs about food. He hadn't, but he said he would try to. He wrote a song called "Let's E.A.T.," which was a good fit for the project, but a couple weeks later he sang a song called "I Think about Sex" at *Cast Party*. The word *food* was in the next-to-last line of the song, and that's all it needed to qualify for *One Meat Ball*, so I swapped it out with another song. "I Think about Sex" is one song that takes listeners by surprise on this compilation.

Another singer/songwriter I heard at *Cast Party* for the first time was Mary Liz McNamara, doing her song "Bacon." It was probably a year later that I started putting *One Meat Ball* together, and I knew that song had to be part of it. Mary Liz also included her candied bacon recipe in the cookbook, with the comment: "Sometimes two wrongs *do* make a right."

Including songs by Ray Jessel and Mary Liz McNamara on one of my compilation projects made me especially happy, since I believe a good song is a good song, and the best songs cross all musical genres, like "It Was a Very Good Year."

I first heard Maude Maggart's voice on Ray Jessel's debut album *The First 70 Years*, and it was at *Cast Party* that I finally got to see her sing live. I've since attended a number of her one-woman shows: *The Songs of 1929*, *The Songs of 1933*, *The Songs of Irving Berlin*, *Good Girl/Bad Girl*, *Dreams*, and *Parents and Children*. In New York, Maude performs at the Oak Room at the Algonquin Hotel—it's a very expensive night out, but thrilling.

Maude spends months not only meticulously researching the songs she chooses, but also the entire era when they were written. I've compared an evening of Maude Maggart at the microphone to attending a history lecture given by the most glamorous history professor you will ever meet, accompanied by some of the most beautiful singing you will ever hear. I knew Maude for a year before I knew she was Fiona Apple's sister. I hope someone writes a musical that could star both of them—I think they already have the perfect title: *Good Girl/Bad Girl*.

One of American music's most wonderful interpreters and smartest entrepreneurs, Michael Feinstein, is a frequent guest, and he even celebrated his birthday at *Cast Party* (though he rarely performs—he just loves to watch the show). I've seen novelist/screenwriter and star of *Die Mommy Die!* Charles Busch in the house. Singer/producer Jamie deRoy pops in— she does a hilarious parody of a *Sound of Music* song—"I Am Sixty Going On Seventy." Jamie is one of the producers who brought the thrilling British musical *Coram Boy* to Broadway (I saw it three times) and also the brilliant one-man play *Thurgood*, starring Laurence Fishburne. Another night Lucie Arnaz, daughter of Lucille Ball and Desi Arnaz, was coaxed onstage. She said, "I'll sing a song that's a little jazz, a little country. Did you know my dad was from a little country?" Jon Hendricks, of the famed trio Hendricks Lambert & Ross, has been spotted in the crowd.

One night in January 2008, Tony Bennett was in the audience. I got there late, and as I came in, I saw a limousine with its engine running out in front of Birdland—always a sign that there's someone important inside who might need to make a quick getaway. But that limo sat there for more than two hours. Tony didn't sing, but he had come to *Cast Party* with an a capella group called Mosaic that he had done a TV appearance with earlier that day. At one point Jim Caruso gave Tony Bennett the mike, and he talked to the audience from his seat, saying he was so happy to see so many young people who were as in love with the Great American Songbook as he was.

Christine Ebersole, winner of the 2007 Tony for Best Actress in a Musical (*Grey Gardens*), stops in frequently. Billy Stritch is her accompanist, too, so she's been a *Cast Party* fan for a long time. A friend of mine went to high school with Alby Maysles, who, with his brother David, filmed the late-1970s award-winning documentary film *Grey Gardens* that became the basis for the musical and then the HBO film of the same title.

Back in 2000 my friend mentioned that Alby wanted to see Dame Edna, so I took him as my guest. Alby, who has a big fluffy head of white hair, laughed so hard and totally loved Dame Edna's show. At the end, when Dame Edna chose lucky audience members to come onstage, Alby had caught her eye and was one of the chosen few. I felt so proud being the connecting link between those two artistic powerhouses.

Christine Pedi is a *Cast Party* regular—she's an accomplished actress/singer/comedienne who toured the world with *Forbidden Broadway*. She was the first one to ever "do" Christine Ebersole as Little Edie Beale of *Grey Gardens*. That might not play in Peoria, but in Manhattan they screamed with laughter.

Phoebe Snow has stopped in to sing at *Cast Party*, and so has Janis Ian, who lives in Nashville these days. Janis sang her Grammy-winning hit "At Seventeen" to the delighted crowd, and then followed it up with "My Autobiography," which sports such lyrics as "I've led a fascinating life / Had a husband, and a wife . . ."

David Buskin, who was half of Buskin & Batteau in the 1980s, then a third of the comic trio Modern Man (and now back with Batteau again), is also working on a theatrical piece called *Boomers* with prolific singer/songwriter Jake Holmes. They've tried out some of the songs in front of the *Cast Party* crowd.

Oscar winner Celeste Holm (yes, Margo Channing's best friend in *All About Eve*) often is in the audience and occasionally sings, too. Her husband, Frank Basile, is an opera singer with a deep, romantic baritone voice. One night they sang the sweetest version of the standard "True Love."

David Ippolito, "the guitar man of Central Park"—a New York fixture since the 1990s—has made *Cast Party* his winter home when it's too cold for him to sing outdoors in the park.

Which brings me to another "crash and burn" *Cast Party* story. I met David downtown on the Chelsea Piers at a Hurricane Katrina benefit concert the fall of 2005. David plays not far from Central Park West and the entrance at West Seventy-seventh Street, but since most weekends I'm on the road, I had never seen him. We instantly hit it off, and I told him he should come to *Cast Party* some Monday. I was sure the crowd would love him.

That's an understatement. He is one of those performers who commands the room just by approaching the microphone. He even wrote a song about *Cast Party*, called "I'm a Cowboy Who Hates Country" ("Dolly Parton can stick it / I've got tickets to *Wicked* / I'm a cowboy who hates country").

Like me, he's gotten into the habit of trying out new material at *Cast Party*, and one night he brought in a song called "Tom Cruise Scares Me" that was an instant hit. A few days later I was doing a show in Boston. That song of his kept running through my head, so I asked him to e-mail me the lyrics—I was pretty sure I had the chords down pat—because I wanted to sing it that weekend.

Each verse was about something that scared David—and I found there were a couple of verses that didn't scare me. David is scared of Oprah and Wolf Blitzer, but not me. If I cut those verses, though, the song was too short, so I wrote new verses about things that scared me—the Weather Channel, Kenny Rogers, Republicans.

That weekend I did my new version of "Tom Cruise Scares Me," and it went over very well. I called David and sang a bit of it over the phone, but he told me my melody and chord changes were very different from his. (Oh, he wasn't mad or anything; he just noticed that mine was different.)

So the next week at *Cast Party* we were both there, and I came up with an idea that I pitched to Jim Caruso: have David sing his version of "Tom Cruise Scares Me," then immediately following, have me do *my* version of it. Then the audience could hear the folk process in action, and maybe even vote for which verses of both songs to combine to make a *third* version of the song. Jim looked rather dubious about this, but he trusted me and said okay.

This is an instance where I should have thought things through a little bit more. My song as it stood shared half the verses of David's song—so half of my song would be funny verses the audience had *just heard* three minutes before. That's not good, for starters.

David sang "Tom Cruise Scares Me" and totally KILLED. The audience *loved* it. However, something bad happened during David's performance that I hadn't anticipated. My song was still so new and so fresh that the melody hadn't set in my permanent memory bank yet. As I was listening to David, my melody slowly faded, then evaporated, and then it was *gone*.

I should have gone to plan B, except I didn't have a plan B. I was so set on trying this back-to-back experiment that I made the crucial mistake of not being prepared with more than one song that night. When Jim called my name, I started singing "Tom Cruise Scares Me," except that I was playing *my* chords but singing *David's* melody.

The looks on the faces in the audience? Confusion and perplexion (is that a word?), but I plowed ahead anyway. As I realized what I was doing—one set of chords, different melody—*my* chords went away, and I started fumbling all over the neck of the guitar. There were no laughs, just blank stares of "what the f*#?" as I stumbled my way to the end of the song, which was greeted by—oh, no!—the dreaded, pitiful golf applause.

As I was about to unplug my guitar to make a hasty retreat, Jim bounded onstage and stopped me. "Do another song, Christine," he said, "do one that you *know*."

This was a first. I was getting an encore because my song bombed. I had *never* seen this happen at *Cast Party*. And this is where my lack of a plan B really torpedoed me. And my frequent use of the capo.

I wasn't using a capo on "Tom Cruise Scares Me," so I didn't bring one onstage. To do another song, I needed to choose one written in first position on the neck of the guitar—and truth be told, I don't have a lot of songs like that. Yes, Van Ronk's words about relying too much on my capo came back to haunt me. I was being given the rare chance to redeem myself the same night I tanked, and I had to think of something *quick*.

It hit me. I'd play "Why Do I Write Songs I Cannot Sing Well"—it was the perfect place for that goofy song. When I sing that song, I start out singing it badly, then playing it badly, and then it slides into bad Spanish and a ridiculous sing-along. I'd be commenting on what just happened to me—it would be *great*.

So I started that song, but then something *really* bad—not *funny* bad—happened. The vocal mike started to sink very, very, very slowly. So slowly that is was almost imperceptible. But I knew it was happening, and I had to start adjusting my stance at the mike so the audience could hear me.

I hoped that Jim would see what was happening—maybe he'd run on-stage and tighten the mike—but either he didn't notice or thought that coming onstage would disrupt my song. So I kept singing, slowly sinking along with the mike, but not so much that the audience realized what was wrong. All the mike-sinking was taking my focus off the song, and I suddenly realized that it wasn't getting any laughs at all. Eventually, the sinking seemed to have stopped, but it left me in a very uncomfortable position, standing with my knees bent.

Finally the song was over, and I left the stage to—holy crap, not again—more of the dreaded golf applause. I can't tell you how humiliating this felt. Oh, there were some in the house who knew I was just having a bad moment, but there were plenty who had never seen me before, and what an awful introduction *that* was.

I slunk up the aisle to my table. Jim had resumed his duties as emcee, and now I witnessed a legendary *Cast Party* tradition I had heard about but had never seen firsthand: when someone brings the show to a screeching halt—like I just did—Jim will ask the most famous performer in the house to come onstage to save the show. Often there are Broadway performers enjoying their one day off not performing. Jenna Russell, star of the most recent revival of *Sunday in the Park with George* came to *Cast Party* many times. One of those times I asked her if she was going to sing. She said, with her clipped British accent, *"Dahling . . . I'd rather be boiled in nuclear waste!"*

The night of my fiasco, the biggest star in the audience was Liza Minnelli, and now Jim was doing his best to coax her out of her seat. If I wasn't embarrassed before, I sure was now. Liza strolled to the stage as the crowd went crazy. She and Jim kibitzed a bit, she powwowed with Billy Stritch, and then she launched into—I don't even remember what song it was.

I was intent on just getting out of there, so I slowly started to inch my way along the back wall. I had gone about 10 feet when my cell phone started to ring. I froze, hoping no one would notice it was me. For God's sake, Liza Minnelli was onstage, saving the show that I just ruined! I was wearing a light linen outfit, and my cell phone was in my front pocket—lighting up my shirt as it rang.

People turned away from the stage—*they turned away from Liza Minnelli*—to see me frozen in fear against the back wall with my pocket lighting up as my phone rang.

"It's *you!*" someone yelled. "Your songs sucked, and now you're ruining Liza Minnelli's performance!"

I fumbled for the phone so I could stop the ringing. It was Andrew from Seattle—yes, the guy I usually call when my career has blown up in my face. This time *he* was calling *me*. Was he psychic?

I quickly hit "ignore" on my phone, then turned and ran out of the club, hailed a cab, and didn't show my face at Birdland or *Cast Party* for two weeks.

I know now that was foolish of me. When you are part of a show like this where everyone does a single song, whatever happens—good *or* bad—is quickly forgotten when the next performer takes the stage. I'm not the only one who has run out feeling humiliated, that's for sure, but having a bad moment onstage is something that happens to everybody in this business. Likewise, when you have a great moment and the crowd goes crazy, that doesn't change your life, either. It's about working steadily, working hard. I always encourage performers to take risks onstage—the day you stop taking risks is the day your performance starts to grow stale.

One night Bonnie Koloc from Chicago stopped in—she, along with John Prine and the late Steve Goodman, were considered the trinity of singer/songwriters in that city. That night she didn't have her guitar with her and didn't want to use mine, so instead she sang a stunning version of the Hoagy Carmichael and Johnny Mercer standard "Skylark" with Tedd Firth and Steve Doyle backing her up.

Like Bonnie Koloc, Hilary Kole is a singer/songwriter well versed in the Great American Songbook—it's Hilary's sultry voice you can hear singing "Lullaby of Birdland" on Birdland's Web site. She often fronts a sixteen-piece big band at Birdland, but because she's a songwriter, what I love most is when she sits at the piano and accompanies herself. Remember her name: *Hilary Kole*. Her lovely debut album was released in 2009—it's called *Haunted Heart*. Because her album is a big hit in Japan, Hilary is seen less and less at *Cast Party* these days; she traveled there three times to do concerts in 2009.

Another fine songwriter who plays piano is Garth Kravitz, and meeting him at *Cast Party* set me off on another long-running theatrical adventure. In early spring 2006 he told me he would be in a musical called *The Drowsy Chaperone* opening in April, and that Sutton Foster was the star. I bought tickets for the third preview performance, and as I settled into my seat, my thought was, "For Sutton's sake, I hope this will be a hit . . . but if it's not, she'll have to do more concerts and maybe sing my songs!" Yes, that's a selfish thought, but it's what I was thinking.

When the performance was over, I knew I was in trouble. It had been a few years since I became addicted to Dame Edna's Broadway show, but I knew I wanted to see this show again. And again. And again. All told, I saw *The Drowsy Chaperone* sixty-seven times during its Broadway run. I know because I had all my tickets photocopied, laminated, and turned into place mats that I gave to each cast member when the show closed a year and a half later.

Luckily, the kind producers of this show had a nightly "lottery" for the front-row seats—twenty-two seats that were sold at a discount for twenty-five dollars each. Not only did I win that lottery many times, I became friends with others who, like me, couldn't get enough of *The Drowsy Chaperone*. At the lottery we would team up—if your name was drawn, you could get either one or two tickets—so joining forces doubled our chances. Three *Drowsy* addicts I became good friends with are Robert Britton, who at the time worked at *People* magazine; an Upper East Side nanny named Jamie Skirvin; and a college student from Tennessee named Annie Govekar.

Since I tried to see it once a week, I guess you might say that while it ran *The Drowsy Chaperone* was my religion. Hell, I'd rather give *them* money than the Catholic Church anyway, and I did find the show uplifting and inspiring. While some audience members might be disappointed to see that an understudy was going on for one of the leads at a particular performance, I loved watching the understudies strut their stuff. Like with Dame Edna, I learned something new about live performance every night.

The Drowsy Chaperone won the most Tony Awards in 2006, much to the chagrin of the producers of *Jersey Boys*, who thought they were going to sweep until this little upstart of a show came along.

The songs in *Drowsy* were written by Canadians Lisa Lambert and Greg Morrison. On my album *Happydance of the Xenophobe*, I recorded a folk version of "As We Stumble Along," the big number sung by the drowsy chaperone herself, brilliantly played by Beth Leavel, who won the Tony that year for Best Actress in a Musical. Every night she stopped the show with "Stumble," and every night Danny Burstein would stop the show with the song "I Am Aldolpho," which he sang with Beth. He was also nominated for a Tony, but it went to someone else that year (noooooo!).

During the curtain call, if Garth Kravitz spotted me in the front row, he'd give me a little wave. Later he told me that the cast played a game called "Where's Christine?" where they tried to figure out exactly which seat I was in based on my laughter. (I can't help it! The show is really funny!) Since its Broadway run, I've traveled a couple of hours outside Manhattan to catch touring productions of this show.

Eventually Sutton (who was also nominated for a Tony in *Drowsy*) left to play Inga in *Young Frankenstein*, and Danny Burstein left to play Luther Billis in *South Pacific*. Danny was nominated for a Tony once again, and once again it went to someone else, but as they say, it's an honor just to be nominated, especially since *South Pacific* was the most honored musical of 2008. Danny's portrayal of Billis had a lot to do with that. As I'm writing this, I have seen *South Pacific* twenty-five times.

Early in the run, one of my favorite things to do after the show was to strike up conversations with others who had just seen it and ask if any of them happened to see *The Drowsy Chaperone*. If they said yes, I would say, "Did you recognize the actor who played Billis? He was in *Drowsy*." *Every single time* I have said this, the person would respond, "No, I don't remember him. Maybe he was out the night I saw it."

And then I'd say, "Do you remember Aldolpho? The Latin lover? '*I am . . . Aldolpho,*'" I would say with his Spanish accent. The look on their faces was priceless.

"*Billis* was *Aldolpho?*" they'd exclaim with disbelief. Unless someone told you, you'd never know it was the same actor. In the original program for *South Pacific*, Danny Burstein's bio only mentioned he was in *Drowsy*, not what part he played. I convinced him to add that, and he did.

I have come to study *South Pacific* the way I did *Drowsy*. I've watched Paulo Szot, William Michals, and David Pittsinger all play the role of Emile DeBecque superbly and watched the incomparable Kelli O'Hara play the part of Nellie up until her fifth month of pregnancy—by pure luck I caught her very last performance—then watched newcomer Laura Osnes take on that part and make it her own. Watching major parts change actors makes me all the more appreciative of Danny Burstein as Billis, who is rock solid. I can't wait to see what he does next.

Everybody I took to see *Drowsy* loved it. One of them was Steve Wozniak, the cofounder of Apple. He was in New York during October 2006 promoting his autobiography, *iWoz*. A few months earlier, Janis Ian had tipped me off that he was a big folk music fan—and I'm a longtime Apple user—so we started corresponding. When his promotion itinerary included New York, I convinced him to take a few hours off to be "Guest DJ on a Segway" on my XM radio show (he actually brought a list of five hundred songs he wanted to play, but producer Bill Kates made him whittle it down to twenty-eight). I also spirited him away to catch a matinee performance of *Drowsy*.

He loved the show so much that he cried when it ended—oh, it's not sad, it's just very sweet, and he's a sensitive guy. I had e-mailed some of the cast members that Woz was going to be in the house for that Sunday matinee, and they all wanted to meet him. But he is shy, so that didn't happen. I also tried to get Woz to sing backup on a song at *Cast Party*, but that also didn't happen. However, if you caught him on Kathy Griffin's TV show *My Life on the D-List*, and then later on *Dancing with the Stars*, it looks like he's gotten over a lot of his shyness.

Beth Leavel has been working steadily ever since *Drowsy* closed. She was in *No No Nanette* at New York City Center's Encore Series and stopped the show every night in the second act with a big blues number—I saw that one twice. After that, Beth took over the part of Frau Blucher in *Young Frankenstein* from Andrea Martin. By the time she joined the cast, fellow *Drowsy* castmate Sutton Foster had already left to star as Princess Fiona in *Shrek: The Musical* (another Tony nomination for Sutton). Then Beth took on the part of Donna Sheridan, the single mother in *Mama Mia* (the part Meryl Streep played in the film), and eventually she will play one of the leading roles in a brand-new musical called *Minksy's* heading for Broadway.

I can't wait.

All these theater adventures can be traced back to the day I said hello to Garth Kravitz at *Cast Party*. My two young *Drowsy* pals, Jamie Skirvin and Annie Govekar, are now webmasters for Danny Burstein and Beth Leavel, and I hired Annie to design the CD package for my live concert *I Don't Make This Stuff Up . . . I Just Make It Rhyme*. So they have found a way to constructively channel their love for *Drowsy* and the actors who starred in it. And I found a wonderful new graphic designer to boot.

Another memorable character I met at *Cast Party* was a singer/dancer named Bob Dolphin. Bob was one of those irrepressible sprites who lived to sing and dance—every song he ever sang at *Cast Party* contained a break in the middle where he would tap dance. For the first couple of years he simply tap danced on the carpeted stage, but Jim Caruso had a small square tap floor built for Bob's eighty-second birthday. It was kept behind the curtain, and whenever it was Bob's turn, either Jim or Steve Doyle would lug it out.

Bob never sang the same song twice, and the crowds at *Cast Party* loved him unconditionally. For many years Bob was a makeup artist, and he was known as the original "eyebrow man" who did many of the top movie stars of the day—Katharine Hepburn and Greta Garbo were just two of his clients. After I got hooked on *Drowsy*, I knew that Bob would love it, so I encouraged him to enter the lottery for front row seats. Well, he did, and later that day he left this message on my voice mail, which I transcribed and e-mailed to the cast (I was told it was tacked up on the call board for all to read):

> Miracle of miracles, I've never won anything in my life, ever, and last night I won a seat to *The Drowsy Chaperone*, so I did get in on the lottery deal, and brought in another gentleman, he was my "companion"—is that what you call it? A man from Maine who had also never won anything in his life and was trying for

the lottery, so we made a pact to bring each other in if either of our names got called. And it was "kids night," so there were *sooo* many people trying for the lottery. But I won! I won! It was thrilling—we were nearly out of our minds with joy. The tap dancing! The music! And you are right—that show is show business if I've ever seen it. The people there—the entire cast—is of the highest kind of delivery. I was stunned. Aldolpho with the streak in his hair, what a phenomenal performer, and the woman who looks like Judy Garland, the bride, and of course the Drowsy Chaperone herself—we were delirious with joy. You made two people awfully happy, and I wanted to thank you a million times over for recommending this show! It's a seamless piece of great art. When the cast at the end embraces the interlocutor, I cried, and I think the man from Maine did, too, but I'm not sure and didn't want to look and embarrass him. And the leading man— the groom—has such good looks and talent, but more than that captures you with his warmth and kindliness and a decency that makes him a really viable leading man like you just don't see these days. The whole show is like the Lord—assuming there is one—handed me a gift.

Bob Dolphin always sat at the same table whenever he came to *Cast Party*—he sat alone, on the second level. He had lots of friends who offered him a seat at their tables, but he didn't like to talk during the show and wanted to just focus on the performers. When he was totally blown away by a singer, rather than clapping he would raise up both arms straight over his head and wiggle his fingers very fast. I'm taking sign language classes, and whenever we "clap" for each other like that, I often think of Bob. If you saw him doing that after *your* performance, you felt very good indeed.

Bob Dolphin was a dear, dear man, who died in November 2007 while visiting relatives in California. I still have a voice mail message from him, and I don't have the heart to erase it. All the *Cast Party* regulars still talk about him, and it feels sad to see a stranger sitting at Bob's table on Monday nights. But he would agree that the show must go on.

One night when I got to *Cast Party*, Jim Caruso was apoplectic. A very famous movie star, who had just left at the end of the early show, had planted a big kiss on Jim's lips and whispered in his ear, "Oh my God, I'm so sick, I can't believe I was able to get out of bed today." Then she coughed and sneezed her way out of the club. Poor Jim! The next day I wrote him a song promoting the idea of bowing politely when you greet someone. It's called "Bring Back the Bow." For a long time I had been thinking about writing a song on this topic, but it took that one moment at *Cast Party* to bring it to fruition.

Although I try to attend every *Cast Party* show, some nights I don't perform. I work enough and don't need to show off when I'm home in New York, so I usually only do a song when I am breaking in a new one or re-working an old one. Otherwise I sit and watch and take it all in. I guess Jim Caruso noticed this, so since mid-2007 I've been filling in as guest host from time to time when his performing career takes him out of New York. Broadway belter Klea Blackhurst also guest hosts—she's very funny and does a fantastic job. So does producer Scott Siegel (he even changes outfits over the course of the evening). It's hard work to fill Jim's shoes because he is such a natural comedian, so when I host my prime objective is, as I tell him, "to keep the franchise going." *Cast Party* is *his* baby, so I do my best, and I let my favorite songwriters know that I'm hosting.

When I guest host, I leave my fancy Grit Laskin guitar over on a stand with the understanding that any guitar players are free to use it if they don't have their own guitar with them. But one night that idea backfired. It was the night that singer/songwriter Tom Chapin came by with Jon Cobert and Michael Mark, his two sidemen (who also performed solo in the show). My guitar was next to the piano, toward the back of the stage and out of harm's way—I thought. But when operatic soprano Jenny Lynn Stewart performed an energetic version of "Ed Sullivan" from *Bye Bye Birdie*, she flung her arms out dramatically and hit one of the microphone stands. The microphone smacked my guitar and knocked it onstage.

Tom Chapin, who was at one of the front tables, jumped onstage without thinking and picked up my guitar as Jenny Lynn continued on with her song. He looked closely at it, then looked over at me and shook his head slowly in a dark, dramatic way. *Oy vey*. After putting the guitar back on its stand and moving it all the way to the back of the stage, this time really out of harm's way, he returned to his seat. Jenny Lynn kept singing, oblivious to what was going on behind her. At the end of the night, I looked closely at the guitar and could see that it had a fresh new crack in it. Jenny Lynn was mortified, but I wasn't mad at her. One of the responsibilities of the host of *Cast Party* is to be the microphone wrangler, and I should have moved those mikes myself, but I didn't. I also told her that I've always had a thing for Ed Sullivan, so now I have a permanent reminder of him in my guitar.

I took it to Noria, the go-to guitar repair guy in Manhattan, and happily found out that the crack was a minor one, costing just a hundred dollars to fix. When you have a working guitar, even such a fancy one like my Laskin, getting dings in it goes with the territory. My last mishap cost $700 to fix, so this time I was relieved. And Jenny Lynn Stewart and I have become good friends, which might not have happened if she hadn't sent me so many e-mails apologizing for the accident—which I kept telling her wasn't her fault.

The last year of his life, legendary songwriter John Wallowitch visited *Cast Party* four times. He wrote more than two thousand songs in his lifetime, recorded by the likes of Tony Bennett, Dixie Carter, and Blossom Dearie. The last time he visited Birdland he sang one of his most clever, popular songs, "Bruce," and then said to the audience: "I have a new song for which I have just written one line so far. But I don't know if it's worth writing a whole song on this topic or not." He then sang, "Just because you're old, fat, ugly, and gay doesn't mean you belong onstage in a cabaret. . . ." Then he stopped and said, "What do you think?"

A week later John did a house concert for sixty guests in the Upper West Side living room of singer/songwriter/music-biz guru Ann Ruckert, where each guest contributed money at the door. At the end of the night, John walked out with over a thousand dollars. That concert was taped—the title of the album is *Miracle on 71st Street*—and you can't help but get chills when you hear the final lines of the final song: "Into the night the roadway bends / I see a light and nothing ends . . ." because John died a few weeks later. I never got to see him to do a whole concert, so I am so grateful to Jim Caruso for creating a weekly event where someone like John was so welcomed, and I'm grateful to Ann Ruckert for recording him.

On any given Monday night I've heard more wonderful, accomplished singers at *Cast Party* than I can remember—on my Web site I have a page devoted to the list of performers I got to see for the very first time there. I wanted to include it here, but there's just way too many names, and every week the list grows!

I've also become friends with some music fans who regularly come to *Cast Party*. One of them is a man we all call Russian Michael. One night after the show he took me to a dark, crowded underground bar in Greenwich Village called Marie's Crisis where the patrons stand around for hours singing show tune after show tune. I'd never seen or heard anything like it before—a hundred people swigging beers and singing "I Get a Kick Out of You," then segueing into "Oklahoma!" then "Everything's Coming Up Roses" at the top of their lungs.

One night when I was on tour in California, Michael called me and held up the phone at Marie's Crisis so that I could hear the pianist sing my song "Good Thing He Can't Read My Mind." It was 2:00 a.m. in California, 5:00 a.m. in New York.

One night David Ippolito brought to *Cast Party* one of his best friends, concert promoter Sid Bernstein, the man responsible for bringing the Beatles to America—not to mention the Rolling Stones and Herman's Hermits. He spent the evening all night at one of the front tables, had a ball as people came by to pay their respects.

Another night actress Joyce Randolph came to *Cast Party*—she was Trixie on *The Honeymooners*. She was all dressed up, sat right in front of the stage, gave each performer her undivided attention, and stayed to the very end of the show. Even Jim Caruso's mother, Pat, comes to *Cast Party* from time to time. He started out his career performing with her in seafood restaurants in Dallas, Texas. She doesn't sing, but she plays standards on the piano and has such a lovely feather-light touch on the keys.

Two *Cast Party* regulars who never sing—or play—are Scott and Barbara Siegel, perhaps the hardest-working couple in the New York theater world. They produce the Broadway by the Year concerts at Town Hall, along with the Unplugged series and the annual Nightlife Awards, they are nominators for the annual Drama Desk Awards, and they have authored forty-seven books. I've been in the audience for most of their shows—I didn't see my first Broadway musical until I was twenty-five years old, so I have a lot of catching up to do.

The Siegels' dedication to theater and music is complete—they don't own a television, and every night they attend live events in theaters and cabarets of all sizes—including a stop at *Cast Party* every Monday night to leaflet the crowd for whatever their latest venture is.

I really knew I was in the right place that night during the summer of 2008 when Barry Humphries, aka Dame Edna, strolled in to *Cast Party* with Michael Feinstein and sat at the table right next to mine. As fate would have it, my name was the next one called. I had been sitting there nursing a cranberry and seltzer, guitar in hand, prepared to hit the ground running to sing— for the very first time ever—"The Goldfish Whisperer," which I wrote with Sutton Foster. And now I had to sing it in front of my idol, Barry Humphries.

The fact that I didn't faint on my way to or from the stage, and remembered all the words and chords, is a testament to my four years of *Cast Party* experience. (Though I did give a copy of the lyrics to Jenny Lynn Stewart, who promised to shout them out should I get lost. But it wasn't necessary. *Whew*.)

I feel so lucky to have read Erik Piepenburg's article about *Cast Party* that ran in the *Times* during the summer of 2004. What if I hadn't? Where would I be now? On my albums *folkZinger* and *Happydance of the Xenophobe*, you'll hear twenty musicians whom I met at *Cast Party*—and I even quote Joan Crowe, another singer I met there, in the liner notes: "Seize the day . . . but go out at night!"

If you don't live close enough to New York City to stop in at *Cast Party*, why not start your own regular Monday-night soiree at a local club? Or do it Tuesday nights, like Mary Jo Mundy does in Los Angeles at the Gardenia. Looking back, I can see that Jack Hardy's Monday-night songwriters' dinners and now *Cast Party*'s Monday-night shows both helped me a great deal to create, and to be part of a community of songwriters. Ultimately, songwriting is a very solitary task for someone like me, so God bless Jack Hardy and Jim Caruso for giving people like me a place to connect with others of my tribe.

TOP LEFT: With Debi Smith, Sally Fingerett, and Camille West on a bad-hair day in 2005. Photo © Anne Safran Dalin. **TOP RIGHT:** A very rare Bitchin' Babes lineup, at the Cheswick Theater in Glenside, Pennsylvania, 1996. Debi Smith, me, Janis Ian, and Sally Fingerett. Megon McDonough was starring in *Always . . . Patsy Cline* in Chicago, so Janis subbed for her. Photo: Christine Lavin Collection **MIDDLE:** Rare photo of *six* Bitchin' Babes onstage at the Sanders Theater in Cambridge, Massachusetts, circa 2000: Julie Gold, Debi Smith, Sally Fingerett, Megon McDonough, Camille West, and me. Photo © Rob Pownall **LEFT:** Next to "room service," "sold out" are the 4BBs favorite two words. 1996. Photo © Sally Fingerett

TOP LEFT: Recognize these guys? They're Canadian superstars, circa 2000. A free CD to the first ten people who can identify them; e-mail me at christinelavin.com. Photo © Christine Lavin **SECOND LEFT:** With brilliant singer/songwriters Susan Werner and Michelle Shocked backstage at the Philadelphia Folk Festival in 2003. Photo: Christine Lavin Collection **THIRD LEFT:** Three eminent American songwriters in the Edmonton Folk Festival parking lot, circa 2000. A free DVD to the first ten people who can identify *them*; e-mail me at christinelavin.com. Photo © Christine Lavin **TOP RIGHT:** I surprised Dar Williams midsong at the Edmonton Folk Festival, circa 2000. Photo © Christine Lavin **ABOVE:** The finale at the Falcon Ridge Folk Festival in the mid-2000s. That's Sonny Ochs in white near the center. I'm one person over in a sleeveless black top. Photo: Christine Lavin Collection

TOP: Listening to Dar Williams from the audience at Edmonton Folk Festival, circa 2000. Photo: Christine Lavin Collection **LEFT:** At the Canmore Folk Festival in 2002, Al Williams visits the striped guitar case he built years earlier for my Larrivee guitar. Photo © Christine Lavin **RIGHT:** Finishing my outdoor set at the same Canmore Folk Festival. Photo: Christine Lavin Collection

TOP LEFT: Steve Wozniak in 2006 modeling the "Segway Hand Sox" I knitted for him. Photo © Mark Rupp **TOP RIGHT:** It's a CD cover; no, it's a Halloween mask—hey kids, you're both right! 2005. Photo: Christine Lavin Collection **MIDDLE:** Onstage at the New Jersey Repertory Company, August 2001. Photo © SuzAnne Barabas; courtesy the New Jersey Repertory Company **LEFT:** Taking a break from during a recording session of "French Toast Bread Pudding" in 2006 with producer Brian Bauers, Ray Jessel, and Michael Quinn. Photo © Michael Katsobashvili **FACING PAGE:** Oh my God, do I love this photo of Ervin Drake and me onstage in 2007 in Great Neck, New York, singing his song "I'm a Card-Carrying Bleeding Heart Liberal." Photo © Gordon Nash

TOP LEFT: Sometimes people at my shows say outrageous things: 2009. Photo © James Madison Thomas **TOP RIGHT:** From 1999 to 2002 I did sparkle manicures on audience members before each show—until people complained about the fumes. Photo: Christine Lavin Collection **RIGHT SECOND:** Here I am with musical geniuses Ray Jessel and Aaron Weinstein at Birdland's *Cast Party* in 2009. They are not above making fools of themselves if it's good for a laugh. Photo © Steve Sorokoff **MIDDLE LEFT:** With two of the greatest singers of all time, Klea Blackhurst and Marilyn Maye, at *Cast Party* in 2009. Photo © Steve Sorokoff **MIDDLE RIGHT:** With the Great American Songbook's most glamorous and passionate champion, Maude Maggart, at *Cast Party* in 2009. Photo © Michael Katsobashvili **LEFT:** Onstage with a boisterous pack of "Sensitive New Age Guys" in 2009 in Pinellas Park, Florida. Check out those kilts! Photo © James Madison Thomas **RIGHT:** With jazz vocalist supreme Lodi Carr at *Cast Party* in 2009. Photo © Michael Katsobashvili

350

TOP LEFT: Betsy Franco Feeney, Betty Ann Murphy, and me onstage in 2008. I'm presenting Betty Ann with the book *Amoeba Hop* to thank her for bringing that bucket of swamp water to ninth-grade Biology class so many years ago. **TOP RIGHT:** Backstage in 2007 with pal-for-life Julie Gold. **ABOVE:** How weird is this? Julia Roberts polishing my shoes, Carole King whispering in my ear, and Louise Goffin looking on during the night my acting career began and ended in the late 1990s. All photos, Christine Lavin Collection

TOP LEFT: Janis Ian came to *Cast Party* in 2009, and Jim Caruso loved her! Photo © Steve Sorokoff **SECOND LEFT:** With my dear friend Russian Michael at *Cast Party* in 2009. Photo: Christine Lavin Collection **TOP RIGHT:** In New Haven, Connecticut, in 2002, Dame Edna chose my Uncle Will as her "Queen Elizabeth"! Photo: Christine Lavin Collection **ABOVE:** With Barry Humphries, a.k.a. Dame Edna, at the stage door of Broadway's Booth Theater in 2000. Photo: Christine Lavin Collection

28

GETTIN' USED
TO LEAVIN'

no longer cry anymore
At the sound of "good-bye"
Maybe I'm a little bit cynical
Maybe I'm a little bit wise
Or maybe I'm gettin' used to leavin'
Gettin' used to all the "fare-thee-wells"
Gettin' used to sayin' "I'll give you a call"
When I know I probably never will . . .

(If you are thinking, "She must have written this before she became friends with Ervin Drake," you are correct!)

As our mother has gotten older, all the Lavin kids have worked together to make her golden years more comfortable. My brothers Greg and Ed live in Geneva, and my brother Tom and sister Mary live nearby in Rochester. They and their spouses have played a greater part in her care than those of us who live farther away. For the past few years the rest of us have tried to visit at least twice a year, staying for a week at a time, to keep her company.

I was doing that at the end of December 2006, and after my second day there, I got the feeling that I should move in permanently. I could see how much she seemed to blossom with company, and she ate better when meals were prepared for her. I was the only one of the Lavin kids not married or living with someone, so I was really the only one in a position to do this.

I didn't say anything to my brothers and sisters about what I was thinking at first. I know how impulsive I can be—was this something I really could do? I asked myself if what I was doing between concerts in New York City was more important than what I could be doing by living in Geneva between concerts, and the answer was no. I had moved to New York in 1976 to be part of a Greenwich Village music scene that didn't exist anymore. I was now a part of the *Cast Party* scene, which I loved, but was that more important than taking care of my mother?

Again, the answer was no.

I figured I would still keep performing, though cut back a bit and just do theater concerts, the direction my agent thought I should be going anyway. My business manager had refinanced my apartment a couple of times already and was constantly sending me "stop spending money!" e-mails, so this could be a situation that would benefit my mother and take the mounting financial pressure off me at the same time. But it would be quite a change in my day-to-day living, since by then I had lived in New York longer than anywhere else, and I loved the 24/7 rhythm of the city.

I returned to Manhattan in January of 2007, then put my apartment on the market in February. The asking price was approximately four times what I had paid for it, so even with the refinancing, I would still make a profit—giving me the kind of financial cushion I had never had before, which would also be a financial cushion for my mother. In early 2007 the housing market was still relatively robust, so I anticipated a quick sale.

I hated the thought of leaving New York, but I loved the idea of having no financial pressure. I was curious to see how that would feel, how it would affect my writing, my working. And I loved the idea of my mother not having any financial worries, either.

Because my agent usually books concerts six months to a year or a year and a half in advance, I told her to book fewer shows for the end of 2007 and all of 2008, and any shows she did book should be in theaters. If I was to leave my mother alone, it had to be for a good paycheck, unless it was within driving distance of Geneva.

If my apartment had sold quickly, as I thought it would, and for the amount I thought it would, my plan would have been fine. But it didn't sell quickly or for that high price. We started lowering the price bit by bit—but I just knew it was going to sell soon; I was very optimistic about that—so from April to June 2007 I spent a lot of money (a lot of money for me, at least). You already know I've developed quite a fondness for theater, which is not cheap, and neither is knitting, now that I was frequenting beautiful yarn shops that sold expensive yarns. I took friends out to favorite restaurants and loved picking up the check.

And since this would be my last year in New York, I did a lot of recording, using many of the musicians I had met at *Cast Party*. I had no plans to make a commercial CD recording until I got the letter from Elizabeth Edwards encouraging me to get my song "More Than 1,000,000 Americans" out there. As soon as I read that, I thought I *should* put out a CD, and I thought I could easily afford it since I'd be selling the apartment soon.

It's a classic mistake to spend money you don't have yet, and that's one that I made. But putting that CD on Yellow Tail Records in Seattle—the company run by my friend Andrew Ratshin—was *not* a mistake. Many years ago Allan Pepper introduced me to Andrew and told me he thought we should work together. I didn't see it—we live 3,000 miles apart—but Allan Pepper is right about a lot of things, and this was another one. I figured I'd be leaving New York as it was, so being on a label outside of New York made sense, too.

I'm the first East Coast artist to join Yellow Tail, and I love being part of a completely artist-driven record company. The roster is quite eclectic, and Andrew, one of the most brilliant singer/songwriters I've ever heard, is a very smart businessman, too. I am so happy to be on his label.

The months went by—July, August, September—and my apartment still hadn't sold, despite lowering the price yet again. But as they say, all it takes is that one buyer, and she finally arrived—a college professor from Indiana who had grown up in New York City and now wanted to retire there. She immediately felt at home. Now I could get all my plans in gear. The new owner had to be approved by the co-op board, and it looked like she would be able to move in in February 2008. There was a window where I didn't have any concerts the last week of January/first week of February, so January 29 and 30 would be the big days for my move upstate. I put a deposit down on a mover. I started to seriously pack everything up. I went to Geneva in December and rented a large storage space so that I wouldn't overwhelm my mother's house with my furniture, CDs, and books.

The apartment sale paperwork, however, took longer than expected, and the new owner would now not be moving in until the end of March. The sale still wasn't closed, but I was locked into my timeline due to my concert schedule.

And then something unexpected happened.

It was late Monday night, January 21. I was at *Cast Party;* the show had just ended (it was really early Tuesday morning). I took out my cell phone to check my e-mail and saw there was one from my sister Louise in California, addressed to all of us Lavin kids. I read it sitting at a table at Birdland.

More than a year and a half earlier, my sister had applied on our mother's behalf to the Veteran's Administration. She had just received word that our mother qualified for a monthly stipend as the widow of a World War II veteran. It was nearly a thousand dollars a month, but it came with the restriction that she couldn't have a wage earner living under her roof. So the e-mail from my sister was very matter-of-fact: although the family appreciated my selling my apartment to move in with our mother, now I couldn't. She suggested I get an apartment in Geneva and visit whenever I wanted to, but I couldn't live with Mom.

I sat there at Birdland, furiously typing on my cell phone. I couldn't believe that just like that, everything had changed—was that money more important than having someone live with Mom full time? Didn't they realize that my place had been on the market for ten months before it finally sold? I knew my brothers and sisters were surprised when I had proposed living in Geneva, but no one had objected or told me it was a bad idea.

I wondered if there was more to this—did my mother *not* want me living there? Maybe *they* didn't want me moving in with Mom? Maybe I'm not the caring nurturer I thought I could be? I was reeling. This was eight days before my scheduled move. I had sold my apartment. Where would I go?

For the next twenty-four hours, e-mails zipped back and forth. When there are nine kids there's nine opinions, plus the opinions of interested spouses. There were some who thought my living with Mom was worth more than the government money, but we were overruled by those who thought this was a way for our dad to help our mom from beyond the grave, to help her maintain her independence. I understood that, too. I didn't have much time, but I had to come up with another plan quickly.

To my surprise, part of me was relieved. I didn't really want to leave New York City. I was prepared to because I felt I was fulfilling a family duty, but this new development changed everything. I decided I would find an apartment in New York City, sign a one-year lease, and then reassess the situation and figure out what to do at the end of that year.

The problem with this plan was that I had practically no money in the bank. Oh, I would when the sale closed, but that was two months off. I had spent a lot of money the last year, anticipating the move. That was a mistake. To sign a lease, I would need first and last months' rent, a security deposit, and, if I used a rental agent, that fee, too. I called my friend Martha, and she suggested I check out Craigslist to see what was available.

For some reason I decided I would look for a studio apartment, and I would put most of my possessions into storage for the year. So I looked at tiny, overpriced spaces—$2,100 a month for a dark, cramped 300-square-foot room was pretty typical—down in the area close to Bellevue Hospital. Why on earth was I looking there? The first day of my apartment search, an intriguing thing happened.

I was down on Third Avenue in the Thirties, not far from Bellevue Hospital. The apartments were tiny and dingy. As I was walking down the street, I asked a guy which way the subway was. He told me he was going that way, and he would show me.

As we were walking, I asked him if it was a good neighborhood. He gave me a strange look. "It should be," he said, "but not for me." When I asked him why, he told me that on October 6, 2007, on that same street in broad day-light, a crazy man started stabbing a woman. He intervened and tried to get the man off the woman, and in the process he was stabbed many times. His face was very scarred, he had lost all sight in his left eye and hearing in his left ear, and he had no feeling in the left side of his face. He had just come from visiting the woman, who was still in the hospital, more than three months later. He opened his backpack and showed me newspaper clippings, where he was hailed as a hero on the front page of the *Daily News*. However, he had lost his job as a cook in a restaurant since he could only see out of one eye, and he had no place to live and was staying with friends.

Many were outraged that this Good Samaritan had risked his life to save a stranger and then experienced such hardship, so the newspaper had set up a fund to help him. I asked him how much money they raised for him, and while at one point he knew it was over $16,000, he hadn't re-ceived a penny. He had called the paper many times, just to be put on hold. No one would ever get back to him.

He wasn't asking me for money or even complaining, really—he was just telling me. I was hoping the train would come because I didn't know what to say. But the train didn't come, and then I *did* know what to say—I know a writer at the *Daily News*, David Hinckley, and I would contact him. I gave this man my phone number so he knew I was serious. He gave me his phone number and name, Amarjit Singh, before the train came. He said he would call me the next day.

He didn't call me, but I did write to David and gave him Mr. Singh's phone number. I had only met David Hinckley face-to-face once many years ago but was constantly in touch with him about music events. He was a tremendous help when Dave Van Ronk was sick, and he helped to get the word out about the Peter Paul & Mary/Tom Paxton/Arlo Guthrie con-cert Allan Pepper produced at the Bottom Line that raised such a nice chunk of money for Dave.

In the end, David talked to Martin Dunn, the editor of the *Daily News*, and Amarjit Singh finally got his money. I didn't ask him how much it was (that would have been rude), but he was so happy and thankful. He said he owed money to the people who had put him up over the past several months, so he would pay them and keep the rest in the bank. The doctors don't know if he will regain feeling in his face (the loss of eyesight and hearing is permanent), so he will be undergoing more operations. I hope the paper does a follow-up story on him now that things are going better, thanks to the generous *Daily News* readers.

I don't believe in coincidence, but to be in that neighborhood at that time of night, to ask a total stranger his opinion of the neighborhood, to have that stranger turn out to be a kind soul who risked his life for another total stranger, to have the *Daily News* raise money for him and then not give it to him, and for me to just happen to know someone at that paper . . . ooooh, it was Dad doing another good deed from the Great Beyond.

Now that that was taken care of, I could focus on my immediate situation. After searching intensively for three days, and through sheer luck, I was the first person to see a brand-new apartment the first day it was on the market. On a high floor in the West Nineties in Manhattan, it had an east-facing terrace overlooking Central Park, the Triboro Bridge (renamed the Robert F. Kennedy Bridge), and even the Empire State Building; one bedroom; a beautiful modern kitchen; and an open floor plan, all in a doorman building. I had lived in an apartment with so little light for so many years that I was thrilled to be moving into a space that would be *all* light. The only problem was it was more expensive than I could easily afford— $700 more than what I wanted to spend each month—and I didn't have enough money to pay the first month, last month, security deposit, and broker's fee. The broker and management company understood the sale of my apartment was under way, but the only way I could meet all the upfront costs was if they let me put some of it on my credit cards. However, the leasing company had *never* let a potential tenant do that. I trotted out the fact that my business manager had been forcing me to put money in a retirement fund for years, and I could tap into that if need be. (My business manager goes crazy whenever I say that. If he's reading this, he's screaming, "No Christine! You *can't touch* that money!")

There was one jittery weekend, February 1–3, when I had some checks coming in and checks going out—I was hoping it would make it appear that I had more money than I actually did—and I think that was when the leasing company checked my bottom line. The broker texted me on February 4 that I was approved. I was so relieved. If they had said no, I had no backup plan. Ervin Drake had offered to cosign the lease for me, and so had Harry, but when you cosign, they put you through the financial ringer, too, and I didn't want to subject anybody else to that. I'm an adult. If I didn't qualify, I'd sink or swim on my own and figure it out.

That first night in my new apartment, surrounded by unpacked boxes, I looked around and heaved a sigh of relief. I had a place to live. Then I stepped out on the small terrace and took a deep breath. The whole city was alive out there—a constant thrum, a sea of blackness studded with tiny pinpricks of shimmering light. The Empire State Building's lights were out, except for the bright red blinking beacon on the very top. That part of the skyline looked two-dimensional, almost unreal—jagged angles of buildings all chockablock. I've lived in this city for more than thirty years, and for the first time, standing out there, I felt like I was part of the skyline.

I was trying not to think of the cold hard reality of my situation: instead of cutting my monthly expenses, I had increased them. And because I had first planned to move to Geneva, my agent had booked very few concerts for the next year and a half, under the assumption I'd be living there and have very low overhead. So my income would take a big dive for the next year and a half, and for the first two months in my new apartment I would be paying rent *and* the mortgage and maintenance for my Riverside Drive apartment. I could envision the profit from the sale of that apartment shrinking before my eyes.

Because I still owned the apartment on Riverside, I took my time cleaning it out. I would walk over with my shopping cart; pack it up with office supplies, dishes, and other miscellaneous things I never got around to packing up before the big move; and then I would walk it back to my new place and work on songs in my head. That's how I wrote "Here Comes Caesar the Dog Whisperer," a theme song for *The Dog Whisperer* TV show on National Geographic Television. (They don't know I wrote it, and they probably don't want it.) I came up with the idea when I thought about Gabe and SuzAnne Barabas, who run the New Jersey Rep Theater. They leave the TV on during the day—the Animal Channel—for their pets. I figure other people probably do that, too, so there should be a special theme song for dogs who like to watch *The Dog Whisperer*—one in a key that only dogs can hear. I was so engrossed in writing that song that I walked past my new building and went three more blocks before I realized I had walked too far. So thanks to that song, I pushed my bulging-at-the seams shopping cart an extra six blocks.

I tried it out for the first time at *Cast Party* and learned something interesting. My plan was to sing half of it in dog key, then the second half in human key. The audience laughed like crazy during the dog key, imagining what it was I was singing for the dogs, but as soon as I started singing the lyrics for real, they stopped laughing. Oh, I think the lyrics are still funny, but obviously not as funny as the audience *imagined* they were when they couldn't hear them. I spent a good long time on that song, and it's a damn shame that I just have to move my lips when I perform it onstage.

I was happy having a new song written after only one day in my new apartment, but I was already starting to worry about money, so I came up with a new plan to make extra money over the next year: I would sell my knitting at my shows! Every spare minute I had, I knitted what I call "brain cozies"—it's a headband that can also be worn around the neck (like if you are skiing and get too hot—slide it down around your neck so you don't lose it!). I had knitted about twenty of these when Andrew in Seattle told me I should sit down and work out the math to see if it was going to make enough money so I could stay in my beautiful new apartment.

This is where my fondness for expensive yarn trips me up. I simply refuse to knit with crap; that's the kind of hairpin I am. I use yarns made of merino wool, silk, cashmere, and alpaca. (And, of course, the sequins.) The materials for a typical brain cozy cost approximately ten dollars, though some are fifteen. Each one takes me a day to knit. I brought some to shows to see if they would sell, and at what price.

Trial and error taught me that no one would pay more than thirty dollars, and twenty dollars was the price at which they sold the best. So that meant I could make a potential ten-dollar profit on a brain cozy that took an *entire day* to knit. Thank you, Andrew, for knocking me off that train to nowhere. Knitting and selling brain cozies was not going to save the day. What now?

The first time I used the laundry room in my new building, I spied a flyer tacked on the bulletin board: Universal Pictures was looking for an apartment on a high floor overlooking Central Park for a film shoot. I was on a high floor! My terrace looked out over Central Park! The TV show *Law & Order* had filmed at Martha's store once and paid well for the privilege. I scribbled down the number and called while my laundry was drying, and I was told that the location scout would come the following week to check out my apartment.

I called Sally Fingerett and told her the news. Always the pragmatist, she told me to have someone in the apartment with me in case it was a scam, where a bad guy would come and rob me, then throw me off the terrace. I took her advice and had Samir, the assistant property manager, with me when the location scout from Universal came by, but it appeared to be legit. The scout said that the director (Tony something—he had just directed *Michael Clayton*) wanted larger windows than mine. However, he took at least two dozen photographs of the living room and kitchen, and even more of the view from the windows. Now I had to wait until around April 18—the day of the shoot—to see if the killer view won out over the smaller windows. And the best part? The movie was *Duplicity*, starring Julia Roberts! It would be her apartment. I was going to show the location scout the photo of Julia polishing my shoe in that Cinderella play, but then I didn't, thinking he'd never believe it was real and that I was some kind of nut.

April 18 came and went, with no call. I tried calling the location scout, but there was never any answer. Hmm. Maybe it *was* a scam. Maybe having the assistant property manager there saved me.

In just a few months, I had more parties in that apartment than I had in my old place over fourteen years. The view is too magnificent not to share. On July 4, Andrew; his wife, Hilary; daughter, Emma; and mother, Edith came over for dinner and to watch the fireworks from my terrace. I invited other musicians and friends to stop by, and it became a party— Martha Faibisoff, David Ippolito, Ray Jessel, Joan Crowe, Steve Doyle, Janet Fanale, Jamie Skirvin and Annie Govekar (my *Drowsy* pals), Ervin and Edith Drake, Joe Sirolla, Steve and Eda Sorokoff, my writer pal Jim Bessman. I miscalculated on the fireworks—we could only see the very tops of them over the skyline, so we watched them on TV. We passed the guitar around and entertained each other. The entire room came to a hush when Andrew sang "Just One Angel."

Andrew and Hilary's daughter, Emma, is quite the little chef. We made blueberry popovers and orange-ricotta pancakes. I had also made lemon curd to go with the blueberry popovers, and Emma got the idea to put some lemon curd in the orange-ricotta pancake batter. It was a delicious addition. Emma also helped me bake rosemary-cheese mini popovers that day. She's a budding little Iron Chef, I tell ya!

One bonus of the apartment that I didn't anticipate was the show the sky puts on during thunderstorms. When thunderstorms roll through at night, I turn off all the lights, and if it's not raining too hard, I sit out on the terrace. One night for over an hour there were lightning flashes every two seconds—hundreds of them—so far to the east they were silent, but huge and high and spread out so wide they took up a huge swath of sky. Planes were still landing at LaGuardia—I could see their lights make the long, slow descent in front of the lightning flashes. I bet that made some of the passengers nervous.

The blue color of the sky over Manhattan is also a wondrous thing. One night I was baking and listening to John Wallowitch's last album, *A Miracle on 71st Street*. He's got a song called "Manhattan Blue" that stopped me in my tracks. It's about the color of the sky to the west just after the sun has gone down. What struck me about his song was that I had tried many years earlier, in 1995, to write a song about that same shade of blue that his song was about, but I had never finished it. I went through my files and found what I had written, and after hearing John's song, I knew I had to complete "That Elusive Blue."

I continued to be a part of *Cast Party* every week, occasionally guest hosting, and I traveled out of New York to do concerts, but every month my bank account dipped a little bit more, even as my love for my new digs grew. I cut back in the recording studio. I only bought clothes on sale. If I couldn't walk it, I took a subway; no more cabs. No more picking up the tab at restaurants. No more restaurants. I needed a new plan.

I read an inspiring article about the Pillsbury Bake-Off, where the grand prize is $1 million. But after the million-dollar prize, the finalists receive a measly $5,000. Not good odds. I have what I think is the best chocolate chip cookie recipe ever. It took me a long time to perfect it, and it was included in my now out-of-print songbook that was published in 1992. I looked at the Bake-Off rules carefully, which say a submitted recipe can't have been published. Would a songbook that no longer exists break the rules? And I've tweaked it a bit, so it's even better than the version in my songbook.

In the summer of 2008 I made a double batch of these for an Obama bake sale in Central Park. My new next-door neighbor's four-year-old grandson was visiting, and he helped me mix and taste-test them. I told his grandma, "Years from now he probably won't remember doing this, but make sure his mom knows he helped raise money for Barack Obama's presidential campaign."

The bake sale table was set up opposite the line where people wait for tickets for Shakespeare in the Park, and based on how quickly everything sold, it's safe to say that Shakespeare fans go for Obama big time. I renamed the cookies "Barack-o-late Chip Cookies." You'll find the recipe on my Web site.

As I write this, I'm sitting out on my terrace. It's 6:30 p.m. A soft breeze is blowing, and I know the sun is setting behind me because tangerine-colored streaks of light ricochet off the Fifth Avenue apartment windows across Central Park. To the south, wispy pink clouds hover above the Citicorp Building, the Chrysler Building, the Empire State Building, and all the smaller structures in between.

Harry just called from Jackson Hole. He'll be splitting his time between the courtroom and the slopes, teaching lawyers how to lawyer in the former and teaching senior citizens how to ski on the latter.

I should get up and exercise—I do the two-mile loop around the reservoir, counterclockwise, like the signs tell you to. I've met a lot of other runners/walkers who also do the loop around this time of day, and one told me Jackie O. used to do the loop daily, too, except she did it early in the morning, and clockwise, I guess for security reasons. From my terrace I can see there's a couple hundred people circling the reservoir right now.

I used to think my dream apartment had a terrace that faced west and a gym on the ground floor, but I was wrong. My dream apartment has a terrace that faces east, and an exercise track surrounding the Jacqueline Kennedy Onassis Reservoir in Central Park, which is so much better than a gym.

Okay, the Pillsbury Bake-Off idea isn't going to save my bacon, the film-shoot plan fizzled, and the profit from my hand-knitted brain cozies isn't going to amount to much. What can I possibly do, besides writing songs, to keep the wolf from my door?

I know. I'll write a book.

But first I'll run down to Lincoln Center to see if I can score a last-minute ticket to *South Pacific*.

THANK YOU!
I APOLOGIZE!

Thanks to my concert booking agent, Ann Patrice Carrigan at Poetry in Motion, for getting me out there; to Paul Bartz, who did that earlier in my career; and Tom Rush before that. Thank you to Bruce Newman, who continues to give Memphis lawyers a good name. *Big* thanks to Mark Hawley for his kind support over the years, and to Robert Aubry Davis, Mary Sue Twohy, and Bill Kates, who gave me the opportunity at XM satellite radio's channel 15, "The Village," and John Platt at WFUV to share good music. Thanks to Bob Sherman for continuing to give new folksingers their first airplay. Thanks to these generous heroes who work to support quality music: Dick Cerri, Rich Warren, John Sandidge, Gianni Valenti, Jamie deRoy, Stuart Ross, Jim Caruso, Vic and Reba Heyman, Babs DeLay, Lydia Hutchinson, David Broida, the staffs at Caffé Lena, Passim, the Towne Crier, the Turning Point, the Old Town School of Music, the Freight and Salvage, the Iron Horse, everyone at Rounder Records, Redwing Records, Appleseed Records, Red House Records, Sliced Bread Records, and Yellow Tail Records, and all the producers and house concert hosts around North America who keep music alive. Thanks to Phil Kurnit for taking a chance on recording me all those years ago. And two snaps up to Sally Fingerett, "the Bitchin' Business Babe," for keeping that group so vibrant.

A big hug to Allan Pepper for adding his thoughtful words to this project. Thanks to the radio DJs around the world who play folk music, and to Don White, who inspired and challenged me to write this book. If you can buy only one book this year, please buy mine. If you can buy another, buy Don's—*Memoirs of a C Student*. Buy three this year? Janis Ian's *Society's Child*. Four books? Suze Rotolo's *A Freewheelin' Time*. Five? The late great Dave Van Ronk's *The Mayor of MacDougal Street*, co-written with Elijah Wald. Six? *Nice Rendition: Cheryl Wheeler's Lyrics in Calligraphy.*

A big smooch to Ervin Drake, who continues to inspire us, and to Edith Drake, who continues to inspire Ervin. Thanks, too, to Bill and Janice Kollar.

Thanks to Steve Rosenthal, Brian Bauers, and Phil Klum for their expertise in recording studios, to Irene Young in photo studios, and to Maureen Bennett O'Connor in design studios.

A shout-out to all the road managers I have worked with over the years: Terry Gabis, Tom Slothower, Louise Lavin, Mary "Piglet/Joe Namath" Lavin, Linn Lavin,

Lois Dino, Micah Engber, Jack Gabis, Kelly Macauley, Catherine Robbins, Dan Lillienfeld, Jim Carona, Lisa Regal, Claudia Russell, Janet Fanale, and that Grateful Dead roadie who drove me around California while he smoked a doobie and drove 100 mph (enough said about *that* trip).

Heartfelt thanks to Lisa Clyde Nielsen, Jeff Eyrich, Paula Brisco, Linda Loiewski, and the team at Tell Me Press for giving me the opportunity to publish with them, and to Gail Parenteau for spreading the word.

But also one big apology.

Many years ago the fabulous singer/dancer Anne Reinking was performing a one-woman show at an upstairs performance space in Manhattan. I didn't hear about it until the day of the show. I am a huge fan of hers, and so is my friend Harry. I called the venue but was told the show was completely sold out. The only way to possibly get in was to hope for no-shows at the door.

So that night Harry and I went to the door. It was cold, freezing sleet/rain was falling, and a crush of people was pushing and shoving to get in out of the weather.

This was before computers were sophisticated. The man controlling the ticket line was at the bottom of a big flight of stairs just inside the doorway. He held a long dot-matrix printout and checked off names as people with reservations arrived. Harry stepped up and asked if there were tickets available, and the poor schlub with the printout screamed, *"No! It's sold out! Step aside!"* We immediately did.

The next person behind us stepped up and shouted his name: "Green! Two tickets!"

The guy with the printout looked at the list and then asked, "Howard or Benjamin?"

"Benjamin!" the man said.

The guy with the printout checked off his name and told him to go upstairs and pay there.

Harry immediately jumped back in line and shouted, "Green! Howard! Two tickets!"

The poor guy with the printout didn't notice he had just spoken to Harry thirty seconds earlier. He simply checked off the name and told us to go up the stairs, which we did.

It was a terrific show, marred only by my fear of the Green party showing up and having us arrested.

For the record, I apologize, Mr. Green.

What we did was wrong. It will never happen again.

APPENDIX 1
CHRISTINE LAVIN COMPLETE DISCOGRAPHY

SOLO ALBUMS

Cold Pizza for Breakfast
Yellow Tail Records, 2009; album produced by Brian Bauers and Christine Lavin

"Cold Pizza for Breakfast Redux" / "A Firefly's Life" / "The Kind of Love You Never Recover From" / "Sometimes" (featuring Anil Melwani) / "Here Comes Caesar the Dog Whisperer" / "Too Old for the National Spelling Bee" / "That Elusive Blue" (featuring Robin Batteau) / "Human" (featuring Robin Batteau) / "Attractive Stupid People" / "Not Me Not Me Not Me" / "Odds Are" / "Mencken's Pen" / "Bring Back the Bow" / Christine reads an excerpt from the book *Cold Pizza for Breakfast: A Mem*-wha?? / "Good Thing SHE Can't Read My Mind: A Dude's Eye View"

I Don't Make This Stuff Up . . . I Just Make It Rhyme
Recorded live at Bound for Glory at Annabel Taylor Hall, Cornell University
Yellowtail Records, 2008; album produced by Brian Bauers and Christine Lavin

Phil Shapiro introduces Bound for Glory / "The Most Polite City in the World" / "A Shark in New York Waters" / Sharkman on Malta / "Planet X" (featuring Sal Ruibal) / "Good Thing He Can't Read My Mind" / "I Am Psychic So Are You" / "More Than 1,000,000 Americans" / "Alone Again Naturally" / "Tacobel Canon" / Worst birthdays / Birthday game: Alissa vs. Andrea / "Sunday Breakfast with Christine" / A recipe for everyone whether they want it or not / "The Moment Slipped Away" / "What Was I Thinking (1993–2007)?" / Hidden track (studio recording): "A Shark in New York Waters"

Happydance of the Xenophobe
Yellow Tail Records, 2007; album produced by Brian Bauers and Christine Lavin

"The Most Polite City in the World" / "Happydance" / "Chocolate Covered Espresso Beans" / "More Than 1,000,000 Americans" / "Here Comes Hurricane Season" / "Tom Cruise Scares Me" / "Smokers" / "Russian Michael" / "As We Stumble Along" / "Whipped Cream" (featuring Lodi Carr) / "Why?" / "Reminiscing with the Elusive Gentle Boxer of Love" / Hidden track: "The Liar Sleeps Tonight"

folkZinger
Appleseed Records, 2006; album produced by Brian Bauers and Christine Lavin

"Armageddon" (featuring Ian and Noah Slothower) / "Happiness Runs" / "The Bends" / "Winter in Manhattan" / "Moken Spoken Here" / "Chicken Soup for the Soul" / "Bad Girl Dreams" / "All My Lovin' " / "One of the Boys" / "The Peter Principle at Work" / "(I'm a) Card-Carrying Bleeding Heart Liberal" / "The Accidentals' Surprise" / "Winter in Manhattan" (sung by the Accidentals)

Sometimes Mother Really Does Know Best
Recorded live at the Colorado Springs Fine Arts Center
Appleseed Records, 2004; album produced by Christine Lavin

"Strangers Talk to Me in Colorado Springs" / Rocky Mountain . . . Hi! / "Wind Chimes" / You should have seen the frightened looks on your faces / What kind of ridiculous glamour trajectory am I on? / "What Was I Thinking?" / Martha Stewart . . . Victoria's Secret . . . Bob Dylan . . . Pachelbel? / "The Tacobel Canon" / Steve . . . you are so busted! / "A Question of Tempo (When I'm Under Pressure)" / "Planet X" / Planet? Planot? Goofy? / Who are the brainiacs in the house tonight? / Bernice, Carol, and the crowd compete for the science prize / "You Look Pretty Good for Your Age" / Art Jensen, Mr. Colorado Springs / Flashback to 1956: How do you spell Cassiopeia? / Boston Red Sox fans: the most loyal, the most tenacious, yet the most troubled of all baseball fans / "Ballad of a Ballgame" / "The Legal Ramifications of a Crackerjack Vendor Who Works in Yankee Stadium" / "Sometimes Mother Really Does Know Best"

The Runaway Christmas Tree
Christine Lavin and the Mistletones (Gregory Clark, Julie Gold, Ervin Drake, Emily Bindiger, David Lutken, Margaret Dorn, and Andrea Vuocolo)
Appleseed Records, 2003; album produced by Emily Bindiger

"A Christmas/Kwanzaa/Solstice/Chanukah/Ramadan/Boxing Day Song" / "Snow! Medley" / "The Runaway Christmas Tree" / "Dona Nobis Pacem" / "Lamb & Lion" / "The All Purpose Carol" / "Elves" / "Scalloped Potatoes" / "Polkadot Pancakes" / "Tacobel Canon" / "A New Year's Round" / "Th 12 Dys f Chrstms" / "Allelujah/Amen" / "Good Night to You All"

I Was in Love with a Difficult Man
Red Wing Records, 2002; album produced by Steve Rosenthal

"I Was in Love with a Difficult Man" / "Jack & Wanda" / "Strangers Talk to Me" / "Sunday Breakfast with Christine (and Ervin)" / "Making Friends with My Grey Hair" / "Trade Up" / "Wind Chimes" / "All You Want Is What You Want" / "Three-Storied Life" / "Firehouse" / "For Carolyn/Something Beautiful" / "Looked Good on Paper"

The Subway Series: Songs from Above and Below the Streets of New York
Recorded live at the Walsh Family Library, Fordham University
christinelavin.com records, 2001; album produced by Christine Lavin

John Platt introduces Christine / "Waiting for the B Train" / "Doris and Edwin: The Movie" / "Wait! Here's a Better Ending!" / "Good Thing He Can't Read My Mind" / Good thing you couldn't read my mind! / Dallas, TX '63/NYC '99 / "The Sixth Floor/Moon-Rising Tide/We Are the Lucky Ones" / Where is the Mango Princess? / "If We Had No Moon" / Have I got a deli man for you! / "Another New York Afternoon" / "Shopping Cart of Love: The Play" / "The Moment Slipped Away" / "OK, Gang, One More Song (SNAG)"

Getting in Touch with My Inner Bitch
christinelavin.com records, 2000; album produced by Christine Lavin

Choice words from Dave Palmater / "Single Voice" / I venture into the crowd with spelunking lamp on my head / "You Look Pretty Good for Your Age" / Don't make me be naughty / "What Was I Thinking in 1999?" / What Monica L. and Cameron D. have in common / It's dangerous to confide in a songwriter / "Another New York Afternoon" / A late-night IM turns into . . . / "Plateau" / Gene Shay adds his voice to the low fat/no fat debate / "Happy Birthday Maureen" / "Harrison Ford" / "Polka Dancing Bus Driver and the 40-Year-Old Mystery" / "The Piper" / "Getting in Touch with My Inner Bitch" / Megon McDonough, a great singer, inspires an idea / "Adjust Your Dreams/Shining My Flashlight" / "Piranha Women of the Avocado Jungle of Death"

The Bellevue Years
Rounder, 2000; album produced by Christine Lavin

"If You Want Space, Go to Utah" / "The Vacation of Their Lives" / "Giant TV Screen" / "The Danger" / "Tidal Wave" / "Another Woman's Man" / Interview with David Weinstein, 1/22/84 / "Cold Pizza for Breakfast" / "Music/Sport Notes, 1984" / Lady Knights, the Atlantic Ten, & the Atavistics / "Isn't This Just Like Empty-Vee?" / Let's get out of here, Jody / "Camping" (live from General Feed and Seed, 6/14/86) / "Artificial Means" / "The Moment Slipped Away" / "The First Folk Singer on the Space Shuttle" (live with Trumbull and Coor, 11/7/87) / "If I Could Be Sonja Henie"

One Wild Night in Concert
Recorded live at the Blue Moon Coffeehouse, Illinois Wesleyan University
christinelavin.com records, 1998; album produced by Christine Lavin

Words from our sponsor, Darcy Greder / "Oh No" / "They Look Alike, They Walk Alike . . ." / "National Apology Day" / "Flip Side of Fame" / Creating just the right mood for the next song / "The Kind of Love You Never Recover From" / Amanda McBroom at the Rainbow and Stars Room / "Errol Flynn" / The secret fear of songwriters / "Please Don't Make Me Too Happy" / The audience votes / "The Voice on the Relaxation Tape" / Visiting Dallas / "The Sixth Floor" / The day after on a plane to California / "Great Big Bug" / An insomniac at night / "The Wild Blue" / "Dream/Summer Song/Gotta Twirl"

Shining My Flashlight on the Moon
Shanachie, 1997; album produced by Steve Rosenthal

"Shining My Flashlight on the Moon" / "Two Americans in Paris" / " 'Honey, We Have to Talk' " / "I Want to Be Lonely Again" / "Music to Operate By" / "Happy Divorce Day" / "Polka-Dancing Bus Driver and the 40-Year-Old Mystery" / "Robert and Annie in Larchmont, New York" / "If I Ruled the World" / "As Bad As It Gets" / "Snackin' " / "The Scent of Your Cologne" / "Planet X"

Please Don't Make Me Too Happy
Shanachie, 1995; album produced by Steve Rosenthal

"Oh No" / "Constant State of Want" / "I Knew You'd Call . . . I'm Psychic" / "The Secrets at This Wedding" / "The Sixth Floor" / "Jane" / "Jagged Hearts" / "Scatter New Seeds" / "Waiting for the B Train" / "Something Is Wrong with This Picture" / "*69" / "Please Don't Make Me Too Happy" / "Oh No (Reprise)"

Compass
Rounder, 1994; album produced by Bill Kollar

"Blind Dating Fun" / "Compass" / "Rushcutter's Bay" / "Replaced" / "You Think You've Got Problems" / "Until Now" / "High Heel Shoes" / "Prisoners of Their Hairdos" / "I Bring Out the Worst in You" / "Ten O'clock in Toronto" / "Katy Says Today Is the Best Day of My Whole Entire Life"

Live at the Cactus Cafe . . . What Was I Thinking?
Recorded live at the University of Texas
Rounder, 1993; album produced by Christine Lavin

"Prince Charles" / "We Are the True Americans" / "Dear Dan" / "Bald Headed Men" / "What Was I Thinking?" / I blab about celebrities I have spied / "Doris and Edwin: The Movie" / "Alternate Endings" / I N T E R M I S S I O N / "The Dakota" / "Regretting What I Said" / How the Lord helped me rewrite / "Shopping Cart of Love: The Play" / "Katy Says Today Is the Best Day of My Whole Entire Life" / "What Was I Thinking? (The Dance Mix)"

Attainable Love
Rounder, 1991; album produced by Mark Dann

"Attainable Love" / "Castlemaine" / "Yonder Blue" / "Sensitive New Age Guys" / "Victim/ Volunteer" / "The Kind of Love You Never Recover From" / "Fly on a Plane" / "Venus Kissed the Moon" / "Moving Target" / "Shopping Cart of Love: The Play"/

Good Thing He Can't Read My Mind
Rounder, 1988; album produced by Bill Kollar

"Good Thing He Can't Read My Mind" / "Bumblebees" / "The Santa Monica Pier" / "Waltzing with Him" / "Mysterious Woman" / "Realities" / "Downtown" (featuring Livingston Taylor) / "Never Go Back" / "85 Degrees" / "Somebody's Baby" / "Ain't Love Grand"

Beau Woes and Other Problems of Modern Life
Rounder, 1986; album produced by Robin Batteau

"Amoeba Hop" (featuring Dave Van Ronk) / "Summer Weddings" / "Prince Charles" / "Gettin' Used to Leavin' " / "Camping" / "Ballad of a Ballgame" / "Doris and Edwin: The Movie" / "Roses from the Wrong Man" / "Air Conditioner" / "All I Have to Do Is Dream/A Summer Song" / "Biological Time Bomb" / "The Moment Slipped Away"

Future Fossils
Rounder, 1985; album produced by Mark Dann and Christine Lavin

"Don't Ever Call Your Sweetheart by His Name" / "Damaged Goods" / "Cold Pizza for Breakfast" / "Rockaway" / "Nobody's Fat in Aspen" / "Rituals" / "The Bag Ladies' Ball" / "Regretting What I Said" / "Sweet Irene the Disco Queen" / "Ramblin' Waltz" / "Artificial Means" / "Space Between Rings" / "The Dakota"

Absolutely Live
Lifesong Records/Winthrop, 1981, reissued in 2000 on CD; album produced by Terry Cashman

Producer Terry Cashman welcomes the crowd / "Three Months to Live" / I express my deep concern for tiny animals / "The Amoeba Hop" / What do New Yorkers fear the most? / "Summer Weddings" / Oh no! Here comes a toxic Romeo! Run! / "Add Me to the List" / "The Bitter End" / The F.I.B.S. Club—you may already be a member! / "I'm Mad" / The crowd will "Name That Tune" in 18 notes / "Downtown" / I have mixed feelings about New York / "Getting Used to Leavin' " / Nobody's making disaster films anymore. Bummer! / "Doris and Edmund: The Movie" / I welcome to the stage the fabulous Hilly, Lili & Lulu / "Air Conditioner" / "If I Should Call You" / Shikses, Chicken McNuggets, and Plumpetts / "I've Been Living on Milk and Cookies Since You've Been Gone"

DVD

girlUNinterrupted
Recorded live in Indianapolis
christinelavin.com, 2002; DVD produced by Mark Butterfield

"Strangers Talk to Me" / "Jack and Wanda" / "Good Thing He Can't Read My Mind" / "Da Doo En Ron Ron" / "Harrison Ford" / "Planet X" / "Jeopardy! lyrics" / Who is the smartest person at this concert? / "You Look Pretty Good for Your Age" / Here He Is, Mr. Indianapolis / "Sensitive New Age Guys" / "The King of Indianapolis Is Wayne" / "Mary Helen, Mary Margaret, David, and Michael" / "Making Friends with My Grey Hair" / "Firehouse" / "Wind Chimes" / "Sunday Breakfast with Christine" / "The Polka Dancing Bus Driver and the 40-Year-Old Mystery" / "Adjust Your Dreams/Shining My Flashlight" / Let's give stuff away / "All I Have to Do Is Dream/A Summer Song/Twirl"

FOUR BITCHIN' BABES ALBUMS

Fax It! Charge It! Don't Ask Me What's for Dinner!
Sally Fingerett, Christine Lavin, Megon McDonough, and Debi Smith
Shanachie, 1995; album produced by Sally Fingerett and Dan Green

"My Mother's Hands" (Smith) / "Stars" (McDonough) / "TV Talk" (Fingerett) / "Great Big Bug" (Lavin) / "Shadow" (Smith) / "Microwave Life" (McDonough) / "She Won't Be

Walkin' " (Fingerett) / "Energy Vampires" (Lavin) / "Dreams of Deep Water" (McDonough) / "Muzak" (Smith) / "Clover" (Fingerett) / "What Was I Thinking?" (Lavin) / "Lullaby" (group)

Buy Me, Bring Me, Take Me, Don't Mess My Hair! Volume 2
Sally Fingerett, Julie Gold, Christine Lavin, and Megon McDonough
Rounder, 1993; album produced by Steve Rosenthal

"Oh Great Spirit" (McDonough) / "Bald Headed Men" (Lavin) / "Save Me a Seat" (Fingerett) / "From a Distance" (Gold) / "Sealed with a Kiss" (Lavin with group) / "Butter" (McDonough) / "Graceful Man" (Fingerett) / "Try Love" (Gold) / "Take Me Out to Eat" (Fingerett) / "As Close to Flying" (Lavin) / "(Fun to Be) Perfect" (Gold) / "The Choice" (McDonough) / "Good Night New York" (Gold)

Buy Me, Bring Me, Take Me, Don't Mess My Hair! Volume 1
Sally Fingerett, Patty Larkin, Christine Lavin, and Megon McDonough
Rounder, 1991; album produced by Sally Fingerett and Dan Green

Dick Cerri introduces the show / "Prisoners of Their Hairdos" (Lavin) / "Wake Up and Dream" (McDonough) / "Not Bad for a Broad" (Larkin) / "Ladies Lunch" (Fingerett) / "Good Thing He Can't Read My Mind" (Lavin) / Megon on codependency / "Painless Love" (McDonough) / "Dave's Holiday" (Larkin) / "Home Is Where the Heart Is" (Fingerett) / Christine reads mailing list cards / Sally explains the game show / "She Moved Through the Fair" (McDonough) / Megon draws the next suggestion / "Junk Food" (Larkin) / Sally draws the next suggestion / "Sensitive New Age Guys" (Lavin) / "But Still He Loved Her So" (Fingerett) / "I'm Fine" (Larkin) / Meg channels Patty / "Every Living Thing" (McDonough) / "These Boots Are Made for Walkin' " (group)

COMPILATION ALBUMS

One Meat Ball
CD accompanied by 96-page cookbook edited by Christine Lavin
Appleseed, 2006; Mark Hawley, executive producer

"Blueberry Pancakes" (Annie Bauerlein and Chip Mergott) / "Maple Syrup Time" (Pete Seeger) / "Taylor the Latte Boy" (Marcy Heisler and Zina Goldrich) / "Root Beer for Breakfast" (Vance Gilbert) / "Betrothal" (the Accidentals, featuring Marcia Pelletiere) / "Bacon" (Mary Liz McNamara) / "Orange Cocoa Cake" (Cathy Fink and Marcy Marxer) / "Mocha Java" (Alan Miceli) / "I Think About Sex" (Ray Jessel) / "Tomato Puddin' " (Jeff Daniels) / "Butter" (Megon McDonough) / "Fudge" (Robin Hopper) / "Ten Pound Bass" (Sally Fingerett and Jonathan Edwards) / "The Heartbreak Diet" (Julie Gold) / "Blackberry Winter" (MaryJo Mundy) / "One Meat Ball" (Dave Van Ronk) / "Bottle of Wine" (Tom Paxton) / "Pie" (Debi Smith with Doc Watson) / "French Toast Bread Pudding" (Christine Lavin) / Bonus hidden track featuring Dame Edna

Christine Lavin Presents: On a Winter's Night
Special 20th anniversary edition
Rounder, 2004; compilation produced by Christine Lavin

"Secret Gardens" (Judy Collins) / "Last Night" (Lynn Miles) / "Winter Wind" (Patty Larkin) / "The Storm" (Cheryl Wheeler) / "Wild Berries" (Sally Fingerett) / "Rising in Love" (David Roth) / "When We Were Just Friends" (Bauerlein & Mergott) / "Another Time and Place" (Dave Van Ronk) / "Your Face" (Cliff Eberhardt) / "She's That Kind of Mystery" (Bill Morrissey) / "I Saw a Stranger with Your Hair" (John Gorka) / "In Our Hands" (Kenny White with Shawn Colvin) / "Lancelot's Tune (Guinevere)" (Buskin & Batteau) / "A Lesson in Every Goodbye" (Megon McDonough) / "The Kind of Love You Never Recover From" (Christine Lavin) / "Here We Go" (David Mallett) / "Let Me Fall in Love Before the Spring Comes" (Blumenfeld & Kaplansky) / "Frozen in the Snow" (David Wilcox) / "On a Winter's Night" (Willie Nininger) / "Stars" (Hills, Herdman, Mangsen & Gillette)

The Stealth Project
christinelavin.com records, 1999; compilation produced by Christine Lavin

"Hold Me Tonight" (Red Grammer) / "John's Cocoons" (Michael McNevin) / "Walk on Water" (Diane Zeigler) / "Lounging in the Belly of the Beast" (Electric Bonsai Band) / "Twilight" (Ron Renninger) / "Let the Rain Come Down" (Lori Lieberman) / "Ten Complaints" (Dee Carstensen) / "River Skeeters" (Gideon Freudmann) / "Harrison Ford" (Christine Lavin) / "Adolescent Rant" (Don White) / "Prom Dress" (Deborah Pardes) / "Hi Sal, Have You Checked Your E-mail?" (Grit Laskin) / "The Marijo Tonight" (Jackie Tice) / "I'm Going Back" (Cathie Ryan) / "Love Travels" (Ceili Rain) / "Rust" (Lynn Miles)

Laugh Tracks, Volumes 1 and 2
Shanachie, 1996; albums produced by Steve Rosenthal and Christine Lavin

Disk One:

Andy Breckman tells us how he really feels / "Don't Get Killed" (Andy Breckman) / The Chenille Sisters give us their Bob Dylan update / "Blowin' in the Wind" (the Chenille Sisters) / Welcome to New York (Don White) / "Rascal" (Don White) / Vance rants / "Country Western Rap" (Vance Gilbert) / Act I: Patty Larkin Channels Marlene Dietrich / Act II: Patty Larkin "Hums" "La Vie en Rose" / Act III: "At the Mall," Starring Dietrich/Miranda/Merman / "Blow 'Em Away" (Chuck Brodsky) / "Potato" (Cheryl Wheeler) / Welcome to New York (Greg Greenway) / "Driving in Massachusetts" (Greg Greenway) / Thinking of majoring in English? (Dave's True Story) / "Trollope" (Dave's True Story) / "Microwave Life" (Megon McDonough) / Laugh Track WFUV Laffers—Debbie Kiba, John Kiba, Doris Ruth Oppenheimer, Becka Ribaudo, Joe Ribaudo, Carol-Lynn Wolfe / "(These Eggs Were) Born to Run" (Rob Carlson)

Disk Two:

What is bothering Cliff Eberhardt now? / "Good for Nothing Saint" (Cliff Eberhardt) / "Double Yodel" (Lou and Peter Berryman) / Rob Carlson demonstrates the international insult / "God Loves the Irish" (Rob Carlson) / "TV Talk" (Sally Fingerett) / David Buskin goes out on a limb / "Hotline" (David Buskin) / "Slap Bang" (Betty) / Dave Van Ronk gives himself advice / "Garden State Stomp" (Dave Van Ronk) / "I'm Bored" (Christine Lavin) / "Every Man for Himself" (the Foremen) / Debi Smith on the bodhran, Hags, and Irish Pizza / "Sleep" (Debi Smith) / Tom Paxton explains the '80s / "Yuppies in the Sky" (Tom Paxton & Company) / Bonus track: "The Jackie O. Auction" (Tom Paxton) / Bonus track: WFUV Laughers: Steve Sherman, B.J. Kowalski, and a Mystery Woman

Follow That Road
Martha's Vineyard 2, double album
Rounder, 1994; albums produced by Steve Rosenthal and Christine Lavin

Disk One:
"Wintertide" (Al Pettaway) / "Born a Little Late" (Susan Werner) / "Chase the Buffalo" (Pierce Pettis) / "Hard Day Yesterday" (Kristina Olsen) / "Did You Hear John Hurt" (Tom Paxton) / "The Speculator" (Cathy Fink and Marcy Marxer) / "Magnolia Street" (Buddy Mondloch) / "Deep Country" (Barbara Kessler and Jonathan Edwards) / "These Are the Times" (Red Grammer) / "From My Hands" (Frank Christian) / "Cog in the Wheel" (Diane Zeigler) / "Ashes of Love" (Tom Prasado-Rao) / "Home" (Sally Fingerett with Cheryl Wheeler and Jonathan Edwards) / "Heaven Is Free Tonight" (David Buskin) / "Ramblin' Boy" (Tom Paxton and Tsubasa) /

Disk Two:
"One Day Closer" (Jonathan Edwards) / "Green Green Rocky Road" (Dave Van Ronk) / "King of Seventh Avenue" (Ellis Paul) / "If Love Is a Dream" (Megon McDonough) / "The Great Storm Is Over" (Bob Franke) / "Ballad of a Ballgame" (Christine Lavin) / "Cover Me" (Robin Batteau) / "Flying in the Face of Mr. Blue" (Kate Taylor) / "Gettin' Up Early" (Tom Paxton) / "Wearing the Time" (Susan Graham White) / "Heart on the Run" (Tom Intondi) / "Follow That Road" (Anne Hills) / "Feel Your Feelings" (John Forster) / "Life Is Hard" (Cliff Eberhardt and the Bad Boy Club) / "Menemsha" (Hilary Field)

Big Times in a Small Town
Martha's Vineyard 1
Rounder, 1993; album produced by David Seitz and Christine Lavin

"Big Times in a Small Town" (James Mee) / "Dog Dreams" (Jonatha Brooke) / "Is It Wrong to Feel So Good" (Cliff Eberhardt) / "Entering Marion" (John Forster) / "Nod over Coffee" (Pierce Pettis) / "Further and Further Away" (Cheryl Wheeler) / "Summer of Love" (Pete Nelson) / "Afro-Cuban Lullaby" (Hilary Field) / "The Star Spangled Banner and Me" (David Roth) / "A Folksinger Earns Every Dime" (David Buskin) / "I Am My Dad" (Electric Bonsai Band) / "Chained to These Lovin' Arms" (Patty Larkin) / "A Road Worth Walking Down" (Greg Greenway) / "The Date" (Barbara Kessler) / "Little Piece at a Time" (David Wilcox) / "A Time to Decide/Endless Sky" (Chucky Pyle) / "Shivering/ Tight Jeans/Nursery Rhyme/Round and Round" (David Roth, Kristina Olsen, and Friends)

When October Goes

Rounder, 1991; compilation produced by Christine Lavin

"When Fall Comes to New England" (Cheryl Wheeler) / "Locked Away" (Amy Malkoff and Raymond Gonzales) / "Southbound Train" (Julie Gold) / "Will You Come Home" (Susie Burke) / "When I Need You Most of All" (David Buskin) / "Lie Easy" (Gail Rundlett) / "Island of Time" (Patty Larkin) / "Where Were You Last Night?" (Frank Christian) / "Out of My Mind" (John Gorka) / "Are You Happy Now?" (Richard Shindell) / "When October Goes" (Megon McDonough) / "Gettin' Used to Leavin' " (Christine Lavin) / "The Return" (Sally Fingerett) / "The Long Road" (Cliff Eberhardt and Richie Havens) / "Coming of the Snow" (Rod MacDonald)

APPENDIX 2
1,000 TERRIFIC RECORDINGS I HAVE PLAYED ON THE RADIO

If you find yourself in a funk, I recommend that you play this entire list of songs—but not in alphabetical order. Mix things up! Playing this song list will take you about sixty hours: you could do it in a week if you played eight and a half hours a day. I promise you, by the end of that week, you will not only feel better, you won't even remember what was bothering you.

Accidentals: "The Earth and Man"; "Fire Fire"; "For What It's Worth"; "Gerald Ford Presidential Administration"; "Hodie Christus"; "Hymn"; "I'm Not Going Home for Christmas"; "Love Me Like a Rock"; "Many Voices"; "Poem for a Dog"; "Sunday in the Park"; "Wheel of Time"; "Where or When"

Alarik, Scott: "Morrow"

Allen, Linda: "We Are the Rainbow Sign"

Andersen, Eric: "Before Everything Changed"

Andersen, Tom: "Another Tuesday"

Anderson, D.C.: "Sister Clarissa"; "Your Father and I Have Been Talking"

Anderson, Jamie: "Mama Come Quick"; "When They Know Who We Are"

Anel, Lili: "George Bailey's Lament"; "Voyager"; "Won't You Stay"

Annis, Nick: "Recurring Theme"

Armstrong, Jen: "Day for Peace"

Arnowitz, Suzy: "Hold on to Your Heart"

Artisan: "What's the Use of Wings"

Asher, Lisa: "Galileo"

Askew, Joy: "Lake Calhoun"

Astro Cappella: "The Sun Song"; "The Sun Song: PBS Dance Mix"

Atwell, Tim: "Built for Comfort Not for Speed"; "I Hate Hammers"; "A Quiet Game of Chess"

Avenue Q Broadway cast: "North Pole Global Warming Surf Party"

Barker, Les: "The Civilised World"

Barnaby Creek: "Moving Less Awkwardly"

Barnett, Janie: "On the Water"

Barnett, Judy: "Elena Was Lonesome"

Batalla, Perla: "Salvation"

Bauerlein, Annie: "Blueberry Pancakes"

Bauerlein & Mergott: "Rich in Love"

Beatles: "Day in the Life"

Bedford, Brian: "What's the Use of Wings"

Bellowhead: "Copshawholme Fair"

Beloff, Jim: "Big in Japan"; "Charles Ives"; "The French Café"

Bennett, Arlon: "Be the Change"

Bergeron, Ellis: "City on Fire"

Berryman, Lou and Peter: "After Life Goes By"; "Dupsha Dove"

Bessette, Mimi: "I'm Leaving Tonight"

Blachly, Susannah: "Secret Place"

Black, Mary: "No Frontiers"; "Prayer for Love"

Blake, William Equality: "Time After Time"

Blanton, Carsie: "Ain't So Green"

Blind Boys of Alabama: "The Last Time"

Blumenfeld, Hugh: "Brother"

Blumenthal, Francesca: "Firemen Shopping"; "Queens"

Freyda: "Dreams of Harmony"

Friedman, Dean: "I Miss Monica"; "Saturday Fathers"

Frishberg, Dave: "My Country Used to Be"

Fure, Tret: "The Wedding Song"

Gaelic Storm: "The Beggar Man"

Gallup, Annie: "April 22 Somerville, Massachusetts"

Ganger, Victoria: "Too Much Martha"

Garfunkel, Art: "If I Ever Say I'm over You"

Garin, Michael: "In a Dream I Cried on Oprah"; "If Workers Control the Means . . ."; "World Leader Name Game"

Geyer, David: "You Can't Sit Still"

Gilbert, Vance: "A Case of You"; "Country Western Rap"; "Eliza Jane"; "I Met Ellis Paul"; "Takin' It All to Tennessee"

Gilkyson, Eliza: "Man of God"; "Peace Call"

Gill, Jim: "Banana"; "Yow!"

Gillette, Steve: "When the First Leaves Fall"; "Windows of Heaven"

Girlyman: "Postcards from Mexico"

Gold, Julie: "From a Distance"; "Good Night New York"; "The Heartbreak Diet"; "Merry Christmas (Peace Peace Peace)"; "Tiger in New Jersey"

Goldberg, Eve: "Something About a Sunday"

Goldman, David: "Sorry Said the Moon"

Goldman, Kat: "The Great Disappearing Act"; "Soft Place to Land"

Goldman, Richard: "The Good Years"; "Zsa Zsa"

Goldstein, Teddy: "Four Ninety Nine"

Goodman, Steve: "The Dutchman"

Gordon, James: "Casey Sheehan Didn't Die for Nothing"; "World Gone Mad"

Gorka, John: "Blue Chalk"; "Blues Palace"; "I Saw a Stranger with Your Hair"; "Love Is Our Cross to Bear"

Grace, Leela, and Ellie Grace: "You're Aging Well"

Graff, Randy: "There's a Change in Me"

Graham White, Susan: "A Heart Unarmed"; "Seasons"

Gramins, Ashley: "Godspeed (Sweet Dreams)"; "Rainbow Connection"

Grammer, Red: "Bo Bo See Wattin Tattin"; "Shining Eyes"; "Strangely Wrapped Gift"; "These Are the Times"; "Use a Word"

Granary Girls: "Briar and the Rose"

Gray, Kierstin: "Fire"; "Let You Slip Away"

Great Big Sea: "Fast as I Can"; "Hidden Track"; "Mari-Mac"; "Something to It"

Green, Babbie: "Two Homes"

Green, Dan: "That September Morn"

Green, EJ: "Morning After"; "Sea Water"

Greenbaum, Susan: "Dead End Called Main Street"; "Love Song"

Gregson, Clive: "Fingerless Gloves"

Griffin, Patty: "Living with Ghosts"; "Making Pies"; "Not Alone"; "You Never Get What You Want"

Griffith, Grace: "Exile"; "Hills of Shiloh"; "My Life"; "Quiet Land/Inisfree"; "Sailing/Ships Are Sailing"; "Shape of My Heart"

Griffith, Nanci: "Everything's Coming Up Roses"; "Three Flights Up"

Guthrie, Woody: "Ticky Tock"

Haines and Leighton: "Does This Mean It's Over"

Hairspray Broadway cast: "Tracy Turnblad's Big Bad Holiday Rap"

Hall, Mary Gordon: "Babe Alone"; "Soul Affair"

Purpose and Kaplansky: "Ring on My
Hand"
Putman, William: "Plastic Flowers"; "TV
Trained"
Raman, Chip: "Little Mighty One"
Rankin, Kenny: "Here's That Rainy Day"
Ratshin, Emma and Andrew: "The Night
That I Was Born"
Ray, Kevin: "God Save New Orleans";
"Karaoke Town"; "Your Gay Friend"
Reader, Eddi: "Ya Jacobites"
Redding, Lipbone: "Old Tattoo"
Reed, Lou: "Trade In"
Renninger, Ron: "Dreams of Nothing";
"Flowers in the Sidewalk"; "Half Time
Band"; "Pickle Pickle Wee Wee Tar"
Rent Broadway cast: "Seasons of Love"
Riverdance: "Slip into Spring"
Roberson, Steve: "This Little Romance"
Robertson, Cally: "Beautiful Love"; "Po-
etic Justice"; "Tomorrow Night"
Robertson, Cally and Mae: "Smile"
Robertson, Mae: "American Tune";
"Forever Young"; "Summer of My
Dreams"
Roche Sisters: "Weeded Out"
Roche, Suzzy: "Sweetie Pie"
Rogan, Billy: "Frank and Andrea"
Rogers, Garnet: "The Painted Pony"
Rogers, Lisa: "Jesus and Jesus"
Rogers, Stan: "Northwest Passage"
Romanoff, Steve: "Teach Your Children
to Sing"
Rosing, Val: "Teddy Bear's Picnic"
Rosser, Chris: "David and Marie";
"Deeper Than My Own Name"
Roth, David: "Bake Sale"; "Kids"; "Mas-
ter's Degree"; "Morning Person";
"Nights at the Chez"; "The Ranch of
All Compassion"; "Rising in Love";
"Round and Round We Turn"; "Taller
Than My Hair"

Rusby, Kate: "Merry Go Broom"
Russ and Eli: "Never Did No Wanderin' "
Russell, Catherine: "Offering"
Russell, Claudia: "Dance"; "Oh Califor-
nia"; "Stars"
Russell, Thomas George: "Van Ronk"
Russell, Tom: "Beat Folk"
Russell, Vickie: "Take Care of You"
Sage, Rachel: "Hunger in John"; "My
Word"
Saint John, Barbara: "Emily"
Sato, Shinobu: "John Hurt Medley"
Savoca, Karen: "Sunday in Nandua"
Savory, Tanya: "Big Town"
Schindler, John: "Don't Fit In"
Schmidt, Charlie: "Why Henry"
Schmidt, Claudia: "Remember"
Schneckenburger, Lissa: "The Irish Girl"
Schwartz, Eric: "The Grill Is Gone"; "I
Don't Know You"; "Me and Jenny and
the Lovely Marilu"; "Moishe the Kid";
"Only Be"
Seat of the Pants Band: "Once in a Life-
time"
Seay and Pinkster: "Think Third World"
Seeger, Peggy: "Polonium 210"; "Vital
Statistics"; "You Men out There"
Seeger, Pete: "Maple Syrup Time"; "Sail-
ing Down Golden River"; "Take It
from Dr. King"
Sexton, Martin: "America"; "Black
Sheep"
Shaber, Sam: "Honey"
Sheridan, Cosy: "The Losing Game"
Shindell, Richard: "Are You Happy
Now"
Shocked, Michelle: "Anchorage"
Shonti Elder: "Rolling Fog"
Siegel, Dick: "My Sweet America"
Siegel, Peter: "My Commentary on Pri-
vate Ryan"
Simon, Carly: "In the Wee Small Hours"

APPENDIX 3
STEVE WOZNIAK: GUEST DJ ON A SEGWAY

As a bonus, here is a song list from Steve Wozniak, who was a guest on XM radio's *Slipped Discs* with Bill Kates and me on October 2, 2006. At the time Steve was doing a publicity tour for his autobiography, *iWoz: Computer Geek to Cult Icon: How I Invented the Personal Computer, Co-Founded Apple, and Had Fun Doing It*. Steve is a diehard folk music fan and listens to XM channel 15 "The Village" all the time. He even sleeps with the radio on: he says that songs will wake him up, he'll write down what is playing (thanks to the LED readout that accompanies most tunes), and then he'll go right back to sleep. In the morning—sometimes having no memory of it—he sees song titles and artists' names written down, and soon he starts Googling.

At first I asked him to read some of his book on the show (he agreed), but then I asked him to be a guest DJ. Little did I know that that was one of his lifelong dreams. A few days later he e-mailed me that he had five hundred songs he wanted to play.

I asked him to narrow down his list to, say, twenty-eight songs. A good rule of thumb is that you can play twelve songs an hour. Since I thought the show should run three hours, I allowed time for him to read from his book. We gave the show a title: "Guest DJ on a Segway." Woz is a Segway enthusiast, so we arranged for him to park his vehicle in the coffee room. At the last minute his schedule changed and he didn't bring the Segway, but we kept the title anyway.

Woz had a lot to say—about a lot of things, not just music. The show ended up being more than four hours long. Bill Kates and I knew we had one of the most important inventors of the twentieth century in front of a microphone, and we didn't want to limit him. Co-hosting a show with Steve Wozniak as the guest was one of my proudest moments on the air—up there with interviewing Ervin Drake, Dave Van Ronk, and Jeff Daniels.

Thanks, Steve, for letting me include your selections here in my book. By my reckoning, you have 472 more songs to go. We're waiting!

Amos, Tori: "A Sorta Fairytale"
Baez, Joan: "Winds of the Old Days"
Bern, Dan: "Lithuania"
Berner, Martha: "Good Company"

Black, Mary: "Speaking with the Angel" and "Katie"
Brodsky, Chuck: "Unbridled Reins"
Chambers, Casey: "Captain"

Chapman, Beth Nielsen: "Sand and Water"

Cohen, Leonard: "Suzanne"

Dylan, Bob: "One Too Many Mornings" and "Percy's Song"

Gilkyson, Eliza: "Coast"

Griffin, Patty: "Florida"

Griffith, Nanci: "Good Night, New York"

Kaplansky, Lucy: "The Red Thread"

Kennedy, Pete and Maura: "Half a Million Miles"

Kingston Trio: "Four Strong Winds"

Lavin, Christine: "Robert and Annie in Larchmont, New York"

Leitch, Donovan: "Catch the Wind"

Lightfoot, Gordon: "Sit Down Young Stranger"

McLean, Don: "Vincent"

Morrissey, Bill: "Birches"

Peter Paul & Mary: "Blowin' in the Wind"

Rogers, Garnet: "Shining Thing"

Simon & Garfunkel: "The Sound of Silence"

Stuart, Marty: "Three Chiefs"

Waits, Tom: "Big Joe and Phantom 309"

INDEX

ABOUT THE AUTHOR

Over the past twenty-five years, between concert tours in the United States, Canada, and Australia, Christine Lavin has recorded twenty solo albums (*Good Thing He Can't Read My Mind* won the New York Music Award in 1991 for Best Folk Album) and produced nine compilation CDs showcasing the work of songwriters whose work she loves. She started learning guitar at age twelve by watching lessons broadcast on PBS. Although she can't read music, her songs have been performed by Broadway stars Betty Buckley and Sutton Foster, cabaret diva Andrea Marcovicci, the a cappella darlings the Accidentals, and many others. The lyrics to "Planet X" are included in *The Pluto Files*, a novel written by Neil deGrasse Tyson, director of the Hayden Planetarium . . . despite the fact that Christine earned a D in Astronomy in college.

Visit Christine online at www.christinelavin.com and www.christinelavin.net.